Early Modern Literature in History

General Editors: Cedric C. Brown, Emeritus Professor, University of Reading; **Andrew Hadfield**, Professor of English, University of Sussex, Brighton

International Advisory Board: Sharon Achinstein, University of Oxford; **Jean Howard**, Columbia University; **John Kerrigan**, University of Cambridge; **Katie Larson**, University of Toronto; **Richard McCoy**, CUNY; **Michelle O'Callaghan**, University of Reading; **Cathy Shrank**, University of Sheffield; **Adam Smyth**, University of London; **Steven Zwicker**, Washington University, St Louis.

Within the period 1520–1740 this series discusses many kinds of writing, both within and outside the established canon. The volumes may employ different theoretical perspectives, but they share a historical awareness and an interest in seeing their texts in lively negotiation with their own and successive cultures.

Titles include:

John M. Adrian
LOCAL NEGOTIATIONS OF ENGLISH NATIONHOOD, 1570–1680

Robyn Adams and Rosanna Cox
DIPLOMACY AND EARLY MODERN CULTURE

Jocelyn Catty
WRITING RAPE, WRITING WOMEN IN EARLY MODERN ENGLAND
Unbridled Speech

Bruce Danner
EDMUND SPENSER'S WAR ON LORD BURGHLEY

James Daybell and Peter Hinds (*editors*)
MATERIAL READINGS OF EARLY MODERN CULTURE
Texts and Social Practices, 1580–1730

James Daybell
THE MATERIAL LETTER IN EARLY MODERN ENGLAND
Manuscript Letters and the Culture and Practices of Letter-Writing, 1512–1635

Maria Franziska Fahey
METAPHOR AND SHAKESPEAREAN DRAMA
Unchaste Signification

Andrew Gordon
WRITING EARLY MODERN LONDON
Memory, Text and Community

Kenneth J.E. Graham and Philip D. Collington (*editors*)
SHAKESPEARE AND RELIGIOUS CHANGE

Jane Grogan
THE PERSIAN EMPIRE IN ENGLISH RENAISSANCE WRITING, 1549–1622

Johanna Harris and Elizabeth Scott-Baumann (*editors*)
THE INTELLECTUAL CULTURE OF PURITAN WOMEN, 1558–1680

Constance Jordan and Karen Cunningham (*editors*)
THE LAW IN SHAKESPEARE

Claire Jowitt (*editor*)
PIRATES? THE POLITICS OF PLUNDER, 1550–1650

Gregory Kneidel
RETHINKING THE TURN TO RELIGION IN EARLY MODERN ENGLISH LITERATURE

James Knowles
POLITICS AND POLITICAL CULTURE IN THE COURT MASQUE

Edel Lamb
PERFORMING CHILDHOOD IN THE EARLY MODERN THEATRE
The Children's Playing Companies (1599–1613)

Katherine R. Larson
EARLY MODERN WOMEN IN CONVERSATION

Monica Matei-Chesnoiu
RE-IMAGINING WESTERN EUROPEAN GEOGRAPHY IN ENGLISH RENAISSANCE DRAMA

David McInnis
MIND-TRAVELLING AND VOYAGE DRAMA IN EARLY MODERN ENGLAND

Scott L. Newstok
QUOTING DEATH IN EARLY MODERN ENGLAND
The Poetics of Epitaphs Beyond the Tomb

P. Pender
EARLY MODERN WOMAN'S WRITING AND THE RHETORIC OF MODESTY

Jane Pettegree
FOREIGN AND NATIVE ON THE ENGLISH STAGE, 1588–1611
Metaphor and National Identity

Fred Schurink (*editor*)
TUDOR TRANSLATION

Adrian Streete (*editor*)
EARLY MODERN DRAMA AND THE BIBLE
Contexts and Readings, 1570–1625

Mary Trull
PERFORMING PRIVACY AND GENDER IN EARLY MODERN LITERATURE

The series Early Modern Literature in History is published in association with the Early Modern Research Centre at the University of Reading and The Centre for Early Modern Studies at the University of Sussex

Early Modern Literature in History
Series Standing Order ISBN 978–0–333–71472–0 (Hardback)
978–0–333–80321–9 (Paperback)
(*outside North America only*)

You can receive future titles in this series as they are published by placing a standing order. Please contact your bookseller or, in case of difficulty, write to us at the address below with your name and address, the title of the series and the ISBN quoted above.

Customer Services Department, Macmillan Distribution Ltd, Houndmills, Basingstoke, Hampshire RG21 6XS, England

Politics and Political Culture in the Court Masque

James Knowles
Professor of Renaissance Literature and Culture, Brunel University, UK

© James Knowles 2015

All rights reserved. No reproduction, copy or transmission of this publication may be made without written permission.

No portion of this publication may be reproduced, copied or transmitted save with written permission or in accordance with the provisions of the Copyright, Designs and Patents Act 1988, or under the terms of any licence permitting limited copying issued by the Copyright Licensing Agency, Saffron House, 6–10 Kirby Street, London EC1N 8TS.

Any person who does any unauthorized act in relation to this publication may be liable to criminal prosecution and civil claims for damages.

The author has asserted his right to be identified as the author of this work in accordance with the Copyright, Designs and Patents Act 1988.

First published 2015 by
PALGRAVE MACMILLAN

Palgrave Macmillan in the UK is an imprint of Macmillan Publishers Limited, registered in England, company number 785998, of Houndmills, Basingstoke, Hampshire RG21 6XS.

Palgrave Macmillan in the US is a division of St Martin's Press LLC, 175 Fifth Avenue, New York, NY 10010.

Palgrave Macmillan is the global academic imprint of the above companies and has companies and representatives throughout the world.

Palgrave® and Macmillan® are registered trademarks in the United States, the United Kingdom, Europe and other countries

ISBN 978–0–230–00894–6

This book is printed on paper suitable for recycling and made from fully managed and sustained forest sources. Logging, pulping and manufacturing processes are expected to conform to the environmental regulations of the country of origin.

A catalogue record for this book is available from the British Library.

A catalog record for this book is available from the Library of Congress.

Typeset by MPS Limited, Chennai, India.

Contents

List of Illustrations vi

Note on Frequently Cited Texts vii

1 Introduction: 'Friends of All Ranks'? Reading the Masque in Political Culture 1
2 'Vizarded impudence': Challenging the *regnum Cecilianum* 21
3 'Crack Kisses Not Staves': Sexual Politics and Court Masques in 1613–14 53
4 'No News': *News from the New World* and Textual Culture in the 1620s 93
5 'Hoarse with Praising': *The Gypsies Metamorphosed* and the Politics of Masquing 131
6 ''Tis for kings, / Not for their subjects, to have such rare things': *The Triumph of Peace* and Civil Culture 173

Notes 210

Select Bibliography 263

Index 283

List of Illustrations

4.1 Title page of *A courtly masque: the device called, the world tossed at tennis* (1620) (Folger Shakespeare Library, Washington, DC, STC 17910)   107

4.2 Vellum binding of Arundel copy of *The Masque of Queens* (1609) (Huntington Library, California, RB62067)   123

4.3 Manuscript listing of Robert Burton's bound collection of plays and pageants (Bodleian Library, Oxford, 4° T 37 Art)   128

6.1 *The Honour of the Inns of Court Gentlemen* (1634) (Crawford Collection, National Library of Scotland)   200

6.2 *The Honour of the Inns of Court Gentlemen, The second part* (1634) (Crawford Collection, National Library of Scotland)   201

Note on Frequently Cited Texts

Jonson

All references are to *CWBJ* cited below.

Some use has also been made of *Ben Jonson*, ed. C. H. Herford, P. Simpson, and E. Simpson, 11 vols. (Oxford: Clarendon Press, 1925–52) and *The Complete Masques*, ed. S. Orgel (New Haven: Yale University Press, 1969).

Libels

Unless otherwise stated, copies of libels are drawn from *Early Stuart Libels: An Edition of Poetry from Manuscript Sources*, ed. Alastair Bellany and Andrew McRae. Early Modern Literary Studies Text Series I (2005) <http://purl.oclc.org/emls/texts/libels/>.

Frequently cited texts

Chamberlain Letters	John Chamberlain, *The Letters of John Chamberlain*, ed. N. E. McClure, 2 vols. (Philadelphia: American Philosophical Society, 1939).
Court Masques	David Lindley, ed., *Court Masques* (Oxford: Oxford University Press, 1995).
CSPD	*Calendar of State Papers, Domestic, James I* (1856–72) Calendar of State Papers, Domestic series, of the reigns of Edward VI, Mary, Elizabeth, (James I), ed. R. Lemon with addenda ed. M. A. E. Green, 7 vols. (London: Longman and Co).
	Calendar of State Papers, Domestic, Charles I (1858–97) Calendar of State Papers, Domestic series, of the reign of Charles I, 1625–[1649], ed. J. Bruce and others, 23 vols. (London: Longman and Co).
CSPV	*Calendar of State Papers, Venetian* (1864–1947) Calendar of state papers and manuscripts, relating to English affairs, existing in the archives and collections of Venice, and in other libraries of northern Italy,

	ed. Rawdon Brown and others, 38 vols. (London: Longman and Co).
CWBJ	*The Cambridge Edition of the Works of Ben Jonson*, ed. David Bevington, Martin Butler, and Ian Donaldson, 7 vols. (Cambridge: Cambridge University Press, 2012).
ES	E. K. Chambers, *The Elizabethan Stage*, 4 vols. (Oxford: Clarendon Press, 1923).
HMC Downshire	Historical Manuscripts Commission (1925–95) *Report on the Manuscripts of the Marquess of Downshire, preserved at Easthampstead Park, Berkshire*, 6 vols. (London: HMSO).
HMC Portland	Historical Manuscripts Commission (1891–1931) *The manuscripts of His Grace the Duke of Portland preserved at Welbeck Abbey*, 10 vols. (London: HMSO).
HMC Salisbury	Historical Manuscripts Commission (1883–1976) *Report on the Papers of the Marquess of Salisbury*, 24 vols. (London: HMSO).
JCS	G. E. Bentley, *The Jacobean and Caroline Stage*, 7 vols. (Oxford: Clarendon Press, 1941–68).
Whitelocke, *Diary*	Ruth Spalding, ed., *The Diary of Bulstrode Whitelocke, 1605–1675* (Oxford: Oxford University Press, 1990).

1
Introduction: 'Friends of All Ranks'? Reading the Masque in Political Culture

If early modern audiences regarded masques as 'tied to the rules of flattery' to 'commend the King' and 'speak in praise / Of the assembly', modern critics have often regarded them as tied to the rule of monarchy.[1] This book presents a different approach, placing masques within a broader 'political culture', the varied ways in which political ideas and practices are represented, communicated, and debated across society. It also locates these texts within 'masquing culture', the interplay of texts, forms, spaces, and personnel that shaped this key element of early modern culture and which, also, opened it to voices and forms beyond the royal court.[2]

Historians and literary scholars have been divided between those who regard this period as, largely, defined by its monarchy and by a politics that is 'court-centred, elitist, and consensual', and those who have seen a more geographically and intellectually plural culture.[3] This book posits a more contested and permeable context for the masque, where differing ideas and ideals of government existed, arguing that masques engage with politics, with difference and even with dissent, rather than replicating royal ideology or rehearsing factional power-play. It explores how Jacobean and Caroline masques, understood as part a broader and more fluid 'political communication', became conduits for debates about political principles and sites for discussions of the role and nature of political authority. Masques could also become vehicles for opinions and ideas that existed beyond the court, responding to the plurality of the early modern era. Masques operated not just as sites of political debate or counsel but, crucially, instantiated an ongoing experiment with how to articulate such dissent and what limits there should be to criticism and critique. In this period, vigorous intellectual and political debates, often expressed in language quite alien to courtly tact and negotiation, are also articulated through the particular repeated concern for the boundaries of civil speech, or what Maskerado in *Love Restored* describes as how to speak 'truth under a vizard'.[4] In this context, to debate how to speak politics is, itself, to speak politics.

Although there have been some notable challenges to the consociation of monarchy and the masque, and some persuasive and important modifications to our understanding of court culture and how it operates, the masque has been consistently associated with an apparent movement towards absolutism and the centralised state.[5] Thus Stephen Orgel, who more than any other has revived sophisticated study of the English masque, characterises the form as combining new spectacular resources with the 'reappearance' of Divine Right theory that transformed the audience into spectators of 'visions of a harmonious commonwealth' achieved by 'mimetic magic'.[6] Following Orgel, one current strand of masque interpretation links the images of monarchs 'set on stages in the sight and view of all the world' to a highly theatricalised society, defined by a 'Royal Theatre' that enacts the whole state in microcosm.[7] The 'profound ethical statements' of the masque, a combination of Platonism and Machiavellianism, then lie in 'the triumph of an aristocratic community; at its center . . . hierarchy and a faith in the power of idealisation'.[8] Re-energised and extended by new generations of scholars inspired by Foucault's compelling and violent theatrics of power, the masque has been the defining form for a bleak reconceptualisation of a totalitarian early modern culture. Shaped by 'absolutist theatricality', such approaches echo Jacob Burkhardt's 'state as work of art', disempowering even as it entrances.[9]

Despite this persuasive and coherent view of masques as power performed as beauty, paradoxically, much current masque scholarship stresses the failure of the form. More and more marooned in an illusion of power, if the magic of the masque was designed to ward off incipient political collapse and war, the monarch often appears to have been the only one enchanted. Regarding such approaches as manifestations of *'ex post facto'* (after the fact) readings of the 1630s in the light of the Civil Wars, Martin Butler, neatly dissects the 'logical circularity' in interpretations that laud aesthetic significance and assert political inadequacy.[10] Even if such approaches cannot be applied easily to Jacobean texts, it remains unfortunate that masques have been too often slotted into narratives of the evolution of parliamentary sovereignty and long-term causes for the English Civil Wars that depended on a model of emerging conflict between Crown and Parliament, divergent court and country values, and an increasingly isolated court. So, just as they echo civil war newsbook propaganda and Walter Scott's novelistic excoriation of the Stuarts, such critical contextualisations make conflict inevitable and render masques an ineffective and decadent distraction.[11]

This narrative of chronic, emergent conflict has come under considerable attack; according to some historians, Britain, ruled by a vigorous and innovative court, was largely consensual and pacified.[12] In this context, more revisionist masque criticism has celebrated the efficacy of the masque within a vital court culture. Martin Butler's subtle and nuanced interpretations have insisted on both a more functionalist approach that highlights how masques work – and also fail – inside court society through faction, through power-broking, and through jostling for precedence. Royal power can never be assumed but must always be negotiated or improvised, and is never 'an uncontested monopoly'.[13] Attention to this factional context of the masque stresses the 'permeability of Whitehall', the connections to localities, and the 'cooperation and consent' of the governing classes that illuminate the circulations of power.[14] Encouraged by New Historicism, whose language of power and improvisation it borrows, masque criticism has explored in detail the contingencies and specific occasions of many masque, often with startling results. Often these studies have articulated a carefully and historically contextualised consideration of the politics of the form, an emphasis upon the tensions between contingent meanings (what Jonson termed 'present occasions') and the powers of idealisation and mythification (the 'removed mysteries'), alongside more sceptical assessment of the efficacy of the royal image or the unquestioning acceptance of absolutist ideas.[15]

Of course the problems in masque hermeneutics extend beyond 'a simple difficulty of historical perspective'.[16] Nonetheless, shuffling the pack of historical cards produces a different sense of the political game in the early modern era and enhances our understanding of the rhetoric and form of the masque. Although contextual study has diversified how masques might relate to court culture, the investigation of the masque's discursive frames, especially of genre, has been more constraining, often settling within an overarching rhetoric of consensus. Martin Butler, in particular, argues that inherent in the form are limitations imposed by the 'exclusiveness of the court event' and 'constrained by rules of tact'.[17] Drawing on Renaissance ideas of panegyric as an educative vehicle that, as Pliny claims, 'teaches through praising', this approach requires 'tactfully articulated' advice.[18] Compliment inspired to improvement by presenting ideals of behaviour and countered any impression of flattery by recalling its recipient to codes of good behaviour or obligation. How far such tact constrains the possibility for counsel is suggested in the balance between 'criticism' and 'compliment' that Kevin Sharpe traces in the Caroline masque, where 'constructive criticism rather than opposition' shapes the form.[19] Even Thomas Scott's formulation that 'Kings are content in plays and masks to be admonished of various things' places control in monarchical hands suggesting, as with the masque, that exactly the context of court performance which allows commentary that would be suppressed elsewhere contained the implications of that criticism by its very privilege.[20] In current masque scholarship the overriding emphasis on tact, or criticism from within the court system, on the 'courtly negotiation', and on power rather than politics, has limited the implications of the transactions the masque represents and embodies.[21]

Neither the court nor panegyric were, however, the only frames available. Outside the court, in different circumstances, other masque writers and other masquing modes pushed fewer compliments and provided more critique. Counsel was one of the motors of early modern society, and the acquisition of the skills to counsel and the exercise of those skills form one of the defining characteristics of early modern manliness.[22] At a personal level, it was conceived of as a duty, and rulers were obliged to receive 'tendered honest opinion' in a 'spirit of likeness and equality'.[23] At a political level, the rhetoric of counsel informed a link to ideas of free elections and free speech (however imperfectly conceived and achieved), and at an institutional level parliament claimed the place of counsel.[24] Recently, David Colclough has argued for the importance of debates over freedom of speech in a variety of arenas in early Stuart public life (sermons, parliamentary debates, manuscript miscellanies) and the centrality of 'the duty as well as the right to speak frankly' for humanist adaptations of the *vir civilis*.[25] Bacon's description of an ideal counsellor, which acknowledges the requirement to be 'faithful, and sincere, and plain, and direct', also posits the problem of unwelcome or over-frankness, so that to counsel, especially in Bacon's practical essay, effectively requires strategy and negotiation.[26] As Colclough's own work charts, *parrhesia*, the central rhetorical trope for speaking boldly, becomes an act of self-exculpation for speaking (too) boldly; it has also been argued that codes of decorum and propriety act as a significant brake on counsel's frankness.[27]

Other writers, however, stressed honesty and sharpness over reticence. Surveying the impact of classical rhetoric on political culture before the 1640s, Markku Peltonen has pointed out the preference for adversarial debate as part of basic classical training, often rooted in public persuasion of the populace, which undermines the idea of tact and consensus pointing to a culture in which 'division rather than unity' fuelled politics.[28] Many humanists followed Erasmus in *The Praise of Folly* who warned: 'If you think that no-one should ever speak freely or reveal the truth except when it offends no one, why do physicians heal with bitter medicines and place *aloe sacra* among their most highly recommended remedies?'[29] Erasmus advocated the usefulness of obliqueness and play in counsel, so that erudite humour became a means to convey frank speech, but his espousal of direct, even offensive speech, and the degree of bitterness permissible in counsel, also became staples of early modern intellectual debate. The traditions of Lucianic and Erasmian learned play that colour Jonson's texts often focus on how to provide counsel or critique.[30] Indeed, two of the masques that most centrally debate the boundaries of tact and scurrility in political culture, *Love Restored* (1611) and *News from the New World in the Moon* (1621) draw upon Lucianic satires.[31]

Given Ben Jonson's role as the main masque poet, the ways in which we understand masques cannot be separated from interpretations of his work and career. Even studies that have argued for a more 'the potential for a radical and subversive' Jonson who used his movements between court and public theatres to articulate a sceptical and questioning attitude towards politics, employ the masque evidence of more conservative trends in his thinking.[32] Yet, as made by Jonson, the antimasque/masque structure holds the possibility for dialectic while his designation of masques as 'poems' points not only towards seriousness but also towards reason and argument that are at odds with some of the more mystical interpretations of masques.[33] Even at the height of his masque-making Jonson's masques are filled with conditionals: the deities that embody power are not automatically aligned with the monarchy, creating a 'fictional distance' between the ideals and actuality of power.[34] Sometimes, indeed, the negotiation between contingencies ('present occasions') and mythifications ('removed mysteries') that the form required either breaks down or is exposed, as in the collapse of social harmony in the revels dances for *Love Restored* (see Chapter 2, p. 21), or in the irresolvable challenge faced in *Neptune's Triumph* (1624) of representing the collapse of the King's policy to marry Prince Charles to the Spanish Infanta as a success.[35]

Framed by critical distance, both in the performances and in the textual versions, the masques carry reminders of the less than perfect performances that often occurred and which the written texts equally often repaired: *The Haddington Masque* quarto notes it reassembles the epithalamion 'made to be read an entire poem' that had been 'sung in pieces between the dances' (277–8). In *Pleasure Reconciled to Virtue* (1618) the folio text turns the revision of the antimasque generated by the King's boredom at the original (seen by many critics as some of Jonson's best masque-poetry) as a royal command performance 'with . . . additions'.[36] If the printed masque book offered the opportunity to repair the deficiencies of performance, even the apparent textual fixity found in the folio, with its careful evasions and erasures, can be challenged. Much as *The workes* (1616) would have avoided the occasion for *Hymenaei* and the *Barriers at a Marriage*, other texts in circulation attested to this masque's origins in 'the auspicious celebrating of the marriage-union, between Robert, Earl of Essex, and the Lady Frances, second daughter to the most noble Earl of Suffolk'.[37] Faced with such uncertainties, it is perhaps unsurprising that Jonson's later poems, in particular, present a poet 'hoarse with praising', forced to worship that 'idol of the revels', and at risk that he 'may / Lose all . . . credit with my Christmas clay / And animated porcelain of the court'.[38]

Counsel was central to Jonson's conception of his role as poet and he was fond of citing the equivalence of monarch and poet.[39] In *Discoveries*, which is substantively concerned with learning and counsel, he claimed:

> I could never think the study of wisdom confined only to the philosopher, or of piety to the divine, or of state to the politic. But that he which can feign a commonwealth (which is the poet) can govern it with counsels, strengthen it with laws, correct it with judgements, inform it with religion and morals, is all these. (*Discoveries*, 740–3)

Julie Sanders has noted the ambiguity of the poet's claim to 'feign a commonwealth', which is, of course, not necessarily a monarchy, but the over-riding concern lies in shared, communal values.[40] This includes active engagement with the 'improvement and security' of the country that typified what Richard Cust, borrowing from contemporary terminology, calls the 'public man'.[41] Jonson's refusal of the designated roles of 'philosopher', 'divine', or 'politic' (politician) evident in the first sentence places the poet closer to this early modern ideal that is also characterised by 'outsider' status.[42] As a counter to Jonson's confidence about the myth-making possibilities of the masque announced by the heroic 'men-making poets' (345) supporting the House of Fame in *The Masque of Queens*, this ethical sensitivity, which also informs the anxieties of counsel found in *Discoveries*, can also be seen in the more questioning assessment and constant reshaping of masque form which typifies his masque-writing career. The Jonsonian scepticism towards the 'short bravery of the night', particularly if viewed through the lens of a pointless celebration of an already collapsing political system, registers continuing and powerful concerns with the efficacy of the masque and with how far his counsel has been able to articulate criticism.[43] Jonson's debates with Chapman, Daniel, Middleton and most of all, Inigo Jones, long recognised as crucial to shaping and defining the masque's hermeneutics and form, should be understood as part of Jonson's responsiveness to external critiques. These debates over masque form suggest that contemporaries regarded masques as not simply delightful or profitable, but also as meaningful and effective. Crucially, and especially for Jonson, his concern with the power of the form contributes to the urgent, vexed, and continued highly political debate over finding a language through which current issues and ideas can be explored and represented at court.

Political culture

Recent readings of the masque have grown in sophistication in response to the revisionist revitalisations of the significance of the court and faction, patronage and political place, and of individual patrons. Yet the current awareness of a vigorous court culture has also been accompanied in both critical and historical studies by insistence upon an all encompassing will to consensus has ultimately been depoliticising. The re-evaluation of court culture and the fascination with the politics of 'patronage and place' has often concentrated attention on factional manoeuvres rather than political debate; cultural production has become the adjunct of aristocracy.[44] Where politics existed, interest lay within the court and its factions; conflict, debate, and especially 'opposition' were marginalised as the concerns of a minority and, in the case of the last term, derided as an anachronistic impossibility.[45] The narrowness of such approaches has been noted by many critics and historians. Malcolm Smuts, in particular, envisaged a more 'poly-centric' Jacobean court, highlighting the possibility of political and cultural divergence amongst its constituent parts, not only the three royal households but also the varying factions, endowing court culture with a degree of debate and dynamism.[46]

To understand the masque and its significance we need to return the form to a political culture that recognises the vitality of a multi-centred society ruled but not dominated by the court, with more diverse voices and forms that could, on occasion, permeate even the closed court world. Political culture can be best understood as the socially embedded ways in which political ideas that were once seen as the preserve of elites and expressed through explicit public statements (tracts, treatises of principle or philosophy, or records of institutional processes, such as parliamentary debates), were reshaped into assumptions, beliefs, and behaviours, often barely acknowledged or directly articulated, that guided political actions across different classes, genders, religious affiliations, and geographies.[47] Political culture encompassed 'identity formation' processes (what elsewhere gets called 'Renaissance self-fashioning'), as groups shape their own identity or are identified by others in a shifting and dynamic manner, but also allows that 'serious, meaningful politics happened in surprising places, in curious forms, and unfamiliar languages'.[48]

So recent historical work has reasserted the role of the parliamentary as central to political life in the Jacobean and Caroline periods and illustrated the different models of power and divergent understandings of the role of parliament in operation. Other work has stressed the political plurality and engagement of different localities and communities beyond Westminster and Whitehall.[49] Indeed, studies of local structures, such town councils and parishes, reveal not only 'citizens within subjects', but a deep-rooted concerns with civic participation, self-governance and the public good, understood within a tradition of 'ubiquitous' republican discourse that enacted participation more through office-holding than the franchise, existing alongside, and even independently of, monarchy and its prerogative powers.[50] These approaches, highlighting the complex interactions between rhetoric or discourse and cultural practices, posit a more pluralistic political culture in which the monarchy is not the sole reference point.[51] Sometimes referred to as 'post-revisionist', this dynamic model seeks to capture a mobile and various political culture which links specific case studies with micro-histories as well as with broader narratives of historical change.[52] Examining 'a number of centres of power at once', post-revisionist approaches explore tensions between centre and localities and 'the interactions between these arenas' of politics to suggest that the structuring binaries of early modern political culture are polarities in discussion not 'concrete separations'.[53] Such more flexible and mobile models of culture echo elements seventeenth-century somatic and medical discourse, which argued that 'the health of this body was frequently to be secured through a dynamic, even difficult process of purgation or purification'.⁵⁴ The ultimate aim may have been physical and social harmony, even consensus, but that emerged from a complex and continuing process of difference and balance.⁵⁵

This renewed interest in a broader political culture has highlighted issues of dissemination and communication as questions of information networks but also the material and cultural dimensions of books and reading have acquired new significance in understanding political awareness beyond the Whitehall walls.⁵⁶ Indeed, the concentration on two related phenomena, news culture and libelling, has generated a major reformulation of early modern political culture as far more conflicted.⁵⁷ The social circulation of a wider range of printed and manuscripted texts and a range of 'newsworthy' texts from parliamentary separates to poems, contributes to a broader political awareness, especially in the 1620s and 1630s. The centralisation of news in London, and its permeation into the 'middling sort' provides the impetus to far more divisive kinds of rhetoric, often rooted in what has been called 'conspiratorial paranoia'.⁵⁸ This news world disrupts the hierarchical information flow from court to localities with 'horizontal circulations' which not only appealed across social groups, transgressing the boundaries of literate and illiterate, oral and written, but which also supported a 'political sphere' in an 'emergent civil society'.⁵⁹ The dominance of conflict rather than consensus, moreover, challenged the boundaries of what can and cannot be spoken.⁶⁰ These social circulations were often characterised by the omission of 'consensual phraseology and polite restraint' and the substitution of more robust forms of discourse.⁶¹

Some sense of the 'savage guerrilla war in manuscript' that operated by the end of the 1620s can be heard in suggestions, albeit in a pro-Spanish match tract, that the Armada had been prompted by the 'Philippicae and invective in every pulpit, ballets [ballads] and libels in every press'.⁶² Later, in 1637, Archbishop William Laud lamented the level of abuse he received when, in one political demonstration, his Star Chamber speech against Prynne was displayed nailed at one end, singed with fire and its corners cropped and bearing the inscription, 'the man that puts the saints of God into a pillory of wood, stands here in a pillory of ink'.⁶³ Laud's 'pillory of ink' provides a powerful instance not only of the impact of libelling, but evokes the struggles for authority conducted through the presentation, appropriation, and re-appropriation of images, ideas and texts. The sophisticated inversion of a symbol of authority reminds us of the existence of a vibrant popular political culture and consciousness in social groupings beyond the court.⁶⁴ Significantly, for forms like the masque, the language of these libels challenged the modes of civility and rational discourse that so engaged

Jonson, yet many of these texts emerged from, or were circulated by, the very circles in which he moved.[65]

In critical studies the 'social text' and the 'sociology of texts' have become axioms. Jonson has, himself, always been recognised as a key figure in the development of literary print culture, but more recently Harold Love's studies of manuscript circulation have provided a more nuanced sense of publication (performance, manuscript, print) that illuminates Jonson's own more strategic uses of different kinds of print (quarto, folio), his employment of manuscript paratexts, and his own involvements in manuscript circulation to supplement and even subvert print. That masque texts, songs, sections of masques, and various types of description became currency in social exchanges that operated geographically and politically far beyond the court and the implication of the masque in news and news networks seems easy to establish.[66] Much of the information we have about masquing originates with newsletters: John Pory's professional productions, the correspondence of John Chamberlain and Dudley Carleton, and the diplomatic dispatches of various representatives have all been mined to furnish interpretations of the masque. This dissemination of masque-material in provincial newsletters meant Jonson's texts (or news of them) circulated through political and social networks alongside political tracts or commentary, sometimes as part of the same letter, and in many cases close to or amidst the libellous verses.[67] Manuscript was not solely about privileged dissemination, indeed it was often associated with dissident texts and networks, and even the widespread circulation of parliamentary materials carried some residual sense of transgression as what was meant to remain private was allowed public voice.[68]

This emphasis on communication has reshaped how the narrative of the period, and particularly, the movement towards the crisis of the 1640s, can be understood. Peter Lake and Steven Pincus have proposed that the early modern period from the 1580s onwards saw a series of crises (1590s, 1620s, 1640s, 1690s) when the developing political communication allowed for a 'post-Reformation public sphere' in which conflicts were articulated initially inside the regime, but later also including those beyond the landed elite.[69] Many of the earliest manifestations of this public politics were part of a 'communicative political game' in which ideas of public good and religious truth dominated. Interestingly, the second eruption of this public sphere occurs around Cecil's Great Contract (1610) when popular grievances and an 'enhanced' discussion of royal prerogative not only scuppered the proposal but led to the release of Cecil's memoranda to the king on the need for financial retrenchment as a response to a tide of libels against the beleaguered first minister.[70] What started as an attempt by the regime to appeal to various publics fostered the development of a political public sphere in which the disputes of the 1620s over international religious conflict, royal policy towards the Spanish match, and the connections between the cost of war and the royal finances, were fuelled by the proliferation of newspapers and other forms of political communication.

This model of an episodic and irregular public sphere is much more contingent, comprising the 'occasional and opportunistic opening up and shutting down of debate on a limited set of issues', and differentiates between sorts political eruption (parliamentary crisis, court scandal, national political crisis) and the varying dynamics, emphases, and outcomes of each event.[71] The connections within these public spheres bring together specific events (the Great Contract), forms (libels, circulation of documents), different arenas (court, parliament, news networks), political issues and principles (royal finances, prerogative), and the political process (role of counsel, discourses) combining both detailed and local micro-histories with broader national and issues and ideologies. Lake and Pincus also stress the 'central' role for 'performances and collective political actions' in this creation of a new political awareness and it can be seen that both public theatre and political ritual have a place in this system.[72]

To situate the masque in this framework allows the reconnection of 'present occasions' and 'removed mysteries' so that in a more permeable and polycentric political culture masques register not only within the court, but interact with other texts from other political arenas, through their performances, their textual manifestations (from manuscript separate to printed masque book), and their symbolic associations. We can also recognise, still, the importance of factions and personal representations and performances in masques, but also trace their filiations with broader political debates or involvement in political events, such as the court scandals that themselves become sites of political debate.[73]

Centrally, the emphasis in early public spheres on counsel directs us towards questions of how politics can be spoken. Here the permeability of early modern politics requires us to focus not just to the substance of debate but also on its means and medium, and how difficult, often challenging and uncivil ideas and voices, might be accommodated within the more decorous forms of the masque. Such concerns become a key part of the meaning of masque occasions and texts. The resulting situation is parallel to that seen in theatrical censorship in this period, as Richard Dutton has argued:

> A 'state' view on many of the central religious and political issues of the day was a meaningless concept . . . censorship aimed to keep the commentary within the limits tacitly accepted at court itself; it insisted on a suitable fictional veiling of topical issues, so as not to cause specific offence either to individuals of note or to friendly foreign powers; it required respect for the existing constitutional establishment, and showed concern for public order . . . the margin of what was permissible was that much greater, as long as all involved subscribed to the system of authority itself.[74]

These parameters suggest that the boundaries of speech were under continual negotiation, much like the communicative game that constituted public discussion of policy for much of the 1610s. In this situation there is no simply accepted standard of civility to be breached, but the 'civility situation' must be created anew or reasserted in each instance. Such fluidity endows poet and masque a mediatory role evident in the continued testing and balancing of the boundaries and pressures around what can be articulated, how, and where that characterises the Jonsonian masque and especially in its self-conscious paratextual positioning in relation to other writers, occasions, and forms. The shifting forms of the masque, and the striking responsiveness evident throughout Jonson's masque-texts, embody processes of testing out the boundaries of licit and illicit speech as civility situations are established and negotiated.

Historical approaches to this early modern public sphere have traced a fitful development through a series of discrete but interconnected crises, starting in the 1590s, but erupting around particular issues in 1610, 1614, and 1621 (and then later in the 1620s and the 1640s). This book mirrors these moments of crisis through case studies of masques from these specific years, many of which are also attached to the summoning of parliament (1611, 1614, 1621), but supplements this by the consideration of incidents within court culture, such as the eclipse of Robert Cecil, the Carr–Howard match, the consolidation of George Villiers' role as royal favourite and the inception of Prince Charles' public career. This last occasion suggests how parliamentary and court events might coalesce, but on other occasions the debates instigated through masquing culture remain more autonomous. Modern political culture tends to associate debate with parliamentary or legislative bodies, but within the kind of political culture created by early modern courts, events within the ritual calendar provided opportunities for reflection of the interdependencies of ceremonial and politics. In fact, the steady occurrence of masques staged every Twelfth Night provided a continuous space for political representation not available through parliament and allowed these ceremonial forms to take on a greater political significance.[75] The final example discussed, *The Triumph of Peace*, responds to the political issues raised by the King's coronation in Scotland in 1633, but also to the re-launch of the monarchy that had been attempted in 1630–31 with a return to the Jonsonian masque.

From this it will be clear that this political culture resembles but does not map directly onto later versions of the public sphere. In particular, ideas of its 'public' nature need modifications. Some elements of this political culture would, if only partially, satisfy modern ideas of 'publicness', such as the interaction of published texts (pamphlets and masques) or publicly disseminated forms (libels and newsletters). Other dimensions of the early Stuart public sphere inhibit open debate or locate particular kinds of discussion or debates in inaccessible settings such as aristocratic households. Just as we will see with the exploration of the kinds and limits of language to be used, these differences between the fixed, open, and deliberative conception of a modern public sphere and this political culture are precisely part of the process of forming and shaping the different public spheres that eventually contribute to creating (in indirect and complex ways) more recognisably modern ideas of the public sphere.

The case studies in this book, then, represent moments of early modern political culture, moving outwards from the Twelfth Night masques to examine how the masques interact with a range of other political texts (treatises, libels, plays, masques) from different social groups (lawyers), and different performance spaces (country house, inns of court, public playhouse). It culminates with a moment of dialogue between key parts of the establishment (the court and inns of court) that openly debates political issues as *The Triumph of Peace* presents a very different view of royal powers and legal restraint. The thrust of this book is to highlight how this is not simply an aberration, but that the frequent availability of masques in other arenas fostered the interplay between different kinds of masquing and different political viewpoints. To claim masques, as Jonathan Goldberg does, as an 'inherently royal form' understates their connection to the web of other masques, rituals, and ceremonies which were key elements in early modern political culture.[76]

The masque and political culture

Consideration of the masque as political form has always been constrained by the view that ultimately it cannot be a site for serious political debate as its modes are over-reliant on panegyric and persuasion rather than analysis. As David Lindley has noted, 'characteristically the masque does not debate, but asserts: meaningful dialectic was, usually, inhibited'.[77] Yet this, perhaps, underestimates how far early modern rhetorical culture combined deliberative and demonstrative forms of rhetoric: analysis was often supplemented by praise and blame. David Colclough has argued, indeed, that such uses of praise and blame were important constituents of early modern civil society especially in a culture deprived of arenas for civic expression, such as parliament.[78]

Jonson's own conceptualisation of the masque as poem has already been noted, but other elements of these events, such as design, also have rhetorical underpinnings. Dance, for example, an element often relegated in modern discussion, could also be treated as a form of persuasion so that, as *Apologie de la Danse* argues, dance 'est une eloquence muete . . . bien plus forte et plus persuasive que celle de Ciceron'.[79] The cultural interweaving of allusions and meanings found in early modern masquing culture, heightened by the dialogue between masques and other more clearly contentious forms that this book traces, encourages persuasion and debate. These 'curious forms and unfamiliar languages' of a different political culture point towards the distinctive ways in which political dialogue and communication might have operated in a hierarchical and ceremonialised culture.[80] If, as has been suggested in recent work on public discourse in the early modern period, the key features of open and equal access and rationality that we associate with a post-Enlightenment public sphere may only have been partially available, then assertion either in the form of persuasion, praise or blame may still have contributed to a different kind of dialogue and debate.[81] Debate, as its etymology suggests, could also be about dissension conducted through opinion, invective, and disagreement.

One element that points towards Jonson's engagement with the potential for broader political debate lies in his particular awareness of audience. Jonson's fascination with finding the right audience, interpreted as part of authorial self-fashioning, is often envisaged in exclusionary terms. Yet at both ends of his career Jonson shows specific concern with how occasional texts might be understood. Jonson's *Ben Jon: His Part of King James his Royall and Magnificent Entertainment through his Honorable Cittie of London* (1604), enunciating a new style of royal entertainment, balances awareness of the dignity of the occasion with a need to convey its meanings to the broader audience that such events attract and who must be entertained and instructed.[82] Jonson defends his method as combining both the 'expression of State and Magnificence (as proper to a triumphall Arch)' and the 'Site, Fabricke, Strength, Policie, Dignitie and Affections of the Cittie'; he continues:

> The symbols used are not, neither ought to be simply to *hieroglyphics*, *emblems, or impresas*, but a mixed character, partaking somewhat of all, and peculiarly apted to these more magnificent inventions, wherein the garments, and ensigns deliver the nature of the person, and the word the present office. (*Royall and Magnificent Entertainment*, 203–7)[83]

This passage counters any straightforward sense of literary exclusivity either in terms of audience or means of signification. The key assertion here concerns a desire to avoid the need for over-explication associated with popular culture in the form of the 'truchman' or with the use of labels ('"This is a Dog", or "This is a Hare"') but Jonson also seeks devices that 'without cloud or obscurity declare themselves to the sharp and learned' (211).[84] The passage swerves away from exclusive, exclusionary, and esoteric symbols, creating a new 'mixed Character' that relies on the 'garments and ensigns' (props?), and 'word' (inscription) to 'deliver' meaning to the audience.[85] So, rather than an explicator narrating to the audience, or mystical symbols elevating the audience, Jonson posits an essentially rhetorical or dramatic model, especially if we understand 'word' in the passage not just as the motto or inscription, but the range of verbal elements, including speeches. This revelation of meaning 'without clouds' through dramatic narration supports greater understanding by the audience.

The passage, in contrast to *The Masque of Blackness* where the 'mute hieroglyphic' is chosen against the 'imprese' because of its 'strangeness, as relishing of antiquity' (222–3), highlights Jonson's concern to speak to those who are 'sharp and learned'. Jonson not only moves away from social hierarchies but also articulates one of the widely recognised difficulties of these public entertainments. In *Pageantry and Power* Tracey Hill provides a succinct account of the varieties of misprision that occurred in civic ritual and illustrates how different pageant-writers, responding the problem of how to address such a heterogene audience, stressed the verbal, the visual, and the popular in differing degrees. Echoing these concerns, on this occasion both Thomas Dekker and Jonson doubted the ability of the multitude to grasp abstruse classical allusion, but they diverge in their depiction of audience response. Dekker, while recognising the significance of the visual and popular in civic ritual, stresses how 'streets paved with men' enjoyed the spectacle, and dismisses those 'whose heads would miserably runne a wooll-gathering, if we doo but offer to breake them with hard words'.[86] Jonson, instead, moves away from present audiences to removed readers, and as he rewrites the performance as book, imagines an entirely different audience, especially in the quarto text that appeared at the time. Even as the quarto moves on, invoking a readerly experience where author and reader 'turn over a new leaf with you' (583) and progress to 'the pegme' in the Strand, Jonson returns to the twinned issues of readership and audience and develops a potential national audience:

> Thus hath both court-, town-, and country-reader our portion of device for the city; neither are we ashamed to profess it, being assured well of the difference between it and pageantry. (*Royall and Magnificent Entertainment*, 578–80)

In the 1604 quarto this passage, removed in the folio, follows directly from some of the most innovative typographic imitation in Jonson's canon, replicating the Roman altar and the inscription on the closed gate (548–77). Jonson's note, in turn, is marked out by its decorated initial 'T' and by its own specific type-forms, where the readership, yoked together by a short dashes, unites a broad spectrum of readers against the cynical 'wry mouths' of the spectators 'of the time' who can only see (and criticise) the 'mechanic part yet standing (580–1)'. While concerned to differentiate himself from the pageant-writers, Jonson also imagines an audience of 'court, town and country reader' which is not only geographically broader but also more socially and intellectually diverse.[87] In so doing, he situates himself as a poet with a national audience. The passage anticipates the differentiation between body (here 'the mechanic part') and soul in *Hymenaei*, but this inaugural essay in pageantry, in contrast, uses a skilfull manipulation of the dual performance and textual versions of the occasion to announce not 'removed mysteries' but a shared reading experience.[88] As with the earlier passage, spectating, gazing, and wondering are linked to a failure to understand, while reading and absorbing the 'device' are linked to the proper appreciation of meaning.

Jonson's attitude to audiences shifts across the timeline of his career, the genre of the text under discussion, and even, as Julie Sanders suggests, in the context of specific audiences on particular occasions.[89]

Indeed, in texts such as *The Masque of Queens*, Jonson's evocation of the poetic nature of the masque also invokes how 'a writer should always trust somewhat to the capacity of the spectator' with 'inquiring eyes' and 'quick ears' (*Queens*, 85–6), and posits a belief in the validity of ephemeral art forms and the capacity of the audience at odds with some views of Jonson as a 'literary exclusionist'.[90] While *The works* (1616), may have edited out the metropolitan reader and recast sections of the masques and entertainments to accentuate royal connections, the volume also catalogues a range of readers and audiences bound together by 'enquiring eyes' and 'quick ears'.[91] Even at the end of his career, returning to the masque in the context of a more isolated monarchy, Jonson's concern with the public and publication surfaces in the prefatory epistle 'To make the spectators understanders' to *Love's Triumph Through Callipolis*. In the first masque quarto of the Caroline period, itself a deliberate act of audience generation, Jonson restates the public role of masques as 'mirrors' that 'ought always to carry a mixture of profit with them no less than delight' (3–5). Strikingly, Jonson advocates collective engagement, not just from the 'lords and gentlemen called to the assistance', but in the description of masques as 'public spectacles'. Even as the epistle balances between constraints issued by the 'honour of [the] court' and the 'public' nature of the occasion, the publication seeks to bring the 'excellence of the exhibitors' and a wider audience together (1–7).

As is discussed in Chapter 6, the return to full-scale masquing, even employing the Jacobean masque-poet, may contribute to the Caroline ceremonial re-launch in the early 1630s (see p. 174 below), while the reinstatement of the large-scale publication efforts of the first decade of the Jacobean era with elaborate texts and commercial printers, may also suggest an awareness of audiences beyond the performers and those present. The shift from 'spectators' to 'understanders' may have been implicit in performance, but it is explicit in the printed text, the redaction of the event available to those beyond the court, echoing the ideal that these events were 'donatives of great princes to their people' (4). Yet the movement from the present performers to the removed readers also transforms the level of engagement as the superficial spectators are required to be textual understanders.[92]

The question of how and how far masque audiences understood what they saw and heard stretches back to Aby Warburg's sceptical response to Jacob Burkhardt's Florentine 'community of meaning' whereby audiences instantly comprehended complex allegories.[93] The masquing culture of the Jacobean and Caroline court encouraged audiences to become understanders, through a plethora of explicatory texts, the rehearsal process, the communal memory of previous performances, the textual realisations, and in performances that required audiences to evolve a double consciousness of performer and role. Although there is room for miscomprehension, mis-performance, and the whole panoply of accidents to which performance is prey, the numerous responses, especially in Chamberlain's newsletters and other political commentaries suggest that there were plenty of understanders at court and beyond. Often times, as with *The Irish Masque at Court* or *Pan's Anniversary*, the correspondence reported directly political and dissenting reactions. This book explores how this understanding allowed masques to contribute to the political culture of the Jacobean and Caroline periods, becoming sometimes the conduit for debates about political principles, for discussions of the role and nature of monarchy and political authority, and also about the opinions and ideas that existed beyond the court in the wider nations, ideas often expressed in language quite alien to courtly tact and negotiation.

This book, rooted in James VI and I's own sense in *Basilicon Doron* of the monarchical stage as a site of scrutiny rather than adulation, explores this potential for debate. It highlights moments of strain in the interaction between the masque and political culture, where the pressures on the form and the debates around its purpose are more urgent and explicit and where the questions of how to speak politics, how to engage in a political culture, erupt into the open. It begins with *Love Restored* (1611) as this offers an opportunity to explore how masquing responded to widespread parliamentary criticism of the court around the Great Contract and key questions of prerogative. This chapter illustrates not only the overlapping issues that fed political culture, combining matters of political principle and personal criticism of Robert Cecil, but also the potential for interaction between the civil discourses of the masque and the ruder world of libellous poetry echoed in its fiction where country comes to court.

The transactions between the world of libellous verse and the masque are developed in a discussion of the masques surrounding the Carr–Howard marriage in 1614, again exploring the interaction of uncivil language and the masque, but imagined here as ultimately pacified by the King. *The Irish Masque* debates language and civility in politics but applies its strictures not only in Ireland but to the rest of the kingdoms. The masques of this season are also implicated in a difficult and competitive set of factional relations, and intertextual rivalries between masque-writers and patrons, but the explosion of libellous verse and commentary beyond the court can be used to show how masquing became more permeable and open to responding to the scurrility and sexualised language through acts of generic transposition as sexual libel re-emerges as epithalamic masque.

The second half of this study examines how Jonson's increasing involvement with publication and his awareness of the growing news market in all its forms shapes the later masques. The central masques of this section, *News from the New World in the Moon* and *The Gypsies Metamorphosed* mark different interactions with the vibrant political culture that developed in the 1620s. In the political crisis created by the Palatine situation and parliamentary controversies in 1621, Jonson's masques were deeply engaged in the political debates, functioning as part of a sophisticated campaign of self-presentation orchestrated by Buckingham and his followers in response to the political denigration attempted by a shifting collation of opponents and sceptics. The 1620s saw a conscious response to libels that went beyond mechanisms of control or suppression and instead attempted counter-propaganda through responses and neutralisation, and masques belonged to these strategies as much as many other forms of more direct political debate such as polemical poetry.

Throughout these explorations of the masque the interaction between different writers, masque-models, and performance spaces focuses how masquing belonged to a broader, more contentious political culture. Space – or rather spatialised politics – has been at the heart of how the masque has been understood, especially in the link between perspectival space and Divine Right politics.[94] Yet the complexity of court structure, with its different households (dramatised in *The World Tossed at Tennis*), and the multiple purposes of courtly space as – literally – the space of government would suggest that the issue for the royal household was more about how to achieve control of the spaces and maintain order and privacy in what were, in essence, places of public business. There is a long tradition of using the halls of palaces for theatre and political debate, and even custom-built chambers, such as the Banqueting House, had multiple functions.[95] Thus, David Howarth's study of the Banqueting House highlights the judicial functions inherent in the building's architectural forms, while Chris Kyle has shown how Westminster Hall, filled with a 'microcosm' of early modern society (lobbyists, petitioners, lawyers, servants and above all crowds), operated as an 'open and accessible public space'.[96] Some of the implications of this revised spatial politics are raised in Chapters 4 and 5, especially in the context of the 'running masque' and the importation of its politics through *The Gypsies Metamorphosed*.

The final section of the book examines the involvement of the masque, and different masquing styles and spaces, in direct political debate in 1633. Shirley's *The Triumph of Peace* with its use of processional elements, its wide publication, and its paratextual materials illustrates how the masque, even in the Caroline period, might speak to a wider political nation. Shirley consciously echoes earlier Jacobean texts and their critical understanding of the role of masque as counsel and critique. But, crucially, Shirley's text responds to the calculated gesture of Jacobean nostalgia in Charles I's own restoration of the Twelfth Night masques. *The Triumph of Peace*, thus, intervenes in debates about the nature of kingship and the relation of monarchy and populace, illuminating a vibrant political culture in 1633 that demonstrated levels of political engagement and analysis fully capable of challenging the court and its policies.

The sophisticated manipulation of imagery and present occasions in *The Triumph of Peace* modifies any monolithic view of Caroline masque, especially in its formative period of 1630–34, but also suggests how this political culture could allow both nuanced debate and also the grounds for agreement, so that conflict and consensus may have coexisted within texts. Indeed, Shirley's masque requires us to revise our understanding of tact as a force in the control of critique in masque, because in Shirley's hands tact becomes a way to enable the articulation of controversial issues. In this sense, tact as a practice of politeness might seem inimical to debate, but in the context of a more adversarial and even hostile political culture – described by Gervase Clifton in 1637 as 'civill warres' – it gestures towards the kind of rational, measured discourses and discussions associated with the later modern public sphere.[97] Likewise, the consensus that is often vaunted as a feature of Caroline culture, can also be considered more rigorously, not just as challenged, fragile, and temporary as suggested in the halcyon imagery, but also as a process which contains and retains the traces of negotiation and conflict. Masques belong to the creation of this consensus, as the commissioning process of *The Triumph of Peace* so clearly shows, yet they also create 'civility situations', spaces in which difficult ideas or controversial modes of speech can be shaped into effective and acceptable tools of communication. In this reading masques are tools not toys.

2
'Vizarded impudence': Challenging the *regnum Cecilianum*

> I'll bring you where you shall find Love, and by the virtue of this majesty, who projecteth so powerful beams of light and heat through this hemisphere, thaw his icy fetters and scatter the darkness that obscures him. (*Love Restored*, 180–4)

Recent scholarship has celebrated *Love Restored* as a 'striking example of Jonson's skill with matters contingent', fashioning an acceptable text and political compromise from unpromising materials and situation.[1] Certainly, at the climactic moment its harmony was shattered when the carefully negotiated ordering of partners and dances that made up the revels was destroyed by Lady Essex and Lady Cranbourne who refused to dance, leaving the men 'alone and [to] make court to one another'.[2] Although this offers a classic demonstration of how individual courtiers and factions could (and often did) undermine the ideals of the fiction, this chapter concentrates on the broader implications of *Love Restored*'s engagement with voices outwith the court.

Although a 'negotiation' between differing court interests and factions, *Love Restored* also encompasses more difficult fractures in the Jacobean polity. Beyond the ramifications of tensions between Cecil's supporters, the King's entourage, and the bedchamber staff which reflected national, and often trenchantly expressed anti-Scots sentiment, *Love Restored* also deals with the limits of royal power.[3] Indeed, the 1610 Parliament and the campaign of libels and documentary responses that surrounded the Great Contract provide a key instance of the early Stuart public sphere where discussions of a government proposal appealed to wider publics (especially in Parliament), triggering waves of response and counter-response that culminated in the release of documents shedding light on one of the most concealed areas of *arcana imperii*, royal finances.[4] While the collapse of the 1610 Contract deal did not spell the end of the *regnum Cecilianum* ('the reign of Cecil'), temporary royal disfavour may have encouraged the first minister's vilification in popular poems, many of which date from the time of the masque's performance.[5]

Love Restored, this chapter will argue, echoes and refracts the questions of royal power and its limits heard in the parliamentary debates. It shadows and mediates not only their language but also the less respectful and rational terms of the anti-Cecilian libels. Indeed, in this context, *Love Restored* proposes an active role for the masque as counsel and mediation, bringing together the differing opinions and forces in the debates, and speaking difficult truths to those in power. *Love Restored* employs these critiques of Cecil as a means to explore the political function of the masque in a national political debate, but also uses the explicit reshaping of masque form and method to examine the role of praise and detraction in civil society.

The 'icy fetters' of failure

Love Restored, In a Masque at Court, staged on Twelfth Night 1612, marks a crisis in the masque as the dejected Masquerado – the masque personified – faces his potential audience to explain that they have no musicians and the boy playing Cupid has lost his voice.[6] Without harmony and love, there can be no masque, and worse follows when a figure, dressed to look like Cupid, denounces the 'unprofitable evils' of such a 'false and fleeting delight', ordering Masquerado to leave. A contemporary audience would not have strained to recognise the issue here about the costs of masques as, shortly before *Love Restored* was staged and having already borrowed from the City of London, the King had resorted to the expedient of forced loans under privy seals to keep the Crown temporarily solvent. Although the difficulties over royal finance had been growing since 1603, the immediate cause of this cash crisis lay in the collapse of the Great Contract, Robert Cecil's scheme to provide solid and long-lasting foundations for the royal finances. In response to fiscal crisis Jonson offered a 'budget' entertainment, replacing the complex mythographical fables characteristic of early Jacobean texts, not simply with a masque about why there won't be a masque, but with a masque restored to its true form.[7]

Austerity is the mother of innovation: in *Love Restored* the large-scale antimasques of earlier years are reduced to a three-hander conversation, prose replaces verse, and elaborate, mechanical scenic effects, such as the House of Fame (*The Masque of Queens*, 1609) or Oberon's palace (*Oberon*, 1611) are supplanted by an entry for Cupid and his masquers in a chariot that may even have been recycled from previous masques. Significantly, *Love Restored* substitutes lesser courtiers – 'gallants chosen out of the King's and Prince's Men' – for aristocratic masquers or the Queen's ladies. Described in the final printed text as 'Gentlemen the King's servants', *Love Restored* marked the first appearance of the bedchamber staff as main masque performers, and uniquely mixed staff from Prince Henry's and the King's households (see pp. 30–1 below for a discussion of individual masquers).[8] Significantly, the masque pivots on Cupid and the final masquers, who are not only 'ten ornaments' individually, but each ornament also combines to 'each courtly presence grace' (228–9).[9] Specific differentiated roles are attached to individuals in a way not seen in the earlier masques where the final entries tend to involve symbolic groups; in *Love Restored* the collective outcome and identity depends on active individual embodiment.

The full title, *Love Restored, In a Masque at Court*, claims a key role for the form as political instrument ('in a masque') and suggests that the source of restoration lies outside the court.[10] Leah Marcus has noted how the masque elevates Goodfellow, 'the plain country spirit' (50), as the external agent, the 'subtler spirit' and 'better discoverer', who restores love *to* the court, invoking an idealised country that helps correct and purge the imbalances of the body politic.[11] To claim that the court, 'unable to diagnose what ails it', requires external support opens a significant contradiction between the claims of political efficacy and the sense of failure that attaches to the court ('Are these your court sports', 46). Indeed, this failure is reflected in the impotency of Masquerado who can neither perform ('I would I could make 'em a show', 1) nor fully understand ('Either I am very stupid, or this is a reformed Cupid', 155). The masque's world in 'icy fetters' (183, also 173–5, 196–7, 206–11) encapsulates the bleak political and financial situation as well as the difficult position for masque and masque writer trying to negotiate between irreconcilable forces. For all its bravura performances and dizzying meta-theatrical commentary, the masque bespeaks fragility and uncertainty: 'Though I dare not show my face, I can speak truth under a vizard' (4–5).

This possibility of failure invests the attempt to bring love to the court with urgency but, even as Robin acts to discover Plutus and restore Cupid, he makes Masquerado and the mortal world the vehicle of that restoration: 'if you had wisdom, he had no godhead' (178). So *Love Restored* invokes the political nation as a counterpoise to the frozen world of the court and posits a new kind of politics where individual ethics and collective virtues must coexist. The language of love from political discourse is restored to the masque, not just through its invocation, but through a process of redefinition that outlines new forms of politics. The final song of *Love Restored* differentiates between resolutions based on laboured negotiation or contract (mortal politics) and those rooted in free will, or 'strife / Of duty', which recognises mutual reciprocity (love politics). Significantly, though, this ending is itself 'a morning dream' (251) as Plutus is merely banished to his caves, dismissing 'how bitterly the spirit of poverty spouts itself against my weal and felicity' (155–6). *Love Restored* ends on a conditional, fragile, and fleeting dream requiring concerted and continued effort to be realised.

'The canker of want': prodigality, royal finances, and the masque

> Nor shall those graces ever quit your court
> Or I be wanting to supply their sport. (254–5)

Love Restored resonates with the question of 'supply', the parliamentary term for revenue. From Plutus' invective against 'superfluous excess' (151–2) through to the image of a frozen world, the questions of who shall pay for the masque are foregrounded. Even the language of love echoes the contemporary debate, and two years earlier in a speech to Parliament James reminded members that their duty was to supply him, but how much to provide 'must come of your loves'.[12] Love as a metaphor for political loyalty was a commonplace of the period, but in *Love Restored* the interconnections of masque, money, and love become the present occasion for a stringent meditation on the roles of obedience and counsel. James I's speech, with its balance of duty to supply and the demonstration of loyalty through the extent of that supply, is paralleled in the differentiation between resolutions based on free will and those based on negotiation or contract. These are expounded in the final song of *Love Restored* which hymns the 'motion of love begot' which inspires grace and obedience: 'But ask not how' (262).

The financial problems of the Jacobean state can be summed up simply: too much monarchy, not enough money. As early as 1604 the cost of maintaining the royal households in the magnificent style to which they wished to become accustomed had caused consternation in the Council and criticism beyond.[13] Structural and strategic features exacerbated the problem: even Elizabeth I had struggled to live within her declining revenues, while the usual excuse of warfare to justify taxation had largely evaporated with the Treaty of London (1604). By 1610 her successor, with three royal households to maintain, was forced to relinquish substantial revenues from the Duchy of Cornwall as Prince Henry came of age, requiring not only a separate establishment, but also money to meet his architectural ambitions.[14] There was also a need to find the contingency funds that might be required if war did develop in Cleves-Jülich.[15] Cecil's initial survey of the King's monies in 1608 calculated the cumulative debt as about £600,000, with annual expenditure of £375,000 outstripping revenues of £300,000.[16] Although by 1610 Cecil had reduced the debt to £300,000 and the annual deficit to about £50,000, using a variety of financial controls and extra-parliamentary taxation such as the imposition on imports of luxury goods (which raised about £75,000 per annum), this progress towards solvency could not be sustained. Indeed, the reliance on prerogative taxation measures in the absence of sufficient parliamentary income caused 'great distraction and scandal' among the populace.[17]

Cecil's plan, the Great Contract, proposed that key aspects of royal fiscal prerogative (the King's ability to raise money without Parliament's agreement) would be signed away for a permanent tax base. Under this exchange a lump sum would dissolve the Crown's current debts and an annual income would be raised in perpetuity.[18] Recent historical research on the Contract has suggested that Cecil's ultimate aim was a 'revolution' in government that would resolve the tension between parliamentary and prerogative finance, creating a bureaucratic state run by the Council and funded by Parliament, and a much reduced household where offices, such as the bedchamber (see p. 28 below), ministered to the King's domestic needs but retained only a restricted political role.[19] The Contract exposes a debate around principles (prerogative against Parliament finance), and political negotiations which are not simply between court factions, but which engaged different if still overlapping sections of the state structure, the court with its factions and internal structures, the Council and bureaucracy, and Parliament.

Cecil's bargain, which involved an unpalatable upfront payment of unprecedented amounts, was first obstructed and finally defeated by a combination of parliamentary wariness over the King's attachment to prerogative powers (especially taxation), factional politicking within the court (the difficulty of aligning all the interests on the Privy Council, pressures from other parts of the court such as the bedchamber), and marked scepticism that the King could or would control his reckless bounty.[20] Cecil described royal generosity as an 'Ignis Edax, a devouring fire' of such magnitude that he feared the English Crown might become permanently impoverished unless curbed, while Prince Henry baulked at being married off, in effect, to the highest bidder not only because he 'did not desire to be either bought or sold', but because he also worried the dowry 'would not come into his hands nor be applied for the good of the Crown' but instead 'be scattered by the King's profusion'.[21]

As the negotiations for the Great Contract in its various forms dragged on throughout 1610 the main stumbling block emerged around the royal bounty. With mistrust on both sides, one parliamentarian noted that the debt and subsidy plan risked that 'the like [demands] may spring up again the next year and so wee be forced to redeem them also', while another commented that 'all these courses would be to no purpose, except it would please the King to resume his pensions granted to courtiers out of the exchequer, and to diminish his charge and expenses'.[22] Cecil had expressed similar view to the King in private, even though in Parliament he had listed other causes for royal indebtedness. James, in return in speech and in print, defended the principle of kingly liberality as essential to the magnificence and dignity of the throne: 'I have spent much: but yet if I had spared any of those things which caused a great part of my expense, I should have dishonoured the kingdom, myself, and the late Queen.'[23] He even refuted the idea that he had been over-generous to the Scots, pointing out that the English, his new subjects, would hardly expect gratitude from him if he dealt unfavourably with his old servants and subjects, and arguing that he had 'dealt twice as much amongst English men as I have done to Scottishmen'.[24] James succinctly summarised the situation in a letter to Cecil: 'whenever the tenor of bounty is touched, the Scots must ever be tacitly understood'.[25]

Anti-Scots feelings were visceral and continuous for most of the first decade of James I's reign. Some of the objections to the union, often mounted by Cecil's parliamentary clients (something that the King and his Scots entourage noted and resented) were principled and legal objections, but much was expressed in intemperate and threatening terms. Sir Christopher Piggott's 'invective against the Scots and Scottish nation using many words of scandal and obloquy' spoken in Parliament in 1607 was 'ill-beseeming such an audience ... and very unseasonable for the time and occasion as after was conceived'. Piggot's speech, although widely condemned as 'unadvised and rude', echoes an extensive anti-Scots campaign that even reached the stage.[26] Chapman, Jonson, and Marston's *Eastward Ho* (1605), and Day's *Isle of Gulls* (1606) were topped by the obscure and notorious 'play of the mines', which probably attacked the Scottish silver mine project. Another occasion, reported by the Florentine agent, Ottaviano Lotti, illustrates how public and direct opposition to the Scots had become:

> A poet's work almost caused a very grave scandal, because several players who were acting it on stage performed it so that when one of the characters wanted to make a serenade to a lady he went and gathered various sorts of music, and many people appeared, with viols, violins, lutes, harps, flutes and suchlike, each one of them claiming to come from one part or another of the provinces of England. They were admitted to the band, and all together they made a concord which gave delight. At length someone arrived with a bagpipe which, besides being toneless, made such a noise that it stunned and ruined all the music.
>
> Finally he averred that he was a Scotsman, and he was bundled out and told that he had very little judgment if he thought that so villainous an instrument could harmonize and unite with others so noble and so worthy. The Scots knights who were present to hear the play thought about making their resentment plain right there, but they refrained, and hoped that the king would be greatly moved to anger. But because what I may call the merciful offices of his Majesty to lead these deputies in Parliament toward the union of the two realms have little availed with them, they say that his Majesty had dismissed them all.[27]

Lotti's account of this vivid satire connects such popular occasions directly to the debates in Parliament about the union, but it also (by evoking the enraged 'Scots knights') recalls the concerns about disruption of class hierarchy and even miscegenation that fill the numerous anti-Scots libels that circulated during the first Jacobean Parliament. In 'Jocky is grown a gentleman', clothes mark the man, so that the feckless Scot is 'turned to satin' from 'doublet and breech that were so plain'.[28] The ubiquitous 'They beg our goods, our lands, our lives' was 'everywhere posted' and even travelled as far as the Dutch town of Middleburg, where it was intercepted and sent to the diplomat William Trumbull:

> They beg our goods, our lands, and our lives,
> They whip our nobles and lie with their wives,
> They pinch our gentry, and send for the benchers,
> They stab our sergeants, and pistol our fencers.[29]

The violence suggested in the poem did erupt from time to time. So, in 1612 and in the immediate months following *Love Restored*, William Ramsay assaulted the Earl of Montgomery at Croydon races, the Scots courtier James Maxwell quarrelled with James Hawley of the Temple at a feast for the Duc de Bouillon, a Scot called Murray, and his servants, killed a London sergeant, and, in May 1612, the Scots Catholic Robert Crichton, Earl of Sanquhar, had an English fencing-master, John Turner, assassinated.[30]

One group became the focus for particular resentment: the gentlemen of the bedchamber. Under the post-1603 reorganization, elements of the more informal, French-based, Scots court-system had been imported.[31] Although the new court had been designed to reflect the union of the crowns and the intended union of nations, only appointments to the Privy Chamber were divided equally between Scots and Englishmen. The 1603 structure included an inner chamber, the King's bedchamber, staffed entirely by Scots, and whereas members of the Privy Chamber, the aristocracy, and even councillors like Cecil were constrained by strict rules of entry and decorum, access for bedchamber members was unrestricted and apparently informal. John Holles, who had been displaced from his position as Gentleman of the Privy Chamber, stated the issue baldly:

> The Scottish monopolize his [the King's] princely person, standing like mountains betwixt the beams of his grace and us; and, though it becomes us not to appoint particulars about him, yet we most humbly beseech his Majesty his Bedchamber may be shared as well to those of our nation as to them . . . and that the same Chamber may have the same brotherly partition which all the other inferior forms of the court, the Presence and the Privy Chamber have.[32]

Access to the monarch, as Holles says, provided power and money, and it has been suggested that Cecil's difficulties in holding together the components of the deal were hampered by the requirement he arrange an audience while senior Scots nobles like the Earl of Dunbar had constant access to the King.[33] Some sense of the extent of the massive power and profit accruing to the bedchamber Scots can be gauged in astonishing gifts like the £45,000 given in 1607 to settle the debts of Hay and Haddington, alongside those of the (Anglo-Welsh) Earl of Montgomery. Indeed, under Crown patronage for the whole period 1558–1642, of the twenty-nine individuals who received 75 per cent of all patronage, ten of them were gentlemen of the bedchamber.

Forty-five per cent of all Crown patronage in this period went to nine individuals, six of whom belonged to the bedchamber. In the midst of financial crisis, a further £34,000 paid to clear debts of the bedchamber staff in 1611 caused particular outrage.[34]

In the 1610 session, in addition to a planned petition asking the King to send all the Scots home, several members tied the refinancing of the monarchy to the Scots issue. John Hoskyns claimed 'the royal cistern had a leak, which till it were stopped, all our consultation to bring money into it was of little use', while John More wrote to Winwood stating that the Commons would happily have aided the King but 'that his Majesties largess to the Scots prodigality would not cause a continual and remediless leak'.[35] In November 1610 the French ambassador reported that Parliament had complained about the gifts given to the Scots, wishing them 'mal de mort' and even raised the possibility of a Sicilian vespers directed against them.[36] In short, efforts to resolve royal finances provoked resentment against the Scots: as John More noted in December 1610, 'common discourse' was all against the Scots, alongside a resurgence of anti-Scots libelling and the renewed armed clashes of early 1612. Interestingly, John Chamberlain copied 'They beg our lands' onto the same sheet as one of the libels on Cecil's death, an association that may suggest how Cecil had become identified with the Scots for some, although historians suggest his relations with the Scots were more complex and fraught.[37] Indeed, a prose libel addressed to Lord Haddington pretends sympathy over the attacks on royal 'prodigality and bounty' towards the Scots and suggests, instead, that these 'witty and cunning speeches' which 'name and blame' the Scots are a ruse to distract attention from the originators' own peculation.[38] The libel noted that these 'caterpillars of the kingdom and subtle snakes in the bosom of their sovereign' are led by 'one little person' who disguises his own profits from wardship.[39]

Cecil seems to have managed his relations with the Scots with skill despite the limitations they placed on his room for manoeuvre. On a number of occasions he had personally intervened to cool disputes, cultivating key figures such as Dunbar.[40] Cecil's opinions about the need to limit the financial rewards for Scots were blunt, but he also rejected 'any frivolous objection', such as the suggestion the Scots should return home: James was their king, too, and they had a right of access and service.[41] Even in 1610 during the heated discussions about the cost of the Scots bedchamber, Cecil had delicately argued,

> we persuade a certain provision for some that are of greatest use, and must be near about your person or adorn your court, neither

propounding a restrain of access to your court or service, for any man that shall repair thither out of Scotland, or dwell here upon his own means; accounting it rather a comfort . . . than a burden to see those that are fellow subjects desirous to behold the face of their king . . . Neither have we a thought to exceed them or any other of your Majesty's servants and well-deserving subjects from the fruits of your bounty . . . But our desires and persuasions tend only to this, that your Majesty will be pleased to make a distinction of men, and to weigh their merits and reward in an even balance . . .[42]

Although expressed in guarded terms, Cecil's proposition was to pay off the debts of the Scots, and in return they would cede their influence.

Love Restored, staged with its cast of Scottish dancers and members of the bedchamber staff linked directly to the King, appears amidst this climate of open critique of Cecil and the courtier Scots. It may be that the suggestions of indecision and negotiation about who was to hold the masque, who was to perform, and who was to pay, reflect an awareness of the fraught situation. The earliest plan seems to have been for a joint masque for the Queen and Prince, although at some stage this transmuted into a masque to be offered by the Prince to the King.[43] Chamberlain's letter points towards a joint masque, but this time between James and Henry with 'gallants chosen out of the King's and Prince's Men'.[44] It is thus possible that *Love Restored* contributed to Henry's charm offensive at Whitehall aimed at reducing some of the tensions over royal finances between the King and the newly established court of the Prince of Wales.[45] If Henry did attempt to control or use *Love Restored*'s agenda, the printed text gives the performers as 'Gentlemen the King's servants', linking the final version to the King.[46]

Unfortunately, the identity of the final masquers who dance the 'ten ornaments' cannot be ascertained. The incomplete list that survives includes two Scots, and one English masquer with Scots affiliations: 'Abercrummit', 'Leviston', and 'Sir W. Bowiers son'.[47] 'Leviston' was probably John Livingston of Kinnaird, a groom of the bedchamber who derived considerable benefit from the sale of recusant lands.[48] He appears on a list of pensioners for Christmas 1611, and spectacularly in March 1612 gained £1000 'as of his Majesty's free gift to betaken out of moneys arising out of the fines and forfeitures reserved for his Majesty's bounties'.[49] In short, he was exactly the kind of Scot of whom the Commons had complained.[50]

The remaining two individuals had reputations as dancers. Although there were several Abercrombies at the Jacobean court, the likely performer here is Abraham Abercromby, a 'Scottish dancing courtier', possibly initially connected to Prince Henry and later to the King.[51] Lastly, Henry Bowyer, the son of Sir William Bowyer of Denham, Buckinghamshire, who may have owed his parliamentary seat to Cecil, died of smallpox in 1614 caused, apparently, by 'over-heating himself with practising' for *The Irish Masque* (another 'medley maske of five English and five Scotts').[52] Henry Bowyer appears to have been on good terms with the Scots as he brokered marriage between Sir Thomas Erskine, later first Earl of Kellie, and the widow of Sir Edward Norris of Rycote.[53]

This prominence of the Scots noted in Chamberlain's letter may well suggest the presentation of a united front, much as had happened in Parliament, against the English who had criticised royal liberality and by implication, therefore, the Scottish courtiers.[54] In this context, the emphasis upon money in *Love Restored* seems calculated not simply to respond to any demonstrable shortage of money but, rather, to use the fiction of stringency to pursue a political point, especially since the Scots and royal liberality were inextricably linked in the English political imaginary. Indeed, the costs of masquing, seen as the signature of the new regime and its Scots adherents, had attracted criticism as early as 1604 when a draft letter from the Council to the King warned against the costs complaining that 'many Christmases pass without any such note, dancing, comedies, plays having been thought sufficient marks of mirth'.[55] The language of these comments is revealingly close to the wider debate on royal bounty and magnificence and the question of what was regarded as 'sufficient' and to whom was clearly a disputed concept. It also suggests that the masque could, handily, stand for a wider political debate.

Indeed, this sense that money in *Love Restored* reflects other key issues in court culture is confirmed if we examine the details of the rest of the 1611–12 Christmas expenditure.[56] Not only was this season marked by almost nightly play productions between 26 December 1611 and 6 January 1612 including *A King and No King*, *Greene's Tu Quoque*, *Cupid's Revenge*, *The Almanac*, and *The Twin's Tragedy*, but the same Chamberlain letter that details *Love Restored* also records extensive gift-giving, gambling, and tilting.[57] Certainly £280 is a small sum in this expenditure, much less than average cost per masque of £1000 to £1500, but pales next to the £1500 Arabella Stuart is reported to have expended on one dress in 1611. Indeed, Cecil presented figures to Parliament in 1610 that suggested the combined cost of Elizabeth I's funeral, the Jacobean coronation, the 1606 entertainment for the King of Denmark, and other diplomatic costs had been £500,000.[58]

Thus the text gave voice to many of the critiques of royal liberality but Jonson's strategy is to associate the desire for 'more frugal pastimes' (141) with 'a reformed Cupid' (155) and with the 'discontented tribes' (229), phrases redolent of strict Protestantism. This ideological antipathy to the masque is driven home by the way that Plutus/Cupid is equally antagonistic to the homely pleasures propounded by Robin Goodfellow thus making cost the explicit excuse that masks more fundamental, less altruistic, objections. Truth is, indeed, revealed from under its vizard, as the strict Protestant appropriations of Truth are shown to be not only mean-spirited and contrary to the necessary liberality of the court and communal social harmony, but also motivated by religious ideology rather than cost-saving. In this sense *Love Restored* stresses the proper use of money, so that economic values such as profit are translated into a 'better' symbolic economy. What Plutus describes as 'unprofitable evils' (31), implying both cost and uselessness, Robin argues create the kind of sociability necessary to civil society. These ties are epitomised by the 'strife / Of duty' (237–8) that Cupid recognises he owes to the royal sun that liberated him from his 'icy fetters' (183), but also the idea of a 'restored' masque.[59] Jonson's terminology rejects Protestant ideas of spiritual and poetic reformation in favour of the revivification and reinvigoration of already existing traditions: this after all is, pointedly, *Love Restored* not love reformed.[60]

Love Restored, then, does not simply defend courtly magnificence, exchanging one sort of profit for another, and nor does it simply navigate any real financial stringency. It takes – even exaggerates – the known financial problems of the court and deploys them to connect the language of those criticising royal bounty with Puritanism, casting the King's reasonable opponents as his ideological enemies. In a classic Jonsonian inversion, Plutus expresses his desire for moderation in entirely immoderate terms, misapplying the language of (in)decorum: Masquerado has 'profaned' the court (27). Indeed, the decision to produce a verbal rather than visual masque, and – as we shall see – to make language and its authority the centre of that masque as well as its medium, may not solely result from Jonson's 'skill with matters contingent' in the sense of making a masque in a court devoid of money, but also posits a highly charged political argument in a court where money and its uses symbolise wider political conflicts. The masque itself becomes a 'restoration' of monarchy, and the proper uses of speech and counsel in civil society.

'A reformed Cupid': *Love Restored* and the poetry of opposition

The attention to language and its use forms a crucial part of the political intervention attempted in this masque. The novel prose antimasque, introducing a mode more associated with everyday, vernacular, and even popular traditions, dramatises the difficulties in achieving directness and even critique in language suitable for court contexts and for address to the King. Although verse and song still embody the final values of the masque and the return to order, the use of prose to 'discover' the false Cupid/Plutus destabilises the straightforward assumption of the higher status of verse: the rational discursive forms embodied in prose are needed to work in concert with the aspiration that 'all the morning dreams are true' (270).[61] Yet, even though Robin proclaims himself an 'honest plain country spirit and harmless' (52–3) in 1610–12 popular voices were far from festive. The appearance of Robin marks an attempt to include but also subordinate those voices and energies so that *Love Restored* demonstrates an unusual responsiveness to criticism from beyond the court.

These issues of decorum and address, but also of the limits of criticism, colour much of the debate over the royal bounty. The rumbling disagreement between King and Parliament over the limits and nature of their discussions is expressed in James' view of some of the Commons' complaints in 1606 as 'pasquils'.[62] Indeed, among Cecil's papers from this Parliament a draft survives of two proclamations, one against the 'excess of liberty' practised during the Parliament and the rumours that surrounded its business, and one reminding subjects against the fomentation of 'murmur and alienation' and that parliamentary liberties were limited to speeches 'in a manner not clamorous or tumultuous' and to Parliament times.[63] This difference between permitted discourse in Parliament and beyond formed a central part of the King's speech to Parliament on 21 March 1610, which contrasted legitimate grievances, whose resolution he regarded as a key feature of Parliament, and 'pasquils', the product of 'grudging and murmuring spirits' which had been aired not only in the House but 'even in many other peoples' mouths' and 'taken up in the streets'.[64] This issue of the proper spaces of discourse – the King talked of England as 'settled in civility' – runs through the masque. In the inverted world that Plutus has created, his critique, filled with the supposed indecorum of these 'vanities' for 'high places' (136) and accusations of impertinence (21) and 'impudence' (26), is itself highly inappropriate and disrespectful.[65] The paradoxes of Plutus' claims are used to suggest that criticism of the royal bounty is itself impertinent and unsuitable, not merely unseasonable, but the 'license of surquidry' (29).

The 'grudging and murmuring spirits' of the parliamentary speech are echoed in the notable emphasis upon Plutus/Cupid as a rough and wild orator: he is 'hoarse', not from the ill-effects of trying to speak while accompanied only by 'wild music' (14–15), but from his voicing of invective. As the dismayed Masquerado asks: 'Ha' you recovered you voice to rail at me' (25). To 'rail' was straightforwardly to speak abusively, but it is a term most closely associated with satire and with the style and stance of libel or 'railing rhymes' as James I would later call them.[66] This precise choice of terminology pins down Plutus as an unsuitable speaker and connects him to the kinds of oppositional writing, the ballads, libels, and satirical petitions, used so intensively in 1610–12 to articulate attacks on the Scots, on royal bounty, on prerogative taxation, and on the failure of the Parliament and King to achieve agreement and consensus.

Cupid's railing, however, has another, more specific resonance which illuminates not only the connection of this masque to wider political culture, but to one of the main vehicles of that culture, the libellous verses that are echoed in the masque's language. After the collapse of the Great Contract, Cecil had suffered 'savage' criticism not only from the King (though in the intervening two years his position recovered slightly), but from numerous, violent 'outrageous speeches' that shocked contemporary observers.[67] Although Robert Cecil's death from cancer exacerbated by a particular form of scurvy that caused him to stink as if rotting alive was capitalised upon in a rather disgusting manner by the libellers, the combination of Cecil's body shape, his supposed sexual misdemeanours (he was often said to have died of the pox), and his political dealings are also found in many of the pre-1611 libels. Indeed, the anti-Cecil texts reiterate his base birth, his corruption and peculation, his taxation policy (often contrasted with his own money-grubbing), his sexuality, and his physical appearance.[68] In one early libel by followers of the Earl of Essex he was called 'Toad'; later he was camel, 'spider-shapen', fox, wren, 'heart-griping Harpy', dolphin, and his 'crooked manners' and 'crooked shape' were equated.[69] Cecil's physical disability allowed him to be cast as 'Robin Crooked back', worse than 'Richard the third, he was Judas the second'. Ultimately, this writer decides there is little to choose between late medieval tyrant king and late tyrannical minister: 'A crooked back great in state is England's curse.'[70] The pun in this title, that Cecil was 'unjustly reckoned', provides a subtler version of other poems that figure the Lord Treasurer as a corrupt, cheating tax-gatherer who fleeced others while preserving himself. This accusation is developed in one of the more sophisticated of the libels, possibly by Sir Walter Ralegh, which may gesture towards Jacobean representation of James VI and I as 'Pan':

> Here lies Hobbinol our shepherd while ere
> Who once a year duly our fleeces did sheer,
> To please us his cur he chained to a clog
> And was himself after both shepherd and dog.
> For oblation to Pan his order was thus,
> Himself gave a trifle and sacrificed us
> And so with his wisdom this provident swain
> Kept himself on the mountain and us on the plain
> Where many a fine hornpipe he tuned to his Phyllis
> And sweetly sung Walsingham to Amarillis,
> Till Atropos paid him, a pox on the drab
> In spite of the tar-box, he died of the scab.[71]

The poem moves seamlessly through financial misdeeds and sexual allegations and ends with the symbolic eruption of corruption in the body. These images of physical disease are explored in 'The Devil now hath fetched the ape' where Cecil is compared to Herod who famously died of 'gangrene of the privy parts' and this attribution of a cause to his dramatic decline to venereal disease implied divine judgement and 'was widely appreciated as a sign of social transgression'.[72]

Throughout the 1600s Cecil appears to have fought 'a defensive war' (to use John Donne's phrase: see p. 37 below) to salvage his reputation. In particular, his role in the destruction of the Earl of Essex may well have caused much of his unpopularity, and beyond the obvious symbolism of the Herodian disease that combined the accusations of monstrosity and personal, moral, and political corruption that haunted Cecil, the post-Essex libels cemented a reputation for political deviousness.[73] So, in the fabulously titled 'Here sleeps in the Lord bepeppered with the pox', Salisbury was depicted as 'a Cecilian monster begot of a fox', an allusion that plays on both his and his father's reputations for political machination.[74] The 'fox' here is both his father, Lord Burghley whose fox-fur gown attracted derogatory comments in several of the post-Essex libels, while the phrase also suggests Cecil is himself a fox.

Punningly, the poem also smears Cecil as a monstrous murderer: the original spelling 'Ciciliane', modernised as Cecilian, is a phonic pun on 'Sicilian', implying that the Essex revolt became a Sicilian vespers by which Cecil removed his enemies.[75]

The Cecil libels represent one of the versiferous explosions that accompany the occasional crises of debate that constituted public political culture in the early 1600s, and like riot they have been seen as 'a form of crisis communication between rulers and ruled', although the ubiquity of the Cecil texts argues for a greater penetration of different social groups and geographical regions.[76] Their prevalence and ferocity was enough to attract contemporary commentary which tended to see them, not always favourably, as marking a shift in the culture of libelling. According to these accounts, the scattered scurrilous verses of the mid-sixteenth century gradually increase in number, intensity, and degree of scurrility, to become an almost constant presence in society which tested the boundaries of civility. Thus, John Chamberlain, writing on the culmination of the libelling wave after Cecil's death remarked:

> The memory of the Lord Treasurer grows daily worse and worse and more libels come as it were continually, whether it be that practises and jugglings come more to light, or that men love to follow the sway of the multitude: but it is certain that they who may best maintain it, have not forborne to say that he juggled with religion, with the King, Queen, their children, with nobility, parliament, with friends, foes and generally with all. Some of his chaplains have been heard to oppose themselves what they could in pulpit against these scandalous speeches but with little fruit.[77]

Chamberlain hints that the power of the libels, in part, lay in their credibility. Cecil had been a consummate politician so that the 'practises and jugglings' that might 'come more to light' and cause the attacks, might well be believed. Chamberlain is very clear, however, about the scale of the problem and the spread of information as the chaplains attempt to redress his reputation against 'the sway of the multitude'.

These libels represent something more than personal invective. For Pauline Croft the publication of pro-Cecil tracts, presumably coupled with the sermons mentioned by John Chamberlain, designed to correct some of the libels and defend his actions over imposition and the Great Contract, constituted a 'concerted attempt' at a posthumous defence.[78] This may itself develop from Cecil's own use of printed propaganda, for example at the time of the Gunpowder Plot, when he even published a response in English and Latin to the 'contumelious papers and pasquils dispersed abroad in divers parts of the City'.[79] During 1610–12, as part of the appeal to pass the Great Contract, an unprecedented tide of political material passed around the nation: in particular, a collection of printed parliamentary material was issued, claiming to have been produced abroad, and defending Parliament's attitude to the Great Contract; attacks on the legality of impositions were circulated in manuscript; and localities would have heard from their returned MPs about the debates as they had been instructed to canvass their neighbours' opinions.[80] These various approaches to political persuasion show how the 1610s saw a campaign to influence public opinion through a range of media ranging from printed royal justifications through to scurrile squibs.[81]

Something of the impact of the Cecil libels is suggested in Chamberlain's letters, and in other correspondents of the period who noted the 'many epitaphs written upon the dead Treasurer', but the most sophisticated and suggestive analysis comes from the poet John Donne.[82] He wrote to Sir Henry Goodyer from Spa:

> Nothing in my L[ord] of *Salisburies* death exercised my poor considerations so much, as the multitude of libels. It was easily discerned, some years before his death, that he was at a defensive war, both for his honour and health, and (as we thought) for his estate: and I thought, that had removed much of the envy. Besides, I have just reasons to think, that in the chiefest businesses between the Nations, he was a very good patriot. But I meant to speak of nothing but the libels, of which, all which are brought into these parts, are so tasteless and flat, that I protest to you, I think they were made by his friends. It is not the first time that our age hath seen that art practised[.] That when there are witty and sharp libels made which not only for the liberty of speaking, but for the elegancy and composition, would take deep root, and make durable impressions in the memory, no other way hath been thought to suppresses them as to divulge some coarse, and railing one: for which the noise is risen, that libels are abroad, men's curiosity must be served with something: and it is better for the honour of the person traduced, that some blunt downright railings be vented, of which every body is soon weary, then other pieces, which entertain us long with a delight, and love to the things themselves. I doubt not but he smothered some libels against him in his life time. But I would all these (or better) had been made then, for they might have testified that the Authors had meant to mend him, but now they can have no honest pretence. I dare say to you, where

I am not easily misinterpreted, that there may be cases, where one may do his country good service, by libelling against a live man. For, where a man is either too great or his vices too general, to be brought under a judiciary accusation, there is no way, but this extraordinary accusing, which we call libelling[.] And I have heard that nothing hath souped and allayed the D[uke] of *Lerma* in his violent greatness, so much as the often libels made upon him. But after death, it is, in all cases, unexcusable. I know that *Lucifer*, and one or two more of the fathers who writ libellous books against the emperors of their times, are excused by our writers, because they writ not in the lives of those emperors. I am glad for them that they writ not in their lives, for that must have occasioned tumult, and contempt, against so high and sovereign persons. But that doth not enough excuse them to me, for writing so after their death; for that was ignoble, and useless, though they did a little escape the nature of libels, by being subscribed and avowed: which excuse would not have served in the Star-chamber, where sealed letters have been judged libels, but these of which we speak at this present, are capable of no excuse, no amolishment, and therefore I cry you mercy, and my self too, for disliking them, with so much diligence, for they deserve not that.[83]

Donne's letter provides considerable insight into thinking about libel among sophisticated and literate readers, notably the pleasure afforded by memorable 'witty and sharp' poems while coarser texts – the more 'sluttish' as another collector terms them – fade away.[84] Libelling is justifiable not only for its 'elegancy', but also as a corrective of men's behaviour ('meant to mend'), acquiring an almost judicial function ('extraordinary accusing') especially for those beyond the easy reach of the law. Donne's strictures against posthumous libelling which cannot achieve 'amolishment' of behaviour ('after death, it is, in all cases, unexcusable') may explain some of the outrage the Cecilian libels occasioned.[85] Donne's purposive reading of libels, however, overlays moral with political dimensions. Donne views libelling as a patriotic duty as in the instance of libels against Lerma (which also suggests a fascinating *pan-European* awareness of political verse) and hints at the possibility of campaigns of libel and counter-libel. Indeed, concern for individual honour and reputation can be subsumed by the possibility of 'liberty of speaking' no matter how uncomfortable.

Donne's interpretation of Cecil's own approach is penetrating. Not only did Cecil ensure the suppression of some libels during his lifetime ('I doubt not but he smothered some libels'), but his friends,

Donne implies, may even be engaged in a subtle campaign of releasing 'some blunt downright railings . . . of which everybody is soon weary'. This evidence of what Donne strongly hints are organised campaigns ('It is not the first time that our age hath seen that art practised'), echoing the modern political arts of the spin-doctor, depends on subtle gradations within libel, and a sophisticated audience awareness of the effects of different types of political poetry.[86] Alongside the recognition of a popular appetite for such verse, Donne even suggests disinformation campaigns whereby the wider population will swallow the 'coarse, and railing one[s]', distracted from the truly powerful texts that 'entertain us long with a delight, and love to the things themselves'.

Donne's subtle tracings of the interaction of aesthetics and politics show the awareness of libels within intellectual and literate circles in the early 1610s. He belonged to the tavern societies, often dominated by lawyers, which offered emerging institutional spaces for political and social discussion. Such informal social groups circulated parliamentary separates and satirical manuscripts, especially political verse, such as the notorious 'Parliament Fart'.[87] Jonson not only participated in one such group, he was especially close to the controversial lawyer John Hoskyns, whom he regarded as one of his creative fathers. One recent study of Hoskyns, who had a reputation for satirical and controversial speech, suggests that his – and his circle's – compilation of manuscripts combines a 'range of responses to political events'.[88] Libels in this view are less an assault on civility than part of a process of definition of the boundaries of free speech and counsel.

Nonetheless, Donne's letter also highlights some significant characteristics of libelling and its reception that differentiate early modern understandings of debate (always tinged with its secondary meaning of 'dissent') from more modern conceptions of free political discourse. Donne admires their 'liberty of speaking' and admits this as part of their power, but he asserts an aesthetic and political judgement in differentiating between the effective, well-written libels – which presumably are those of the literate intellectual classes – and the 'noise' of 'course, and railing' poems. Donne, discriminating between unacceptable railing (blunt, downright, noisy, coarse, non-purposive, and posthumous) likely to provoke 'tumult and confusion', and 'the elegancy and composition' of proper political poetry that corrects as it accuses, gives libelling an important function in political culture by reaching the seemingly untouchable to prick them to self-reform. The invocation of the spectre of disorder and civil unrest often echoed in the ways in which ambassadorial reports cite libellous explosions, illustrates the problematic position adopted by many writers in this period which allows the elegant compositions that would appeal to the literate, but feels much less enamoured of the more popular end of the satirical spectrum.

The Chamberlain and Donne letters testify to a contemporary sense that the Cecilian libels marked a new departure even in a society acculturated, as Donne implies, to campaigns of libel and counter-libel. The evidence provided by the invectives released by Cecil's own death suggests a rapidly evolving pattern with relatively few texts dateable to earlier events in his career, such as his role in the Essex Rebellion.[89] The evidence of this survival shows that certain subjects were more tractable to libellous treatment. As Pauline Croft notes, the Great Contract was entirely ignored but the outpouring of posthumous anti-Cecil libels suggests the degree to which libels had established themselves as important constituents of a wider political culture during the period *c.*1600–10. Although there is no evidence that Cecil's opponents deployed libels in an orchestrated campaign, some of the known transmission networks suggest that they may have aided their circulation, and in return, Cecil's associates certainly circulated poetry, wrote hagiographical tracts, and commissioned sermons in his defence.[90] In August 1612 Benjamin Norton treated Sir Walter Cope's *An Apology for the late Lord Treasurer* as 'a book written in his praise', placing its appearance beside the publication of the 'multitude of epitaphs scarce turning to his praise', alongside the partisan distribution of Cecil's own speeches on the Great Contract, including his attack on royal profligacy, as elements in a concerted strategy intended to redeem his reputation.[91]

In this context, then, certain features of the masque acquire new resonances. From the libels it is clear that Cecil was often deliberately diminished by the use of the diminutive 'Robin', and depicted as 'the robin with the bloody breast', and one of the more sophisticated of the posthumous libels exploits different uses of the name:

> Here lies interred worms' meat
> Robin the little that was so great
> Not Robin good-fellow, nor Robin Hood
> But Robin the devil that never did good.
> He studied nothing but mischievous ends,
> Tricks for his foes, trains for his friends,
> A cruel monster sent by fate
> To devour both country, king, and state

> I care not, nor I cannot tell
> Whether his soul be in heaven or hell
> Butt sure I am they have earthed the fox
> That stunk alive, and died of the pox.

This mock epitaph, that turns the earl into a shape-changing ('Robin the little that was so great') trickster, echoes accusations that he was a Machiavel, an 'old Cicilian fox' who 'plotted' Essex's fall, acted as a 'cunning spinner' and 'With tricks and devices of legerdemain / He played like a juggler with France, England, Spain.'[92] As with the poem, *Love Restored* contrasts different tricksters and trickery, pitting Robin Goodfellow's 'riddles for the country maids' (51–2) against the other well-known Robin about court. Indeed, it is unsurprising that, if whoever wrote 'Here lies interred worms' meat' could think of the comparison between tricky minister and trickster spirit, it is equally possible the contrast might also exist in the minds of the audience.

Other parallels support the links between the *regnum Cecilianum* and the rule of Plutus, depicted as a darkly inverted 'age of gold' rather than a Jacobean Golden Age. Although many of these aspects might belong to generalised characterisations of Mammon's world, some might be attributed more closely to Cecil who, like Plutus, had appeared to draw all power to himself (Cecil was often called 'the great engine of state'). Elements echo Cecilian devices to rescue Crown finances, and the claim to 'dispose of honours, [and] make all places and dignities arbitrary from him' (159–60) appears directed at the newly created baronetcies by which Cecil set such store.[93] The key feature is the proverb that dominates the whole country:

> 'Tis he [Plutus] that pretends to tie kingdoms, maintain commerce, dispose of honours, make all places and dignities arbitrary from him, even to the very country, where Love's name cannot be razed out, he has yet gained there upon him, by a proverb insinuating his pre-eminence: *Not for love or money*. (162–72)

This phrase comes suspiciously close to the motto that had dominated the shop setting of *The Entertainment at Britain's Burse*: '*All other places give for money, here all is given for love*'.[94]

Written in 1609, Jonson's last Cecilian entertainment had attracted considerable commentary which noted the 'immense revenue' expected from the shopping arcade. Indeed, the contemporary accounts of the occasion stressed the opulence of the occasion and the culmination in elaborate gift-giving, and Stow remarked on the stir created by the 'variety of devices, pleasing speeches, rich gifts and presents as then flew bountifully abroad', and the staggering sum mentioned for the Queen's gift is confirmed in the Hatfield accounts.[95] The commercial revenue and even the profusion of gifts are suggested in Robin's anatomy of how Plutus 'pretends to tie kingdoms, maintain commerce' ultimately 'usurping all those offices in this age of gold which Love himself performed in the Golden Age' (157–8). Crucially, Robin suggests how the 'offices' of Love – friendship, loyalty, even the ties of civility – have been replaced by monetary exchanges echoing the unease implicit in the Venetian ambassador's account of *The Entertainment at Britain's Burse*. Suitably enough for an occasion staged in an 'exchange', the Burse suggests the fine – if not blurred – line between gifts and bribes. Cecil made great play of the Burse as symbolising the new world of discoveries he was leading, but also the new state he and the King were building: it was, after much discussion, named Britain's Burse.[96] Here the use of a version of Cecil's motto which claims 'preëminence' and echoes the accusations against Cecil of over-control, trickery, and dishonesty, frames the first minister as a version of Plutus.

There may be a further connection to the world of the anti-Cecilian libels through the emphasis upon physical deformity in *Love Restored*. In the masque, Jonson employs a double representation of Plutus. The fiction depends on Masquerado's mistaking Plutus for Cupid, an error made possible by the iconographic tradition that depicted Plutus as 'a little boy, bare headed, his locks curled, and spangled with gold', so that once he has 'stol'n Love's ensigns' (163) (the bow and quiver of 213), the two kinds of love are almost interchangeable.[97] The masque also, however, juxtaposes the young Money Love with another iconographic tradition, in part drawn from Lucian's depiction of the deformed money god in *Timon*, where Plutus is 'agèd, lame and blind' (224).[98] Jonson, in fact, goes even further and associates Plutus with 'insolent and barbarous Mammon' (184–5), echoing both the Bible and Spenser.[99] Guyon's temptation in Book 2, canto 7 of *The Faerie Queene* by the 'vncouth, saluage and vnciuile wight / Of gresly hew' wearing outwardly dark clothes lined with a grotesque-covered gold lining underpins Jonson's emphasis on barbarism.[100] The failure here of the civil duty of receiving gifts and returning them may be alluded to in Cupid's positioning with the Graces (211) and in his promise to repay his imprisonment with love in the 'strife / Of duty' (237–8).[101]

As we have seen, the emphasis upon Plutus/Mammon's bodily deformity echoes the satires that attacked Cecil, but Jonson complicates the 'nexus of ideas concerning the relation between bodily, moral, spiritual and political corruption'.[102] Goodfellow reveals beauty as well as deformity: Cupid frees himself by shedding 'furs and charms' to appear as naked 'As at his birth, or 'mongst the Graces' (211). Here Robin's clear-sightedness contrasts with the blind Plutus, and with the other Robin around Court, whom the King had castigated as 'a little blinded with self-love of your own counsel'.[103] This clear-sightedness contributes, however, to the distinction between Goodfellow and the mortals, and leads into a moment of sharp invective within the text. Robin highlights the failure of mortals to differentiate Cupids:

> 'Tis you mortals, that are fools, and worthy to be such, that worship him; for if you had wisdom, he had no godhead. He should stink in the grave with those wretches whose slave he was. Contemn him and he is one. (177–80)

Robin's acerbity contradicts the earlier image of the festive spirit. The revelation of the corrupt body beneath the fair surface parallels the process seen in the satires against Cecil just at the point where his bodily illness was becoming an open matter of discussion. Indeed, the image of the stinking body of Money Love may well, for those closest to the masque's first performance, have suggested Cecil's own plight.

Some of these allusions to Cecil's physique and political position can be understood in terms of Jonson's sometimes uncomfortable relationship to Cecil which, perhaps, resurfaced in 1611–12 as he revisited texts written during 1606–9, the period of their most intense connection during preparations for the (abortive) edition of the epigrams.[104] Although these criticisms remained coded (hardly surprising given that, as Cecil's posthumous libellers pointed out, 'The little-great . . . was so feared / who in his life none durst think evil'), *Love Restored*, in its concern with access may prefigure Jonson's bitter claim to William Drummond in 1619 that 'Salisbury never cared for any man longer nor he could make use of him.'[105]

Although some aspects of *Love Restored* suggest that its critique is specific, even personal, aimed at courtiers like Cecil and the bedchamber Scots who have benefited from the King's bounty, the masque moves away from the private invective of the libels and towards a political critique that connects the national situation and individual behaviour.[106] This can be seen in 'the strife / Of duty' which should motivate the courtiers to repay with support, and this thrust towards broader implications may explain the shift away from a collective final masque to the individuated virtues for each of the ten masquers, the 'spirits' of the court: Honour, Courtesy, Valour, Urbanity, Confidence, Alacrity, Promptness, Industry, Ability, and Reality. Each of these 'ten ornaments' refuses to 'strive for place', and their 'harmony', combining together, represents the antithesis of those who 'rudely' demand position and precedence. This designation, connecting personal and group ethics, looks forward to Jonson's description of the masque as 'royal education' in *Pleasure Reconciled to Virtue* (201). It restores the masque by moving from general and collective roles seen in the earlier texts (see above, p. 23) to individual performances whereby the masquers are required to measure themselves against their roles. Cupid's speech suggests strongly this will be a restorative process: 'As music them in form shall put / So will they keep their measures true' (246–7). The musical form, the masque itself, will bind them into individual behaviours to produce collection action: 'Till all become one harmony' (248). In this context, the pairing of the ornaments is fascinating as each virtue (honour, valour, confidence, promptness, ability) is balanced by a virtue of process or behaviour (courtesy, urbanity, alacrity, industry, reality). If these 'spirits of court' are, in fact, danced by James' much-criticised bedchamber, the virtues defend their role (confidence is, for example, trustworthiness), ending with their two key characteristics, ability and loyalty.[107]

The emphasis on the personal servants to the monarch and their defining virtue of ability and loyalty echoes some of the murmurings against Cecil but also provides a more fundamental critique of the *regnum Cecilianum*. Implicitly, Cecil's contract, where rights are exchanged for money has failed due to the lack of loyalty; the proper love of subjects to monarch will be the only force to resituate money in its rightful position of 'slave'. Potentially, this makes Cecil a double target, both for failing to use his riches to help the Crown which had funded him so handsomely, and for failing to understand the politics of the Great Contract, stressing a monetary bargain rather than relying upon a requirement to love and obey. Cecil's politics is a failure of his regime, much as Plutus' reign is interrupted, and of his approach to politics through contract rather than love and obedience.[108] This is manifest in the implications of Cupid's military entrance, in triumph and the reclamation of his lordship and 'rites' (201), reiterating the significance of proper forms of obedience (rites) but also the powers (rights) that accompany them. Rites are, in this instance, also masques and the punning connection points towards *Love Restored* as vehicle of a claim about the civic role of the masque and masque-writer in which 'rites' and rights are intertwined, both as manifestations of the right of counsel and political role of rites.

'The motions were ceased': restoring politics to the masque

For all its hopeful title and its invocation of the charitable spirit of Christmas festivity, complaint and criticism dominate *Love Restored*, suggesting the uneasy and unstable tensions in the masque between communal celebration and critical self-examination. Even as Robin Goodfellow invokes festive pleasures, his struggle to achieve admittance and the verbal force of Plutus' attack threaten to overwhelm love and restoration. The masque sequence barely contains some of the darker aspects of the fiction, and Mammon's near triumph highlights the close affinities of Plutus' age of gold with Pluto's hellish realm. Contention – another of the key aspects of Mammon's cave ('murders, treasons, rapes, his bribes', 215) – continually threatens to surface, and this fragility is heightened as Cupid, in defining 'courtly grace', alludes to the norm where courtiers 'rudely strive for place / One to precede the other' (230–1). Even the transformation to honour offers a continuing struggle, a 'strife / Of duty' which Cupid offers to the King.

This unsettled ending exposes some of the tensions between critique and celebration in the masque. The difficulty of the contingent conditions that the masque, and *Love Restored* in particular, must negotiate raises the central question of how masques might be an effective political form that blends rites and rights. It is as if, at this crisis point, the masque is rebalanced – restored – in its own terms, to include the darker and sharper critique necessary alongside praise to achieve an effective political intervention marked in Goodfellow's injunction to mankind to 'Contemn' Plutus (180). This critique echoes both Lucian's *Timon* dialogue (the submerged 'source' for this masque) and the Erasmian 'bitter medicines' of frank speech offered in advice to monarch and court.[109] Significantly, the injunction to Masquerado to 'Contemn' Plutus and so make him a slave stresses the role of speech as action in shaping and making the world.

Although the masque section opens with the prediction that 'beauties will revive' true Love in court, the action is more complex and less complete. At Cupid's behest Goodfellow banishes Pluto, but he continues to menace from his caves, and as we have noted, the masque conspicuously alludes to former disputes even as it invokes the hope that 'music them in form shall put'. Indeed, as David Lindley has pointed out, *Love Restored* imagines the subjugation of Plutus and Cupid's triumph:

> The majesty that here doth move
> Shall triumph, more secured by love
> Than all his earth, and never crave
> His aids, but force him as a slave. (232–5)

The inference that James will 'never crave / His aids' and can compel the obedience of money through love seems both to allude to the Great Contract ('His aids'), its failure, and the King's ultimate prerogative that could demand obedience. Although Cupid says that he 'owes' the debt of duty to his liberator, there is no sense of a mechanism by which love will impel others to follow his example, apart from by 'force'. On one hand the passage reads as a suitable subjugation of the 'slave' Money Love, but its implications – especially in a political world beyond the masque – are oppressive.

These were precisely the issues that the debates over impositions had exposed in the fourth parliamentary session that ran from February to July 1610. The widespread understanding that royal power should be exercised through recognised channels, guided by models of kingship and stewardship, functioned as a powerful cultural brake on more instrumentally absolutist views. Royalist absolutism was further moderated by a vigorous tradition of parliamentary thinking that twined together the issue of their freedom to debate and liberty so that 'the exercise and defence of freedom of speech were signs of liberty as well as ways of maintaining it [liberty]'.[110] In the early Jacobean period, however, the reliance of royal finances on extra-parliamentary taxations based on prerogative powers gave impetus to the discussions. Impositions (the name for non-parliamentary taxes) more than any other subject raised the question of that liberty and the right to offer frank advice and counsel and were seen as touchstones because they threatened to uproot 'the ancient liberty of this kingdom, and . . . your subjects right of propriety of their lands and goods'.[111] The most radical of these speeches, presented during the fissiparous session in spring 1610 concluded that we do not possess any such liberties, since to 'take away the liberty of the subject in his profit or property' is to 'make a promiscuous confusion of a freeman and a bound slave'.[112] Drawing extensively on the language of Roman republicanism, these speeches argue that 'the very existence of prerogative powers reduces us to a level below that of free subjects'.[113] Thomas Wentworth brought the issues of free speech and personal freedom together, arguing 'if we shall once say that we may not dispute the prerogative, let us be sold for slaves'.[114]

The 'promiscuous confusion' of freemen and slaves is echoed in the identity confusions of the masque and in its repeated invocation of slavery (179–80, 183, 235). The image of love 'confined by . . . tyranny to a cold region' and the 'icy fetters' leads to the evocation of Muscovite oppression. As Daryl Palmer notices, the lineage of this trope can be traced to Sidney's 'slave-born Muscovite', but Jonson has transformed metaphor into matter by linking Muscovite tyranny to Plutus as an image of the 'commercial speculation and courtly penury' that dominated the Jacobean court.[115] Yet, although money matters, particularly in the context of the growing Russia trade, the language of these sections constantly equates Mammon's rule with 'arbitrary' government (169). Mammon controls 'all places and dignities', and he 'walks as if he were to set bounds and give laws to destiny', imagining mankind enslaved by the worship of this 'earthy . . . idol' (176, 187). The language of the parliamentary debate – widely reported at the time – seeps into the masque, but it has been inverted, so that rather than royal prerogative enforcing slavery, it is the failure to love properly that has made slaves of men. The bodily deformity created by Mammon's assumption of 'enforced shape' and his lameness and blindness are transferred to his self-created slaves (175, 224), whose inability to dance or to recognise his tyranny, demonstrate their servile state. Again, such images appear in the parliamentary speeches where tyranny unmans the nation. Thus, according to Thomas Hedley, free men, 'their bodies more able and fit for soldiers', also labour better and supply the monarch with greater and more assured supply, especially in time of war.[116] In the masque, Cupid, feeling the 'heat that inward warms', sheds his furs and restores the national body, as the 'spirits of court and flower of men' with 'flamed intents' display 'True valour' (239–40, 250).

This appropriation of the languages of parliamentary debate – and the more daring reversal of its polarities – arises in the constant discussion of language and the limits of speech and counsel that inform both the fiction and the form of *Love Restored*. The question of what might constitute frank counsel and its limitations were often raised during the session, and amidst these debates, as James chided the Commons for allowing that 'my words by railing speeches be slandered', sometime during 1610–12 Cecil drafted a proclamation against insolent speech and writing. Commenting on the King's speech in May 1610, Chamberlain regretted that 'our monarchicall powre and regall prerogative [is] strained so high and made so transcendent' but still quibbles at the 'bold passages' that originated in the House, concluding with the wish of many that 'this speech might never come in print'.[117]

The limits of free-speaking and satire explore parallel issues as both Robin and Plutus counter-charge each other as uncivil, as speaking beyond the bounds of decorum, and even as speaking as libellers:

> Alas! How bitterly the spirit of poverty spouts itself against my weal and felicity! But I feel it not. I cherish and make much of myself, flow forth in ease and delicacy, while that murmurs and starves. (155–8)

Although the passage oscillates between the discussion of the 'flow' of money and the starvation of poverty, the debate is also cast in textual terms, so that part of Plutus' invective defines Goodfellow as one who 'spouts' and 'murmurs'. 'Murmuring' was much associated with the articulation of political discontent (a murmurer was someone who complained against political authority); and although 'spouting' was mainly associated with empty speechifying it could also be associated with disputation and other forms of aggressive speech.[118] Indeed, the language of the text is frequently filled with terms that define abuse, the proper kinds of language, and the access that decorous speech provides or indecorous speaking precludes: 'vizarded impudence' (26), 'impertinent folly' (21), 'licence of surquidry' (29), 'insolent and barbarous' (184–5).

This concern with speech as power and the proper use of speech is echoed in *Love Restored* which is full of speech in action, from the 'charms' that entrap Cupid (208) to the comic inventiveness that manifests the power of 'so good words' (66). Words also circumvent Goodfellow's exclusion, or rather survive the violence of 'non-entry' (67) and translate it into comic speech. Against this verbal dexterity, the porter's staff, which sets in motion the comic sequence of assaults each of which culminates in failure and in physical violence, usurps the role of speech and 'spoke somewhat to that boisterous sense' (67).[119] For violence to supplant speech, in the context of a masque that dazzles in its linguistic inventiveness, suggests both the fragility of festivity in its inability to enter and also its potential failure: at the end Robin, having suffered 'despair' only slips by 'when all invention – and translation too – failed' (126). Although seen in comic terms, the failure of court festivity is followed by an image of the proper (and more acerbic) festivity represented by Robin, first nearly concussed by the mechanics of court festivity, and finally nearly excluded by the violent incivility that suffuses the court.

It is perhaps surprising to talk in such terms of a masque that is so joyously comic, yet the linguistic self-consciousness of the masque, and the uncertain poise between failure and success, even in the antimasque, makes for a more tense and uncertain outcome. On one hand, the verbal precision of the masque stands against, perhaps even rebukes, the looser language (in all senses) employed in the flood of libels that were, to use Donne's terms 'tasteless and flat' rather than 'witty and sharp'. By voicing dissent in a language that shows 'elegancy and composition' (again, Donne's terms), the poet can replace the libeller, achieve more, but without the disruption that the noise of libel generates. In this scenario frank counsel and communal celebration are not exclusive opposites. On the other hand, having posited this case for the poet as mediator, the core fiction of the antimasque dramatises the difficulty of being heard as the country spirit strives to enter the court. Access, so often seen in terms of hierarchy and the ambassadorial disputes that frequently turned masque performances into thwarted negotiations, here concerns how proper, 'sharp and witty' festivity might attend the court when excluded both by social rules and practices (the porter) and by the frozen world of failed court festivity (Masquerado/Plutus).

Of course, this issue of access is then cast in comic terms: Robin excluded by the porter trying his shifts to enter; the citizens' wives who have snuck in; and the allusion to Thomas Coryat's entrance to a masque in a trunk (79–80). Beyond the comic assault on Inigo Jones in the mechanics of the masque noticed by Leah Marcus, the very business and mechanics of court festivity – all that expensive scenery – has become an obstacle to the admission of the proper, sharper spirit of festivity.[120] But the image of the near 'mazarded' (76) spirit who 'must come in at a door' (78), also turns the whole issue back towards the audience and participants: they must invite this spirit in in order for the charm to work. We have here the internal contradictions of the form laid bare: festivity which aspires to harmony and social cohesion also often rejects deeper and more penetrating kinds of festive wit. Moreover, in a parallel to the insistence on personal will in the masque, here in the antimasque, individuals have to decide to invite Robin to enter.

This poetic independence and authority, created through engagement with civic debate informs what we might call the politics of access in *Love Restored*. The critical contentiousness of national debate, translated by Jonson's restoration of the masque, needs to be heard but depends also on the engagement of the masquers and the will of the audience. In laying out these tensions and contradictions, *Love Restored* places the masque as a point of mediation, offers a moderated poetic independence, but also turns the completion of the masque's argument and education over to those watching. In so doing, it balances the positions of the different competing participants, the patron, and of the voices in the national debate. Even as it seems to align itself with the position of the King and the bedchamber in favour of prerogative powers, and certainly the royal right to demand obedience, it also stresses the 'strife / Of duty', the competition of duties to serve, to counsel, to govern, that should replace mere compelled or contracted obedience. To be true courtiers, and true men, it is necessary to recognise limitations (especially on bounty), and to act and cooperate to support the potential harmony offered by the throne. These duties also apply to monarchy and all are reminded of the need for mutual agreement if the 'icy fetters' of Plutus are to be avoided. Importantly, this balance will be achieved and maintained not by mimetic magic, but by individuals acting virtuously themselves and in concert with others: 'Till all become one harmony' (247).

This invocation of harmony can, of course, be read as a manifestation of royal order, but its articulation through Cupid establishes critical distance from straightforward alignment with the King, while the actual creation of harmony is through the actions of the dancers aligned with the music. As harmony requires the unification of different voices, the music that 'them in form shall put', also evokes the way in which the masque combines the different voices of the political nation and produces order from them. In this sense civility of behaviour (243–4) and language are yoked together ('urbanity', 'confidence' are key courtly values), and suggest the ways in which civility operates in a double fashion, tying together monarch, aristocrats, and dissidents and regulating their behaviours.[121] The whole passage is tinged with the language of temperance, so that the placing by music ('As music') is completed by their continued self-control ('So will they keep'), bringing the 'graces' to court. The penultimate song picks up this mutual movement of the Graces (267–8), perhaps recalling the Spenserian moment in *The Faerie Queene* when the vision of the three Graces embodies the 'friendly offices that bind', and offering a redefined form of courtesy to the Jacobean court.[122] Here the performance of the harmony brings together ethical self-discipline and political restraint while the words of the song themselves in their use of 'measures' and 'proportions true' bring together all the elements, the different actors and voices, 'in form' (245).

This recognition of poetic independence modified by the need for active participation and audience understanding conjures up a less assured and fixed voice and role for the poet than has been traced in *The workes* (1616). In suggesting a role for the masque in mediating between the various agents and factions, and the principles and positions they embody, it points up the limits of its own intervention: for festivity to function requires a competent and reactive audience. In turn this, perhaps, suggests that the Jonsonian scepticism about the 'short bravery of the night' is born less of ethical discrimination operated against those already seen as flawed, but rather articulates the difficulty of the festive task. Part of the problem derives from a public culture that is forming and reforming itself and finding ways in which 'measures' and 'proportions' (212, 213) can achieve harmony. The fluidity of this situation requires an equally dextrous and inventive response from the masque, so the title of *Love Restored* carefully recalls Protestant ideas of reformation, but reformulates them as 'restoration'. The masque puts 'in form' (211) the kinds of language and behaviour that would make a restoration of social and political harmony possible – it moves towards consensus – while recognising, incorporating but not absorbing, the variety of voices needed to make harmony. Out of exile, failure, incivility, and violence, and through the temporary opportunity of the masque, it offers the possibility of civil debate: 'Now let them close their eyes and see / if they can dream of thee' (282–3).

At least one observer saw the parallel dilemmas of counsel and the need to create civility early in Jonson's career. Even before the run of great masques for Anna of Denmark and Prince Henry, Sir John Roe explored the same questions in his epistle to Jonson, addressed to him in the aftermath of their joint expulsion from *The vision of the 12. goddesses* in 1604.[123] Roe juxtaposes trustful truth-telling in 'true friendship' against the noisy and barbarous court that drowns out counsel.[124] 'The state and men's best affairs are the best plays / Next yours' echoes contemporary concerns about the expenditure, the 'unthrifty rout' who 'increase / In riot and excess as their means cease' (lines 19, 22–3), and looks forwards to later articulations of the irreligiosity of masques in a way that Cupid's reclamation of his 'usurped rites' in *Love Restored* also seems concerned to counter. Centrally, Roe translates physical exclusion into a symbolic exile that affirms Jonson's worth. The 'unthrifty rout' not only wastes money but also shows an inability to hold 'learning'. This intellectual bankruptcy is contrasted with 'true friendship', the foundation of a proper state, and while the ever-moving 'rout' of masquers and hunt-followers should be allowed to 'pass' into obscurity, the poet stands as one centre of civil intercourse. The failure to allow access signals not only how the court 'all your [Jonson's] studies flout' but also how the voices of reason, civility and, pointedly – given Roe's Protestantism – faith, are excluded. The final lines which place Jonson (perhaps rather exaggeratedly) as victim, 'the bruised reed' and 'smoking flax', also offer a more aggressive promise for the future as the biblical quotation concludes 'he shall bring forth judgement unto truth'.

In *Love Restored* the refusal of access dramatises a rejection of the basis of the civil state in hospitality, festivity, and shared discourse. In this sense, the masque echoes Roe's remarkable sense of the poet, so often seen as an insider, read as an outsider.[125] In the contrast between friendship and 'counsel' and a court addicted to 'riot and excess' the sheer intractability of Jonson's pursuit of patronage, needful but destructive, is encapsulated and the fragility of the vision of royal education exposed in the jeering rejection of the poet and his ideas. Roe's poem focuses on the excluded poet, but in *Love Restored*, through the initial failure of the masque and the intervention of Goodfellow, these exclusions become part of the contentiousness of masques. The contention concerns the carving out of a poetic independence within civic society, the charged demarcation of what can be said, and the mapping of where the boundaries of political discourse lie. Already, in *Love Restored*, a drama of access, the question of inclusion and exclusion has radically shifted away from Whitehall and the entrée to the royal apartments, away from Westminster and the energies of the dissolved Parliament, and, instead, focuses on an emergent political nation.

3
'Crack Kisses Not Staves': Sexual Politics and Court Masques in 1613–14

The discussion of *Love Restored* in Chapter 2 established the interconnections between libellous politics and the masque. It also advanced an argument for the masque as civil instrument that could both appropriate, and yet still also articulate, some of the external criticism of the court, particularly the implications of the prerogative powers employed to sustain its damaged finances. This debate over prerogative and the political principles evoked by such discussions may have been filtered through the role of the bedchamber and the invective against Cecil but, as some of the parliamentary speeches suggest, these discussions voice divergent views of monarchy and its powers. Even to discuss such matters was, itself, a controversial and political act, and so the concern with 'proper' language in *Love Restored* aligns with two interconnected political issues: the dilemma of counsel (when and how to speak difficult truths), and the concept of freedom of speech. Parliamentary debates over freedom of speech claimed that the ability to speak in defence of such speech was a key demonstration of that freedom, and the masque's concern with civility in language (and its opposite, violence in action) stems not only from the tense situation that surrounded the occasion but also from its role as part of public debate. In a situation where the possibility of public debate is emerging, if fitfully, then the boundaries of acceptable discourse, especially in the charged world of Jacobean rhetoric and invective, become key political concerns in themselves. As was suggested in Chapter 1 (pp. 12–13), these shifting and fluid public spheres do not share the rationalist and regulated system found in the post-Enlightenment public sphere.

In *Love Restored* discussion of how to talk politics becomes a profoundly political act; in *The Somerset Masque* parallel concerns arise during the intensified eruption of public debate over the Overbury affair (1614–16).

As with the case of the Great Contract, this scandal revealed some of the fault lines in the Jacobean polity, and the celebratory masques became entangled in public discussion about the alliance. Recent detailed critical and historical work on the Howard match and the Overbury scandal not only furnish more nuanced contexts for studying the entertainments of the 1613–14 season, they also illuminate the interaction of politics of differing kinds in multiple arenas: the Irish Parliament, the English Parliament, the court, public political cultures. These transactions are registered in different media ranging from printed forms, through to manuscript circulations and political prints, employing printed pamphlets, trial transcripts, documentary collections, ballads, and libellous verse. The most striking feature lies in the further development of a more contested public political culture in which masques were implicated. Indeed, the complex dialogue between different texts and auspices – Howard texts, the King's masque, the Queen's entertainments – promotes factional manoeuvring *and* political debate.

It has often been argued that the Overbury scandal had broader effects and marks one of the key development points for political consciousness. Christopher Hill and Lawrence Stone connected it to the rise of 'country' sentiment, the agglomeration of anti-court values they saw as producing the disillusion with monarchic corruption; David Underdown argued that a toxic mix of popery and gender inversion operated; and, most recently, the detailed study by Alastair Bellany has highlighted the damage done to the King's reputation for impartial justice.[1] Certainly, the scandal resurfaces in print publications in the 1640s and appears to have undermined the legitimacy of the Stuart regime.[2] The personal nature of the scandal illustrates how the personal and the political intertwine in Jacobean court society, so that the libels with their personal slanders were more than just titillating, they went to heart of the regime's fitness to rule.[3]

These ethical issues, the connection of personal behaviour and political action, are embodied in the masque, certainly as conceived by Jonson, but in the case of the last text of the sequence, Jonson's *Irish Masque* (29 December 1613 and 3 January 1614) the concerns are centred on how to address such sensitive issues. Indeed, the emphasis in Jonson's *Irish Masque* on civility and decorum echoes contemporary concerns about 'uncouth' subjects and voice and their circulations in broader culture. The role of the Irish bards this chapter suggests represents, then, not simply a 'complacent reassurance' of the court but engages with urgent questions of the limits of political discourse for all the four kingdoms, even though the Irish setting caused concern at the time and retains uncomfortable resonances.[4] Again, the role of civility here is to forge an agreed means of speaking that allows proper public debate and instantiates reasonable behaviour.

All the commons wonder

> The relation of the magnificence of my lord Somerset's marriage is too large to be here inserted. (John More to William Trumbull, 7 January 1614)
>
> There was never the like bravery and vanity seen as hath been the most part of all these unholy days. (Sir John Throckmorton to William Trumbull, 11 January 1614)[5]

It is unsurprising that the ambivalence expressed by the diplomat William Trumbull's correspondents about the marriage of the royal favourite Robert Carr, Earl of Somerset and Frances Howard, Countess of Essex and its lavish celebration has persisted. Over seven days between 26 December 1613 and 6 January 1614 Campion's *Somerset Masque*, Jonson's *A Challenge at Tilt, At A Marriage* and his *Irish Masque at Court*, the anonymous *The Masque of Flowers*, sponsored by Francis Bacon, and Middleton's now lost *Masque of Cupids* were all performed. In addition, in a connected manoeuvre, Anna of Denmark staged Samuel Daniel's pastoral, *Hymen's Triumph* (3 February 1613), to mark the marriage of Jean Drummond, her first lady of the bedchamber, to the Earl of Roxburgh.[6]

The specific political and cultural tensions presented by the Carr–Howard nuptials have been overshadowed by the later events of the sensational trial of the Earl and Countess of Somerset for the murder of Sir Thomas Overbury in 1615. In 1613, however, concern centred on the nullity and divorce of the Earl and Countess of Essex (formally ended on 25 September 1613), and on the rapidly succeeding marriage between the Earl of Somerset and the divorced countess (26 December 1613). As another of Trumbull's correspondents commented: 'all the Commons wonder at the accident; let them look to it whom it most concerns'.[7] Calvert's letter evokes the climate of gossip that surrounded the match, especially the inference (confirmed at the later trial) that the new Earl and Countess of Somerset's relationship had been adulterous.[8]

This marriage carried immense political significance. It brought together the royal favourite, Carr, and the pro-Spanish Howards, tilting the balance of power in many areas of policy-making and court life from both the 'patriot' faction that favoured Protestant allegiances, and also from the Francophile Scots courtiers with whom Carr had previously been associated.[9] Contemporaries heralded this major factional realignment, and the Earl of Northampton's description of the bride, Frances Howard, as a 'dainty pot of glue' uncomfortably conveys how the marriage bonded her father, Thomas Howard, Earl of Suffolk, and her new husband.[10] In the male power politics of the Jacobean court Frances Howard *was* little more than adhesive.

As Trumbull's correspondence shows, the celebrations were controversial both for their lavishness and their perceived inappropriateness. Other contemporary sources reveal considerable factional manoeuvring, unease, and tension around the celebrations alongside the Queen's barely concealed distaste for the marriage. These fractious relations emerge throughout the various entertainments, and especially in Queen Anna's sponsorship of *Hymen's Triumph* which diverges in its presentation of marriage from the Carr–Howard marriage texts. Indeed, Campion and Daniel's texts, in particular, debate sexual mores through differing representations of Hymen and Cupid, and they question the forms of the masque, contrasting the King's 'newborn creatures' (155) with the female recreations of the Queen's court.[11] The gendered debates embodied in this group of texts between entertainments staged by the King and Queen reached beyond the royal households and the factions of the Jacobean court to engage with the political nation and its diverse voices. Calvert's letter noted that 'all the commons wonder' and this public debate was intensified by the lavishness of the celebrations, such as the massive horseback and carriage procession of courtiers who went to Merchant Taylors' Hall to see Middleton's *Masque of Cupids* on 4 January.[12]

The most recent historical study, Alastair Bellany's *The Politics of Court Scandal in Early Modern England*, stresses the complexity and multiplicity in the representations of these events. Bellany details not only the ambivalences evident in many of the accounts but also outlines the potential for the scandal to legitimate as well as de-legitimate the monarchy. Among the significant features Bellany traces is the emergence of 'relatively large, socially diverse publics [that] had consumed a steady flow of news and comment about the scandal'.[13] Each of the different moments that contributed to the broader fabric of the scandal attracted satirical and political commentary in a wide range of media and forms, and the 'flash-points', such as the nullity, divorce, and marriage, in particular, generated a veritable explosion of libelling and political versifying often expressed in highly sexual, scatological, physical, and graphic detail.[14]

Contemporary commentators noticed this phenomenon although their comments are tinged with embarrassment and ambivalence. So, in 1616, Robert Niccols described how the widespread discussion of the scandal:

> Had set loud Fame upon a lofty wing,
> Throughout our streets with horrid voice to sing
> Those uncouth tidings, in each itching ear.[15]

The image of Fame's 'horrid voice' captures some of the impact of these libels and suggests the transgression of both physical and discursive boundaries as 'those uncouth tidings' pass 'throughout our streets'. The 'itching ear' of public appetite lends a near venereal quality to the news-dissemination as the libels infect the body politic as much as sexual misconduct was supposedly rewarded with physical infection.[16] Some sense of the violation caused by the gradual accumulation of salacious detail is conveyed by the 'horrid voice' and the 'uncouth tidings' which involve not only what is said but how it is spoken and how transmitted.[17] The sense of social dislocation and disharmony is palpable but still Niccols locates these voices in 'the Forum', recalling a much more respectable history of republican political debate.

The events and personalities of this scandal highlight many 'embarrassments' for contemporaries and for modern historians and critics. David Lindley's evocative term captures well the unease over the highly sexualised and charged language that the Carr–Howard wedding provoked. These nuptial entertainments, especially the *Challenge at Tilt* and the *Somerset Masque*, responded to this climate by translating the highly sexualised language about Carr, the nullity, and the Carr–Howard alliance from the libels circulating contemporaneously into the licensed discourses of the masque. Thus, although the effacement – literal and political – which Lindley traces in these texts has an important role, other strategies that either face down or translate criticism of the marriage were also deployed.

'The most potent favourite of my time': Carr and the Jacobean favourite[18]

> You know the *primum mobile* of our court, by whose motion all other spheres must move, or stand still; the bright sun of our firmament, at whose splendour or glooming all our marigolds of the court open or shut. In his conjunction all other stars are prosperous, and in his

opposition mal-ominous. There are higher spheres as great as he, but none so glorious.[19]

Any understanding of the significance of the 1613–14 masques begins with the central role of Robert Carr. As his contemporaries recognised, Carr's marriage marked an important new step not only in the earl's fortunes but also in the role and significance of the favourite.[20] Carr's political role developed from the power vacuum created by the deaths of the Earl of Dunbar, the Earl of Salisbury, and Prince Henry, allowed for an unprecedented degree of influence, and required a redefinition of the concept of the favourite. Such changes not only reconfigured the factional politics of the court, they also impinged upon sensitive medium-term issues including the King's general predisposition towards the Scots (see Chapter 2), and raised the origins of Carr's particular power in royal favour.

In the aftermath of the deaths of 1612, James I seems to have decided to reassert his own power, using Carr as the broker between the two dominant court factions, moving decisively away from the combined forces of minister and Privy Council to the bedchamber favourite.[21] This decision, combined with the increased distribution of royal bounty, gave Carr a new power and significantly altered the meaning of the role of the favourite. As Bacon noted in 1616 'it is no new thing for Kings and Princes to have their privados', but Carr emerges as a very novel figure in English terms, 'a politico'.[22] Indeed, Linda Peck has argued that both James and Carr may have imitated Spanish models, notably the dominant political and cultural position of the Duke of Lerma. Thus while James drew upon the centralised bounty of the Spanish court, Carr adapted Lerma's policy of aristocratic display and collecting. Carr has, in recent studies, emerged as a key figure in the collecting of Italian, especially Venetian, art and sculpture in England, a cultural trend which was not only 'avant-garde' but associated in some contemporary minds with the ideal of 'magnificence'.[23]

Carr transgressed many boundaries at the English court. He was a Scot raised to the English peerage, he moved from the bedchamber to the bureaucracy, and later in his role as Lord Chamberlain he broke the English rule separating the inner and outer chamber heads in the court structure.[24] This dual position, which granted him unrivalled control over patronage and access to the King, was recognised and the Venetian ambassador reported that 'he [Carr] is to dispose of everything' and that James made all policy decisions with him, confiding in Carr 'above all others'.[25] James I wrote to Carr in similar terms asking 'do not all court graces and place come through your office as Chamberlain . . .' and pointing out Carr's 'infinite privacy' with him.[26]

This highly ambiguous 'infinite privacy' with James was the root of Carr's power. A letter from the Earl of Suffolk describes the complex overlapping of personal and political connection in Carr's rise, commenting 'Carr is now most likely to win the Prince's affection and doth it wondrously in a little time'. Suffolk progresses rapidly from how James 'leans on his arm, pinches his cheek, smoothes his ruffled garment' to political realities: 'where it endedth, I cannot guess, but honours are talked of speedily for him'.[27] This unstable combination of personal and political power rested on royal 'affection' and acquired the emotional dynamics of intense erotic relationships making it almost impossible to disentangle the personal, the political, the emotional, and the, at least potentially, sexual elements in such connections. Moreover, such intimacy, given its transgression of the normative boundaries of the court, rendered Carr both powerful and vulnerable.

Carr's very position embodied a whole nexus of these difficult and contested relations, and the subsequent marriage itself also exposed further fault lines in Jacobean culture, not least the shadowy connections between nationality and manliness. His close imbrication in a series of relations with other men (most notably Sir Thomas Overbury, the Earl of Northampton, and the King), which were the very basis of power, also laid Carr open to suggestions that might range from undue influence through to accusations of unnatural sexual practices. Carr's relations with Overbury seem to have occasioned most comment and Roger Wilbraham described Overbury as 'Somerset's bedfellow, minion and inward councillor' while Francis Bacon commented on their 'excess . . . of friendship' claiming that Overbury had made Carr his 'idol'.[28] The confusion of different roles (bedfellow, minion, councillor) encapsulates many of the anxieties which attended inter-male relations in this period and which were especially pronounced in offices with strong elements of close personal service, like the secretaryship which supplied so much of Carr's influence. In this respect Bacon's suggestion of 'excess' in these relations resonates as this was often one component or trigger for accusations of 'sodomy', a complex and conflicted term which might include same-sex sexual practices among its repertoire of misdemeanours.[29]

Many of the social and political positions which Carr occupied, from page to privado, from companion to counsellor, and his rapid transitions between them, made Carr particularly vulnerable to suggestions of inappropriate influence that quickly could translate into accusations of unacceptable conduct. As the figure of the friend, one of the cornerstones of Renaissance homosocial relations, threatened to overlap with the reprobate category of the 'sodomite', a dangerous duality informed both personal connections and the fundamental power relations in patronage and clientage.[30] Indeed, the situation parallels that outlined by Eve Sedgwick in her analysis of the 'double-bind' of male homosocial relations in the nineteenth century, whereby male entitlement and advancement required men to engage in close relations with other men which, also, always risked the accusation of inappropriateness or immorality.[31]

Both the annulment and Carr's rise to power through the bedchamber increased awareness of the power of male sexuality at the Jacobean court, perhaps accentuated by the contrast with the latter years of Elizabeth's reign. Jacobean culture seems to have been characterised by a broad sexualisation of culture, not only in the eroticised languages of power and alliance, but in the interconnection of political and bodily metaphors, an element exploited by the explicit sexual languages of contemporaneous political poetry often heightened at crisis points such as the Carr–Howard match. Whereas Lindley reads this versiferous explosion as an expression of misogynist anxieties about female sexuality it seems that *male* sexuality is equally implicated given both the specific nature of the nullity and divorce and also the general culture, heightened at court, of a society where manliness, the idealised male body and male bonds, underpinned political discourses, structures, and most of all, power. Current critical interest may have focused on Frances Howard, but the embarrassments felt by Jonson (and other writers at the time) give equal weight to the fraught territories of male relations derived, in part, from the origins of Carr's preferment in royal favour. Some of the opprobrium heaped on Frances Howard and on the marriage articulated displaced anxieties about Carr, his social and ethnic origins, the nature of his rise to power, and the ambivalences that surrounded male favourites in Jacobean culture, so that the repeated invocations of fertility which characterise many of the poems and masques that surround this match often appear to stem less from epithalamic convention than the urgent need to contain Carr's potentially disruptive political and sexual desires and relations.

Despite the often graphic nature of many of the libels, especially those directed towards Frances Howard, speculations about the origins of Carr's power could not be expressed except in indirect and mediated forms, and so various kinds of displacement operate in the Carr–Howard match and its surrounding texts, registering the intense sexual anxieties around the match and, especially, concerns about manliness and male sexual performance. These libels become coded ways of articulating not only what the Essex–Howard divorce and the Carr–Howard match reveal about national manliness, but also what the implicit and more controversial question of Carr's relations and desires, sexual and political, with other men might suggest about the operations of power at the Jacobean court. The situation, indeed, parallels that outlined by McClung and Simard's revealing discussion of the critical vilification of Donne's Somerset epithalamium, which argues that the anxieties expressed by critics about the Carr–Howard wedding reflect displaced unease over the potentially sexual nature of the relations between Carr and James.[32] Although McClung and Simard are primarily concerned with modern critical writings, similar contemporaneous discomforts can also be traced in the commentary on the wedding masques. In this respect, the 'open secret' which the Somerset match threatened to articulate was not only the corrupt, sexual underpinnings of the Jacobean court which would expose one of its iconic marriages as a sham, but also the subtle interconnections of male power relations and other, interdicted, male relations which could be classed as 'sodomitical'.[33]

'The defence of a good prick': nullity and libel, 1613–14

One of the key points established by both *The Trials of Frances Howard* and *The Politics of Court Scandal* concerns how later writers have confused the chronology of the Overbury affair and compounded attitudes and discourses from after the revelation of the murder, poisonings, consultations with cunning women, and the accusations of witchcraft, with the earlier situation and the controversy around the Carr–Howard marriage.[34] So, although Overbury had died in September 1613, the main subjects of discussion in the autumn of 1613 were the nullity, the divorce, and the rapid remarriage.

Calvert's view that 'all the Commons wonder at the accident' typifies the widespread repetition of both gossip and written discussion of these topics.[35] Other letters dated May and June 1613 show the extent of this interest but also an awareness of the wider implications of the marriage, one of the writers noting how as well as spoken gossip 'it is written also of their annulling the marriage', while another worries that 'Thus you see the little care taken at home of all things; our government as well ecclesiastical as politic will become a scorn and byword to all nations.'[36] The nullity case, which centred on whether the Earl of Essex was sexually capable or whether he was solely impotent with Frances Howard for whatever reason, involved a royal commission of bishops taking evidence about the earl's sexual ability, a virginity test for the countess, and countless rumours about the causes of the failure of the marriage.[37] Indeed, Archbishop Abbot reported that he had been 'by a good friend informed' of an extraordinary scene in the Earl of Essex's chamber when, in the presence of 'five or six captains and gentlemen of worth', the earl had refuted the evidence of his incapacity by 'taking up his shirt, [he] did shew to them all so able and extraordinarily sufficient matter, that they cried out shame of his lady'.[38] It is not only that the Earl of Essex either displayed the size of his genitals, the strength of his erection, or masturbated in front of this audience 'of worth', but that the performance itself became a matter of report.

Contemporary commentary on the divorce was not restricted solely to gossip and newsletters but also emerged in libels which also yoked together the issues of reputation, reportage, and male potency. Thus one libel commented:

> This dame was inspected but Fraud interjected
> A maid of more perfection
> Whom the midwives did handle
> Whilst the knight held the candle:
> O, there was a clear inspection!
>
> Now all foreign writers, cry out on those mitres
> That allow this for virginity
> And talk of ejection and want of erection:
> O, there is a sound divinity![39]

'Talk of ejection and want of erection' was widespread and the poem hints that national manliness has been impugned by the spread of news of this trial by 'foreign writters'. Certainly Archbishop Abbott noted that 'since that time much sport had been made at the Court and in London' about the titillating sexual details.[40] Members of the Howard faction referred to Essex as 'my Lord the Gelding' while Northampton teased Carr, claiming that to decipher his handwriting caused less pain than 'that which a man takes in cracking a sweet nut to taste the kernel, or but like the pain which my Lady Frances shall feel when the sweet stream follows'.[41] Northampton even urged Carr: 'If my lord would draw his sword in defence of a good prick it were worth his pains.'[42]

Although Frances Howard's body was the centre of the examinations for sexual capacity, the issue also reflected upon Essex and his manliness, and even if the reports of his public display of sexual capacity are nothing more than rumour, the very prevalence of such rumours remains significant. Equally, the reflection on manly capacity – if expressed through images of female sexual desire (often figured, in fact, as depravity) – also fills the libels that can be associated with the nullity and marriage, and are not only directed at Essex but also at Carr. Thus in 'Lady changed to Venus dove' which imagines Frances Howard as 'Venus dove', the 'sport of both night and day' in seducing Carr is contained and justified by a productive marriage in which 'Plants enough may . . . ensue'.[43] Yet the poem closes with bawdy punning in which 'Some-are-set and some are laid / If none stand, God morrow maid!' This question of the two earls and their ability to 'stand' (or not) is handled in a less witty fashion in 'From Catherine's dock their launched a pink' as Carr is urged to 'mend her keel / To stop her leak and mend her port'.[44]

The graphically sexual language of the libels and their concern with male performance held particular dangers for Carr, for besides the potential to exacerbate national tensions they also focused potentially unwelcome attention on Carr's sexual nature and desires. Indeed, Carr's position made him the frequent target of politico-sexual innuendo, and one poem depicts Carr as a bubble:

>When Carr in court at first a page began
>He swelled and swelled into a gentleman
>And from a gentleman and bravely dight
>He swelled and swelled till he became a knight
>At last forgetting what he was at first
>He swelled into an earl and then he burst![45]

Given the context of the other sexualised libels circulating at the time, the 'swelling' here can be read as sexual as much as titular, and the poem continues that sense of 'excess', in power, wealth, dress, and manners, which surrounded Carr. The 'burst[ing]' here may be an ironic image of the very detumescence with which the Howards taunted Essex. Indeed, such sexual punning informs many of the poems about James and Carr, and these often deal in sexual innuendo about the exact means of the favourite's rise to power:

>Let any poor lad, that is handsome and young,
>With *Parle vous France*, and a voice for a song,

> But once get a horse, and seek out good James,
> He'll soon find the house, 'tis great near the Thames.
> It was built by a priest, a butcher by calling,
> But neither priesthood nor trade, cou'd keep him from falling
> As soon as you ken the pitiful loon,
> Fall down from your nag, as if in a swoon:
> If he doth nothing more, he'll open his Purse,
> If he likes you, ('tis known he's a very good nurse)
> Your fortune is made, he'll dress you in satin,
> And, if you're unlearned, he'll teach you dog Latin.
> On good pious *James* Male Beauty prevaileth
> And other men's fortunes on such he in-taileth.[46]

This parodic 'Advice to the sons of men' connects sexual and religious deviance (Wolsey's palace) and concludes with an obscene pun which meshes Carr's new-found fortune with sodomy: sexual 'in-tailing' leads to financial entailing.[47]

Even the apparently heteroerotic Carr–Howard match reflected upon manliness and the male body. The sexual and political impotence represented by the failure of the original Devereux–Howard marriage – which had inaugurated the Jacobean union – compounded the shadowy sense of national prowess under threat. These *male* implications were only strengthened by the links between Carr's advancement and James' preference for 'Male Beauty'. So, paradoxically, the solution for a 'crisis' in personal and national politico-sexual potency lay in the marriage of the Scots male favourite of the king, whose very position threatened to expose the overlapping discourses of patronage, friendship, and sodomy in the Jacobean bedchamber. In these circumstances the insistent invocations of fertility throughout the 1613–14 masques seem highly pointed.

Rude boys and white staffs: the 1613–14 masques and sexual crisis

> Hold your tongues!
> And let your coarser manners seek some place
> Fit for their wildness. (*Irish Masque*, lines 134–6)

The Carr–Howard masques addressed directly the climate of rumour and the political libels in a strikingly explicit manner.[48] Using the sexual licence permitted within epithalamia these masques translate libellous bawdy into the more decorous language of fertility, countering imputations of sexual decadence and impotence with an image of a revitalized Jacobean union, extended in the *Irish Masque at Court* to include the 'civilising' project of the Irish plantation. These verbal translations acquire absolutist implications in the *Irish Masque* where Jonson deploys the ideal of decorum to differentiate between civil and uncivil speech about both marriage and plantation, dismissing the rebellious Irish and political libellers of the Carr–Howard match as barbarians.

On the surface, however, the masques, tilts, and ritualised hospitality marking the nuptials enacted a reconciliatory politics designed to re-found the Jacobean union and heal some of the intense factional disputes that had seethed throughout 1612–13. Chamberlain describes a 'late pacification of the court' and each event carefully deployed English and Scots, mixing members of opposing factions.[49] Most importantly, Queen Anna was persuaded to countenance the nuptials, a major victory as she had intermittently feuded with Carr despite a formal reconciliation in 1612.[50] Anna cordially loathed Sir Thomas Overbury.[51] Indeed, although as a Catholic Anna should have shared many of the foreign policy aims of the Howard faction, she sided with the Protestant patriots (notably Pembroke and Southampton), and she was in dispute with Northampton over Greenwich Park at this time.[52] Northampton even feared that 'enflamed with passion and rage [and] out of her hatred to me' she might 'disorder the main state of the proceedings'.[53]

Some sense of the protracted negotiations (the precise details of which are unclear) can be gleaned from the numerous references to planned wedding dates for Carr and Frances Howard, the original plan to hold the wedding and its celebrations at Audley End, the Suffolks' main house, and the decision to hold both wedding and entertainments at Whitehall.[54] Although the documentary evidence to delineate exactly what kind of deal was struck between the King and Queen (and the relation of that negotiation to other subsidiary arrangements between the factions) is lacking, the correspondence of the period allows a picture of the transactions involved for the main protagonists. For Carr and the Howards, the advantages were obvious, and it appears that the marriage would 'reconcile him [Carr] and the house of Howard together', and Northampton, even as he saluted Frances as a 'dainty pot of glue', expressed his pleasure to Carr that the proposed marriage was bringing him and Suffolk together.[55] For the Queen, whatever gains she made, perhaps linked to the dispute with Northampton over Greenwich Park, her presence provided some legitimacy to the match. John Chamberlain summed up the protracted discussions:

> The marriage was thought should be celebrated at Audley End the next week and great preparation there was to receive the King, but I hear that the Queen being won and having promised to be present, it is put off till Christmas and then to be performed at Whitehall.[56]

Chamberlain's phrasing links the Queen's 'being won' to the changed venue and timetable, suggesting that Anna sought to thwart the Howards of their greatest triumph by insisting on London and a neutral venue rather than a Howard house, while also inconveniencing Carr. Combining the Carr–Howard wedding celebrations with the Christmas festivities could also be passed off as a sensible economy in a court stretched by the Palatine wedding celebrations and aware of the Crown's fragile finances while permitting both King and Queen to continue to manoeuvre and assert their different views of events. Thus, although observers noted a 'general reconcilement in this conjuncture' the Queen's sponsorship of an alternative marriage, between her maid of honour Jean Drummond and Lord Roxburgh, carefully distanced her from her husband's behaviour:

> All the talk now is of masking and feasting at these towardly marriages, whereof the one is appointed on St. Stephen's day in Christmas, the other for Twelfth-tide. The King bears the charge of the first, all saving the apparel, and no doubt the Queen will do as much of her side, which must be a masque of maids, if they may be found, and that is all the charge she means to be at, saving the bride's wedding gown and the marriage bed, wherein she will not exceed £500, for she sayeth her maid Drummond is rich enough otherwise as well in wealth as in virtue and favour.[57]

In contrast to the 'magnificence' lavished by James on his bedchamber favourite, Anna salutes the marriage of her lady of the bedchamber with an insistence upon 'virtue'; and she pointedly invited the Earl of Essex to the feast.[58] Contrary to the claims of parsimony, the feast was especially magnificent, and Holles reported that 'so many either came or were invited that a table stretching the whole length of the gallery was filled. She herself [the Queen] sat at the board's end and by her stood the whole time my lord of Essex.'[59] Whether the congress of courtiers was itself a mark of disapproval of the Carr–Howard match, or pointed support for the Earl of Essex, the Queen's position at the head of her table in the new refurbished gallery of Denmark House asserts her independent position and separates her from her husband.[60] Reports that the Queen actually spent £30,000 on the occasion may suggest she also chose to demonstrate her financial power.

Contemporary descriptions of the Carr–Howard masques shimmer with barely concealed tensions and factional rivalries momentarily contained, instancing precisely the diplomatic and factional negotiations involved in court masques. The nuances of these negotiations are significant because the Queen's role in the leading masque for the occasion, *The Somerset Masque*, stretches the boundaries of the masque form, and places her in such a complex and contradictory position that some have suggested that she was probably 'obliged' or 'constrained' to 'enact her approval' of the match.[61] The evidence of a 'general reconcilement', combined with Chamberlain's description of the winning of the Queen and Northampton's awareness of her ability to 'disorder' his plans, perhaps tends more towards hard bargaining and delicate balances to negotiate even a temporary consensus. Indeed, the requirement to acquire the Queen's public approval acutely shows that certain kinds of power lay in the Queen's adept hands. So, although it is perhaps tempting to regard *The Somerset Masque* as a product of the King's coterie, and the Queen as manoeuvred into acquiescence and disempowerment, the insistence on 'pacification' (see p. 65 above) in the contemporary accounts points towards much greater influence for the Queen, something that is, in fact, acted out in the masque.[62]

So, given the rhetoric of consensus that was sought in the marriage and presented in some contemporary accounts, the strength of the Queen's position lay in the possibility that she might not act. Had the Queen refused to countenance the match, the whole question of the positions and histories of both bride and groom would have been unveiled in a very public forum, and the rumours that were simmering would have been, to some extent, confirmed. Nothing in the contemporary record of the performance suggests that the Queen demurred in any way, although it is tempting to speculate that she may have enjoyed the palpable technical failures of the masque. Her subsequent actions, in countenancing an alternative wedding, suggest that her strategy was one of a nuanced difference and separateness that accentuated her own status and position. So, in effect, using the ideal of consensus to some extent to her own advantage, it seems that although the joint participation of James and Anna was supposed to stress the exemplary unity of the royal marriage, the entertainments created a gendered dialogue, focusing especially upon the roles of Cupid/Venus and Hymen as the tutelary deities of desire and marriage which opened up the question of the marriage and its origins and nature as effectively as any overt gesture of defiance.

Campion's *Somerset Masque* formed the linchpin of these debates, and the final scene of this masque, the 'artificially presented' depiction of London and the Thames (*The Somerset Masque*, p. 273), also suggests how the text acknowledged its complex relation to the contemporary political situation, literally offering the court a world beyond itself. In this engagement with a world beyond the narrow purview of the court the Queen's intervention has a crucial function. Thus, the fiction of Campion's masque, that the twelve knights summoned to celebrate the nuptials by Fame were prevented by the intervention of sorcery that created a storm and conjured away six in a flash of lightning and transformed the remaining six into golden pillars, exploits the quest of the chivalric hero for the virtuous lady but also echoes Anna of Denmark's own wedding voyage.[63] The sea-voyage echoes romance motifs, most notably Phaedria in her gondola on the Idle Lake from *The Faerie Queene*, although there may also be a recuperation of the bawdy uses of ship imagery used to denigrate Frances Howard in several of the contemporary libels.[64]

Although the squires' and knights' ostensible purpose is to celebrate 'This nuptial feast', the intervention of the sorcerers forces them to seek the Queen's help to release the knights and subdue the global 'confusion' created by the spells.[65] This displacement of the quest away from the marriage and onto the Queen's powers echoes the almost entire absence of references to the specific occasion in the text, and suggests how the masque shifts attention away from the difficult marriage of a woman already noted for her questionable behaviour, and onto the figure of the inherently virtuous and fertile queen whose presence acts to ensure the validity of the marriage.

This dual strategy of translation and displacement also applies to the antimasque as the libellous attacks on Carr and Howard are associated with the machinations of the enchanters and enchantresses Error, Rumour, Credulity, and Curiosity. Each of these figures wears costumes suitable to their distortions of truth: 'a deformed vizard', 'a skin coat full of winged tongues', 'a cap like a tongue, with a large pair of wings to it', 'a skin-coat full of eyes', 'a fantastic cap full of eyes' and a 'habit painted with ears, and an antic cap full of ears' (*Somerset Masque*, p. 271). The prominence given to Error and Rumour suggests precisely the gossip and libels which surrounded the match, while Curiosity and Credulity embody the voyeurism which attended the annulment proceedings. These varieties of false speaking and hearing are contrasted with the 'blest ears' of the Queen and the audience (*Somerset Masque*, p. 269).

Anna's role develops this association of the libels with witchcraft. Invoked as 'Bel Anna', the name created for her in Jonson's *Masque of Queens*, her presence rather than the King's validates the marriage, and draws upon her powers depicted in the earlier text: in *Queens*, Anna banishes the 'envious' witches who 'Mix hell with heaven' making 'Nature fight / Within herself' (123–4). Like the witches of *The Somerset Masque* who create 'confusion' (*Somerset Masque*, p. 272), the witches in *Queens* deployed 'Ignorance', 'Suspicion', 'Credulity' to encourage 'Two-faced Falsehood', 'Murmur' and 'Malice', 'Slander', and finally 'black-mouthed Execration' (92–105). Whereas in Jonson's masque Anna merely embodies the virtue spread by Fame, in Campion's text she is the active participant. Thus in *The Somerset Masque*, Anna not only undoes the 'Knotted spells' but in accepting the sacred tree brought in by the three Destinies she liberates the knights and releases the 'Good spells' (*Somerset Masque*, pp. 272, 274). The emphasis upon Anne's 'manifest' 'glory in th'effect' and the role of 'Virtuous Dames' (*Somerset Masque*, pp. 272 and 273) appropriates her female virtue to support this male-centred match as she both banishes the malicious and distinctly libel-like spells and also releases the poetic energy for the celebrations.

Speaking and singing become symbols of the proper use of language in the masque contrasted to the 'knotted', contorted words of the enchanters and witches. Mortal speech is depicted as insufficient ('my tongue's too weak to tell' explains the First Squire), until supported by the action of the Queen in completing the Fates' song and directions. By plucking the branch, the enchantments – the false speaking of the sorcerers and sorceresses – are broken and

> While dancing rests, fit place to music granting
> Good spells the Fates shall breath, all envy daunting
> Kind cares with Joy enchanting, chanting. (*Somerset Masque*, p. 274)

The evil magic that has trapped the knights is replaced by the 'enchanting' and 'chanting' of the Fates, their harmonious and ordered singing voices contrasting with the hate-filled spells of the witches ('all envy daunting'). Indeed, this process of divine harmony and song supporting mortal speech then action is represented in the masque as the squire repeats the final words of the chorus that provides the main motivation of the masque ('By virtuous Dames, let charmed knights be released': *Somerset Masque*, p. 272) and by the final speeches:

> The Second Squire.
> All blessings which the Fates' prophetic sung,
> At Peleus' Nuptials, and what ever tongue
> Can figure more, this night, and aye betide
> The honoured bridegroom and the honoured bride.
>
> All the Squires together.
> Thus speaks in us th'affection of our good knights
> Wishing you health and myriads of goodnights.
> (*Somerset Masque*, p. 276)

Against the calumny offered by envy the bride and groom are offered the 'prophetic' song of the Fates and 'whatever tongue / Can figure more', a process replicated in the good wishes then spoken by the four squires on behalf of the redeemed knights. The allusion to the nuptials of Peleus and Thetis may not only suggest the magnificence of the feast, but also the outcome of the marriage, the birth of Achilles. The mythographer Abraham Fraunce noted that the wedding was associated with both 'the 'generation of things' and the exclusion of Eris, the goddess of 'Discord, the only cause of dissolution.[66]

The emphasis on female agency throughout the masque is striking, and even though Hymen is invoked, the masque ends with Venus: 'The sea-born goddess straight will come' (*Somerset Masque*, p. 276). In a masque dominated by the female figures of the three Destinies (Fates), Eternity, and (possibly) Harmony who is accompanied by 'nine musicians', the Queen enacts the power of divine harmony, and her agency is not contained by the 'Men-making poets' (345) of Jonson's *Masque of Queens* but is asserted in her acceptance of the 'Sacred Tree' (*Somerset Masque*, p. 272).[67] This tree, which contemporary documents identify as an olive, was an emblem of the fruitful wife and had previously been used in *Minerva Britanna* (1612) to salute Anna not only as a mother but as the protectress whose 'outstretched arms' will 'shield and shade the innocent from harms, / But overtop the proud and insolent'.[68]

Clare McManus has used the ambivalence of the olive image to argue that the masque appropriates elements of the Queen's personal iconography and subordinates them (and her) to the King's command as part of a wider strategy which sees the masque replicate elements of her former masquing, such as her association with maritime imagery, and transform it into a representation of her enforced acquiescence in the masque.[69] While Anna's power may ultimately be subordinated to that of her husband, the masque repeatedly represents her agency and the significance of her willingness to 'shield and shade' the marriage.

The importance of the Queen's role is stressed by a series of formal innovations that reshape the masque. Centrally, Anna substitutes for the King, replacing him as the normal focus of the performance. The main episode that pivots the action – the taking of the branch and its presentation – literally requires her involvement but also locates her as the centre of the masque. Her gesture also crosses the bounds of the masque fiction as she bridges the masque and court worlds, so that her action acquires significance both in the world of realpolitik and in the masque's myth world.[70] In this way the Queen is not only the dancer and presenter as she had been in Jonson's earlier masques. She becomes the focus of the masque, not simply as a spectator but as an actor who operates in both the court and masque worlds.

This role is a manifestation of her position as a consort queen, and in this masque she literally and symbolically brings together the two worlds of the masque. Indeed, she bridges the factions of the court as the 'Nobleman' (*Somerset Masque*, p. 273) to whom she presented the magic branch was the Lord Chamberlain, the Earl of Suffolk, while the ultimate recipient was the Earl of Pembroke who, having accepted the tree, led out the Queen to dance.[71] The choice of Pembroke as lead dancer would appear to be significant as he was not the highest ranking masquer (this was the Duke of Lennox), but he was the leader of the Protestant patriot faction. In a text that also emphasises the role of the Queen's 'blest hands' or 'sacred hand', her hands literally bring together the court and the masque, joining the factions together as she hands the 'divine-touched bough' to Suffolk and is handed out to dance by Pembroke (*Somerset Masque*, pp. 272–3). In this moment the Queen becomes the connection between the factions and, implicitly in the image of scared touch, she takes on the royal, medicinal role, binding the court together.

The central place afforded to Anna also requires a series of displacements. Although the Countess of Somerset is noted as being invited to dance, her husband is nowhere mentioned, and while this masque ostensibly celebrates her marriage and deploys a panoply of epithalamic effects, most of the action centres on the Queen.[72] Similarly, in contrast to Anna's central and active role, James only features as the passive recipient of the First Squire's praises and this diversion away from the King's role and the repeated insistence upon Anna's virtue may seek to deflect some of the contemporary unease over James' connection with Carr, the nullity, the reputation of the bride, and the 'toward' marriage. Yet, even amidst the repeated injunctions to and celebrations of heroic procreativity (suggested in the allusions to the marriage of Peleus and Thetis which produced Achilles), Carr's entanglements cannot be entirely suppressed.[73] Thus in the 'Fourth Song, a Dialogue of three with a Chorus after the Second Dance':

> I. Let us now sing of Loves delight,
> For he alone is Lord to night.
>
> II. Some friendship betweene man and man prefer,
> But I th'affection betweene man and wife.
>
> III. What good can be in life,
> Whereof no fruites appeare?
>
> I. Set is that Tree in ill houre,
> That yields neither fruite nor flowre.
>
> II. How can man Perpetuall be,
> But in his own Posteritie?
>
> CHORUS
> That pleasure is of all most bountiful and kind,
> That fades not straight, but leaves a living Joy behind.[74]

Lindley argues that these lines show that Campion is 'self-evidently not concerned about any homosexual relationship which might have subsisted between Carr and the King or Carr and Overbury' and on one level they do continue the theme of fecundity, emphasising 'fruites' over 'pleasure'.[75] Yet this pleasure is not only between man and woman, but explicitly in the friendship of 'man and man' which some 'prefer'.

Although the decorum of the masque would not permit direct allusion to the precise connection between Carr and James (let alone the recognition of it as an alternative 'pleasure'), the marriage – as we have seen – is founded upon male bonds and male power alliances. Campion's text is oddly contradictory in this respect, dominated by 'Love's delight / For he alone is Lord tonight' (p. 274), stressing the role of Cupid over Hymen, so that the language of this song constantly pushes at the boundaries of the unsayable as the inter-male 'friendship' which some 'prefer' reminds the auditors of the connection between this preference and preferment. Later, the song which seems to celebrate fructification alludes both to 'posterity' and 'behind' almost as if recalling the libellers' puns on 'in-taileth'.

The threat of disruption that Carr's advancement and marriage created is perhaps suggested in the lengths to which the King went to negotiate a settlement with the Queen, to bring the masque in from Audley, its first proposed location, and to announce the pre-eminent favours he was offering to Carr. The diplomatic invitations may have described the masque as a 'private' occasion, but Finet reassured the London diplomatic corps that 'his Majesty was pleased to cast upon one of his most favoured Servants to have the marriage solemnised in his own house, and to invite to it whom he should think fit at his Princely pleasure'.[76] This public demonstration of royal favour was continued in the finances and the casting. *The Somerset Masque* was not only (and apparently entirely) funded by the King, it also differs in its choice of performers from the other post-1612 masques which were usually staged by the 'King's gentlemen and servants', the members of the bedchamber and other associates of the personal court, as was the case with *The Irish Masque* on 1 and 6 January 1614.[77] In this case, the status of the masquers was noted by observers: Ferdinand de Boisschot describes them as mostly '*Condes del Reyno*' (Lords of the Privy Council), although as with other of the Somerset entertainments considerable effort was made to balance the court factions.[78] In this sense the *Somerset Masque* represents something of a throwback to the early unionist masques with their deliberate balancing of Scots and English participants, although here the equilibrium sought is between the Howards and anti-Howard faction, notably in the prominent roles given to Suffolk and Pembroke. This layering of motives and agendas perhaps explains some of the complexities of the masque, and as much as key features of the masque and its surrounding occasion point towards royal agendas, some elements point towards its origin as a Howard masque, such as the choice of Campion, a writer linked through his patron Sir Thomas Monson, to the Howards.[79] Campion's involvement suggests not only their influence, but the continuation of the campaign from the summer of 1613 to seek commonality with the Queen.[80]

The same motivation may apply to the use of French forms in the masque. David Lindley notes that the emphasis upon enchantment rather than myth in *The Somerset Masque* parallels developments in the *ballet de cour* and that the musical style, especially of 'Bring away that sacred tree', may follow continental models.[81] The choice of French form holds multiple agendas, including self-differentiation from the Jonsonian masque, but may have been designed to appeal to the Queen who supported a band of French musicians and staged a *ballet de cour* in her own Chamber at Denmark House in 1617.[82] Nevertheless, as Clare McManus has suggested, this French style may have held more coercive possibilities as many of the ballets had enacted the submission of royal women to the will of the male monarch.[83] Unlike Campion's summer *Entertainment at Caversham*, which also followed French ballets in stressing the priority of sociability and dance over words, here the non-dancing Queen is manoeuvred rather than obliged, into a 'general reconcilement in this conjuncture', even if temporary, with the Howards.[84]

Although these factional and political issues were central to the meanings of the masques for contemporaries and have been the foundation of much modern masque criticism, the political rationale that underlay the masques was not simply the representation and resolution of internal political divisions, but a response to outside opinion. So, while on one level the use of Fame in *The Somerset Masque* is shaped by intertextual relations with *The Masque of Queens*, and the style of the masque with a contentious interaction with the Jonsonian masque, the Queen's action in undoing the spells replicates her actions in attending the masque and countenancing the match. The primary focus, then, extends beyond the factional politics to the world of the libellers, fragments of whose texts and language constantly surface and are appropriated in the masque.

A similar double focus on both court factional politics and wider political debates can be seen in Jonson's *A Challenge at Tilt*. Although Jonson may not have produced a masque directly celebrating this marriage, his *Challenge at Tilt* provided a symbolic core for the entertainment sequence that marked the wedding. Thus, *A Challenge*, like Campion's masque, pursued a dual strategy of reconciliation and containment: on one hand it stresses the reciprocity of love and continuing the court unity expressed during Carr's installation as an earl earlier in 1613; on the other hand, it contains the languages of sexual desire, here seen as the legitimate desires of bride and groom, links them to the proper rites associated with procreation, and recasts them in a classical form that lends dignity and purpose.

A Challenge at Tilt restages the *Barriers at a Marriage* performed for Essex and Frances Howard in 1606, making the second marriage a continuation of the King's union policies, and a direct, potentially successful, replacement for a failed union. As with other elements of the celebration that were staged in highly visible symbolic locations, such as Whitehall, this part of the marriage celebrations was highly public and may have been designed to affirm Carr's position in royal favour and to announce royal support for the match. The Challenge was preceded by running at the ring by the King, Prince Charles, and Carr, and was performed in the more open space of the tiltyard.[85] Moreover, to reinforce unity the two Cupids' 'champions', representing bride and groom, were drawn from the differing court factions so that the Howards fought in the groom's colours while Pembroke and Montgomery wore the bride's livery.[86] This theoretical reconciliation may have been ruffled by the actual performance: one diplomatic dispatch suggests several noblemen refused to participate. Moreover, the Carr–Howard match marked a major shift towards the pro-Spanish and pacific factions at court, and a fair segment of the audience must have been conscious of the uncomfortable implications of the tilt.[87] Essex, the impugned party in the divorce, was a leading martial figure and more associated with stricter Protestantism, and alongside the Earl of Pembroke was an exponent of military intervention against Catholicism in Europe.[88]

We cannot be sure that the text as performed may not have contained more direct material that was edited out during 1615–16, although what survives refers to 'strife' and 'difference' at court in conscious recognition of the difficulty of the process in which it was engaged. The performance of the tilt enacts this process of reconciliation. Tilting, even though it required considerable martial skills, was a highly regulated and aestheticised form of warfare and ultimately embodied a submission to the laws of chivalry and royal authority. As such it was an ideal vehicle to mythologise the resolution of disputes. Thus, the public backing offered to the marriage is balanced by the recognition that the marriage has produced tensions, and the text of A Challenge uses the debating Cupids to gloss the marriage as the unification of two types of desire, just as the performance sought to unite the differing court parties.[89] The bipartite structure contributes to this approach, so that the 'challenge' announced on 27 December presents the two Cupids 'striving' for supremacy, while the 'tilting' staged on 1 January opens the new year with further contentions which are then resolved, first through the ritualised actions of the tilt, and second through the intervention of Hymen who insists they must both surrender as 'this is neither contention for you, nor time fit to contend' (145–6). The important feature here is the regulation and eventual resolution of strife, so that this is not a marriage without strife, but one in which the right kind of contention, the 'strife wherein you both win', as to who loves most 'begets a concord worthy all married minds' emulation' (171–2). Debate and disagreement are subsumed in civility and transformed from a potential source of discord into the basis of higher harmony.

Although the controlled expression of tensions and their ceremonial resolution may not have entirely worked in the actual performance, this strategy was used to submerge both the potential embarrassments of the occasion, and to translate some of the more widespread concerns about the nullity and the marriage through the appropriation of the language of sex and desire. *A Challenge*, to a remarkable extent, reeks of sexual tension, with joking references to unregulated sexual appetite and even sodomy.[90] In the dialogue in which Eros and Anteros, representing Carr and Howard, struggle for precedence, Eros is characterised by his 'excellent beauty' that is 'right worthy' (154) of his mother Venus, which recalls Carr's own handsomeness.[91] Equally, the second Cupid, standing for Lady Howard, refuses to give way: 'Thou cannot put modesty into me, to make me come behind you though; I will stand for mine inches with you as peremptory as an ambassador' (12–13). Both these allusions seem to court disaster, reminding the participants of Carr's 'Male Beauty' which 'prevaileth' with the King, while the bawdy also echoes the kinds of accusations about Frances Howard's indecorous behaviour and the language of the libels which depicted her as 'a lusty filly', 'growne so wide / theare is a passage for a Carre to ride'.[92] Indeed, the second Cupid claims that he even 'made her language sweeter . . . upon her tongue' (42–3) than that of Mercury, transforming Frances Howard from a figure tainted with female forwardness and the slanderous tongues of libel into a figure of female eloquence whose god-defeating 'tongue' outdoes male understanding.

Although the refutation of the libeller's language, and even its representation and appropriation are not as clearly present as in Campion's *Somerset Masque*, Jonson's bawdy Cupids relentlessly portray raging, even outrageous, desire 'playing in your bloods like fishes in a stream, or diving like boys i'the bath, and then rising on end like a monarch and treading humour like water, bending those stiff piccadills of yours under this yoke, my bow', sentiments which are regarded as 'most stiffly spoken, and fit for the sex you stand for!' (84–7, 131). This reiterated sexual allusion and punning in *A Challenge*, like the Campion masque with its strategy of containing the libellous innuendo around the Carr–Howard nuptials, corrals desire within the bounds of acceptable marriage and discourse, the 'glad solemnities' marked by what the first Cupid calls 'proper rites' (23). These 'proper rites', those that are suitable to the occasion and thus also decorous, are by implication contrasted with the improper use of speech in the libels and satirical commentaries.

Part of the tactic is to cast Carr as Aeneas, a Venusian figure. The concluding explanation by Hymen suggests that desire will now be regulated within marriage and that love and presumably the marriage will 'flourish and prosper' (166–7) with children, a further dynastic extension of the implicit Carr–Aeneas parallel. Hymen's intervention sanctions desire just as the text absorbs the bawdy of the libels and translates it into a more courtly setting and marriage. Even here, however, the dialogue negotiates the tensions created by the match:

> And may this royal court never know more difference in humours, or these well-graced nuptials more discord in affections, than what they presently feel, and may ever avoid. (176–8)

The prayer-like conditionality of this closing sentiment marks how far the Carr–Howard match had stretched the harmony of the court. This closure, moreover, illustrates one of the problems in this strategy for, as in *The Irish Masque*, simply to turn the libels into fescenine verses and to translate the tensions within the court into 'difference in humours' belittles genuine concerns about the political implications of the alliance.

The appearance of the Cupids in *The Challenge* and the containment of desire within marriage are repeated in many of the masques and epithalamia surrounding the Carr–Howard match. Often the Carr–Howard marriage is depicted as expressing true love in contrast to the failed dynastic Devereux–Howard union: as early as June 1613 Chamberlain recorded how 'the world speaks liberally that my Lord of Rochester and she be in love one with another'.[93] So the repeated emphasis upon Cupid in many of the masques, especially in *The Challenge* and Middleton's *Masque of Cupids*, may register this aspect of the relationship.[94] Certainly, the reconciliatory role assigned to Hymen in Jonson's text continues the dialogue between the entertainments for the Somerset wedding over its tutelary deity, each text exploring the balance between Cupid and the restraining forces of social order. Campion's masque, for instance, stresses the roles of Cupid and Venus (the 'Sea-born Goddess'), combining 'Hymen' with 'Amor', although the potentially disruptive qualities of desire are encased within choruses praising Hymen, 'Charms' which are 'enclosing' and 'closing'.[95]

The events surrounding the Carr–Howard match involve an unprecedented degree of public speculation and discussion and, interestingly, the court solemnities despite their official status as 'private' acquired public dimensions, not only in the processions and the tilting, but also in the language of the entertainments. Rather than avoidance or effacement these masques are centrally concerned with containment, displacement, and translation, echoing the bawdy discourse of gossip, refuting its truth, but also recuperating some of its language in order to restrict its implications. In particular, *The Somerset Masque* contains Carr's subversive potential, especially in the emphasis upon procreativity in marriage. Figuratively and verbally Campion and Jonson's two texts make the 'defence of a good prick' that Northampton had urged upon Carr by more violent means. Yet, as in Niccols' later tract on Overbury, there are also signs of strain as the negotiations and factional deals that underpin the occasion constantly threaten to unravel, and a recognition that the public discussion generated even by the 'towardly marriages' has pushed at the boundaries of what is acceptable in public discourse by engaging with the libellous poetry that circulated around this match. Jonson's final masque for the 1614 season itself engages with the question of the limits of public discourse.

'Sing then some': *The Irish Masque at Court*

In comparison to the other Carr–Howard texts Jonson's *Irish Masque at Court* has sometimes seemed anomalous, concerned with political debates about Irish settlement rather than the celebration of a marriage. The Irish fiction has not met with approval: John Chamberlain regarded the masque as a 'mimical imitation . . . not so pleasing to many, which think it no time (as the case stands) to exasperate that nation by making it ridiculous'.[96] More recently it has been described as either an unsuitable use of the intractable and uncomfortable problems created by Jacobean policy in Ireland to celebrate the ephemeral marriage of a court favourite, or as a 'charade designed to amuse a non-Irish audience'.[97] Yet, many features of *The Irish Masque* are designed to refute or reformulate the aesthetic strategies found in *The Somerset Masque* and to modify its political agenda.[98] The final section of this chapter suggests these allusions help illuminate how *The Irish Masque*, despite its rather sparse references to the marriage, engages with the nuptials and their political ramifications in a critical manner.[99] It has been noted that early modern 'English representations of Ireland were in point of fact representations of England', and in *The Irish Masque* a nuanced view of Irish civility supports similar discriminations about England and its civilisation.[100] By disaggregating simplified and homogenised notions of 'the' Irish, Jonson relates the uncomfortable and difficult Irish political and cultural situation to key political issues around obedience to royal will and the limits of civility and civil discourse.[101] The role of the poet as embodied in the figure of the bard represents a particular kind of civic and political discourse, not only in Ireland but across England and Scotland, and crucially reflecting on the would-be 'civilisers' and courtiers as those they claim to improve.[102]

In many ways *The Irish Masque* is a rewriting of the earlier Anglo-Scots union masques, and Jonson was not the only writer to link the Carr–Howard match and union politics. The anonymous *The Masque of Flowers*, sponsored by Francis Bacon and staged by Gray's Inn, draws parallels between this match and the renewal of Anglo-Scots union, and is perhaps designed to bear out Bacon's view of colonisation as a providential and heroic labour worthy of the ancients, bringing 'savage and barbarous customs to humanity and civility'.[103] In Bacon's masque an elaborate tree-filled garden, presided over by garden gods whose charm envisioned a renewed, fertile and civilised Britain, embodied not only marital fertility but the return of a new unionist world: the 'rude and waste' are repaired and the marriage 'mends all things' to make 'Britain fit to be / A seat for a fifth monarchy'.[104] Such formulations are also present in the *Irish Masque*, so if Ireland submits to the 'music of . . . peace' the king will 'in her all the fruits of blessing plant' (*The Irish Masque*, 132, 138). The imagery here also seems to parallel one of the more sympathetic unofficial verses about the marriage, which envisaged the marriage as the restoration of natural order, arguing that 'Plants enough may hence ensue / Some-are-set where none ere grew'.[105] Such images, implicitly of plantation, commonplace both in colonial and epithalamic rhetoric, are displaced as *The Irish Masque* moves away from the ideal and the prophetic towards a more earthy, but also less certain, sense of the parallel situations in marriage and plantation.

There were good reasons to be tentative. Speaking in April 1614, Sir Ralph Winwood warned the House of Commons that 'the late rebellious parliament of Ireland has awaked Tyrone out of his sleep' and conjured up the possibility of a papal invasion of Ireland.[106] While this was undoubtedly overly alarmist, the Irish Parliament of 1612–13 had witnessed extraordinary disruption when, after an attempt to prevent the installation of the Protestant Sir John Davies as speaker, Sir Arthur Chichester complained to the King of the 'contempts and insolencies' of the Irish Catholic parliamentarians and their 'malignant and crooked' nature. Another dispatch noted the 'great contempt and disorder' and 'noise' in Parliament, while a further missive condemned the 'offensive and contentious' opening of Parliament.[107] A largely Catholic delegation that had travelled to court to persuade the King of Irish loyalty had been confronted by the King's demand for a public declaration in his presence of their loyalty to him or the Pope. Indeed, James castigated their behaviour: 'you have carried yourselves tumultuously, and . . . your proceedings have been rude [and] disorderly'.[108] When the required obedience was not forthcoming, he promptly imprisoned two members of the delegation.[109]

Jonson's more Tacitean masque explores the issue of civility in the parallel contexts of England and Ireland, but whereas *Flowers* relies on an idealised and generalised hope that some of the divisions occasioned by the match might now be resolved, Jonson particularises the Irish situation and insists upon decorum in speech and behaviour, rejecting both the sexual and scatological innuendo which has characterised the commentary surrounding the nuptials and also the 'rude and disorderly' proceedings in Ireland.

This sterner, but also more nuanced view emerges from the opening of the antimasque with its derogatory depictions of the comic and disordered servants (Dennis, Donnell, Dermock, and Patrick) of the party of Irish ambassador-masquers, arrived to mark the 'great bridal' of 'ty man Robin' (49–50). According to their servants, the masquers have supposedly lost all their clothes ('te prishe of a cashtle or two upon teir backs', 63) during a storm on the Irish Sea so they must dance in their 'mantles' (67). This use of traditional Irish garb incorporated into the masque already differentiates the text from some of the plantation writers who regarded the mantle as unacceptably barbarous. Jonson's nuanced approach continues in the 'civil gentleman of the nation' (114–15) who takes over the celebrations, introducing first a bard, and then the masquers, who dance in their cloaks, finally revealing 'their masquing apparel' (156). These masquers are notably loyal (something they protest regularly, as in 81–97) and not simply the barbarian 'other'.

Although the final bard's song that marks their transformation into 'newborn creatures all' (155) under the 'spring' of the King's 'presence' (152–3) echoes rhetoric linked to the Jacobean project to 'civilise' Ireland and replace the Old Irish with the New Irish, the footmen criticise the 'few rebelsh and knavesh' (95) who discredit the Irish nation with their recalcitrance.[110] While much of the comedy draws on the comic stereotype of the Irish footmen (especially their mock-Irish accents and their naïve wonder at the court and the King, 13–16), they are linked to the Pale and to the royal household: Dennis, for example, is a servant to the royal costermonger (5–6). In the context of derogatory representations of the Irish as feckless and purposeless, these footmen not only represent the labouring and middling sorts, they also, even though they and their masters are 'poor' (70), are not simply disorderly. Thus, even though their dance is 'rude', that of their masters is 'solemn'.[111]

A parallel distinction can be found in the treatment of their language. On one level their talk of 'ty man Robin' is jokily over-familiar and their initial reluctance to speak along with their marked deference to the King distinguishes them from the disorderly. Yet, although they warn each other to 'take heet' (19), their language and behaviour also transgresses the limits of courtly speech. The scatological puns (notably on 'shit' in 105 and 119) and the dance performed 'to the bagpipe and other rude music' (110-11), even though they make a key point about the equality of all men, represent an unacceptable coarseness which needs to be controlled. Thus the Gentleman's admonishment, 'let your coarser manners seek some other place / Fit for their wildness' (123-4), concerns correct discrimination and use in language. The language is not dismissed as barbaric, but 'coarser' and not fit for this place (though suitable for their own 'wildness').

The politics of language, of course, figured in the immediate Irish context of this masque as Barnaby Rich, writing in 1610, had advocated teaching the Irish to speak English rather than Gaelic and connected the advancing 'civility' of the nation, despite their Catholicism, and their 'very good conversation', while Sir John Davies hoped that 'the next generation will in tongue and heart and every way else become English so there will be no difference or distinction but the Irish Sea betwixt us'.[112] Particular concern focused on the 'Bards . . . Rhythmers, and other such lying poets' as Rich names them, who were largely associated with disorderly Irish (Gaelic) culture; Ireneus in Spenser's *View of the Present State of Ireland* had urged the suppression of the bards because they sang of the 'licentious' and the 'most dangerous and desperate in all parts of disobedience and rebellious disposition'.[113]

In *The Irish Masque*, these oppositions of barbarism/civility are complicated and the two central symbols of the masque – harp and bagpipe – are more multi-layered and coded, neither as solely Irish nor as simply barbarous. The sequence of the two dances, first as the footmen dance to the bagpipe and second as the Irish lords dance to the harp, suggests a differentiated but still united culture complete with a deferential final cry: 'Peash, Peash! Now room for our mayshters' (112). Even though articulated in comedy, Dermock's comparison of the Irish mantles as 'fine cloyshs now, and liveries' (116) just like those given to the King's men makes Irish dress and court livery parallel and equal. The associations of the bagpipe are not solely ethnic or derogatory and may be associated with the footmen's class.[114] Indeed, the only reference to specifically Irish music comes from the harps and, in this case, the harp-playing bard brought in by the Gentleman exemplifies the civil Irish rather than the barbarian. In contrast to the attitudes found in many plantation writers, the bard in *The Irish Masque* is characterised as a prophetic figure, urged to 'Sing . . . some charm . . . / That may assure thy former prophecies' (139–40). These prophecies are to be spun out of the King's deeds in ending 'unnatural broils' and instituting 'the music of his peace' (130, 132).[115]

Jonson's use of the harp has attracted adverse attention and Philip Edwards regarded it as absurd that the bard should sing for the English polity that had extirpated Gaelic culture. The harp, however, does not solely represent a subordinated culture;[116] not only was the harp used in both Scots and Irish culture but it was also adopted at the English court by several aristocrats including Robert Cecil who may have learned to play on a harp gifted to him by the Countess of Desmond in 1597.[117] Both Anna of Denmark and James I supported harpers: Daniel Cahill was employed in the Queen's household before 1610, and Cormack McDermott appears in the King's household list of 1605.[118] There is every sign that the instrument was widely appreciated in England, and Bacon commented that 'No instrument hath the sound so melting and prolonged as the Irish harp.'[119]

Irish identity in *The Irish Masque* is, then, more complex than simply a rejection of Ireland as barbarous; indeed, the 'civil gentleman of the nation' and the bard instructs not only the Irish but also the English who have not, yet, recognised that James will end 'our country's unnatural broils' (130). 'Our country' may appear to refer to Ireland but the sense of shared culture and the ambiguity of the referent also allows it to apply to England. In this context the phrase 'unnatural broils' forms another point of contact between England and Ireland, as it offers a vision of a nation at war ('deafened with the drum', 131), but at this point, despite the parliamentary disputes, and the threat of invasion if war did break out with Spain, there were no hostilities. In 1614 'broils' seems much more likely to allude to the parliamentary dissension and what the King called the 'rude and disorderly' proceedings. Indeed, the connections between the 'knotty beginning' of the Irish Parliament, the English court context of factional contention, and the English climate of political rumour and libels around the Carr–Howard match can be seen in the parallel terms used to describe the different kinds of debate and dissent.[120] Later in the same year Chichester was concerned by the rumourousness of Irish culture in a way that echoes perceptions of the English itch for news during the Overbury affair:

> They were never so much devoted to superstition, nor so discontented generally, never more rash and raving of their tongues, nor so ready with their ears to listen unto rumours from abroad . . . and unto speeches of reproach and criminations against rule and rulers from the lowest to the highest.[121]

Although this letter discusses one of the many invasion scares that exercised the authorities, it illuminates broader concerns about the impact of rumour, libel, and dissent, along with the fear of potential interruptions of 'solemnities'.[122] This shared aspect of English and Irish culture is perhaps confirmed in the masque when the footmen reveal that they have arrived for the celebrations because 'Tere vash a great newsh in Ireland of a great bridal' (48–9).

To discover the authorities in Dublin and London shared anxieties about 'great newsh' comes as no surprise, but it also suggests how the Irish fiction in Jonson's masque may reflect on the English situation, and the 'knotty beginning' of the Irish Parliament and the disrupted ceremonials form a neat parallel for the Carr–Howard nuptials. The rudeness of the Irish footmen's speech (especially its scatology), and the use of the bagpipe (often associated with rough rhymes) can be seen as ways of representing aspects of the verse around the Carr–Howard match. Interestingly, then, the careful distinctions about the Irish and the role of lower-class voices here suggest a much less condemnatory attitude towards libels and the unofficial politics of rumour and news culture. Such writers and opinions may, ultimately, like the footmen, be required to depart but for all their coarseness they are loyal.

This brings another Tacitean twist to the differences between the treatment of dissenting voices in *The Somerset Masque* and *The Irish Masque*. In Campion's romance-based masque the Queen 'undid all knots' and so these voices are smoothed by the actions of the 'vertuous Dame' and the malicious spells are undone in a process that encloses and transforms them to harmony.[123] Yet, as Jonson's more outward-looking text adopts the more rationalist approach found in Tacitus, it also adapts some of its harshness. Even as James' 'gladding face' (127) countenances and, therefore, legitimates the masque, creating an unsurpassed harmony, Jonson achieves his harmony by expelling the disharmonious. This dual-aspect approach proffering a more open recognition of dissentient voices is balanced by ruthlessness in political actions: the viewpoints may be valid, but the threat cannot be allowed to remain. The image of the Orphic bard leading the nation towards civility, inspired by the monarch, stands as a rebuke to the English libellers and promoters of discord. There is a crucial shift here from *Love Restored*, alluded to in the final songs' images of a world 'lately fettered . . . with ice' (*Irish Masque*, 163), where uncivil voices could be incorporated, as here they must change.

The different tone seen in *The Irish Masque* registers a darker political climate. The disquiet over the marriage and the advancement of the Howards and later the deeply contentious sittings of the Addled Parliament had contributed to the rumorousness of the culture. As Michelle O'Callaghan has suggested, a number of writers evidence the concern with how to speak in this climate, especially after the imprisonment of George Wither.[124] Even though the King had hoped 1614 might be 'a parliament of love', it was clear that those hopes and the kind of world envisaged by *Love Restored* had dissipated.[125] Texts such as Chapman's *Andromeda Liberata* (1614) sought to address the 'violent hubbub' of uncontrolled rumour-mongering but may only have succeeded in provoking more reaction.[126] *Andromeda Liberata*, rather obviously, depicts Andromeda/Frances rescued by Perseus/Robert from the monster/whale, a figure that echoes the depiction of public opinion, or rumour, as monstrous creature.[127] The poem castigates the 'ungodly vulgars' who seek nothing but seditious news and in the dedication to the earl and countess and in the epistle to the 'prejudicate and peremptory reader' Chapman casts the role of poetry to stand against the 'spleens profane / Of humours errant and plebian', to utter truth and correct the 'opinions proved / By vulgar voices'.[128] Chapman then had to offer a 'defence' of his original epithalamium, *A Free and Offenceless Justification*, which complains of the appropriation of his poems as satire and libel rather than defence. Indeed several manuscript copies of 'There was an old lad rode on an old pad', the poem that most explicitly deals with the physical demonstration of marital nullity, the text is given a false 'imprint' as: 'Imprinted in Paul's churchyard at the sign of the yellow band and cuffs by Adam Arsenic for Robert Rosear, and are to be sold at the Andromeda Liberata in Turnbull Street'.[129] In case anyone had missed the allusion, the false 'imprimatur' names Chapman and the subject of his poem. Chapman's complaint about this text – and presumably others – was to note that others 'setting my song to their own tunes, have made it yield so harsh and distasteful a sound to my best friends'.[130]

The interactions between *Andromeda Liberata* and manuscript libel show how sophisticated and even open the responses to pro-Howard propaganda had become.[131] Chapman's text may have been part of a coordinated campaign of the kind alluded to in Donne's letter on libelling (see Chapter 2, pp. 37–8), although there are also signs of uncertainty amongst the authorities as to how such a climate could be controlled. Thus we know that Chapman's poem was (unusually) licensed by four Privy Councillors and followed upon plans to produce an official defence of the nullity that Winwood claimed would have appeared in print and in English, French, and Latin.[132] Yet while the Earl of Suffolk remained attached to the plan he was persuaded that 'no questioning by writing' was best as 'it might go on to the world's end; for one book might breed another: and so, they whom it concerned should never be in rest'.[133] Proposals to produce an official transcript of the trial were also floated and abandoned. The sense of pressure on writers created by this climate, the difficulty of maintaining the distinctions between illicit and licit speech and writing, and the fear of constant appropriation by enemies and opponents who turn praise to abuse, suggest a robust culture of political commentary but also precisely the difficulty that faced writers like Chapman and Jonson at this juncture. It is interesting to note that Chapman's language of song corrupted by rude music connects to the soundscape of *The Irish Masque* with its attempts to 'Sing then some charm' that can combine rude and solemn music to create royal and poetic harmony.

If *The Irish Masque*, with its preference for civil bards over various forms of ill-speaking and cacophony that permeated the textual culture of the Carr–Howard marriage, responds to the danger of 'unnatural broils', it does not solely locate these forces beyond the court. Indeed, in tandem with *Love Restored*, the issue of violence replacing persuasion also surfaces, especially in the criticism of the Earl of Suffolk. There was already widespread disquiet expressed at the potential for dominance offered to the Howards by the marriage to the King's favourite, and this was compounded by Northampton's apparent attempts to suppress criticism of himself and the match through the arrest of Wither and the innovative (and repressive) interpretation he put on the statute of *scandalum magnatum* in the defamation cases he prosecuted. It is, therefore, interesting to note that even within its jocular criticism of Suffolk, *The Irish Masque* associates the Howards with repressive violence.

The ordering of the hall before the masque, supervised by the Lord Chamberlain, was one of the crucial ceremonial elements of the occasion alongside the carefully negotiated seating of the various envoys (often the cause of much dissension).[134] The antimasque to *The Irish Masque* thus opens with its antithesis as the comic Irish embassy burst onto the stage ('out ran a fellow') and complain of their distinctly undiplomatic treatment at the hands of Lord Chamberlain Suffolk: 'Ish it te fashion to beat te imbasheters here, ant knock 'em o'te heads phit te phoit stick' (9–10). Although the comic portrayal of Suffolk – as Dermock notes "tere ish very mush phoit stick here stirring tonight' (54) – may have been further revenge upon the Chamberlain's exclusion of Jonson and Roe from the masquing hall in 1604, as in *Love Restored* the role of access and its denial symbolises not only the narrowness of the court but also the attempt to exclude external voices (see Chapter 2, pp. 48–9, 51). Even though cast in comic form these lines echo contemporary critiques of the Howards who were regarded as incompetent and even potentially violent by at least one near-contemporary satirist who noted, 'When they are great / They imprison and beat'.[135]

The comic attack on Suffolk, and his displacement in *The Irish Masque*, gains in pointedness in light of his pivotal role in *The Somerset Masque* and Jonson's praise of the royal bardic figure establishes a careful discrimination, or limit upon, acceptance of the new Howard-led order. Interestingly, Daniel's *Hymen's Triumph* recognises the significance of the Howard annexation of the office of chamberlain and its rapid transference to Robert Carr. In the Prologue added to the printed text which appeared in 1615, a disguised Hymen confronts '*Avarice, Evny* and *Jealousy*, the disturbers of quiet marriage' but, although these figures recall *The Somerset Masque*, this Hymen does not combine love and marriage, using instead a lowly habit and a 'white wand' (22–3) to shepherd lovers towards true, marital bliss.[136] The symbolism of Hymen's 'white wand', substituted for the conventional torch, relegates the role of passion; it also recalls the white staff carried by the Lord Chamberlain and belongs to an important discussion of the symbolism of the chamberlain's office. Hymen, the god-shepherd-chamberlain of this household ruled by honour and integrity, contrasts sharply with the two historical chamberlains, Suffolk and Somerset.

In contrast to the bawdry of Jonson's tilt which asked the opponents to 'crack kisses not staves', *Hymen's Triumph*'s 'unusual decorousness of subject-matter' enunciates an alternative view of this incorporation of desire within Hymen's realm.[137] The Prologue establishes 'feminine' 'recreatives' presided over by Cynthia 'Wherein no wild, no rude, no antic sport' is allowed (Prologue, lines 18–21), and these echoes of Jonson's masque distance Daniel and his patroness from the central court masques. The Prologue, in particular, carves out a virtuous female space, the 'fair structure' Denmark House, 'sacred to integrity' where 'honour keeps the door' (lines 51, 49) in contrast to the geographical and social mobility seen in *The Irish Masque*.[138] Throughout, the Prologue lavishly praises the Queen's marital virtue and productivity (lines 20–39) in comparison to the failed or compromised marriages that had just been celebrated.

Neither honour nor the Lord Chamberlain kept the door at *The Irish Masque* as the Chamberlain's role is taken first by the Irish footmen, who themselves order the room for their masters ('Now room . . . room', 112) and then his function as a purveyor of entertainments is usurped by the 'civil gentleman' ('Advance immortal bard', 126). Significantly, unlike the silent Chamberlain of *The Somerset Masque*, this 'chamberlain' not only sets the rules of suitable discourse as censor, but his blank verse establishes a new and decorous order of speaking where rational speech surpasses the undisciplined speech of the footmen and seeks to outdo the 'drum' and 'unnatural broils' (130–1) of dissent. He mediates between the uncontrolled and loyal but indecorous welcome of the footmen and the elevated charms and prophecies offered by the bard.

The careful positioning of the antimasque fiction through the roles of chamberlain and civil gentleman suggests that *The Irish Masque* distances itself from the new Howard regime but without requiring the kind of language used in libels. This critical differentiation continues in the transformation and main masque, aspects of the text sometimes depicted as flawed. David Lindley, in particular, charges the masque with complacency as the audience's prior knowledge of the masquers' real identity as 'English servants of the King' undermines any educative process which might transform the masquers into the ideal potentials they dance.[139] The masquers, however, as Chamberlain makes clear, were a mixture of bedchamber English and Scots (Sergeant Boyd, Abercromby, Achmouty) whose constitution was precisely supposed to embody the union that the King also wanted for Ireland. The mixed origins of the masquers certainly complicate any idea this masque is simply complacent, since involving the English and Scots as a symbol of the union of the crowns allows a reflection not simply on the Irish and their civilisation, but also on the civilising process and its earlier subjects, England and Scotland.

Understandings of British history underwent a major shift in the 1610s with the publication of William Camden's *Britannia* (1610) challenging the mythical descent of the Britons from exiled Trojans (the Brute legend). Instead, Camden offered a much darker vision of Britain civilised through the violent imposition of Roman order. Before the arrival of the Romans, the English and other indigenous peoples were degenerating into violence but only imposed Roman rule returned them to civility, even though that very state was one of servitude.[140] This example of English history also served to undermine ideas of civilised superiority, placing greater weight upon violence as a means for rule, but also reminding the English of their relatively recent acquisition of civility, also through violence.[141] Such examples, full of ambivalences as they were, also applied to the Scots, and the King in *Basilicon Doron* used a parallel series of discriminations to explain an equally rigorous line with his own Gaelic-speaking Highlanders.[142] This context suggests that the masque is far less complacent than the simple English/Irish binary would imply, and provides a triangulated reminder to all three elements, English, Irish, and Scottish, of their potential for incivility. And although the suggestion of violence is ever present in drum and broils, it also offers a strikingly pacific view of plantation, achieved not immediately through violence but 'by and by' through the 'music of . . . peace' (151, 132).

This question of civility, or rather of the target of the civilising process, is explored further by the masque's innovative form developed from that of *Love Restored*. In that masque, as here, the absence of scenery and magical physical transformation turns attention onto the human, and onto individual and collective action. Here an even sparser masque and a transformation achieved through the removal of cloaks, seems to reveal the 'fiction' of the masque, not because the masque offers a charade, but because it makes the civilisation of the English, Scots, and Irish parallel. What unites them and makes transformation possible is 'the presence of a King', so that more than stressing the superiority of English or Scots, they are reminded they are all 'goot men, tine own shubshects', 'a great good many o' great good shubshects' (83-4) under the King who makes them 'newborn creatures all' (155). Just as the Irish have been transformed, so now the English and Scots: 'all' have been made or remade by the King at one point or another. The submission here is not of Irish to English culture, but of all the cultures of the British archipelago to King James.

This emphasis on the role of the King, on his central powers in the creation and bestowal of honours, is in tune with the Tacitean analytics that the masque deploys. Indeed, given that the masque was danced by at least two of the bedchamber staff, Achmouty and Abercromby, in honour of the most prominent and successful member of the bedchamber, the very performance pointedly asserts the King's prerogative.[143] Carr, as a 'newborn creature' like the Irish ambassadors is neither unclothed nor naked but, like the masquers, he is created in his new robes by royal intervention. To feel the benefit of royal power, not only must subjects 'do their all' (144) and avoid behaving like the 'shubshects' of Ireland (and elsewhere) who carp at royal policy, but they must also 'honour that which he [James] doth love'.[144] The inference is that 'That which' James 'doth love' is Carr, so that while proper obedience lies in recognising that Carr's position is created by James' favour (his love), to thwart or even question the favourite's position, a manifestation of royal power, is to fail to be a good subject and to become uncivil, and even a barbarian.

In many ways, this is the most alienating aspect of the politics of *The Irish Masque at Court*, which closes with a vision of absolute obedience that requires complete submission: 'Obedience doth not well in parts' (149). The insistence upon total rather than partial submission ('in parts') to royal power not only rejects the Irishman's defence of his partly rebellious nation (or any other part of the nation that would make the same claim), it also focuses upon the control of the 'parts'. These 'parts' can be abstract, in the limited (partial) loyalty that has been offered, or more geographical as in the parts of Ireland such as the Pale that have remained loyal, but also in the body parts which need to be united in a vision of loyal bodily unity. This unified social, political, and physical body radically shifts the masque away from the language of the libels and their crude naming of body parts and the concentration of the libellers upon sexual parts and 'in parts' is dismissed as uncivil.

So, while it has become commonplace to describe Jonson's attitude as 'complacent', this verdict underestimates the complexity of the entertainments mounted during the Carr–Howard match and *The Irish Masque* in particular. The masque embodies and seeks to negotiate many of the strains surrounding Carr, his marriage, and the factional shifts that occurred due to the nuptials. In a personal monarchy, where power is largely distributed through favour, dealing with individuals and factions is not a distraction from serious political matters but the vehicle of political action. Yet beyond this, *The Irish Masque* in particular, registers the problems with growing Howard power and the possible damage to royal reputation that the situation presents. In this sense the masque offers a harsh and analytic Tacitean view of royal power, but the Irish 'shubshects', their reminder of different cultures and voices that make up society, also evoke the oppositional voices that already were raised around the scandal and its implications for the government of the wider nation. Even as the masque uses the Irish situation to remind the whole nation of the fragility of its recent civilisation, and the dangers of disorder wherever it occurs, the voices are not dismissed as unacceptable; they are merely 'coarser' in their language than befits a court.

This stress on the 'shubshects' and their role in obedience, however, also offers the possibility for a more limited view of royal power; there is enough of a gap between the royal will and the human enactment of that will to imply that what is willed may not happen. Something of this is suggested even in the Gentleman's speech that summons up the bard, in its use of conditional forms: the charm he will sing only '*may* assure' the prophecies which will need to be enacted by distinctly mortal figures who 'if they had much more / Would do their all' (143–4). In this respect the masque articulates a reserved praise that still maintains royal power but recognises the frailty of its human instruments and also insinuates the suggestion that the King's desired transformation of the nation will require efforts of individual will which may be beyond the capacity of those called upon to act. So, whereas the King wields power to 'end our country's most unnatural broils' (130) and argues that, like the plantation in Ireland, this match is designed to produce 'the fruits of blessing' (138), and that this royal Orphism, the power to civilise and replace 'barbarism' (137) with 'harmony' (134) applies as much to England as to Ireland, the masque also shows how difficult that task will be.

The conclusion of the civil gentleman's speech articulates a double position that places royal power and the subject's obedience at the centre of the masque, and also recognises the human limitations in the exercise of that power:

> Sing then some charm, made from his present looks,
> That may assure thy former prophecies,
> And firm the hopes of these obedient spirits,
> Whose love, no less than duty, hath called forth
> Their willing powers; who, if they had much more,
> Would do their all, and think they could not move
>   Enough to honour that which he doth love. (139–45)

Although criticism of royal policy shows failure in obedience and in the duty of loving subjects to support both the Irish plantation and the Carr–Howard nuptials, the conditionals suggest the possibility that this ideal might not be achieved.

Our concentration upon one dimension of the Irishness of this masque perhaps distracts us from the impact of *The Irish Masque at Court* which like *Love Restored* brings into the court arena voices and social groups that have not been seen or heard before in the masque. The appearance of the Irish, their differentiated positions, and the failures and tensions in their treatment in the masque, brings forward, again, the engagement with forces beyond local and factional politics. The Irish fiction allows Jonson to highlight questions about the limits of what might be spoken, and how it might be spoken, and also to raise the issue of how far an idealised royal absolutism depends on rather more mortal and less satisfactory individuals. Indeed, rather than complacently glossing over the problems represented by the Carr marriage, the Irish settlement, and the discontented voices that were raised around them, Jonson engages with those voices, offering the ideal of obedience, but an awareness that it may not be achievable.

This awareness of outside forces and voices and how they challenged the world embodied by the masque is especially suitable for a masque that belongs to an entertainment sequence that helped bring the masque into a broader public consciousness. The Palatinate marriage that had preceded the nuptials of 1613–14 had been celebrated with an unprecedented number of masques of unmatched magnificence and provoked a large number of printed descriptions of the events, copies of the masques, and eye-witness accounts. Indeed, in the 1613 Palatinate celebrations, the masque had become a highly public event, with a huge procession from the house of the Master of the Rolls, along Fleet Street and the Strand, culminating at the tiltyard preceding the performance of *The Memorable Masque* (1613). The 1613–14 sequence appears to have sought to rival that celebration, but with the effect that even as both occasions propelled the masque into broader consciousness, the issue of cost also came to the fore. As early as 1609 there had been mutterings about the cost of the masques, and a planned joint masque by the four Inns of Court for the Carr–Howard match had collapsed due to their prior 'extraordinary expenses'.[145]

The reach and complexity of the wider awareness of the masque is demonstrated in a letter from Francis Delaval to his Northumbrian brother Sir Ralph:

> Such news as is here is that my Lord of Rochester is made Earl of Somerset, and this Christmas shall marry the Lady Francis Howard, daughter to my Lord Chamberlain, which was divorced from my Lord of Essex, the King doth please to solemnise the said marriage with a masque at his proper charge, performed by divers Earls and Lords, and besides there is two masques more, all being a means to make the Chequer poor, but at last the poor subject shall pay for all . . .[146]

These early indications of a critique from outside the court of extravagances that wasted public funds have auspices that convey the complexity of the politics of the masque: Francis Delaval was attached to the household of Sir William Knollys, later Earl of Berkshire, one of the crucial figures in the Howard attempts to build bridges with the Queen.

Political events in 1613–14 played out in a number of interlocking arenas, including the two Parliaments, the court and its different households, the legal process, and in the various forms of print and manuscript dissemination that spread information not only geographically but also through a range of social groups. Indeed, one study has characterised 1614, in particular, by its 'rumourousness' and noted how extra-parliamentary debates before the opening of the first session determined the course of the initial debates. Moreover, although historians differ over what went wrong in the short-lived 1614 Parliament, even the most revisionist agree that the Addled Parliament presents a considerable challenge to pacific ideals. Some of this conflict was clearly a return to previous issues, to matters of principle such as parliamentary liberties and royal prerogative, which suggest a far more divided and even ideologically charged debate. In a culture in which the circulation of parliamentary separates had become common, and where a wider political nation was addressed by a monarch aware of the potential for the presentation of his case, the masques of the period take on a new significance which is not limited to simply reproducing an untroubled royal ideology, nor solely addressing a quiescent and limited audience.

4
'No News': *News from the New World* and Textual Culture in the 1620s

> I think I have it complete; for I have both noted the number and the capacity of the degrees here, and told twice over how many candles there are i'th' room lighted, which I will set you down to a snuff precisely, because I love to give light to posterity in the truth of things. (*News from the New World Discovered in the Moon*, lines 20–3)

News from the New World Discovered in the Moon (staged 6 January and 29 February 1620) makes 'great newsh' its subject.[1] In dealing with 'news culture' in its broadest sense, *News* illuminates how Jonson's masques of the 1620s, under increasing pressure from shifting political and patronage contexts, negotiate the political tensions generated as the Palatinate crisis divided national opinion. Indeed, the two performances of *News* may even straddle the publication dates of the first corantos, the single-sheet newspapers initially printed in English at Amsterdam but produced in London perhaps as early as February 1620, which carried much of the foreign news to a wider population.[2] Predating *The Staple of News* by some six years, *News* merits far more attention as an examination of the nature of the masque and masque making that asserts the 'neat, clean power of poetry' (94) in public discourse.

The Palatine crisis, regarded by many historians as a key moment in the fissuring of the culture of consensus and as another step in the emergence of a public news culture, illustrates the connection of elite and popular politics, and of religious tensions and political debate. It is here that the 'communicative political game' seen in the 1610s in the interconnections of the masques to libels and to the broader print and pamphleteering culture, gathers force into national political debate.[3]

In this instance, news, in its early modern blend of reportage and novelty, binds together the various aspects of *News from the New World*.

Developed from a staple of popular print culture, imaginary travels to fantastic locations, the masque's moon-journey is combined with recycled Protestant apocalyptic interpretations of the 1618 comet as a harbinger of the Palatine crisis. Thus, *News* presents a double-aspected moon: in the antimasque the moon is associated with insubstantiality, fantasy, delusion, and lunacy; in the masque, the moon-world embodies the poetic imagination inspired by royal knowledge. *News* closes with not only the revelation of sovereign power, embodied in the interaction between the royal sun, King James, and the royal son, Prince Charles, it also dispels the false clouds of moon news (according to the Second Herald, 'They do all in clouds there'). The comic, sublunary powers and motions of charlatans like 'Cornelius Dribble' (70) are replaced with true knowledge and the perpetuity of royal power, itself a reflection of the timeless, harmonious motion of the universe (261–5).

As announced by the Second Herald this new world is paradoxically 'no news' (271).[4] The paradox is that the 'no news' of royal truth, stability, and harmony, is itself news to the giddy world of the news-speculators. News in a wide range of forms – *News from the New World* combines orality, manuscript, and print, and even encompasses the print or political cartoon – becomes a way to explore much broader issues of political culture and communication for which news, as both a print medium and as a culture in pursuit of endless novelty and new markets, stands as handy symbol.[5] In evoking this culture, *News* illuminates the power of print, the potential for democratic exchange across geographies and classes, but also the potential disruption print and its commodification cause for ideas of reliability and truthfulness.

These contradictions in the attitude towards news culture suggest, in turn, that *News* embodies a tentative and conflicted response to the emergence of popular print culture. Like Jonson's late plays, the later Jacobean masques have often been associated with royal policy, a rejection of the engagement of ordinary people in political debate, and a 'thoroughly reactionary' set of attitudes.[6] As Julie Sanders and others have pointed out, however, news is formally diverse, likely to 'bridge' different social groups and ideas, and both represents and also creates a much broader and shared culture.[7] This is not to argue for an espousal of popular politics – popularity was far too problematic an idea in this period – but rather the recognition of greater fluidity and permeability in political culture, especially at points where national interest was provoked.[8]

News from the New World in the Moon redefines the role of the masque.[9] Faced with the difficulties of navigating the turbulent streams of politics at court in the 1620s, *News* responds to the new configurations of court power and favour but also to the demands of the new print world that the masque depicts. The desire to find 'understanders' and a capable audience takes on greater urgency in this fissiparous world. So, even though the masques of the early 1620s are mistrustful of popular political opinion, some aspects engage much more closely with current political issues, particularly how the very business of news functions as a way of understanding and exploring politics. The interconnectedness here between the masque and news culture illuminates a struggle to demarcate a new function for the masque evident in the responses to the running masque inside the court, but also to the more public masque, Thomas Middleton's *The World Tossed at Tennis* (1620–1) possibly staged for Prince Charles. Jonson accommodates changing conceptions of the masque as political form, recasting the masque's transformative pivot, but also assaying a more exploratory and experimental approach, that both responds to the external critiques of his masque-making and also signals new forms of masque publication after *The workes* (1616). The core concern is with the ways in which external events, but also other kinds of publication, other versions of the masque, other venues and arenas pressured Jonson. Indeed, Jonson's late Jacobean texts engage in a lively debate about masque form as a way of responding to the political culture that emerged in 1619–21.

Charting the 'news' world

At the point where *News from the New World* is staged in early 1620 the tensions created by the Palatinate had only started to emerge. Texts such as Abraham Gibson's sermon *A Preparative to War* and Middleton's *Masque of Heroes* (both 1619), fuelled by the presence of the Bohemian envoy Achatius zu Dona to lobby for military support, agitate for intervention. By the end of 1620, however, the foreign diplomatic corps was reporting vocal dispute: 'the kingdom has never had its eyes so wide open and it has never been so teeming with ideas and grievances as now'.[10] In late 1620 Thomas Scott's *Vox Populi* purported to unmask Spanish deceits and the King was forced to issue a proclamation against 'excess of lavish and licentious speech in matters of state'.[11] As 1620 and 1621 progressed, the King and his ministers were frequently attacked and James even complained of a 'republicanising' tendency in his people.[12]

The political crisis of the early 1620s comprised, in reality, three interlocking, extended, and multi-faceted problems. First and foremost, the international and domestic ruptures created by the Palatine match, the invasion of Bohemia, and later by the marriage plans of the Prince of Wales brought together international affairs and warfare, national identity and religious politics, and domestic issues in an unstable mixture. This was compounded by the second related structural issue, namely the changing nature of the court occasioned by the rise of George Villiers and the emergence of the Prince of Wales as a political force.[13] The third factor, the emergence of a vibrant news culture, reported such matters and generated a far more contentious climate, and also marked a changed awareness of the popular market for printed materials in the early 1620s. The printed news culture may itself have reported the international situation, but it also offered opportunities for new kinds of writing and publishing and new forms of politicised debate.

While the shifting patronage patterns of court life required constant negotiation, the international situation was specific and acute. Frederick, the Elector Palatine's assumption of the Bohemian crown in June 1619 jeopardised the peace of Europe and threatened to bring Spanish troops from Flanders and Bavaria into conflict with Frederick's Protestant allies. James VI and I, caught between his alliances with his son-in-law and his treaty obligations to Spain, worked to prevent war and persuade Frederick to relinquish his Bohemian crown as long as the Spanish forces only retook Bohemia leaving the Palatinate alone. The international crisis had a domestic dimension as Frederick was regarded as a Protestant hero and considerable sympathy existed for military intervention to support him, something that would, inevitably, require parliamentary supply. This reliance on Parliament was unwelcome to King James and potentially involved investigation of the royal finances and other policies.

If, as has been argued, these years see the early emergence of a popular political consciousness, *News*, then, explores the effects of the greater circulation of information about foreign and later domestic events. In this sense the masque parallels the broader discussion of the effects of the new media culture seen in Edmund Bolton's sequence of projects for a royal academy, variously dated *c.*1617–24, which included proposals that a royal society should control foreign publications, the 'Italian Polidores, Hollandish Meterans, rhapsodical Gallo-Belgici and the like' which were on sale in London during the late 1610s.[14] Other measures being considered *c.*1619–21 included a proposal from the newsletter writer John Pory and the Keeper of the State Papers, Sir Thomas Wilson, for an official news gazette to provide the populace with news 'most agreeable to the disposition of the head and principal members' of the state.[15] When the first of the two proclamations against 'licentious' speech was issued on 24 December 1620, Sir Francis Bacon, who drew up the proclamation, also wrote to Buckingham about the 'general licentious speaking of state matters' on 16 December 1620.[16] Writing and speaking about matters of state, the tone of public discourse, and the methods by which information circulated were, then, clearly significant issues in the early 1620s.

Jonson's news from the moon – a world filled with lunacy, transitoriness, and insubstantiality – encapsulates how far this differed from a rational world of civil political discourse. In the same year as *News* was danced, Robert Burton commented on how this new world offered such profusion of news of 'weddings, Maskings, Mummeries, Entertainments, Jubilees, Embassies, Tilts and Tournaments, Trophies, Triumphes, Revels, Sports, and Plays' that it threatened madness and melancholia.[17] This flood of material produced two related contexts for masque-making. First, this development of a news culture and especially the new availability of printed news-sheets, redefines the literary system in which Jonson operated. Even if the pre-1616 masques, despite some clearly commercial origins, had been marked out as elite publications, the masque books printed in the 1620s threatened to merge with the flood of pamphlet material, acquiring 'pamphletary dimensions'.[18] Second, the symbolic economy of the book shifts. No longer can the book be associated with ideas of fixity and authority but drifts towards associations with cheap print. In this world, where print revels in novelty and unreliability, ideas of 'textual legitimation' are contested.[19] It requires a redefinition of forms and audiences parallel to the kind of coterie building undertaken in the 1600s.

News in *News from the New World* is not simply plural but various, defined only by 'men's diverse opinions' (45). The three figures of the antimasque, Chronicler, Factor, and Printer, represent differing audiences (court/gentry, civic/mercantile, and the wider populace), different modes of news, and allude to a plethora of types of information: news-flashes from the country (26, 35), wonder pamphlets (35), 'relations' (47),[20] chronicles (18), and, above all, gossip (39).[21] The Factor, the 'superlative' (32) among the three youths is, crucially, a supplier of manuscript news, but the most credulous is the Printer who even believes the fantastical images seen in books, such as the 'castle i'th'air that runs upon wheels with a winged lantern' (190–1).[22] This image may also stand for another news phenomenon, the political print, which also starts to appear in England in the 1620s.[23] Often scatological as much as satirical, these prints could be passed from hand to hand or, occasionally, displayed in taverns and some diaries record the exhibition of scurrilous pictures.[24] Jonson knew the phenomenon and even mentions the notorious 'The Devils Arse a Peak' print in 'An Execration Upon Vulcan'.[25]

This trinity of news-gatherers embody the appetite for news and the news culture that stretches across 'friends of all ranks, and of all religions' (29). Ironically, even as situated on the cusp of the single-sheet serial coranto revolution, these news-mongers focus, largely, on older modes of news. They trade instead in gossip or the recycled legends, like the Sussex serpent from popular pamphleteering, as part of the double-edged joke that these men who are consecrated to 'news' novelty are largely plagiarists. The claimed novelty is then exposed as one of a series of unreliable evidences about their audience and their content. For commercial purposes they claim to represent different markets, but as the Printer argues, they are ultimately in the same business. He explodes the Factor's claims to social superiority, comparing his pamphlet 'lies' for the 'common people' with the more socially exclusive world of manuscript newsletters and the gossip in St Paul's aisle (38–40) as differing only in who makes the untruths. He also confronts the Second Herald's contention that 'nothing's good anywhere but what's to be sold' (12–13), with an insouciant, 'Indeed, I am all for sale' (14).

The potential for news culture to undermine the social hierarchies and belief systems of early modern England can be seen in the creation of a national audience in 'news for all the shires' (31–2), and in the commercial imperative that undermines claims of truthfulness and reliability: 'Ill give anything for good copy, now, be't true or false' (16–17). Thus, the Chronicler, the grinder out of the drudgery chronicles of (mainly) city deeds and leaders, who must produce his daily quota of historical blockbuster of 'three ream of paper at least' and even turns to candle snuffings to supply his news, still inflatedly claims to be 'the light to posterity in the truth of things'.[26] Garbling Cicero's affirmation of history as *'lux veritatis'* (light of truth) only shows how the commercial imperative contributes to the sense of the unreliability and lack of credibility in news. The printer's own claim to know the castle in the air because he has 'seen it in print' (192–3) captures the confusion that this world has created. The reliance upon merely seeing rather than reading and understanding suggests how ambiguous the idea of 'in print' has become and how ideas of authority that might have accrued to the printed book have been undermined by commodification. Indeed, as the Chronicler notes, 'I ha' found it far harder to correct my book, than collect it' (64–5). Its only point of reason in 'a world of these curious uncertainties' (96) is when the Factor and the Printer argue over who should have 'pleasure in the believing of lies' (49), and the Printer triumphs because he 'speaks reason' (52) in spreading this pleasure to all.

The class dynamics of this section of the masque are also complex as the three heralds and the news-gatherers shift from abuse ('coxcomb', 'dull tradesman') through to a mocking politeness of address ('sir', 'gentlemen') and culminate in describing them as 'a fine', 'finer', and 'finest youth', terms which are later echoed in the roles taken by the masquers. This fluidity of social position, which continues in the gender confusions of the moon-world (249–55), suggests that one of the effects of the news culture has been to break down the hierarchies of society, or rather reveal the shared tastes and interests of 'friends of all ranks and religions' (29). So, what is striking at the start of the 1620s is how news culture transforms (infects?) the whole body politic rather than concentrating on one social group as gullible or lacking in judgement.

Alongside the issue of reliability, the question of how to distinguish truth and falsehood is central to the moon-world. Some of this problematic is embedded in the power attributed to 'fant'sy' throughout the masque. On one hand, fantasy encourages the suppositions and wayward imaginings that produce the 'fantastical creatures' who inhabit the moon (193), such as the 'fantastic lovers' (197) who outdo sublunary lovers in their uncontrolled behaviour.[27] On the other hand, fantasy represents the transformative power of imagination, either 'Endymion's way' through 'rapture', and the power of poetry as dream, or through the satirical visions of Menippus and Empedocles.[28] These 'dreams that have honey, and dreams that have stings' (*Vision of Delight*, 54) offer two possibilities for poetic creativity, the imagination of the golden world or the more astringent analyses of satire's 'salted jestings . . . and merry conceits of good words to make men laugh and to discover . . . vicious men'.[29] So as much as 'fantasy' marks the power of imagination to dream and to criticise, the recycling of the term encapsulates the problematic differentiation between legitimate imagination, illegitimate fantasy, and ephemeral and illusory phantasms that characterise the news world. Moreover, the means of discrimination are also inverted as the order of senses is overthrown just as the Printer credits what he has 'seen in print'.[30] Usually, Jonson's concern would be to have an audience 'wise / Much rather by your ears than by your eyes' (*Staple of News*, 'Prologue for the Stage', 5–6), but in *News*, initially, the 'exercise of the eyes' in the masque replaces the exhausted 'ears' of the antimasque (262–3). In this way the main masque enacts a recuperation of the senses as the masquers have to 'collect' their sight 'dazzled by the light' (292) and then regain the proper use of their ears (344–8). This sensory re-education is achieved by a return to the book not as commodity but as symbol of authority. As the masque progresses and light is shed onto the dark imaginings of print, so first the masquers are instructed to 'Read him [the King] as you would do the book / Of all perfection' (279–80), a phrase that encompasses the monarch as perfect text, but also imagines a 'book of perfection' materially and intellectually the opposite of the recycled approximations of the news world. Finally in Fame's song, the proper ordering of the senses is restored as 'All ears will take the voice' (316), and the combined employment of the senses provides a 'more noble discovery' that will be 'worthy your ear, as the object will be your eye' (273–4).

The choice of the book as symbol of royal order has specific resonances given James VI and I's 'indomitable faith' in the power of debate.[31] In James VI and I's *Workes* (1616) Montagu's epistle to Prince Charles offers royal writing as a 'pattern' but in the general preface he defends the King against accusations of engaging in a trade, first with a 'cloud of witnesses' of other writer-monarchs, and then with the pronouncement of the pen as the adjunct of the sword, arguing 'we have seen with our own eyes the operation of his Maiesties Works in the consciences . . . of men [and] there have been those that have been converted by them'.[32] The authority of the book and King are twined together in Montagu's preface, as the world of cheap print and libel is 'blasted by the breath of His Maiesties books'.[33] Later in his *Meditation* on 1 Chronicles, James described his work as 'a certain testament of my upright and honest meaning'.[34]

This alignment restates the claims of the book as royal and printed authority but also revisits the masque's key concern with the circulation of information. Reading the royal 'book of perfection' informs the 'measure', that is the standard or truth, but also its correct movement, the 'measure' of the dance. The masque's kinetic politics, where movement marks order and proportion, is inspired by the King whose 'fullness' (perfection) will 'win your grace'.[35] The stately, ordered movement contrasts with the volatees, whose antimasque dances are the ultimate symbol of this 'moonshine' world. Their hopping movement and name suggest they are associated with airy emptiness, but also with irrationality and caprice.[36] In the motive politics of this masque their erratic movements contrast with the ordered and hierarchical motion of the spheres, establishing the difference between the flows and harmonies of royal information and the jerky circulations of commerce.

The world presented in News from the New World differs from the venereal 'itch of news' associated with libels but the emphasis on fantasy is no less corrosive, undermining rationality and sense. Yet unlike the darker imaginings of 'Fant'sy' in *The Vision of Delight* where 'civil society' becomes a flea circus (91–8), here Jonson does not simply dismiss the moon-world. While the masque imagery chimes with contemporary fears that public debate and news culture stimulated what was seen as confusion and madness rather rational debate, he offers the 'neat clean power of poetry' as an antidote.[37] Against the paranoid conspiracies associated with early modern ideas of popularity, the engagement of 'friends of all ranks, and of all religions' treats the question as one for the whole of civil society. Although it is only tentative within the masque, there is a sense of a more problematic world of different audiences who deploy different discourses, which challenge the conceptualisation of a 'civil' society, and who require engagement rather than rejection. The overall thrust towards the re-education of the ear, traced through the authority of the royal book, presents an image of the King as authoritative writer, supported by his poet, who offers 'measure' and 'proportion', a rational response that deflates the fantasy world of news-gathering.

So, unlike the earlier masques, such as *Love Restored*, *News from the New World in the Moon* does not engage directly with the uncivil world of 'free speaking', rather it analyses the impact of news culture that is both reporting and creating a more contested politics. Faced with the growing political divisions of the 1620s, Jonson reasserts the public role of poetry to define the fame of monarchs and men but he makes poetry the vehicle for the education of the next generation. In so doing Jonson engages in debates about the Palatine war, expressed through images of military heroism, and places the court masque and its education in opposition to the masques written for those outside the court, especially by Thomas Middleton. From this debate stems an important reshaping of the masque's structure that changes the emphasis on the pivotal moment of transformation between antimasque and masque that complicates homogenised readings of the Jonsonian masque. Here, in the early 1620s, Jonson responds to and debates with other masque writers to redefine the form and its political role.

Beyond negotiation: 'news' and royal education

Inseparable from the foreign policy issues that underpinned this masque, the season of 1619–20 also celebrated Prince Charles' attainment of his majority. Recasting some of the entertainments for his elder brother Prince Henry, often perceived to be more militantly Protestant, many of the events staged in this season stressed Charles' militarism. Unsurprisingly, then, even though not necessarily conceptualised as a 'programme', the various elements of the season – masque, tilt, informal entertainments – echo each other and the King's published work. James used his *A Meditation Upon the 27, 28, 29 Verses of the XXVII Chapter of St Matthew*, printed early in 1620, to consider the nature of royal inauguration, and *News* combines this with references to the King's advice manual for Prince Henry, *Basilicon Doron*.[38] Described as a 'powerful revalidation of divine monarchy' the *Meditation* forms the centrepiece of a debate over inaugural politics that provided Jonson with an opportunity to examine the nature of the masque and the function of ceremonial.[39]

Education, of course, formed one constant of Jonson's conception of the masque as counsel or education through praise throughout his career. If *Pleasure Reconciled to Virtue* was designed to demonstrate how 'royal education' (201) could reconcile opposed forces, in *News* the educational focuses are Prince Charles as Truth and his followers as embodiments of the 'music of . . . peace' (228–9). *News* contrasts the fantasy world of the three youths, the Printer, Chronicler, and Factor, with the 'youths' attached to the Procritus, Prince Charles (228). In contrast to the epicenes of the moon-world, the masquers embody proper royal manliness; in contrast to the erratic volatees who 'hop from island to island' (261), the stately movements of the Procritus and his followers demonstrate 'measure' and 'harmony' (313, 315). The Prince's title, originally given to sons of the Roman emperor, derives from the Augustan reorganisation of the *iuvenes*, youths of military age, into a group designed to instil Roman values, a military ethos (especially equestrian exercises), and the importance of imperial service.[40] This title compliments the King as a new Augustus and salutes Prince Charles as a recognised leader of youth.

In contrast to the elaborate parliamentary installation of Prince Henry, Charles' inauguration as Prince of Wales had been notably low key, and the King had worked to contain any independence in the court of his son. In the early 1620s the similarities between Prince Henry and Prince Charles were perhaps more apparent than their differences. Charles was notably a military prince: in 1619 he offered Frederick 'not only to assist him with my countenance, but also with my person'; and by late 1622 this position hardened into a request to his father for permission to lead 'some brave Enterprise abroad to recover at least what we have lost' at the same time as he was learning pike drills.[41] Charles was instructed in the workings of model war-engines, and dedicators of works such as *The Tactics of Aelian* (1616) and *Five Decades or Epistles of War* (1622) may have relied on the Prince's known military interests.[42] Indeed, his period as Prince of Wales led easily into the 'Rex Bellicosus' of his early reign.[43]

In fact, the Prince's first tilt on 24 March 1620 was mounted with such magnificence, costing over £6500, that it actually attracted some criticism that recalls some of the concerns over Prince Henry's activities.[44] Chamberlain noted that the Prince was practising daily for the tilt by March 1620, commenting how the Prince 'begins his tyrocinium at the tilt'.[45] The phrase he uses is highly suggestive as the 'tyrocinium' was the period of military education expected of Roman nobles as part of readiness for military governorship. Charles announced his military prowess in the elaborate parade through the streets that combined his Artillery Band, members of his household, and five hundred of the London trained bands, all of whom accompanied the Prince as a mark of their 'special esteem . . . for his worth'.[46] This public – and publicised – event attracted 'crowds of people' and contrasts with the situation in 1611 when the King had forbidden Henry to ride through the city.[47] As with the Twelfth Night masque, diplomatic manoeuvring over place and proximity continued at this tilt, and although the ambassadors of France, Spain, Venice, Savoy, Holland, and Bohemia were all invited, the French ambassador declined to attend as he could not be 'placed to his minde' as the Spanish ambassador was seated by the Prince's tent.[48] What is striking here, as with the politics of texts from the same season like the running masque, is how nuanced suggestions and inferences are presented, often to a broader audience, through such events. Here, it is also worth noting that the processional route from Denmark House to Whitehall, an enactment of homage to the King, balances the more interventionist stance that his followers could have excited.[49]

The masque shows careful distancing from the ideals of *Oberon*. Where Jonson's masque for Prince Henry had become a negotiation between different conceptions of royal power, *News* subordinates negotiation to reconciliation.[50] The noble youths who danced alongside Charles 'imitating Procritus' endeavour' (283) genuflect to the heritage of Henry's household, that academy of 'young nobles submitted to the severest discipline and entirely devoted to the pursuit of glory', but they also derive their virtue and force from the royal sun, 'the body whence they shine' and to whom they are subordinated. If the next generation is 'a new race', they are the King's 'own, formed, animated, lightened, and heightened' (274–5). The imagery here stands in contrast to the moonlight seen in *Oberon*, where it is unclear if Prince Henry drew his light and power from the King (the royal sun) or from Elizabeth I whose 'heir' he was as a fairy prince: in *News* the masquers are 'animated, lightened' by the light 'reflected by you on them' (249–50).[51]

The highly public affirmation of 'pure harmony' (315), however, perhaps conceals a more complex set of positionings that had appeared across the range of 1620–1 entertainments. Thus, even though the masque closes (for the moment) an equally public set of political moves, the occasion takes on the air of a ritual reconciliation, which although it cements agreement, also restates there has been disagreement. This delicate balance, the public agreement to agree, and the acknowledgement of points of debate as well as contact, suggests truce rather than concession. Indeed, *News* constitutes a public affirmation of consensus made all the more pressing by the Prince's own diplomatic manoeuvres around the Bohemian crisis and his warlike stance. It was continually reported that the Prince 'expresses himself with wonderfully good affection to the cause' and both he and Buckingham worked towards greater support for the Palatinate.[52] The Prince may have desired to intervene 'more for his sister and religion' than for other reasons, as the Venetian ambassador put it, but later he was described as 'more enthusiastic' than anyone else at court for intervention.[53]

The negotiation enacted between King and Prince is most clearly seen in the moment in *News*, when warmed into new life by the royal sun 'which alone is able to resolve and thaw the cold they have presently contracted' (285–7), the masquers 'descend and shake off their icicles' as the royal sun transforms them. As with Prince Henry's earlier masques, such as *Oberon*, the designs accentuate the perfected manly body of the courtiers, contrasting the effeminacy of the epicenes and the gender inversions of contemporary society that are satirised in the prose induction, with the heroic bodies of the courtiers. The icicles melting suggests that they are sufficiently warmed (that is martial and manly) by the royal sun, but that they are temperate, neither overly militant, nor softly effeminate. The patterned cuirass seen in the only design that has been associated with this text may dress the masquers as modern descendants of Augustan *iuvenes*.[54]

Interestingly, these differences between king and prince were publicly enough known for the Venetian ambassador to interpret the contemporaneous publication of James I's pacific *A Meditation Upon Matthew* as designed 'to keep the Prince humble'.[55] The King's *Meditation* uses the mock coronation of Christ to analyse the 'inauguration' of a monarch, warning his son of the duties of kingship.[56] At one point James compares the situation of monarchs in their pomp to that of Damocles, possibly a fit metaphor for his situation in the Palatinate crisis, and while praising the active desires of youth ('Youth should be active and laborious'), the King also stresses the importance and limitation of prerogative power.[57] The text reads as admonition to the Prince's military enthusiasm, even at points recalling his own earlier advice to Prince Henry, warning Charles to ensure that he is able to execute his laws: 'For a King carries not his sword for naught, but it must neither be blunt . . . nor yet must it be ever drawn'.[58] Throughout, *A Meditation* demonstrates an acute awareness of the role of spectacle. In one passage the King compares Christ's trial before Pilate with the public acclamation at a coronation, noting, in particular, the significance of Christ's appearance in 'places of most public resort' as 'it is very fitting that he, that is to be acknowledged the head of all sorts of people, should be invested in a place where all sorts of people may convene and concur to doe him homage'.[59] As so often, although James is commonly depicted as publicity shy, he reveals an acute awareness of the symbolic topographies of ceremony, and also of the potential of public display in the establishment of monarchy.[60]

It has often been noted that James VI and I had been acclimatised by his Scots political upbringing to the idea that he might debate key ideas through his speeches and writings. Indeed, one of the King's many iterations of stage imagery in *Basilicon Doron* proclaims 'one of the maynes for which God hath advanced me on the lofty stage of the supreme throne is that my words uttered from so eminent a place . . . might with greater facility be conceived'.[61] This image of the King as engaged in public debate runs throughout much of his writings and actions, from his dictation of proclamations, through his use of printed tracts to advance his policies, to his poems on the 1618 comet and against the 1622 'Commons' Tears' libel that circulated widely in manuscript.[62] As pressure increased in the divided situation of the Palatinate, and especially after the fractious second session of Parliament in November and December 1621 where freedom to speak had been hotly contested, James sought 'by communicating to all Our people' to offer 'the reasons of a resolution of State'.[63] In such contexts, it is unsurprising that Jonson's masques appropriate the royal image of the book to suggest the 'neat, clean power of poetry' as another arm of royal argument. This deployment of public statements goes beyond the more covert kinds of strategies inherent in the 'communicative political game' that typifies the mid-Jacobean public sphere, and points towards an attempt to employ reason to defeat the more 'fiery and popular spirits' identified in the Commons. In terms of the masque the shift of emphasis away from dealing with manuscript libels towards printed texts, and away from issues of decorum to those of dissemination, suggests the ways in which ceremonial culture was being used not simply to propagandise the monarchy but to argue its case. The development is clearest in the juxtaposition of masque and meditation we see in the 1621 season, perhaps itself an extension of the interaction of masque and sermon which occurred relatively frequently in the period, which points towards not only a more outward-looking role but towards *public* and published discussion.

The re-reformation of the masque: news and clarification

During this early phase of the Bohemian crisis the masque cannot be separated from other texts, genres, and occasions, and the 1619–20 season of masques and entertainments is marked by its involvement in this wider network of public textual interventions. This may be a function of the serious political implications of the Bohemian crisis and the extraordinary intensity of the diplomatic manoeuvring taking place.[64] The highly ambivalent view of news depicted in the text, perhaps, criticises 'excitable and ill-informed militancy' that characterised these years, advancing what was, in effect, the royal thesis that a more strategic and pacific policy should prevail.[65] Equally, although elements of *News from the New World in the Moon* respond to pressures from outside the court, and even offers a further step in a public debate, this masque – in comparison to the running masque, for instance – exhibits the restraint and tact that were required by a state occasion. The measured tone, the stress on ordered and hierarchical movements, the steady flows and harmonies of royal information, contrasts with the erratic, empty, hopping volatees. This motive politics itself embodies a response to the more febrile discussions beyond the court, so that the very form of the masque conveys not simply closure but enacts a process of control answering to the pressures from beyond the court world.

In light of this public contest over policy, Jonson's response to Middleton and Rowley's *The World Tossed at Tennis*, published in mid-1620 but planned for a performance sometime in the busy 1619–20 season, and staged by Prince Charles' Men, illustrates the extent of this development.[66] *The World Tossed at Tennis* espouses a more interventionist approach to the Palatine, and differs from Jonsonian form, at key points attacking his conception of the masque and its audience. If *The World Tossed* was designed, as the title page claims, to be presented by Prince Charles' Men before the King and Prince at Denmark House, the play may mark part of the Prince's advocacy of military preparedness.[67] According to the title page (Illustration 4.1),

Illustration 4.1 Title page of *A courtly masque: the device called, the world tossed at tennis* (1620) (Folger Shakespeare Library, Washington, DC, STC 17910)

after the cancelled performance, the play was also 'divers times presented to the contentment of many noble and worthy spectators', offering the intriguing possibility of a public performance of a masque-like text designed for royal consumption being resituated in the public arena as part of the debate within the political establishment.[68]

Set in a decayed society, *The World Tossed* offers a markedly more activist stance to counter decline: the Scholar and the Soldier (representing arts and arms) are both neglected; Time laments his abuse in revels that ignore his passing; women erase his signs through cosmetics and Deceit and Pride rule in the 'frenzy of apparel' (368); and, centrally, 'Minerva's Altars are all ruin'd now' (210). This strange hybrid – part morality play, part masque – presents a notably Protestant view of a world declined away from Simplicity towards Deceit (conceived in religious terms, 520, 607, 723–7), only to be rescued by a righteous king advised by a Flamen and Law. Although the text shares some of the concerns of *News*, in particular the fantastical figures of the Five Starches who represent the pursuit of fashion and the confusion of sexual identity that had been the subject of controversy in 1619–20, it also argues explicitly for intervention in the Palatinate.[69]

Thus *The World Tossed* includes a scene in which Pallas insists that – as befits her dual nature – wisdom and valour 'are mutual co-incidents' (173) and shows the Muses leading on the Nine Worthies as 'precedents for all future ages' (298). Indeed, the masque closes with the Soldier heading to 'the most glorious wars / That e'er fam'd Christian kingdom' (878–9) in the Palatinate. The duality of war and peace returns in these lines which are balanced by the Scholar's decision to settle in 'a land of most glorious peace' (880), although the 'doubly decked' royal head has already arrived, while the 'glory / Of noble action' will 'bring white hairs upon thee' (885–6). The Scholar and the Soldier take each other's hand and exchange their respective virtues (prosperity, glory) while their speech suggest that the King's learning has produced peace, but that the Prince's future will produce 'noble action'.

Having presented the 'wish' for the 'glory / Of noble action', the Scholar addresses the audience and call on them to confirm this desire:

> Present our wish with reverence to this place
> For here't must be confirmed or 'tas no grace. (887–8)

This wish requires confirmation to achieve 'grace', but who confirms that future ('our wish') remains open. On one level this is simply a variant of the call for applause at the end of a play, but in this context to announce that future hope is not simply guaranteed by the presence of the King as in Twelfth Night masques, but rather it is confirmed by 'this place', moves legitimising power away from the monarch. If 'this place' is the King's throne then 'grace' descends from the monarch, but given the staging for Prince Charles in Denmark House, the line could also suggest the house and its inhabitants. Furthermore, if we accept the idea that *The World Tossed* was 'presented divers time' to 'many noble and worthy spectators', then the lines seek approbation – and legitimation – by applause from the crowd.

The auspices for the performance and the way they are represented in the text seem to continue a nuanced distancing from the King's policies. The 'Induction', spoken by three boy actors as the royal palaces of Richmond, St James, and Denmark House, highlights locations associated with Prince Henry and Queen Anna. The main location, Denmark House, passed on to Charles in 1619, given its associations with his mother, and her own use of dramatic entertainments and masques, on occasion, to criticise her husband's policies and court, is highly symbolic. The opening welcoming dialogue alludes to the Queen's restoration of the building (30, 80), but stresses the charitable and hospitable nature of the place, characterising it in more civic and religious terms than the other royal residences. Although each house has its role according to the seasons, Denmark House explicitly seeks to unite the royal palaces together in 'employment seasonable' (48), which may gesture towards a more inclusive court, united under the roof – and policies – of Denmark House.

The World Tossed at Tennis was also staged by a company that had already presented controversial political material in 1619–20 in the form of a (lost) play that showed a king with two sons one of whom he killed on suspicion he was plotting to murder him only to be dethroned by the other son.[70] While the Venetian ambassador, who noted the 'absolute liberty' of the players, may be correct to connect the cancellation of *The World Tossed* with the King's ire, any disfavour was short-lived as there are continued payments by Prince Charles to the company for providing plays through 1620–4.[71] Indeed, as a play in the repertoire of Prince Charles' Men, it seems possible that *The World Tossed* articulates the Prince's concerns for the Palatinate some of which were unpalatable to the King.

Perhaps, however, the most striking feature of this text lies in the claim of multiple ('divers') public performances, not just for the 'royal royal'st guest' (Q1620, title page; 72), but on the public stage, and continued in print so instituting a public debate through theatrical texts over the Bohemian crisis. In so doing, almost every feature of Jonson's literary masque texts is inverted in *The World Tossed* which revels in its multiplicity of performances and audiences. The title page offers Middleton and Rowley bracketed as having 'invented and set / down' the text against the hierarchy insisted upon by the Jonsonian quarto, while the title page is resolutely a popular woodcut that recalls the form of political satires of the period. The dedication to Charles Howard, Lord Effingham, and Mary Cokayne, daughter of the Lord Mayor, glosses over the cynical view of contemporaries that the wedding united 'honour' and 'money' as Howard had none, to cast the match as a military union that brought together a family representative of Elizabethan heroism, and the 'Lord General of the Military Forces' of the City of London.

If the marriage brought together city and court, the pamphlet casts its audience as equally diverse. Indeed, Simplicity's 'Epistle' before the text echoes the Jonsonian concern with spectators and understanders by immediately offering the 'well-wishing, well-reading understander' and the 'well-understanding reader', and his own role stands against the accusations of Jonson's undue complexity.[72] The contrast between the simplicity of the greeting and Jonson's laboriousness is more than another personal sideswipe in the parodic version of Jonson's career (11–14), as it also alludes to the ideal of civility: this poet – and this work – cannot ever be accused of 'scurrilous or obscene language' (15–16). The allusion to Jonson's 'contentious texts' and his own biting attacks on other masque makers turns Jonson's own techniques and words on him, but makes a serious point about how masques are cast as civilised and yet often are as covertly abusive as the types of language from outside the court usually cast as uncivil. Here the title of a 'Courtly Masque' suggests that this device, not a 'Court Masque' or staged 'at Court' in the Jonsonian parlance, is still 'courtly', that is, civil and so 'lights but where he stands' (Prologue, 16).

At the end of *The World Tossed at Tennis* the masque having been 'tossed in the world' (Epistle, 7) is offered as 'vendible' despite being so rarely seen. This neat reversal of Jonsonian valuation, where scarcity and rarity contribute to value, is not used to dismiss the 'glorious shapes' of masquing, but rather is made more memorable by its availability and the reader and spectator are enjoined to 'Invert the proverb now' and remember the 'seldom seen' (Epilogue, 8–9). Middleton and Rowley's 'masque', 'device', or 'entertainment' is above all a 'short and small treatise' (Epistle, 4–5) that aligns itself with the world of popular print and provides an argument for the popular understanding of an engagement with the masque as a representation of not only 'where he stands' but the 'hope for many ages' (877).

Interestingly, as a physical object, *The World Tossed at Tennis* has a hybrid form which echoes its claim to 'lay claim to none, yet all present' (9). The first issue, without the woodcut, inevitably comes closer to a Jonsonian masque quarto, especially the dedicatory epistle and the use of Latinate forms such as 'Prologvs' (sigs. A3, B1), and yet the second issue with the additional illustration casts some elements as the antithesis of the Jonsonian masque quarto, as both title page and picture stress joint authorship and collaborative theatrical work. The style of the illustration and the typefaces consciously merge with the world of cheap pamphlets where Jonson differentiated his printed texts through their austere and classical typography. The quarto of *The World Tossed* provides an antidote to Jonsonian anxiety and a response to his masque quartos, by establishing three different audiences (royal, the joint dedicatees, and the 'gentlemen' readers and spectators. The Epilogue, forced to 'confess that we have vented ware not always vendible' (1–2), deliberately offers a commercialised, non-elite masque text.

Political transformation: the forms of the masque

A more noble discovery worthy of your ear, as the object will be of your eye. (*News*, 221–2)

If Middleton and Rowley's *The World Tossed at Tennis* suggests a public and courtly role for masque beyond the court, *News for the New World in the Moon* reshaped masque form to produce its accommodation with the world represented by this potential for wider political engagement. Indeed, by re-examining the form of *News*, it is possible to observe both an important defence of the role of poetry in the world of letters – in public debate – and a further recognition of different perspectives beyond the court.

The moment of scenic transformation in *News* marks a subtle but significant shift in the Jonsonian masque and its interaction with voices and forms from beyond the court. On one level the transformation presents a puzzle as no designs survive – not even for a 'place of light' or some sort of moon 'bower' for the masquers. Significantly, none of the surviving documents provide any information about a final masque set, so much so it is tempting to suggest that, like *Love Restored*, this masque avoided elaborate architectural sets and chose different ways to convey its ideas.

If some aspects of *News* echo *Oberon*, others are closer to *Love Restored*, which also offered 'better' discovery. 'Discovery' and the judgement it requires underpins *News* and the discriminations made between the false discoveries of the news-mongers and the true discoveries of the masquers. This shared fascination with 'discovery' suggests that, like *Love Restored*, *News* can be seen as a 'defence' of masquing, a theoretical justification through masque performance of the purpose and meaning of masques. *News* not only experiments with form, it also responds to voices beyond the court, such as Middleton's more public masques, and these extramural pressures mould the politics of the masque and masque form. *News*, in particular, represents Jonson's response to criticisms within the court of his masquing, but also to masques from beyond the court and, especially, to Protestant reformations of the masque.

Jonson's theorisation of the masque predicted a binary and exclusionary structure. The masque depends, as Jonson outlined in *The Masque of Queens*, on the contrast between 'the spectacle of strangeness' (13) and the vision of order, in *Queens*, the 'magnificent building figuring the House of Fame' (322–3). It also required that the antimasque world be removed or translated by the vision of masquing order. The core of the masque, then, lay in opposition and contest between the world of antimasque and masque, and although such a structure might lend itself to debate, in most cases the arrival of the masque was epiphanic.

In practice, however, Jonsonian antimasques were more formally various and their moments of translation more complex and less absolute and often responded to specificities of occasion and situation. They are often experimental and exploratory. One reason for this, as John Peacock has argued, is that despite sustained meditation on the nature of the masque, Jonson 'never worked out a definitive form for the antimasque', partly because of his contradictory theorisations of its function.[73] Thus, in the prefatory material to *Queens*, although Jonson allows the antimasque to be a 'spectacle of strangeness' he also insists upon decorum and purpose, either defined in Horatian terms by which 'no object of delight [may] passe without his mixture of profit and delight', or else in Aristotelian terms of rational mimesis where the 'strangeness' is controlled by decorum or the 'whole fall of the device' (14). Jonson's broader insistence upon masque as 'argument', designed to appeal to understanding and knowledge rather than pleasure and revel, fuels the division between profit and delight, and between two opposed conceptions of the antimasque, either as unrestrained variety or as contained dialectic.

The tension between the rational and mimetic and unrestrained and imaginative antimasques becomes acute in the early 1620s. On one hand stands *The Masque of Augurs* (1622) with its dismissive attitude towards the fantastic; on the other stands *Vision of Delight* (1617) which had celebrated the phantasmagorical, fantastical strain of antimasque. Indeed, the opening dialogue of *News* plays out precisely this tension. The news-mongers belong to the world of the Jonsonian comedy, and the use of prose and modern, topical materials, associates them with realism (in the Aristotelian sense of the mimetic), while their pursuit of the fantastic seems to dramatise the way the fantastic infiltrates – if not infects – both the mimetic world and the actual world.

Jonson's decision to integrate the antimasque into the overall structure of the masque ('the current and fall of the whole device') heightened the importance of the pivot between the two sections and also gave meaning to the revelation of the central scenic feature or machine of the masque. Jonson never explicitly theorises masque-transformation but the two earliest examples map differing possibilities. In *Queens* the transformation between the disorderly scenes of the antimasque and the ordered world of the masque is instant and complete: 'on the sudden was heard a sound of loud music', and at 'one blast' the hags and hell-scene 'vanished, and the whole face of the scene altered' (334–7).[74] This key, transformational moment in Jonsonian masques was largely a moment of exclusion or expulsion, so that even in *Pleasure Reconciled to Virtue* that advances a more conciliatory fiction, Hercules dissolves the 'grove' that conceals disorderly festivity (104–5) and chases off the pigmies (137–8).[75]

Alternatively, the pattern provided by *Oberon* (1611) favours a similar scenic transformation (the dissolution of elements in 'Melt earth to sea, sea flow to air' (220) that accompanies the revelation of the 'bright and glorious palace' (98)), but the satyrs remain to offer homage to Oberon, ceding their position to him ('Give place and silence' commands the Sylvan (237)). *Oberon* offers transformation rather than explusion, as the satyrs are civilised by the 'new nature' (273) revealed in Oberon and his nation of fays.[76] This 'transformative' masque is largely associated, however, with Campion rather than Jonson, as in *Lord Hay's Masque*, and *The Lords' Masque*, although it also figures in the *Essex House Masque* (1621) and the running masque, and in two of Jonson's masques, *Lovers Made Men* and *The Gypsies Metamorphosed*.[77] In several of these texts, although the antimasquers are metamorphosed, this change is justified and modified by their rank as, in both *Lovers Made Men* and *Gypsies*, the antimasque roles were taken by aristocrats.

News from the New World in the Moon complicates masque form as it juxtaposes the two modes of antimasque and introduces a transformational movement rather than exclusionary moment as antimasque gives way to masque. This difference is most marked in its setting: the moon in *News* is dual-aspected, both fantastical and delusional, and inspirational (see above p. 94), linked both to false, sublunary knowledge and to royal (as it were real) knowledge. On one hand, it influences the news-mongers in their lunatic fantasies and produces the volatees who epitomise the fantastical, but on the other hand it is also the inspiration for the poetic voyage and the imaginary account of the moon-world that exposes the news-mongers' folly. Moreover, 'speculation' on the moon and the monarch also produces the truth embodied by the masquers. A similar ambiguity can be seen in the heralds who are neither entirely antimasque nor masque figures: as *comic* news-bearers they seem to provoke the foolish youths and might, in that context, be thought of as antimasque figures, yet they are equally 'the muses' heralds' conveying both the poetic moon-world that the poet imagines, and the King's new universe. The heralds also act as presenters (213–17, 219–30, 293–6) explicating the action, a role that owes something to earlier masque forms, and in effect they cross the antimasque/masque boundary. This dual nature is suggested in their gradual transition between prose (212–13, 219–30) and verse (214–17, 293–6).

Although *News* does not carry the process as far as the later *The Gypsies Metamorphosed* (August 1621), perhaps constrained by the formality of the Twelfth Night masque, like the later Villiers masque, *News* partially dissolves the distinction between antimasque and masque. Indeed, it offers a much more complex world where fantasy and imagination, false truths and Truth, and false and true discoveries (means of knowing as well as things known) all coexist. In this mixed world, peopled by hybrids such as the half-human and half-fowl volatees and the half-man/half-woman epicenes, the poet takes on a mediatory function. The 'neat, clean power of poetry' is to clarify the kinds of truth available, and through the proper use of the imagination to discover not only false knowledge, or true knowledge, but to show how to perceive and how to discriminate. So the poet's journey to the moon described by the heralds (166–269) uses imagination ('the wings of his muse', 166) to reveal the news-mongers' folly and credulity, just as poetry also offers 'the more noble discovery' of the royal masque of Truth. When governed by reason, poetry becomes the means to discriminate between kinds of knowledge, and the poet becomes a figure who not only reveals falsehood, but also provides the vehicle for the display of Truth.

The primarily visual metaphors of 'discovery', 'presentment', and 'clarification' are linked to the education that the masque seeks to represent, not only the royal education embodied in the masquing youths, but the education offered by poetry to the masque audience and which the masque, with its central moment of revelation and clarification, performs. Thus, in *News*, the visual metaphors that permeate the text in part result from the fiction; they also enact a fascination with perception and methods of understanding. The false perceptions of the fantastical youths are fuelled by their reliance on *camera obscura* (61–4), 'perplexive glasses' (65), Pythagorean moon-writing, and a plethora of even less credible means of perception, from the 'mathematician's perspicil' to Rosicrucian intelligence (73–5). The false means of viewing (and thinking) by implication lead to false perceptions and discoveries, which can only be clarified by true discovery, verbal and visual. This goes to the heart of the masque's concerns about audiences, but also to the central point of its fiction about the correct perception of news, so that what seems novel and newsworthy is revealed, when viewed correctly, as 'no news'. Significantly, however, although the fantastical youths and their credulity are shown to be lacking, they are not excluded from the masque: their errors are cleared and they are educated. Similarly, *News* also allows the importance of spectacle and the visual discovery that 'clears' the clouds of mis-knowing and 'helps the presentment' (217).

This highly self-reflexive strand in *News* that runs through not only its fiction but also its consideration of modes of perception and, by implication, its construction of a suitable audience of true discoverers, has particular resonance for Jonson's masque-making and his adjustments of masque form at a point of particular difficulty in his career. Although the final section of the masque stresses harmony, the masque also closes with a more contested evocation of the power of Fame that 'keeps that fair which Envy would blot out' (352). The final 'masque' section of *News* draws on Protestant iconography that depicts Truth as the daughter of Time, while also rejecting the apocalyptic presentation of history, and in so doing, Jonson re-reforms Protestant reformations of the masque in presenting his royal 'Masque of Truth'. In so doing, Jonson replaces the apocalyptic struggle for Truth to emerge, with a truth supported by Fame but assailed by Envy. Jonson may have known the depiction of Truth assailed by Calumny, Envy, and Discord in Geoffrey Whitney's *Choice of Emblems* (1586), and he had already considered the role of Truth as 'time's witness' in his 'The Minde of the Front' which prefaced Ralegh's *History of the World* (1614), the engraved title page of which shows Good and Ill Fame presided over by the eye of Providence, and supported by Truth.[78]

On one level the presentation of Truth and the competing roles of Fame and Envy concern the political context of the masque and the apocalyptic interpretations of history pursued by many of the Bohemian supporters. Yet, at another more local level, Jonson is also concerned with the role of writing in revealing Truth, and so 'Envy' may also allude to the attacks on his reputation throughout 1618–21. In *Poetaster* (1601) Jonson had brought Envy on stage to demonstrate her malice and ill-will achieved through mischievous 'wrestings, comments, applications' (Induction, 24), in a play that also raises – acutely – the problematic relationship of writing and artistic freedom to imperial power.[79] In this later masque, Envy's appearance reprises some of the same issues, but also turns more directly not only to his detractors but also to his competitors. As we know, Drummond's *Informations* and the letter that mentions Jonson's delight at the news that other masques had failed suggests his sensitivity in 1619–20 to other masques, other masque-writers, and alternative masque forms.[80] Given that, in 1620, he was also contending with the running masque and its critique of his writing, the 'Envy' that may have threatened to 'blot out' the 'fair' may well have applied to his own texts in the new competitive arena created by changing masque fashions and patronage patterns.

Again, among contemporary masques, Middleton's *Inner Temple Masque, or Masque of Heroes* (January or February 1619) appears to have attracted Jonson's particular attention. As has long been recognised, Middleton's text alludes to the failure of *Pleasure Reconciled to Virtue*, casting Jonson as a 'silenc'd bricklayer' in phraseology redolent of the fate of Puritan ministers which would not have pleased the author. Jonson appears to have responded in *News* by characterising Middleton as 'a woman's poet' (114), echoing the claim that the *Inner Temple Masque* was 'made for ladies'.[81] As ever this personal sparring marks deeper disagreements that seem to centre on the differing visions of education developed in the two masques. In particular, the Inns of Court which functioned as a 'third university', 'the largest single group of literate and cultured men in London', possessed a distinctive masquing culture which did, at key points, express disquiet with official policy.[82] As enthusiasts for the Palatine marriage in 1613, members of the Inner Temple and Gray's Inn planned to stage the remarkable *The Masque of Truth* that treated the marriage as part of an anti-Catholic alliance, while in 1619 the *Inner Temple Masque* was critical of James I's failure to intervene in the Palatinate and offered a much more militant sense of heroism.[83]

Even though it was staged before the Palatine crisis had escalated, the appropriately named *The Masque of Heroes* registers this interest in the presentation of the Nine Worthies as military figures. Certainly, in *The World Tossed at Tennis*, the Worthies have taken on a distinctly activist stance, symbolising a fame that should be aspired to and which exemplified how 'Men strive to know too much, too little to do' (*The World Tossed at Tennis*, 308). In both these texts, then, Middleton's version of the future was distinctly more martial and in *Heroes*, Harmony presents the Worthies as embodiments of 'heroic virtue' (344), defined as 'human good' (326). In key lines which Jonson's masque answers, they are to,

> all descend to have their worth
> Shine to imitation forth;
> And by their motion, light, and love,
> To show how after times should move. (329–32)

The language of 'motion, light, and love' is of course the staple of the masque world, but Middleton has appropriated the court language and turned it to more militant and Protestant uses, arguing that the appearance of the Worthies will 'Raise Merit from his ancient slumber' (345). Jonson may have baulked at these claims to military prowess, especially coming from outside the court, and the military tenor of *News*, represented in the royal education offered to the youthful followers of the Prince, responds to the more strident militarism of Middleton's masque by reasserting manly military preparedness but in the service of peace.[84] *News* offers a royal knowledge and harmony that predicts a different version of noble youth and hope for the future.[85]

Jonson's responses to masques staged beyond the court illuminate further aspects of masquing culture, notably how different spaces could be used to articulate differing political and aesthetic viewpoints, or indeed how a form associated with the court could be appropriated for 'courtly' entertainments aimed at a wider audience. Much of the emphasis on space in masque criticism has posited the absorption of different places within Whitehall into monarchical space. Indeed, the spatial politics of the masque have often been seen as embodiments of absolutist tendencies with monocular perspectival sets built for solely royal pleasure and to demonstrate a controlling monarchical gaze. Yet, as these texts in different arenas employed in the 1619–21 seasons suggest, the poetics of masquing space extends beyond the mono-spatial theatres of absolutist power towards contested arenas and spatial permeability. *News*, in its relation to a series of public discussions in a wide range of media, shows how the masque, highly sensitised to the meanings of space, also incorporated the different meanings provided by different performances and traditions. Indeed, the 'running masque', with its shifting performance spaces in a variety of aristocratic homes linked together by the procession to and from the various venues, and used to articulate nuanced political positions and semi-official messages on the margins of the court, provides the strongest evidence for the possibility of different meanings created by different spaces.[86] This 'masquing culture' in which a highly sophisticated audience accounted for the performance space in their interpretation of texts perhaps is unsurprising given the intensely personalised nature of early modern court culture, but the interplay between masques in other spaces, such as the semi-public spaces of the inn, or the public stage space, allows circulation of ideas between court and other cultures.

Indeed, it is not unreasonable to suggest that, in a culture sensitised to the meanings of social spaces, and more attuned than modern readers to the significance of rank and access in the hierarchical organisations of space throughout society, performance and signification were intimately connected with space. In this case, the different ideas instigated by the Inns of Court, by civic ritual, by masques in the homes of specific patrons, and even in the different royal houses – such as the palaces who introduce *The World Tossed at Tennis* – signal different political positions. In drawing on both the '*mundus alter et idem*' of satire and on the paradoxes of utopian writing to imagine his moon-world, Jonson's *News* confirms the complex layering of spatial meaning in masques and masquing culture.

These meanings may be traceable in this particular masque's own performance space as, due to the destruction of the Banqueting Hall, the occasion was moved to the Queen's Presence Chamber at Whitehall. Although one motive for this transposition will be practical (the rooms were empty after the death of the Queen), the occupation of the late Queen's space could also have been used to imply a subtle shift in the political position of the masque, closer to Prince Charles, but also recognising the alternative views and voices that the Queen and her court had patronised.[87] These voices included not only masque writers with whom Jonson disagreed (Campion, Daniel), but also forms of masque-writing that he found less conducive, and policies that were more sympathetic to European involvements. The Queen's court had, at times, hosted disagreements with the direction of royal policy, and even worked as a conduit to opinions and ideas beyond the normal purview of the court; here it seems Jonson occupies, literally and metaphorically, the same ground.

Many of the spaces employed in masque stagings, such as great halls, were socially mixed and associated with political debates. Even more exclusive spaces such as the Banqueting House, were not only 'intended for festive occasions, for formal spectacles, and for ceremonials' but also were designed to echo the classical basilica, associated with public administration and deliberative justice.[88] The multiple social and spatial meanings of these places, even if only available to a limited circle, complicate the assumption of monovocal or monocular monarchical spaces.

The use of different spaces, moreover – within and outside the court – highlights how, in the early 1620s, the masque is much less exclusionary. It suggests a form permeable to outside interests, but also a structure that avoids expulsion and uses education and clarification as its presiding metaphors. The focus is on how information is disseminated, but also on how it is understood, again highlighting the possibility of changing modes of perception rather than simply excluding voices that are seen as disorderly or unacceptable. The vision of a news culture involving 'friends of all ranks, and of all religions' (29) makes such exclusions far harder to posit, and instead recognises the need to debate and educate as key to shaping this emerging culture into something akin to civil society.

Beyond the first folio: masques, margins, and print culture

One of the ironies of a masque built on cheap print, and that holds the 'book of perfection' as its central symbol of order, is the lack of quarto publication for *News from the New World in the Moon*. It is not alone: among the post-1616 masques, *Christmas His Masque*, *The Vision of Delight*, *Pleasure Reconciled* (and its revised antimasque *For the Honour of Wales*), *News*, and *Pan's Anniversary* are also without quarto texts.[89] Setting aside whether the absence of quartos for these masques is strategic or accidental, where quarto texts were printed, scholars have tended to argue that the later masque quartos were not commercially produced and have followed W. W. Greg's designation of them as copies 'printed for private distribution on the occasion' for a 'privileged' audience.[90] The evidence for this rests, in part, on the reading of Jonson as a literary exclusionist in the 1620s. Yet, as this chapter has been arguing, such assessments underestimate the evidence of the engagement of the masque in an active and disputatious political culture. As *News* itself shows, masques also inhabit this world of commerce, so while the 'neat clean power of poetry' is advanced as the antithesis of commercial distribution by competing with news, it also belongs to the news world. So beyond the discussion of news, and indeed becoming part of the news by being transmitted through the news, the masque itself, as a form of textual production and, thus, part of the very market it describes, further implicates the masque in this news culture. Not only might the masque discuss the news, be part of the news, but the most likely method of its dissemination – the small quarto pamphlet – situates the masque alongside any other cheap print text. This play between the fiction of the masque and the actual textual and commercial situation of the masque as cultural object raises the role that masque-making might achieve in this textualised universe. Jonson's masque represents an early attempt to explore not only the implications of a mass news-market for political consciousness, but how elite textual forms, like masques, might fare in the print marketplace.

Most discussions of masque as printed text have begun with the massive achievements of the folio *The workes of Benjamin Jonson* (1616) which have rightly dominated discussions of Jonson's creation of a print identity for himself and his works. As the subject of considerable amused derision at the time, the folio has variously been depicted as a demonstration of the stability and reproducibility of print-technology that allowed Jonson to self-canonise as classic writer; as the site of the creation of a 'bibliographic ego' that marks a new kind of possessive authorship in which Benjamin Jonson is the 'onlie begetter'; or as a volume enmeshed in the complex shift between patronage and marketplace, its texts regarded as either fissured with evasions and repressions marking the political contingencies of its creation in its 'interstices and silences', or as providing a 'stylistic or intellectual constancy' that hemmed in its readers on an 'authoritative and stable terrain'.[91]

With a few exceptions the masque quartos have been neglected, although in the two groups of Jacobean quartos, 1606–9 and 1622–5, Jonson constructs differing presentational strategies and narratives aligned with differing conditions of consumption. While consideration of Jonson's use of the arts of publication has recognised, for example, the innovative qualities of the elaborate play quartos of the 1600–11 period, the folio-centric focus of many discussions still compacts Jonson's subtle deployments of different forms of publication – through performances, manuscripts of various kinds, and printed books – into a rigid binary between theatricality and textuality.[92] Surveyed as a whole, Jonson's masque texts show subtle and strategic use of the varieties of publication.[93] In particular, in the quartos of the 1620s – markedly sharing the changing print conditions of the news world – the form and appearance of these texts differ from earlier instances.

Jonson achieved two great innovations in printing the masque in quarto. The first was to produce composite ceremonial collections with strikingly varied and presented contents: *Ben Jon: His Part of King James his Royall and Magnificent Entertainment through his Honorable Cittie of London* also contained the 'Panegyre' and the 'Entertainment at Althorp', *Hymenaei* and the *Barriers* form one volume, and *The Character of Two Noble Masques* also contains *The Haddington Masque*.[94] Indeed, when placed in this context the *Masque of Queens* seems strangely singular, perhaps marking the importance attached to the particular text. In their earliest published forms these royal entertainments and masques were often presented with startling typographical features, such as the inscriptional typeface used in *Ben Jon: His Part of King James his Royall and Magnificent Entertainment through his Honorable Cittie of London*, or the elaborate marginalia in *Hymenaei, Haddington,* and *Queens*.[95] In some cases these masques predate the complex typography of texts such as *Sejanus*, and provide a model for the folio. This sense of high-status, high-value innovation is confirmed in their physical appearance and composition, not just through the addition of authorial paratexts in manuscript or print (dedications, letters, authorial signatures), but also the use of expensive Italian papers and some with fine contemporary bindings.

The creation of the masque as book, employing the full panoply and specificity of print, functions in tandem with Jonson's other great innovation: the creation of the literary masque. These startling print productions 'developed a descriptive poetry to be reproduced imaginatively and differently through reading' and created 'autonomous meanings' that could be accessed 'irrespective of the performance'.[96] This new literary genre of masque-book enabled Jonson, who frequently cast his masques as 'entire poems', to exploit the potential of print to complete the events and verses mangled in performance to remake or make anew the occasion 'as if, in quarto, the soul of a masque could be raised a spiritual body'.[97] This new genre required a new socially broader audience, but also a community of readers trained to read in new ways by competition between masques and masque-writers. Thus in Daniel's *The vision of the 12. goddesses presented in a maske the 8. of Ianuary, at Hampton Court: by the Queenes most excellent Maiestie, and her ladies* (1604), the attack on 'captious censurers' institutes a theoretical defence of masque ('these punctilios of dreams and shows') that runs throughout the early Jacobean masques.[98] Crucially, this theoretical tilting potentially outstrips the masque as staged and engages those who had not actually seen the masque in an absorbing debate available only through the print text.[99] These perfected quartos conceal considerable contention that shapes a dual centre of interest: the recreated masque and the theoretical disputation. The 1604 composite entertainment volume seems to have sparked a competitive disagreement between publishers and authors over the representation of the King's official entry into London, while Jonson's later versions of the printed text allowed Jonson to triumph over his competitors, especially Jones, by claiming the primacy of his invention.

Although these quartos are produced by commercial publishers and were most likely sold as well as used in connection with performances, the limited evidence we have about ownership suggests that whether presented as a souvenir or purchased later from a stationer, these quartos were resolutely luxury items. Most masques, as might be expected, can be traced in elite hands, often connected to performers, so *Blackness* and *Beauty* can be traced in the library of the earls of Arundel, *Queens* among Sir Nathaniel Bacon's books, and *The Masque of Flowers* in the collection of Viscount Campden.[100] Officials of the royal household also owned texts, notably Scipio Le Squyer who owned a copy of *Hymenaei*.[101] This kind of ownership is best represented by the copy of *Queens* that may have once belonged to the Earl and Countess of Arundel. It survives in a contemporary limp vellum binding, with stamped gilt compartments and centrepiece ornament (Illustration 4.2).[102] These high-quality copies were supplemented by occasional manuscript circulations of complete texts such as *Pleasure Reconciled to Virtue*, sent by Edward Sherburn to Sir Dudley Carleton, the copy of the same masque in Ralph Crane's hand in the Devonshire collection, and *The Gypsies Metamorphosed* (1621), which enjoyed a scribal publication to rival *A Game at Chess*.[103]

Caroline masques that survive in slightly larger quantities confirm this social position. Owners included aristocratic figures such as Lord Herbert of Cherbury (*Love's Triumph* and *Coelum Britannicum*) and Sir Robert Gordon (*Chloridia, Love's Triumph, The Temple of Love*).[104] The Bridgwater family were extensive collectors and their library included gifts from authors, such as *Albion's Triumph*[105] and a copy of Carew's *Coelum Britannicum*, perhaps acquired when his sons danced in the masque.[106] The large collection assembled by Sir Robert Gordon of Gordonstoun was most likely assembled in London during his period as tutor to other members of his family, and returned to Scotland probably in the 1650s when Gordon retreated from royal service.[107]

Many copies can be linked to news exchanges or cultural tourism. The masque as news can be exemplified by the copy of *Chloridia* (not extant) sent by Sir John Ashburnham to Elizabeth of Bohemia.[108] The largest identifiable extant group of copies, from the Mostyn Library in Wales, were assembled by Sir Thomas Mostyn (1535–1617) as well as his son, and arrived in Wales as enclosures in news exchanges or gift-giving, many in an unbound state.[109] Identifiable Mostyn copies include *The Masque of Flowers, The Inner Temple Masque, The Fortunate Isles, Chloridia, The Triumph of Peace, Coelum Britannicum*, and *The Temple of Love*.[110]

Illustration 4.2 Vellum binding of Arundel copy of *The Masque of Queens* (1609) (Huntington Library, California, RB62067)

Several of these local collections attest to either participation in the masques or periodic visits to London and early cultural tourism as was the case with John Newdigate III of Arbury Hall, Warwickshire who was present for the procession for *The Triumph of Peace*.[111] He purchased *Chloridia* and one of the 1634 masques as well as paying for his wife to go to the masque and for 'going to see the maskers pass'.[112] The Hastings family took mayoral pageants back to Leicestershire, and both the Cavendish and Clifford families did the same, although one Clifford purchase belongs to a group of payments at York, so it is just conceivable that masques were on sale in York by 1634.[113] Masques even travelled as far as Germany.[114]

These survivals confirm much of our sense of the early audiences and the place of the printed texts. Most are traceable to those with involvement in masquing, close links to the court, visitors for whom access to a court masque was part of the tourist trail, or to news exchanges. Interestingly, they are not all souvenirs of the occasion, such as the Newdigate *Chloridia* bought sometime after the performance, and there are hints of regional sales. Occasionally, as in the bound volume of *The vision of the 12. goddesses* and Jonson's *Ben Jon: His Part of King James his Royall and Magnificent Entertainment through his Honorable Cittie of London* along with three other 1604 texts from Shirburn Castle, there are suggestions of the concerted, contemporaneous assemblage of texts as a record of key events.[115]

Yet, in contrast to the early quartos and the mainly aristocratic collections we can identify as their owners, the later masque quartos present some puzzling aspects, and their ownership is, perhaps, a little broader. These are the quarto printings of *The Masque of Augurs*, *Time Vindicated*, *Neptune's Triumph*, and *The Fortunate Isles*, probably produced as pre-performance texts, which also seem to take on more of the nature of popular print productions than their predecessors.[116] Certainly, they are markedly different from the other extant post-1616 printed quarto, 'A Masque presented in the House of the Right Honorable the Lord Hay', which carefully avoids revealing the masque's conceit contained in the main title, *Lovers Made Men*. The title alone suggests it was designed to accompany the performance at which the patron's interests superseded those of the author, and the single extant copy, printed on an expensive Italian paper, lacking both printer's and the author's name, more closely resembles the pre-1610 quartos in providing elaborate detailing of occasion and auspices.

The quarto printings of *The Masque of Augurs*, *Time Vindicated*, *Neptune's Triumph*, and *The Fortunate Isles* share common features. None have stationer's names on their title pages, none of them appear in the Stationers'

Register, and they were printed on cheaper pot and other miscellaneous papers. Visually the quartos recall the layout of the masques from 1616, with a spare statement of title, auspices, and date resembling the half-title for 'Masques at Court'. This impression is reinforced by the use of title-page mottoes from Martial in three cases (Tibullus for *Fortunate Isles*), and by marginalia in two cases (*Augurs* and *Neptune's Triumph*).[117] The earliest quarto for *Augurs* is the most austere, lacking a motto and place of performance, and only offering 'the several *Antimasques*' and a date: 'Presented on Twelfth night'. Whereas the 1616 masques (and, indeed the pre-1616 quartos) had trumpeted authorial involvement, these quartos are notably reticent, although we know at least one, *Neptune's Triumph*, was corrected in proof (the proof sheet survives) possibly by the author, and Sir Henry Herbert records that Jonson showed him the copy of *The Fortunate Isles* on 29 December 1624, and that it was 'allowed for the press'.[118] The absence of the author's name from these title pages is striking, although the second state of *Augurs* included a note assigning the contributions of Jones, Ferrabosco, and Lanier, signed 'B.J.'[119] It is possible that the title-page mottoes themselves provided a sufficient 'typographic signature' to signal Jonsonian authorship to the discerning reader.[120]

Although it is very clear that these quartos were prepared before the performance, rather obviously in the case of the unperformed *Neptune's Triumph* which was never staged despite the title page's claims, and although some copies may well have been distributed as programmes at the event (a not uncommon practice), the quartos are not simply tied to their performances.[121] The note added to the second issue of *Augurs* hints at a dispute between the collaborating parties, and may be intended to inform audiences beyond the primary spectators. Most significantly, the employment of black-letter for speeches in *Augurs* can have no relation to the actual performance for, as Jerzy Limon has pointed out, the black-letter satirises Van Goose's pretensions to high art, but only for the reader; in performance some other means (perhaps a stage accent) must have been employed.[122]

Jonson's engagement with the production of these masques, the title-page mottoes, and the expressive use of typography in at least one case, suggest that he had not entirely abandoned the idea of the masque as literary form. What has shifted is the publishing context and the kind of literary text envisaged in that the simplified title pages, the reduced marginalia, and the use of cheap print forms suggest not only a modification of physical presentation but also of the masque's place in the literary ecology of the 1620s in a return towards its pamphlet origins. In the 1600s, the elaborate masque and play quartos establish authority as part of wider strategies of textual legitimation, but in the 1620s, with pamphlet displacing the stage as purveyor of news, and with the emergence of a large market for controversial pamphlets, the masque quartos, while still retaining their role as performance guide, also seek an appeal to the cheaper, pamphletary market.[123]

Interestingly, Joe Loewenstein has recently modified the private circulation hypothesis and argued that Jonson, seeking yet further control of his works, acted as 'publisher' directly, although the copies were for distribution rather than sale.[124] His argument places these publications in the continuing narrative of Jonson's aggregation of textual power, in 'the market's repudiation of Jonson', and in the author's decision to recuperate print publication only in the 1630s after the controversial stagings of *The New Inn* and *The Staple of News*.[125] Yet, it is not clear that the market, at least for masques, did repudiate Jonson: Herbert's entry book implies that, in the case of *The Fortunate Isles*, sufficient numbers were to be printed to require official licence.[126] Moreover, William Stansby, a stationer of commercial instincts, continued to accumulate Jonson copyrights throughout the 1620s, suggesting that he envisaged a market for Jonson's works.[127]

It is possible that, as with the copy of *The Masque of Augurs* recovered in 1930, further masque quartos may emerge or other lost copies of texts may be added to our tallies, and that these may change our sense of how the masque circulated in the 1620s.[128] But if we consider the possible use of scribal publication alongside print production in this period, and that in the 1630s Jonson did return to print for the masque, then rather than regarding the lack of printed texts as a sign of failure, market withdrawal, or diminishing power, it is possible to see Jonson's deployment of the different kinds of publications available to him at different points in his career as strategic. In the case of the print quartos, limited print circulation may have provide a halfway house between fully fledged publication and coterie distribution. Jonson uses both small-scale print publication and scribal dissemination as a means to bring out his material, retain authorial control, and negotiate the complex and aggravated political climate of 1619–24, while also reaching different and even more varied audiences. Printing these masques is neither commercial publication nor private dissemination; it embodies, instead, another gradation in the arts of publication.

In fact, in at least one case, *The Fortunate Isles*, we have some evidence about its ownership comparable to that for earlier masques. Of the eight extant copies, four contemporary owners can be traced, including the first Earl of Bridgwater, whose copy was a gift from an unidentified individual, possibly Edmund Scory, and a copy belonging to the Mostyn family (see above, p. 122).[129] *The Fortunate Isles* also appears in two of the only contemporary bound collections of masques known: Humphrey Dyson's wide-ranging pageants and progresses volume and Robert Burton's volume of 'tracts'.[130] These two volumes provide a rather different sense of the context for reading these texts and suggest a wider dissemination than court circles.

Dyson's volume was part of a library of over 400 volumes; he owned several dramatic texts, notably a copy of *The workes* by Jonson (1616), as well as masques and entertainments including Middleton's *Inner Temple Masque* (*Masque of Heroes*). The bulk of the collection reflected Dyson's antiquarian interests that culminated in the revision of Stow's *Survey of London* (1633). The earliest item in the collection is Daniel's *The vision of the 12. goddesses* (1604) and the latest Dekker, *Britannia's Honour* (1628).[131] The majority of the contents are London-oriented although there are some Elizabethan progress entertainments. Dyson accumulated two copies of Elizabethan royal entries, along with texts from other Jacobean public events (*King of Denmark's Welcome* of 1606; and *Order and Solemnity of the Creation of Prince Henry*, and *Tethys' Festival* both from 1610).[132] Eleven of the twenty-three items are civic pageants by Dekker, Middleton, and Munday (including the fragment of the very rare *Camp-bell*), and interspersed among these are Daniel's *Tethys' Festival*, Campion's *Caversham Entertainment*, and *The Fortunate Isles*.[133] In Dyson's collection masques sit alongside the main run of city mayoral texts associating Jonson's works with a less Whitehall-centred milieu, and may almost suggest a selection on the basis of significant historical events, rather than for the author, the courtly location, or the genre.[134]

A similar variety of material also surrounds the fourth known copy of Jonson's *Fortunate Isles* from the library of the academic and writer Robert Burton. Although this collection (Bodleian, 4° T 37 Art) has lost some of its twelve original texts, a contemporary manuscript list details its original contents (Illustration 4.3).[135] In this instance public theatre plays, with a distinct bias towards the popular dramatists Dekker and Heywood, dominate with copies of *The Golden Age, If you know not me, you know nobody*, and *If this be not a good play the Devil is in it* as well as Wilkins' *Miseries of Enforced Marriage* and *The Knight of the Burning Pestle*. These texts, all quite tightly dated to 1607–11, have more popular – and certainly public theatre – origins, and the only consciously courtly drama is *A King and No King* (1611) and even that played at the Globe.

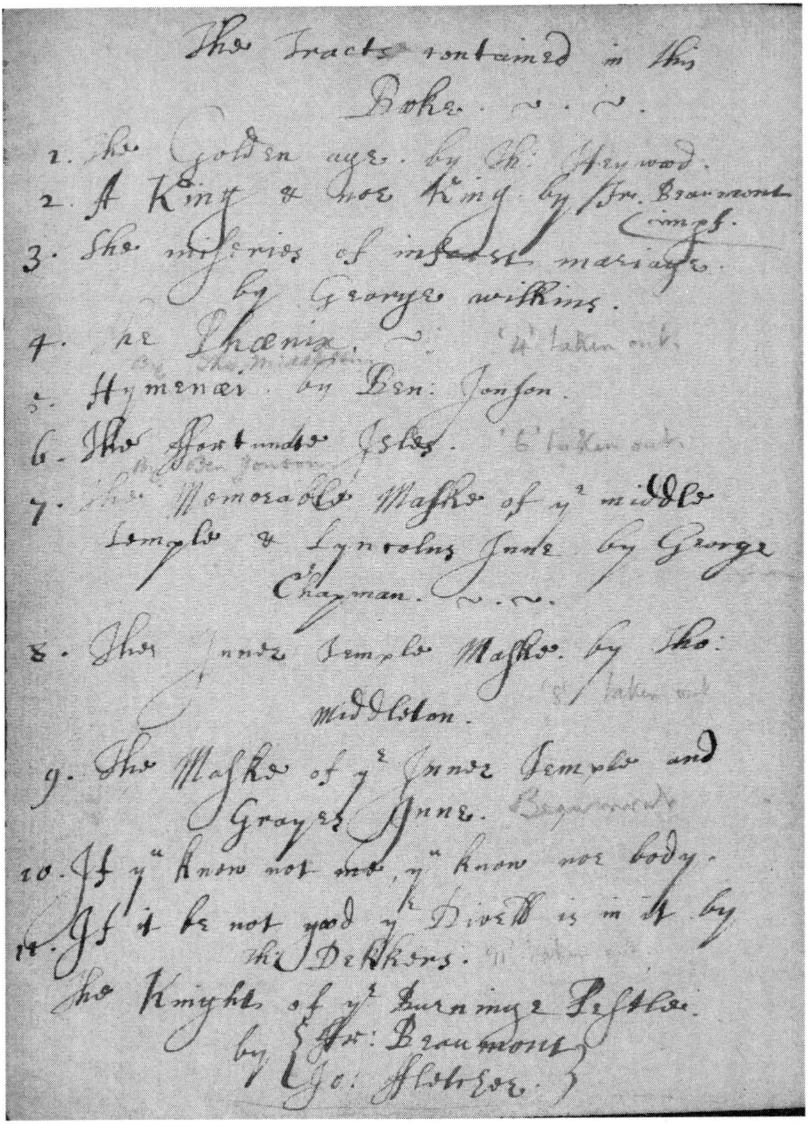

The Tracts contained in this
Boke.
1. The Golden age. by Th: Heywood.
2. A King & noe King. by Fr. Beaumont
3. The miseries of inforst mariage.
by George wilkins.
4. The Phoenix. '4' taken out.
5. Hymenaei. by Ben: Jonson.
6. The ffortunate Isles. '6' taken out.
7. The Memorable Maske of ye middle
Temple & Lyncolns Inne by George
Chapman.
8. The Inner Temple Maske. by Tho:
Middleton. '8' taken out
9. The Maske of ye Inner Temple and
Grayes Inne. Beaumont
10. If yu know not me, yu know noe body.
11. If it be not good ye Divell is in it by
Th: Dekkers.
The Knights of ye Burning Pestle.
by Fr: Beaumont
Jo: Fletcher.

Illustration 4.3 Manuscript listing of Robert Burton's bound collection of plays and pageants (Bodleian Library, Oxford, 4° T 37 Art)

Unlike Dyson's more 'historical' and event-based collection, here the masques belong with other dramatic texts, but from a wider range of auspices, and with a distinct group from the Inns of Court which would have been more pronounced after the earlier binding as the volume originally contained four masques from the Inns.[136]

Given the small sample and the exigencies of survival (even more so for a small vulnerable pamphlet), we can trace a major aristocrat, a provincial gentleman, a London antiquarian, and an Oxford academic as early readers. The owners embody different transmission systems, from patronage, to provincial news exchange, to purchase. It also shows the heterogeneity of the placing of masques within the early modern literary system, from luxury item to cheap print. Although this evidence is very limited and fragmentary, it does suggest the ability to reach beyond a socially and geographically narrow audience. Indeed, its status as a limited souvenir may even have enhanced its newsworthiness, while the greater number of copies afforded by publication may have fuelled the ability to source copies for circulation. Although there is no explicit evidence, some of these copies may well have passed rapidly to other hands and may even have been sold. Certainly in later booksellers' catalogues alongside texts such as *The Triumph of Peace* (still on sale in London and Newcastle in 1656), *The Fortunate Isles* also appears, probably in the quarto text, although some commentators did note the growing scarcity of masque copies by the 1670s.[137]

Even though fugitive survival and limited evidence limit our full understanding of the production of the 1620s texts, it is possible to discern a more shifting approach to Jonson's audience and to the business of publication and print production. Rather than situating *News from the New World in the Moon*, then, within fixed binaries of elite/popular, theatrical/textual, civil/uncivil, we can trace how the boundaries of these oppositions are both mobile and permeable as the whole concept of political culture, and its extension into a public sphere develops. As the technology of print dissemination via pamphlets and corantos develops in the 1620s, alongside the networks of distribution and consumption, so the culture of public politics develops, and so new opportunities and institutions arise. Therefore, rather than imagining a fully formed political culture, we see here a gradual experiment, marked in the uncertainty over speech boundaries and in the anxiety over the implications of such access to political ideas and debate, unfurl. It offers new audiences, their threats and pleasures, and new possibilities for the masque.

Indeed, the final line of the masque turns upon the whole question of audiences and the relation of the masque to the wider world. If the penultimate line of *News* asserts the role of 'Fame that doth nourish the renown of kings' (295), the final line insists on a role in defending royal reputation from 'Envy', placing the masque not only as propaganda, but as a response engaged in debate. The final metaphor of the masque restates the importance of writing and printing in the creation and protection of royal power from the forces that would 'blot out' its fairness. The staining of reputations is caused by worthless, 'blotted' texts while the task of writing is to counter false images as much as to create anew. The metaphor brings together the binarism of darkness/enlightenment initiated by the epigraph ('a world is born out of darkness and sets itself free') and marks the public role of ink, in print or manuscript, in providing either enlightenment or darkness out of its blackness.

5
'Hoarse with Praising': *The Gypsies Metamorphosed* and the Politics of Masquing

> For lack of better news here is likewise a ballad or song of Ben Jonson's in the play or show at the Lord Marquis at Burley, and repeated again at Windsor . . . There were other songs and devises of baser alloy, but because this had the vogue and general applause at court, I was willing to send it to you.[1]

John Chamberlain's letter to Dudley Carleton testifies to the strangeness of Jonson's *The Gypsies Metamorphosed*. Whereas in earlier letters Chamberlain had referred to the 'great provision of plays, masques and all manner of entertainment' that had accompanied James I's visit to Buckingham's house at Burley in August 1621, the uncertain terminology, 'ballad or song' and 'play or show', marks early recognition of how far *Gypsies* disrupted generic and cultural norms. Chamberlain's even vaguer 'devises' continues his classificatory anxiety over the nature of *Gypsies* and is confirmed by the image of its hybridity: these songs and devices are of 'baser alloy'.

Chamberlain's letter testifies to the masque's different kinds of engagement with wider worlds. On one level, Chamberlain's proffered 'ballad or song' exemplifies the elite circulations as authorial and scribal manuscript copies and printed *livrets* were commissioned or distributed as programmes, memorials, or items for collection as part of court news and gossip. On the other hand, Chamberlain's association of this masque with the 'ballad' relocates the masque in the very different news culture and the popular print markets explored in *News from the New World in the Moon*. Although the letter does not identify exactly which part of *Gypsies* was posted to Carleton in October 1621, material from *Gypsies* – the most copied of all masques – moves between elite and popular dissemination. Thus, the most widely dispersed items, the 'Cock Lorel' song and 'The Blessing of the King's Senses', circulated extensively in manuscript in 1620s and 1630 and then resurface in popular print forms in the 1640s and beyond.[2] Chamberlain's testimony of 'general applause' and 'vogue' registers this popularity but also undermines ironic interpretations of *Gypsies* that made Buckingham and the King the dupes of the far more intelligent poet.[3] Current criticism suggests a more controversial and contested text which negotiates the darker dimensions of Buckingham's power without covert scepticism.[4]

Chamberlain's letter captures two other aspects of *Gypsies*. First, the phrase 'song or ballad' conveys the mixture of sung and danced elements that characterised *Gypsies* but which also rendered it so unusual, signalling the different ways in which this masque draws on popular forms rather than courtly dance and music.[5] Ballad is a flexible term but captures this masque's potent affinities with scurrile and popular material more associated with 'alehouse door'.[6] Second, it is not just the ballad but also the 'devises' of the masque that are of 'baser alloy', popular forms, which implies that this masque is itself a new, perhaps more 'popular' form. So, whereas masques such as *Love Restored* and *The Irish Masque* have engaged with and translated the 'railing rhymes' and 'scurrile verses' of early modern political culture, *Gypsies* smelts them into a new base metal. *Gypsies* represents then a changed strategy that depends less on civility than meeting incivility with a new and different 'incivility'.[7]

Taking its cue from the context Chamberlain's letter offers, including the interconnections of elite and popular materials, this chapter undertakes a different reading of *The Gypsies Metamorphosed* arguing that its gypsy material and much of its language draws upon, but also responds to, the upsurge of political commentary, news publication, and various forms of libelling, that characterised the early 1620s. Fuelled by the divisive issues of the Palatinate crisis, and accelerated and impelled by the political rise, dominance, and corruption of the Villiers clan (especially George Villiers, later Duke of Buckingham), political commentary and libel surged. This masque, far from being isolated in the court world translates the language of libel and political debate, as part of a strategy to respond to, and even counter, the pervasive attacks on the Villiers clan. *Gypsies* marks the opening, but also the most ambitious and ambivalent, salvo in a campaign of self-presentation that culminates in Buckingham's employment of his parliamentary popularity in 1624 and the later production of his own propaganda.[8]

As seen in Chapter 4 both the subjects and the boundaries of political discourse were of heightened importance in the summer of 1621.

The 1621 Parliament, already contentious on matters of domestic and foreign policy, faced an explosion of political debate beyond Westminster and Whitehall, and the King had issued proclamations designed to forbid unrestrained discussion.[9] Indeed, the proclamation against 'licentious' speech first issued on 24 December 1620 was reissued at Castle Ashby as the King paused en route to Buckingham's Leicestershire home.[10] Where Jonson's earlier engagements with libelling culture in *Love Restored* and *The Irish Masque* were in the first case exploratory and opportunistic, and in the second instance transformative and exclusionary, *Gypsies* takes as its material and structural principle libellous poetry, engaging directly with the sorts of political discourse found beyond the confines of the court. This becomes even more apparent when the differences between the two versions staged at Burley-on-the-Hill and the revised Windsor version are considered.

Gypsies deploys the different spaces of performance to encourage a more transgressive fiction, to license wider forms to be made into the masque (ballads, 'devises'), but uses the symbolic distance from Whitehall to articulate controversial matters and adopt a deeply controversial language. As seen in Chapter 4, different performance spaces carried potential political meanings in themselves: *The World Tossed at Tennis* moved the masque into the public theatre, while *News from the New World in the Moon* used the late Queen's Presence Chamber with its ghostly associations with her court and its divergent views. The sophistication of such spatial meanings can be traced in the multiple performances of the 'running masque' and its creation of shared intimacies between hosts, performers, and audiences. *Gypsies* is the logical development of this masquing culture whereby the masques interact with other texts but also where masques enacted in different spaces articulate alternate visions of power. Thus Sir Balthasar Gerbier lauded Buckingham's masquing room at York House in which 'as much as could be represented in the great Banquetting Room of *Whitehall*'.[11] By 1621, employed by aristocrats, by the Inns of Court, and by the City authorities, masquing culture extends beyond the royal orbit as different sectors of society competed to use it for their purposes.

'Baser alloy': form, tone, and the strangeness of *Gypsies*

Gypsies subverts the conventions and forms of the two Jacobean genres it straddles. It inverts the norms of the country-house entertainment whereby guests are welcomed through graceful compliments and the presentation of elaborate gifts: here the guests are 'fleeced rather than welcomed'.[12] It also rewrites the masque so that praise of the monarch and the drive towards the revelation of royal power and order are replaced by a dispersed structure with multiple climactic moments. This masque concludes, not with a vision of royal authority as a manifestation of divine order, but with the appearance of the gypsies as their 'real' selves, that is, the members of Buckingham's kindred. While the occasion still closes with praise for the King, if voiced in a novel manner, the transformations are more personal than scenic, and more accidental than the embodiment of a vision of royal power. Despite the alluring sexual energy of the gypsy fortune-telling, shorn of ethical teachings and decorous classicism by the rumbustiousness of the Clowns and the anti-order represented in Cock Lorel's feast, *Gypsies* entirely reverses the transformation into exaltation found in the court masque and questions the genre's central trope of transformation.

During the unprecedented three performances at Burley-on-the-Hill (3 August), Belvoir Castle (5 August), and Windsor Castle (September or October) in 1621 two different versions of the text were generated.[13] At Burley, the occasion commenced with a Porter welcoming the King to the estate (probably several days before the masque itself), while the masque proper presents the Marquess of Buckingham and his kindred as a gang of thieving gypsies. Centred upon the reading of the fortunes of the women of the party, and revelling in lively hospitality of the occasion, the masque manages to create considerable jollity: 'Then let us be merry, / And help with your call / For a hall, a hall!' (BUR 788–90).[14] Alongside the more rumbustious 'Cock Lorel' ballad that celebrated the gypsies' feast at the Devil's Arse Cavern in the Peak District, Burley ended with songs in praise of James. The much-augmented Windsor version, topped and tailed by a prologue and epilogue to be staged alongside the masque, follows the same fiction but transfers the fortunes to a male group of major nobles and officers of state; reduces the stress on hospitality; expands the rustics' dialogue and adds parts for their women; and, finally, extends the final songs to the King with the 'Blessing of the King's Senses'. In particular, where both versions revel in the gypsies' canting language and filching abilities, at Windsor, the comic rustics are humiliated as foolish dupes, while the revised text is markedly more scatological and sexually explicit.[15]

Gypsies, the 'great achievement' of Jonson's late masque-making, has been characterised as a 'vast triumph of vulgarity and wit, crudity and finesse, tastelessness and grace'.[16] Extensive and distinctly 'unwashed bawdry' (*Volpone*, Epistle, 35) is counterpoised with a delicate lyricism in an unstable mixture. It encompasses an astonishingly wide range of influences and forms ranging from vagrancy writings to European *zingaresche*, from folk dances to elaborate sung lyrics, and fluidly moves between prose, octosyllabic couplets, Skeltonics, and complex verse stanzas. Such variety and permeability are striking because they occur-not only in the version staged away from court, where the influence of the informal entertainments that amused the King's entourage might readily be absorbed, but also in the Windsor, that is the court, version of the text. *Gypsies* transgresses in the *public* introduction of bawdy and scatology into the court and even augments them for that occasion.

Strange and heterogene, *Gypsies* bears only the sketchiest of relations to the 'Jonsonian' masque form. Instead of the absolute transformation found in some earlier masques, like *The Irish Masque at Court* that this masque consciously echoes, the gypsies return 'changed' by the simple removal of their exotic disguises to reveal their everyday selves rather than any metaphysical translation of their condition. Thus the Patrico proclaims:

> I can, for I will, . . .
> . . . bring
> The gypsies were here
> Like lords to appear,
> With such their attenders
> As you thought offenders,
> Who now become new men,
> You'll know 'em for true men. (BUR 767, 772–8)

These deeply ambiguous lines undermine the logic of the transformation replacing the exotic and exciting gypsies with the everyday rather than an entrancing vision of a new royal world, while the whole question of whether they are 'new men' is undermined by the performance practice. Against the basic system of the Jonsonian masque that associated the antimasque with professional speaking performers and the masque with silent, dancing aristocrats, *Gypsies* uses speaking (possibly even singing) aristocrats to perform what would, usually, be considered antimasque roles. Indeed, the Patrico's suggestion that they are only 'like' lords (BUR 774) increases the ironic possibilities of this moment as it remains unclear whether they 'are' actually gypsies disguised as nobles, or lords who have disguised themselves as gypsies, now dressed again as aristocrats. Against the normative certainty of the Jonsonian masque, in *Gypsies* nothing is unambiguous, and the claim that the gypsies are 'true men' raises the issue of how they might be so given their shape-shifting and the cry of 'A hall! A hall! A hall!' (BUR 790), associated with the arrival of players, which precedes their reappearance. The text is haunted by questions as to who is performing: gypsies or 'true men' and which might be which?

These uncertain translations are echoed in further structural ambivalences in the masque. While the transformation is the climax of the masque, in this case in both versions the Cock Lorel ballad with its rumbustious lyrics, and 'From a gypsy in the morning' in the Windsor text, overshadows the moment of metamorphosis. *Gypsies* has a dispersed structure with a range of climactic moments, and even if we broadly divide its material by the transformation of the gypsies to courtiers (BUR 799; WIN 938), the material on either side of this structural pivot shows greater variety in subject matter and in style. Thus at Burley, while it might seem logical to regard the section before the transformation as 'antimasque' (BUR 1–799), this would include some of the most lyrical passages of the masque (such as BUR 190–9), while at Windsor the substantial section after the cry of 'a hall, a hall' contains not only the praise of the King (BUR 1043–1114) but the less decorous benediction 'From a gypsy in the morning' (WIN 978–1042). Indeed, at Burley this section for all its novel performances retains integrity and poise as the gypsies join to 'hymn' the King (BUR 809), whereas at Windsor, the Jackman's Skeltonics continue and the 'blessing' and its 'bob' (WIN 970) sung by the rustics, rupture the decorum of the antimasque / masque structure.

In his persuasive treatment of the interconnections between *News from the New World*, the 1620 running masque, and the series of semi-improvised entertainments that developed from the 'bedchamber culture' of the King's personal entourage, Martin Butler also provides some suggestive commentary on *Gypsies* and its performance practice.[17] Many of the likely performers in this masque and in these occasional entertainments overlapped and although they included some senior aristocrats, a miscellaneous and fluid group drawn from the grooms and pages of the bedchamber, the gentlemen of the bedchamber, the members of Buckingham's kindred and faction, the nobles and gentlemen in residence (James' personal friends), and the King's hunting companions, dominated.

The 1620 Salisbury 'show or play of twelve parts' exemplifies the style and personnel of this culture:

> the Lord Buckingham acted an Irish footman with all his habiliments and properties; the Marquis Hamilton a western pirate; the

Earl of Montgomery a Welsh advocate in the bawdy court; the Earl of Northampton a cobbler and teacher of Birds to whistle; the Lord Doncaster a neat barber; the young Lord Compton a tailor; the Lord Cromwell a merryman (also the fool); Sir Henry Rich a curious cook; Sir Edward Zouch a [bearward]; Sir George Goring a perfumer; and Sir William Fielding a Puritan that marred the play.[18]

The description confirms not only transgressive class-roles based on comic stereotypes of often slightly dubious figures (pirates, advocates in the bawdy court, and so on) for the aristocrats and gentlemen but also that, crucially, they *spoke* ('acted'). These performances shaped a joking, body-oriented, bawdy and scurrilous style and their connection to Cock Lorel's feast can be seen in the description of the 1618 pot-luck feast at Newmarket for which the Marquess of Hamilton provided four pigs 'encircled with sausages' or Sir George Goring's 'device' of 'four huge, brawny pigs, piping hot, bitted and harnessed with ropes of sausages, all tied to a monstrous bag-pudding'.[19] Like Cock Lorel's feast these entertainments often tested the limits of taste and decorum in behaviour and speech. The 1617 play of 'Tom o' Bedlam' with 'many pleasant speeches' culminating in a 'scurrilous and base' song led off by Sir John Finet, the Master of Ceremonies did not find royal approval.[20]

This sequence of entertainments depended on intimacy of occasion and familiarity of style. Such familiarity is a key component in *The Gypsies Metamorphosed* but, in the Burley version, it acquires a different inflection from the male-centred entertainments of the King's entourage, as both the Burley text and the surrounding paratextual poems stress the importance of 'family'. Drawn largely from the Villiers cousinage, the 'family' created in this text stems from Buckingham's determination to forge a dynastic heritage and local role in the Midlands for his kin, but also draws in a broad sense on the Villiers clan becoming the King's surrogate family. The Burley version resounds with the King's care for his 'bairns', and the connections between the Villiers family and the 'Bever-ken', and while resident James I wrote two poems commending the 'goodly house' and wishing 'God send a smilinge boy within a while'. The second poem is explicitly entitled 'Votum' (prayer) for 'A Vow or Wish for the felicity / & fertility of the owners of / this house' asking 'Blesse them with fruit delicious sweet & fayre, / That may succeed them theyr vertues rare'.[21] One contemporary newsletter commented on the changed atmosphere at the court with the privy apartments full of scampering Villiers children like 'fairies', and James was notably solicitous to Lady Buckingham during her child-bearing.[22]

The *Diary* kept by Sir Simonds d'Ewes provides an illustrative anecdote of the intimate relations between the King and the Villiers family as part of a discussion that stresses Buckingham's domination over the King in 1622:

> A third story to argue his greatnes was that the other day euen this christmas, the prince the earle of rutland his father in law, his daughter the marquesses wife, the marquesses mother & himselfe plaiing at cards & the king looking on hee openly professed: heere is a father & a sonne (meaning himselfe & the prince) a father & a daughter (meaning rutland and his daughter) & a sonne & a mother meaning Buck: & his mother; the diuell on mee if I know wich I loue best.[23]

Even though told at second hand and with the intention of demonstrating Buckingham's malign control of the King, the story suggests the ways in which the familiarity both presented in and performed by the Burley text and its staging parallels the emphasis on '*dimestichezza*' in the 1620 running masque.[24]

It is in this context that the Patrico's claim that the ballad should be treated as 'merry noise' for 'these mad country boys' is made. The country performance licenses greater freedom than at court and also permits the involvement of rustic figures and broad comedy. The Burley text constantly stresses the latitude granted the gypsies as a 'loyal nation' (BUR 171) of 'gentlemen' (BUR 431), and their transgressions are contained: 'For though we be here at Burley, / We'd be loath to make a hurly' (BUR 775–6). The evocation of 'noise' (both music and disordered sounds) remains 'merry', so that the 'hurly' at Burley never quite becomes 'hurly-burly'.

The location, generic expectations and flexibility, the intimate context of the occasion, and the delicate balancing of the simultaneously trangressive and pleasurable gypsy fiction, allow the Burley version to retain its playfulness without risking the exposure of some of the awkward implications of the masque's language and ideas. That said, some of the material used even at Burley places considerable strain on this playfulness, for where entertainments like the running masque are jokey and dismissive, especially of Jonson's masques, *Gypsies* is often rumbustiously rude. More in the mode of Sir John Finet's 'scurrilous and base' song, the climactic moment of the Cock Lorel ballad strains decorum. While much of the song focuses on a parade of grotesque dishes such as 'Puritan poached', 'Promoter in plum broth', 'A rich fat usurer stewed in his marrow / And by him a lawyer's head and green sauce', the final section explains how the Gypsies' home the Devil's Arse (now 'Peak Cavern' in Derbyshire) was created by the devil's farting. The explosive finale reshapes the form of the masque as much as it dramatises a transformation of the local landscape (BUR 701, 705, 715–16). The cataclysmic fart caused by diabolic over-indulgence that creates the Devil's Arse has no equivalent in any other masque.[25]

In *Gypsies* the antimasque and masque boundary is further blurred by the continuity of the performers as the usual shift from speaking professional players to dancing aristocratic masquers is replaced by a seamless mix of professional musicians and actors working alongside the aristocrats who act, dance, and, possibly, sing.[26] Although much of the text they spoke was teasingly erotic, in the exchanges with the clowns they repeat some of the crudest lines in the text. So, where in *The Irish Masque at Court* (1614) scatology was performed by professional actors, in *Gypsies* scatological comments are repeated by the courtiers-performers. Even if the flexible ethos of entertainments staged away from court is challenged by some of the dialogue in *Gypsies*, ultimately the Burley version with its deft adaption of the 'running masque' retains structural integrity, and the closing section (BUR 800–72) presents graceful and decorous compliments to the King. The Windsor revisions undo the coherence of Burley, and many of the inherent ambivalences in the fiction, especially the nature of the gypsy roles, are accentuated. Indeed, Chamberlain's description at least implies it was precisely the hybrid and bawdy nature of the entertainment that appealed at court. Among those changes, the Clowns are given 'wenches', played by pages, importing the homosocial atmosphere of the bedchamber and hunting entourage into the court.

'We grow a disease': rethinking the Windsor revision

Martin Butler argues that the main thrust of the revisions to *Gypsies* reshapes Burley's Buckingham-centred event into Windsor's James-centred masque.[27] The presentation of Buckingham shifts between the versions, so that at Windsor Buckingham is displaced by the King, the more tentative and conditional stance reflecting not only Jonson's ambiguity towards the favourite and his power but the fluid factional politics of the early 1620s.[28] *Gypsies* thus can be situated as part of the protracted negotiations around Buckingham's power in the 1620s, and constructs the favourite as 'teasingly problematic' so that while his integrity is 'playfully questioned', ultimately, 'under the friendly eye of the king, [Buckingham] is found to be above suspicion'.[29] The Windsor tone is characterised as 'witty rather than disturbing', limited by the considerations of tact, so *Gypsies* more or less successfully straddles two positions, although the move to Windsor unbalances the Burley version and exposes some of the difficulties disguised by the earlier location and auspices.[30] At Burley, in the safety of the country, the favourite and his family are celebrated, thus fulfilling his duty to his patron, but at court the problems created by Buckingham's pre-eminence are registered. For Butler, the Windsor revision reasserts (some) decorum as *Gypsies*, in becoming a James-centred event, is wrestled back into something more recognisable as a court masque.

At the moment, then, most critical attention has been focused on the changes required to restructure the masque, especially after the substitution of male for female fortune-recipients, and while this suffices to describe the normalisation of *Gypsies* in the Windsor version it perhaps underestimates the contradictory results of these changes. If, broadly speaking, the Windsor revision concentrates on three major areas – the fortunes (WIN 324–446), the role of the clowns (WIN 505–703), and the addition of the blessing of the King's senses (977–1042) – current criticism has focused on the structural and tonal change created by the substitution of the male officers of state rather than the significant alterations in the clown roles. Indeed, much of the Windsor revision sharpens the attitude to the clowns and, in turn, produces a more confrontational text which is part of a wider and more aggressive interaction with the culture of debate over the summer of 1621.

The radical difference between the two versions of *The Gypsies Metamorphosed* is apparent even at the opening of the Windsor text that inserts a Prologue possibly even spoken by Buckingham himself. The defensiveness is striking: the Prologue recognises potential criticism ('some will say, . . . we grow a disease') and also the possible discomfort (dis-ease) that the masque and its presentation of the Villiers clan have generated (WIN, Prologue, 16). The source of this anxiety seems to lie in what the gypsy calls 'our boldness' which is absolved by royal favour: 'Forgive us the fault that your favour hath made' (WIN 19–20). On one level the Prologue reiterates the ultimate royal sanction enjoyed by the dis-easeful gypsies, although it also voices the implication that this continued 'sport' sits ill with the new location. This problem of translation – of the movement from country house to court – has further ramifications for the 'boldness' as the Prologue also admits 'I dare be no waster / Of time or of speech / Where you are in place' (WIN 6–8). As the King takes his seat to signal the start of the performance, the audience is reminded that, once the King is 'in place' in Windsor, frivolous speeches and time-wasting can no longer be tolerated.

Some of the ambiguities created in the revision process can be seen in the main substitution in the first half of the masque which exchanges the women's fortunes at Burley for those of the male nobles and officers of state at Windsor. This revision, prompted partly by the geographical relocation of the masque, renders the gypsies themselves more problematic for whereas at Burley their behaviours had been cloaked by their exoticism, and the erotic teasing and sensuousness directed at a (mainly) female audience, at Windsor, where the fortunes involve the great officers of state, the tone is less playful, and its implications more serious. Equally contradictory results can be seen in the refocusing of the text away from Buckingham and towards James, and through which the benefits the favourite has received become expressions of the arbitrariness of royal will supported rather than caused by Buckingham's merits. Echoing contemporary debates both versions manifest some anxiety about the extent of the King's favour, and both emphasise the King's personal intervention. So, whereas the shift of gender and rank makes gypsy lawlessness more apparent, Buckingham's reshaped role renders his favour more conditional upon the power of the King.[31]

This facet of royal bounty had also been stressed at Burley:

> This little from so short a view
> I tell, and as teller true
> Of fortunes, but their maker, sir, are you. (BUR 259–61)

In the Windsor version the King's fortune delivered by the Captain salutes James as 'the maker here of all' (WIN 257). The difference lies not so much in the giver of the fortune as in the role of the recipient. The lines justify both James' bounty and Buckingham's receipt of that bounty, aligning Buckingham more clearly with the monarch and making any act of criticism of the favourite, implicitly, an attack on royal favour. The verse may be much more conditional but the generosity marks royal bounty, a demonstration of proper royal magnificence and the 'large' royal mind, and thus justifies the fact that it 'all desert still overcharge[s]' (WIN 269, 272). At Windsor, moreover, the addition of three extra verses for the Marquess increases his prominence through the size of his part and draws attention to that role ('Myself a gypsy here do shine', WIN 261), but also by drawing attention to his primary role in interpreting the King to the court. This mediatory function is the equivalent of that deployed at Burley where Buckingham acts to unite the locality in praise of the King, and is embodied in the pun that Buckingham will 'tell' the 'fortune' (BUR 260), both narrating and counting out the money. As with so much of the masque there is an echo of the actual situation at court where the bedchamber favourite was the dominant broker of favour and reward.[32]

The Windsor changes, then, instituted a double movement: they accentuate the King's role, make Buckingham subordinate to the royal will, but in so doing elevate him as the primary recipient of royal bounty. The three Windsor stanzas may reorient the masque as more James-centred, but they also locate Buckingham as the King's closest satellite. Indeed, a parallel pattern can be observed in the fortunes for the nobles and officers of state, where senior court figures are all 'attached' to the Villiers clan in some fashion. The most striking illustration of this strategy is found in the Marquess of Hamilton's fortune:

> You should have been a gypsy, I swear;
> Our Captain had summoned you by a doxy,
> To whom you would not have answered by proxy,
> One, had she come in the way of your sceptre,
> 'Tis odds you had laid it by to have leapt her. (WIN 426–30)

Rather like the later co-option of the clowns to sing the King's blessing, by linking Hamilton with the gypsies and by making his role so explicitly sexual he is given a gypsy identity. Similarly, the court officer with whom Buckingham had most problems, the Earl of Pembroke, was given the first of the officer's fortunes but this recognition of his rank is tempered in much of the subsequent fortune which while it praises him as a patron and as a 'second Apollo' (334), concludes:

> You have wanted one grace
> To perform what has been a right of your place:
> For by this line, which is Mars his trench,
> You never yet helped your master to a wench.
>   'Tis well for your honour he's pious and chaste,
>   Or you had most certainly been displaced. (WIN 336–41)

Although the praise of Pembroke registers Buckingham's need to negotiate carefully with his rival, the concluding 'displaced' pointedly reminds the earl that he enjoys his place by the very same favour which now graces Buckingham. Again, in a series of simultaneous manoeuvres the fortune continues the pattern of praising James' role, but also situates Buckingham as (literally) the peer of these great nobles, but also as their better as the recipient of greater royal favour. At times, a certain menace (as in 'displaced') serves to remind the older aristocracy of Buckingham's position, and to stress their shared reliance on the mechanisms of favour.[33] So, even as the significance of royal favour is restated and praises the King for the perspicacity of his judgement and bounty, it also elevates Buckingham, as the beneficiary of favour, as the creature of royal favour, reminding the other nobles of his place in their ranks, and their shared dependence on the King. Rather than being restrained and more decorous, it is possible to interpret Pembroke's fortune as actually more pointed and politically explosive because, in effect, it relegates the Lord Chamberlain even as it appears to praise him.

The delicate combination of deference and polite 'placing' of Buckingham and Pembroke contributes to the kind of 'poetic bridge-building' that Butler attributes to this masque as Buckingham negotiates with his fellow courtiers. Indeed, there is even a slight tilt in the fortunes to encompass a more martial attitude towards continental involvements, notably in the inclusion of a fortune for the Earl of Buccleuch, who had fought with Maurice of Nassau. Nonetheless, this is tempered by the inclusion of three, possibly four, fortunes for those who supported the Spanish match, for Williams, Worcester, Arundel, and (assuming we accept the identification), Cranfield, all of whom, with the exception of Worcester, were either close to Buckingham or owed their offices to him. Yet amidst all this harmony the prominence of the Buckingham associates also serves to remind Pembroke, the most anti-Buckinghamite, and Lennox, after Pembroke the most strongly 'patriot' of the lords, of the favourite's power. On the surface there may be submission and balance, but beneath the surface, a sharper suggestion of a staked claim to primacy as much as parity can be traced. The rhetoric of harmony and constructive engagement created in these texts is seductive but it is constantly disrupted by the awareness of Buckingham's dominant position and his privileged relations with the King.

The second major group of Windsor alterations concentrated on the roles of the clowns. Unlike the changes to the fortunes which were the logical consequence of the change of location and the decision to make the great officers the recipients of fortunes rather than the women of the Buckingham family, the motives for the extensive changes in the clown sequence cannot be associated with the situation or the requisite decorum of the location as they do not simply reduce the verbally and socially transgressive features of the text. Indeed, these changes are very significant and included augmented dialogue, new onstage speaking roles for their 'wenches', and a considerably extended set of speeches for the Patrico and Jackman. Indeed, the Windsor text renders the clowns rather more stupid and, even after they have been robbed, Puppy, the densest of their number still wishes to join the gypsy gang. So, at Windsor the lawlessness of the gypsies becomes, somewhat uncomfortably, the product of the stupidity exhibited by the clowns, while their meagre possessions, which include such items as a religious tract, are mockingly taken and restored.

The changed attitude towards the clowns is established at their much-developed first entrance, one of the points where the revisions cluster, as the response to the clowns is both sharpened and the scatological content of the lines augmented. In the Burley version the clowns entered to debate the nature of the gypsies and prepare their own amusement by the Tom Ticklefoot, the taborer, and Cheeks, the bagpipe-player, discussing the women of the locality in passing. At Windsor, a song for the Patrico and Jackman intervenes after the clowns' entrance and the dialogue is much extended, and parts are provided for their women. The women are celebrated as 'the good wenches' (prostitutes) of Windsor such as 'Frances o'the Castle', 'Long Meg of Eton', and 'Christian o'Dorney' (WIN 506–10) and a sequence of rather pointless scatological jokes is retained. Indeed, one manuscript incorporates an extra phrase which may have been played at Windsor at the point where the Piper and Taborer enter, so that the rather innocuous phrase 'see where he comes' (WIN 504) that follows upon Clod's instructions to Puppy to gather the necessary money to pay the musicians while refusing to contribute himself, now generates Clod's response: 'Why, well said claw a churl by the arse and he'll shite in your fist' and when offered a fart as payment comments: 'Fart? It's an ill wind blows no man to profit! See where the minstrel comes i'the mouth on't' (WIN Appendix, 2A). If, indeed, the purpose of the Windsor revision lay in the restitution of courtly decorum, it is strange that many of the strongest lines, such as 'she hangs an arse terribly', and 'a turd's as good for a sow as a pancake' (WIN Appendix 2B) are also retained.[34]

The changed attitude in the Windsor *Gypsies* is expressed most clearly in the scatological song inserted as the clowns enter, in which the Jackman and Patrico celebrate court taste over local propriety:

> PATRICO   Why, this is a sport,
>   See it north, see it south,
>   For the taste of the court,

JACKMAN   For the court's own mouth.
          Come Windsor, the town,
          With the mayor, and oppose;
          We'll put 'em all down,
PATRICO   Do-do-down like my hose . . . (WIN 450–7)

This 'taste of the court' is the defiance of the local authorities, and this section of the Windsor masque suggests a far more contested culture: 'Let the clowns with their sluts / Come mend us if they can . . .' (WIN 471–2).

Equally, the final section which has the clowns joining in the 'burden' of the King's blessing acquires more complex resonances even though the stated aim is 'to wish away offences' (WIN 971, 973). The song the clowns are cajoled into supporting is designed to protect the King against a series of minor irritants and items known to incite the King's ire or antipathy (tobacco, ling, oysters), but as the heading in one copy supplied by a contemporary reader, 'a prayer for King James, / a character of his humours', perhaps recognises, the 'Blessing of the King's Senses' parodies the Anglican litany in its phrasing and its verse/burden structure that echoes the responses found in the Book of Common Prayer.[35] This suggestion of religious parody in the blessing develops the depiction of the clowns as hypocritical and ignorant Puritans as Puppy regards the Second Gypsy as 'A prophet, a prophet! . . . a divine gypsy' parodying the language of the hyper-religious, while one of the items filched from the rustics is the '*Practice of Piety*' (WIN 658, 637).[36]

This substratum of religious inferences about the clowns tends to heighten the political satire of the text and portrays those who criticise Buckingham and his family as gullible hypocrites as, in reality, wishing to join the gypsy gang. This harsher attitude is accentuated by the omission of the sociability and hospitality that filled the Burley version.[37] Thus, both texts announce that the gypsies 'scorn' to steal from the locals and their claim that,

> We scorn to take from ye,
> We'd rather spend on ye;
> If any man wrong ye,
> The thief's among ye. (WIN 700–3)

The implications of these lines are softened in the Burley version by the later charity and hospitality of the gypsy chief:

> For he we call chief,
> I'll tell you in brief,

> Is so far from a thief
> As he gives ye relief
> With his bread, beer, and beef . . . (BUR 779–83)

The omission of these lines in the Windsor version leaves the 'scorn' of the gypsies unmodified and, indeed, the clowns' choice of religious reading matter, *The Practice of Piety*, is derided:

> As for the ballet,
> Or the book what-you-call-it,
> Alas, our society
> Mells not with piety . . . (WIN 690–3)

Not only do the gypsies reject 'piety', perhaps chosen to mark the Protestantism of the clowns, as foolish and even old-fashioned, but the book which was one of the cornerstones of popular religion is mocked as a 'ballad / Or book what-you-call-it'. These lines are aggressive and uncompromising.

The pattern of changes between Burley and Windsor cannot straightforwardly be linked to a reassertion of decorum nor can they be connected to the compromises created by relocation and a consequent requirement to assert generic limits. While part of the recasting of the masque clearly brought the text in line with other court masques, by heightening the focus on the King and increasing the number of lines addressed in his praise, the situational complexity (or irony) involved in the fortunes accentuates rather than diminishes the gypsies' transgressions. Equally, as Chamberlain's letter implies, the 'vogue' at court was for the 'baser alloy' and the unspecified 'other songs and devices' which argues rather that the increased bawdry and scatology were added to appeal to court tastes: as the Patrico sings 'Why, this is sport, . . . / For the taste of the court' (WIN 450–3).

A parallel complexity of effect can be traced in the 'Blessing' added as part of the refocusing of the masque towards the King and the recasting of the second half of the masque more within the panegyric mode associated with 'masque' rather than 'antimasque'. So, while the blessing of the King's senses may be an attempt at a more inclusive interaction between court and clowns designed 'to wash away offences', the fact that they are co-opted into singing a song that, before it became itself the basis of satirical versions, was already a parody of forms of anti-monarchical satire, creates an uneasy image. Indeed, the sense of the distance between the clowns and now former gypsies is accentuated because here, for the first time, the text asserts the kind of decorum associated with the masque. There is no indication in the text that the transformed gypsies contribute to the blessing, instead their involvement is reserved for the more elevated stanzaic praise-songs at the end of the masque (WIN 1055–1114).

Alongside the reorientation of the masque towards the monarch, and the intensification of the contest between masquers and clowns, another revised area of the Windsor *Gypsies* concerns the language of the clowns' speeches. It might be expected that one potential way in which *Gypsies* could be reclaimed for the decorous and tactful world of the court would be to rein in the bawdy and bodily aspects of the Burley text. At Windsor, indeed, the 'merry noise' for 'mad country boys' (BUR 690–1), cannot be excused by the 'holiday' licence of a summer progress. The changes in these sections not only make the clowns more base, more gullible, more worthy of scorn, and more the object of heightened antagonism, they also augment the bawdry and increase the political bite of the text. Thus, considered as part of a broader politics, the attacks on the rustics and their religion, and the filching that gypsies actually undertake (rather than merely threaten as when they deal with the aristocrat's fortunes), provide the most transgressive moments of the masque which heighten the 'dis-ease' created by the gypsies' negative actions.

At Burley the rustics remain conventional theatrical figures, but the Windsor version endows them with a geographical specificity. Whereas at Burley they are country figures loosely linked to counties around Buckingham's birthplace and home, at Windsor they are much more clearly small-town figures, connected to New Windsor, Eton, Dorney, and other Thames Valley locations.[38] Windsor was closely associated with royal activities, such as hunting and with the Garter ceremonials but, although the town was dominated by the castle, it was also a markedly Protestant settlement with sometimes fractious relations with the royal household.[39] Windsor had been the site of the martyrdom of Robert Testwood portrayed in John Foxe's *Book of Martyrs* and the parish church maintained a reputation for strict observance under its vicar John Martin (1610–33).[40] In 1635 there was opposition to the re-edification of the market cross and Bishop Goodman wrote to the corporation: 'Hath not the Town of Windsor sometimes received a check for Puritanism; in truth I had thought and hoped that all such fancies and humours had been buried with Mr Martin.'[41] These religious tensions were echoed in other arenas, especially in the disputed royal hunting grounds. Windsor Little Park had only been enclosed in 1603 at the

King's behest and there were frequent complaints about the growth of deer numbers and the encroachments of poachers. When the mayor and corporation approached the King in 1624 they were humiliated by his blunt question: 'Why then do you vex me by permitting and suffering your poor to cut down and carry away my woods out of my Parks and grounds and sell the same?'[42]

In some ways the depiction of the Windsor rustics is even more disturbing than the exotic gypsies that have attracted most critical attention as they embody a harsh attitude towards those outside the charmed circles of Villiers kin and court. Their everyday world and language characterise the attitudes of a world antithetical to gypsies. Depicted as at least sceptics about the gypsies, then as critics, and finally as gullible and hypocritical, their treatment, as much as the dismissal of the Irish in *The Irish Masque*, evidences a much more polarised and contentious attitude in the masque. Even if *Gypsies* was more cognizant of, attentive to, and even responsive to, voices beyond the court – they are to be derided.

These contemporary resonances also confirm the shift in the nature of the antimasque that was starting to emerge in the masques of the 1620s. Their lumpen stupidity does not correspond with other, earlier antimasque figures as they are neither truly disorderly in an abstract form, nor are they simply like the deluded inhabitants of the *News from the New World in the Moon*. Rather they seem to spring from the urban world of Jonsonian comedy or, indeed, from the familiar comedies acted by members of the King's entourage such as the Salisbury show with its semi-urban figures. Unlike the figures in the 1621 Salisbury show, however, they are not assigned trades or occupations, they all are cast as feckless youngsters.[43] While the clowns do not present plebeian parodies of those courtly skills, their desire to join the gypsy band, in effect to emulate the gypsies, nullifies their criticisms.[44]

In many ways, the clowns recall the 'Boetians' of the controversial *Pan's Anniversary* staged earlier in the year, particularly in the attitudes to Protestantism and the symbolism of 'rough' music. In *Pan's Anniversary* the 'Prophet' tailor is made ridiculous by his derivation of his wisdom from mouldy old moral tapestries (*Pan's Anniversary*, 99–101), but in *Gypsies*, the allusion to Bayly's *The Practice of Piety* satirises contemporary stricter Protestant devotional practice. This point is reinforced by the juxtaposition with the salacious ballad of 'Whoop Barnaby' highlighting the indiscriminate nature of Puppy and his fellows.[45] Indeed, although *Pan's Anniversary* exhibits an apparently more explicit and extended attack on the Boetian tailor, as an urban artisanal Protestant obsessed with an apocalyptic interpretation of history, *Gypsies* recasts a similar attack in a more allusive fashion. Puppy's outburst in response to the gypsy is a classic example of comic misrecognition and the inappropriate use of learning when he calls the gypsy 'divine' (prophetic). In the Burley text this lack of discrimination followed upon a banal couplet based on a commonplace proverb, but at Windsor the lines are replaced by one of the more sexually graphic instances in the masque:

> You'll ha' good luck to horse-flesh, o'my life,
> You ploughed so late with the vicar's wife! (WIN 556–7)

The effect of the revision is to accentuate Puppy's stupidity in taking the gypsy's sexual joke as a prophecy.

The contrasting treatment of these shared elements in these two masques highlights how *Gypsies*, amidst its much more explicit sexual language and scatology, and even as it satirises the Protestant clowns, takes a different approach. In *Pan's Anniversary* the Boetians are first admonished to 'beware of presuming, or how you offer comparison with persons so near deities' but are forgiven until they return in a second misplaced antimasque and are 'justly' punished by their transformation into sheep (*Pan's Anniversary*, 114–16, 195). Rough music is also more explicitly dealt with in *Pan's Anniversary* where it symbolises the disorderliness of plebeian culture and is linked to the tinker Epam, named for the Theban general Epaminondas, a parody of the militarism espoused by many of the stricter Protestants seeking English intervention in the Palatinate. Although both masques share the 'contempt' (*Pan's Anniversary*, 117) for the plebeians, here where the 'near deities' are themselves disguised as gypsies, in *Gypsies* any dismissal is tempered by a calculated incorporation of the clowns into the masque most notably in the singing of the 'Blessing'.

These slightly differing approaches may reflect different locations and the considerations of public diplomacy, but also register the sensitivity of the situation alluded to by John Chamberlain:

> [O]n Twelfth Day were invited to the masque there, which was handsomely performed, but that there was a puritan brought in to be flouted and abused, which was somewhat unseemly and unseasonable, specially as matters now stand with those of the religion in France.[46]

The issue of what could be spoken 'as matters now stand' with the Protestants in France alludes to the sordid bargain proposed by the extraordinary French ambassador Marquess de Cadenet that England and France join in an anti-Hapsburg alliance, with the French participation ensured by England's guarantee of carte blanche to deal with the Protestants of La Rochelle as French interests dictated and without the threat of English support for their continental co-religionists. It is thus tempting to read the slighting treatment of the clowns in the context of this concern about 'unseasonable' attacks on Protestants and even to suggest that the slightly more covert references may, even in the context of a less public occasion, register Chamberlain's concerns. Although the allusions to the clowns as foolish Protestants are, perhaps, less obtrusive and extended than in *Pan's Anniversary*, they also acquire different resonances because the *Gypsies*' clowns are presented in a particular matrix of ideas, linking the country and county town, popular Protestantism, and especially the discursive world of cheap print and ballads.

In contrast to *Pan's Anniversary* where 'Boetian' popular culture is based on illiteracy (images from tapestries), in *Gypsies* popular Protestantism is rooted in cheap print alongside the popular ballad. This dual textual culture is, as we have seen, one of the sites for some of the emerging political debates in the 1620s, so where *Pan's Anniversary* was controversial for its tactless handling of a short-term issue, the Windsor version of *Gypsies* suggests much longer-term antipathies. *Pan's Anniversary*'s description of the 'puritan brought in and flouted and abused' could equally apply to the Windsor clown sequence, although it has attracted much less attention, but the linkage to popular print culture points towards another dimension of this text, how it appropriates and then redeploys one of the key components of the ballad and cheap print world in the early 1620s: the numerous libels that circulated about Buckingham and his kin. Indeed, there are strong reasons for suggesting that rather than drawing its grotesqueries and scurrility from court forms, *Gypsies* is responding to the pervasive pamphleteering and libelling against Buckingham in a deliberate and even confrontational manner.

Buckingham and libelling culture

The elevation of George Villiers, ultimately Duke of Buckingham, first to the bedchamber and then through the roles of master of the horse, bedchamber favourite, and Lord Admiral has long been recognised as a catalyst for the versiferous explosion of the early 1620s. On one hand, these libels can be seen in the context of the expanding commentary and the news culture developing both through printed news-books and through the virulent libels that greeted the death of Robert Cecil, and the Overbury scandal, and other libelling crises, the number and virulence of the libels now emerges as a progression of expanding commentary.[47] On the other hand, these widely circulated 'porno-political' satires deployed a language unparalleled for its invective and blunt sexual commentary, invoking a distinctively uncourtly and uncivil politics.[48] To counter these attacks and, indeed, create popular support, Buckingham staged a considerable 'public relations' campaign after 1624, when he becomes effectively first minister, to present his own policy position through Parliament. This may underestimate how Buckingham used propaganda tools such as the circulation of copies of speeches, tracts, and poetry commissioned either by himself or his entourage to advance an agenda even in the early 1620s. Indeed, these 'Buckinghamite' texts sought even in 1621 to counter the malign impression created by the libels by using the masque as a vehicle for political self-presentation.[49]

The rapidity of Buckingham's elevation from minor gentry son to earl, marquess, then duke, certainly throws into relief the degree of self-fashioning that could be deployed to remake oneself as an aristocrat, including the implantation of individuals and families to manufacture both lineage and local power bases. Buckingham was not alone in these strategies for self-construction, but his dominance of patronage and his fiscal power helped make the process more clearly visible, whether in art collecting, architectural projects, personal display (such as clothing, jewels, the trappings of magnificence), portraiture, or in literary production. The centrality of family and honour in aristocratic identity fostered further interest in both the presentation of self and family and also their preservation if impugned. Thus Buckingham, notably protective of his mother's reputation, vigorously pursued those who libelled her as Sir Simonds d'Ewes reported in 1623:

> A libell was sett upp at Court against the Marquesse of B[uckingham], worse then the song that went abroad, for which he offered 1,000 pound to know the author. A booke also was sett forth called 'The Chast Matron', in which was discovered all the villanies, witch-crafts and lasciviousness of the old Countesse, the Marquesses mother.[50]

The d'Ewes account is remarkable for the sense it offers of the variety of types of invective directed against Buckingham (libel, song, pamphlet), the range of dissemination methods ('set up', sung, 'sett forth'), and the different audiences and spaces deployed by libel (at court, 'abroad'). Equally striking is the vast reward offered by Buckingham for the apprehension of the culprits.

The range of libels about Buckingham and his kin attack almost every aspect of his activities. In the 1620s, especially during the parliamentary sessions but often outside them, Buckingham's influence and the King's attitude towards the favourite and his family, jostled with foreign policy issues as the main concerns. The widespread survival in multiple copies of the numerous libels illustrates how personal satire became the vehicle for more general critique of government policy couched in terms of personal invective rather than ideological disagreement or critical engagement. If much of the libelling draws on more elevated classical ideas of epideictic rhetoric, its material often drew on traditions of discourse that were distinctly uncourtly and uncivil. The issue of civility in these texts becomes a marker of the boundaries of political expression, used as a variable charge, but also as a signal of the violation of norms, just as the application of apparently 'uncivil' language to Buckingham shows how much his elevation and behaviour have violated the norms of civil society.[51]

In stark and unflinching terms, Buckingham's clan are vilified for their purported Catholicism, their sexual mores, their base blood and lack of lineage.[52] Buckingham and his brothers attracted criticism for their extravagant style, their control of offices, and their political influence, and one early poem, described by its transcriber, John Chamberlain, as a 'prognostication', was more prescient than he realised:

> Above the skies shall Gemini rise
> And Twins the court shall pester,
> George shall call up his brother Jacke
> And Jacke his brother Kester.[53]

The dominance of first the Villiers brothers, then their spouses, and later their cousins was noted in many poems, but most poetic energy centred on George and each of the major political events in which he participated, particularly his voyage to Spain with Prince Charles and the Ile de Ré expedition, inspired more writings often reflecting, as in 'Art Thou Returned Again', a widespread disgust at the favourite's failings. 'Above in the skies shall rise Gemini' provides a grim inversion of the astronomical lore it employs as whereas Castor and Pollux were the signs of a safe and profitable voyage here the only profit will be retained by the Villiers clan.

Many of the poems, such as 'The Warre in Heaven', appropriate the language used by the court for very different ends. James' image of himself as a Jovian monarch – and cultivated by Jonson – has been translated into a far less prepossessing image of a 'Jovial rout' in which sexual order has become inverted so that the planets even start to move in retrograde.[54] This translation of language is augmented by a creative and suggestive use of indirection and inference. Thus, although 'The Warre in Heaven' directly attack Jove's 'white-fac't Boy' whose 'Arse Ioue's marrow so had wasted' for turning 'Loue's pleasures Arse Verse', nothing in the poem provides a precise identification of who, if anyone, might be the poem's referent. Often the potential political meaning is only to be inferred, either from the commonplace parallel of the monarch and Jove, or from the context in which the poem is read. 'The Warre in Heaven' often appears in manuscript commonplace books among other poems attacking James and Buckingham. Context supplies meaning.

Many aspects of the Villiers family's behaviour that fuelled these libels – and the libels themselves – are echoed in *Gypsies*. Their combination of political, financial, and sexual rapaciousness leads to an image of them, like footpads, holding the country to ransom, marrying for gain and rank, and riding off with their booty:

> Harke how the wagons crack
>   With there rich ladinge
> Doll comes vp with her packe,
>   Su's fitt for tradinge.
> Phill: will no longer stay,
>   With her base baby
> What dare the people say
>   When she's a lady.
>   Thes be they, goe so gay
>   In court & citty
>   Would you haue an office pray
>   You must bee thiss witty.[55]

The litany of Villiers cousins all on the marriage market culminates in the wonderful image of the family wagon train overladen with booty travelling the land in search of targets. Speaking of the Countess of Buckingham, John Chamberlain joked that 'in truth she is to be commended for having such care to prefer her poor kindred and friends, and a special work of charity it is to provide for young maids, whereof there be six or seven more (they say) come lately to town for the same purpose'.[56] Others had cause to regret the Countess' ruthless pursuit of financially advantageous matches as another verse summarises: 'They get the devil and all, / That swive the kindred'.[57]

This pursuit of familial advancement through offices and dynastic matches is alluded to in the Burley version of *Gypsies* and the fortunes are largely addressed to Buckingham's sisters-in-law. The Countess of Buckingham's fortune describes her as 'The greatest felon in the land' who has 'stolen so many hearts' that she is 'at all parts / Suspected' (BUR 338, 361, 362–3). Humorous references to the amorous conquests of the ladies were a standard part of the country-house entertainments and other aristocratic amusements such as the 'court of love', and earlier texts such as the 'mock chancery bill' that formed part of *The Entertainment at Ashby* (1607) make similar 'accusations' of amorous rebellion and sedition. On this occasion, however, in the context of widespread critical verse which articulated the link between the family's advantageous marriages and their self-advancement, these platitudes and pleasantries acquire a different, less comfortable resonance. Indeed, as d'Ewes' diary entry shows, one of the most frequent accusations levelled against Buckingham's mother was witchcraft which gives particular point to the Fourth Gypsy's observation 'I cannot tell you by what arts' she operates (BUR 360).

The familial bent for financial peculation is paraded in 'As I went to Walsingham' (*c*.1621) which connects their supposed Catholicism with their financial and sexual rapacity:

> As I went to Walsingham,
>   To that old bawd's shrine,
> Met I Marquis Buckingham
>   And a friend of mine.
> Met Lord beggar Hamilton
>   And Hertford's Scottish Duke,
> Fitz-Howard and close Walden,
>   Sacrificing to St Luke.
>
> As I went to Bedford House,
>   To that puritan shrine,
> Met twice beggar Hamilton
>   And a friend of mine.

The Gypsies Metamorphosed *and the Politics of Masquing*   155

> Met I weak Lord Chamberlain,
>   Doncaster there was he,
> Met I proud Lord Arundel,
>   Foolish Montogomery.
>
> In Council these undertakers break
>   The Spanish match and truce.
> The puritans offer gold and pearl
>   With sacrifices to St Luce.
> As I went to Buckingham,
>   To the queen mother's shrine,
> Met I false Vice-Chamberlain
>   And a friend of mine.
>
> Come, offer up your daughters and faire wives,
>   No trental nor no dirge
> Will open good King James his eyes,
>   But sacrifice to St George.[58]

The poem yokes together the accusation of Catholicism in the Villiers circle with the revival of worship at the Catholic shrine at Walsingham, turning the courtiers into both supplicants and objects of supplication for those who wish to have access to the King. The courtiers are depicted as pilgrims on the way to Walsingham and also as beggars. Although some of the allusions in this poem are rather arcane and its precise political valencies unclear its main thrust attacks the 'undertakers' of the Spanish match, amongst whom it (oddly) numbers Pembroke and Hay, and the corruption of court life, symbolised in the 'twice beggar' Hamilton. What propels the peculation, however, is the crypto-Catholic cult of St George, not the heroic English saint but the corrupt George Buckingham without whom 'no trental nor no dirge' will reach the King.[59] The pun on *the* George, that is the gold coin, accentuates the political critique: money not flesh really achieves results in the Buckinghamite world.[60] This extraordinary image transforms Buckingham into a contemporary Mammon who must be appeased, while the whole poem is suffused by sexual corruption highlighted in the earlier stanza's description of 'the old bawd's shrine'. The poem encapsulates some of the disgust felt by contemporary critics, and even the fear that the world was falling back into the bad old ways.

'As I went to Walsingham' sheds a different light on the depiction of Buckingham and his followers as gypsies for whom, 'All the world is ours to win in' (BUR 64). Much critical ink has considered the connection between these gypsies and both the 'counterfeit' Egyptians, beggars who pretended to be gypsies, and the masterless men who so concerned the early modern authorities. A whole sub-genre of rogue pamphlets had developed to catalogue the types and shifts of rogues (a term which itself appears to have entered legal usage from the literary lexicon), and although some found their antics and their canting language amusing many of the tracts regard them as dangerous vagrants. Dekker's *Lantern and Candlelight* (1608) condemns counterfeit Egyptians: 'They are a people more scattered than Jews, and more hated; beggarly in apparel, barbarous in condition, beastly in behaviour, and bloody if met with advantage.'[61]

The decision to cast Buckingham's family as gypsies has often appeared strange in light of their own rapacious reputation and the generally condemnatory stance towards vagrants, beggars, and gypsies. From this has developed the conviction that the masque must have been ironic, offering a covert commentary on the Villiers clan, although more recently critics have regarded this argument with some scepticism. Marking the ambivalence in Jonson's attitudes to figures who are both 'rogue gypsies' (BUR 436–7) and 'overgrown fairies' (BUR 421), Martin Butler argues that the masque deploys a 'common courtly figure of speech' whereby courtiers on progress imagined themselves as gypsies, and that his playful and teasing presentation renders the gypsies both sexy and exciting.[62] These gypsies belong to a 'royal nation' (WIN 169); they are associated with festive and royal licence (BUR 657–9); and they are 'restorative gypsies' (BUR 651).

This interpretation has much to commend it although, ultimately, to describe this strategy as the 'actualising' of a courtly 'figure of speech' downplays the sanitisation that the masque undertakes. It also underestimates the aggressive revisions traced earlier in the Windsor text that imply a far more combative attitude towards the world of popular culture and specifically the ballad and libel. The rest of this chapter argues that the aggressive tone adopted at Windsor belongs to a calculated response to the libellous versifiers, and that the masque functions as the pointed propagandising of an alternative view and the rejection of an external critique by appropriating and subverting its very language and ideas.

The connections between the imagery of the masque and the libellous poetry do not simply depend upon contextual coincidences. Earlier chapters have noted a sophisticated and growing awareness of the use of varied media to distribute political propaganda, respond to particular events or proposals, and even to cultivate or denigrate individual reputations. Buckingham seems to have been particularly alert to the use of both verbal and visual propaganda to cultivate support and challenge those who criticised him. In the mid-1620s there is some evidence that Privy Councillors, including Buckingham, 'leaked' information about the debates on the forced loan to foster their reputation as 'patriots', and Buckingham's self-presentation shows an opportunistic and occasional uses of masques, poems, paintings, architecture, and the other trappings of aristocratic life to counter opposition.[63]

Buckingham's use of texts seems to have been the most developed. Buckingham's popularity had always oscillated considerably, but his position as national favourite after the return from Spain in 1624 deteriorated markedly during 1625–7, and as he slipped from 'popular hero' to 'pariah', Buckingham sought ways to counter his isolation. Faced with the unexpected war with France in 1627 Buckingham decided to undertake an active role in the expedition against the Ile de Ré, and even appeared dressed in military fashion to convey his new resolve.[64] Moreover, conscious of the popular appetite for news publications, such as the *Mercurius Britannicus* (1625–7) published by the Butter and Bourne syndicate, Jacobean and Caroline officials had started to consider not only control of the press but plans to publish a government newsbook 'to raise the spirits of the People and to quieten ther concepts and understanding'.[65] The result was a series of newsbooks, printed by Thomas Walkley, published 'by authoritie'. Buckingham used newsbooks to cultivate his view of the Ile de Ré expedition, although the final result may have been less positive as, when the scale of the disaster at Ré finally emerged, the criticism against Buckingham was all the more virulent.

During his two-year dip in popularity Buckingham received a crucial offer from a would-be client to execute propaganda schemes which illuminates how an early modern propaganda operation was conceptualised and might have operated. The historian Edmund Bolton wrote to Villiers on 29 May 1626:

> Your Lordship is well known to contend with your accusers upon extreme disadvantages, who are not only armd with most popular pretenses but with all other sorts of witt and weapons . . . to all which you oppose your conscience only, and ye King. They have fresh orators, they have smart poets, they have wise historians, they have searching antiquaries, they have spatious [specious?] philosophers,

they have observative travellers, they have deep discoursers, they have able penmen, they have dextrous swordmen, briefly, what is it which they have not?

If you want the like, nothing is surer than that in this great duel, wherein your Lordship is the single defendant against a multitude, all the choice of a nation your Lordship fights with fewer weapons . . .[66]

Bolton argues Buckingham has lost favour because he has failed to attend to the reading public:

There is scarce any greater cause of your losse with the gentry and better bred sort of our countrey, who universally delight in books, then that of late your Lordship have not seemed to value the generously and soberly well learned, famous for free studies and liberal cyclopaedie. To meet with that evil your Lordship had an offer made . . . for no sort of people under heaven are finally masters over fame and report, but the able writer only.

Indeed, in an earlier proposal offered to King James, Bolton had shown himself as aware of the role of the new media in shaping public opinion, offering to use a royal academy 'to correct the errors and repress the ignorance and insolence of Italian Polidores, Hollandish Meterans, rhapsodical Gallo-Belgici and the like'.[67] Though Bolton's proposal to James was a failure, and the letter to Buckingham may simply recount another abortive project, it provides a fascinating range of propaganda forms: 'smart poets', 'wise historians', 'searching antiquaries', and 'able penmen'. Moreover, amid the general appeal to the chattering and literate classes, Bolton's list also conveys the significance of oral transmission, 'deep discoursers' that might reach beyond the literate few.

Bolton's letter and proposal evidence a sophisticated awareness of a reading public, the necessity of influencing its views, and the importance of writers as 'masters over fame and report'. Furthermore, in the same letter Bolton reveals his interest in what we might now depict as the arts of political spin by stating his 'endeavours to get his friends to appear in the Duke's defence', and he discusses some verses against George Eglisham (the author of *The Forerunner of Revenge*, published in Latin, 1626, in English translation, 1642) which 'are spread in another's name, who is Catholic and ambitious of service'.[68] Buckingham's accounts contain payments for poets although in the absence of details we cannot tell whether these are commissions or ad hoc presentations, but amongst those who 'spread' verses on Buckingham's behalf was Richard Corbett who has recently been credited with shaping a 'trenchant conservative response to the insistent early Stuart expressions of political dissent'.[69] Certainly, Corbett's poems are deeply concerned to rectify a world dominated by '*Corantoes, Diets, Packets, Newes, more Newes,* / Which soe much innocent whitenesse doth abuse'.[70]

Even in the early 1620s official documents express concern at the 'inordinate libertie of unreverent speech' that 'doth dayly more and more increase', and two proclamations were issued in quick succession in an attempt to forbid these interventions in what the King regarded as his prerogative, and as part of the *arcana imperii*.[71] Significantly, in the context of the stagings of *The Gypsies Metamorphosed*, and the subsequent proliferation of copies and responses, the second proclamation was issued as the King was travelling to Burley-on-the-Hill. So great was the King's concern that in 1622 James VI and I himself attacked libellous versifiers stung into action by the (lost) 'Commons' Tears' which accuses Parliament of daring to 'deride' his authority in 'railing rhymes and vaunting verse'.[72] Their intervention is depicted as childish, fantastical, ignorant, uncivil, empty, gossiping, and threatens 'If proclamations will not serve / I must do more'.

Most pertinent to *Gypsies* is the evidence of how Buckingham deployed the masque for propaganda purposes. Throughout his career Buckingham had utilised the masque as a vehicle to display his courtly talents, initially as a dancer, and later as a patron. Many of these masques are known only though terse contemporary descriptions and may have been much like the running masque and other improvised entertainments staged in the early 1620s, but other references suggest a far more elaborate masquing practice fully capable of competing with the Whitehall masques for their intellectual and technical elaboration.[73] In 1626 Amerigo Salvetti reported a masque in which

> the principal spectacle was a marine view representing the sea which divides England from France, and above it the Queen Mother of France, sitting on a regal throne amongst the Gods beckoning with her hand to the King and Queen of Spain, the Prince, the Princess Palatine, and the Prince and Princess of Piedmont, to come and unite themselves with her there amongst the Gods, to put an end to all the discords of Christianity.[74]

Although spectacular display was a crucial dimension to these occasions the participation in the masque, either as host, performer or guest, was also a significant element. If dancing with Buckingham could be

160 Politics and Political Culture in the Court Masque

used to signal allegiance, attendance could be used in more complex and nuanced fashion. Thus at the running masque we know that the King and Prince attended performances at Lady Hatton's (4 January) and at Lord Hay's (8 January).[75] I have argued elsewhere that these guest appearances allowed the King and Prince to sanction the diplomatic messages of the masque and occasion without being directly responsible for them, and that the 'familiarity' created by the masque not only helped to cement cross-factional relations, but furthered Buckingham's own position as 'official unofficial' spokesman of the King. A crucial element in this articulation of nuanced positions was the performance space, and what might be unsayable at court in the public world of diplomacy might, in the context of private houses and '*dimestichezza*', become possible. If in this instance we see the complex exchange of private diplomatic 'courtesy', literally danced out through the masque, on another occasion a more public message was announced. The November 1623 masque by Maynard staged at Buckingham's house and described as a 'gratulation of the Prince's return' was financed by King James. Tom Cogswell has suggested that the masque was intended to reconcile Buckingham and the Spanish ambassadors as relations between them had almost degenerated into open hostility although, if this was so, the depiction of 'des Espagnoliz representees avec des actions dignes de risee' may have been unhelpful.[76]

These masquing occasions were not simply confined to court politics of high diplomacy; Buckingham was also aware of the potential for a broader effect. Thus, in the midst of the controversial preparations for the Ile de Ré expedition Buckingham staged 'a ballet . . . with various interludes, representing the naval armament and its departure from this island' and another in which, pointedly, 'Envy, with divers open-mouthed dogs' heads representing the people's barking; next came Fame, then Truth &c'.[77] Unfortunately nothing further is known of this masque, but the description suggests something that connects very closely with the debate over the limits of civility and tact in discourse and which may also use the kind of imagery which had been associated with Protestant masques such as the 1613 *Masque of Truth*, but reversed so that instead of Truth revealing a religious and even apocalyptic vision, Fame and Truth – presumably – banished the ill-informed and noisome incivilities of the people when faced with Villiers' prowess. The depiction of the dog-headed people accompanied by Envy not only recalls the kind of imagery associated with Spenser's Blatant Beast, but the attitude goes beyond even *The Irish Masque* in suggesting Buckingham's opponents are little more than animals.[78]

This masque has echoes in two other propaganda pieces – this time paintings – created for Buckingham. Both the equestrian portrait of

Buckingham as Lord Admiral and the painted ceiling probably destined for the closet at York House that depicted *The Duke of Buckingham assisted by Minerva and Mercury triumphing over Envy and Anger* specify Envy with her hair of knotted snakes. On the right of the equestrian portrait Charity drags Envy along, while in the closet ceiling Envy, trodden beneath Buckingham's feet, is accompanied in the final version by a dragon and a harpy accompanying the lion which symbolised Anger. The earliest surviving sketch for the picture also included Fame blowing her trumpet, a feature that would have brought painting and masque into even greater concord, although in the final version Fame disappears to be replaced by trumpet-bearing putti.[79] Interestingly, the three Graces at the left of the picture offer Buckingham a crown in addition to his laurel victor's wreath and the palm of victory, perhaps to suggest the personal qualities that bring him to Honour and *Virtus* who await him in the celestial temple painted above. Mercury in the painting appears not simply as the messenger of the gods but functions as a god of rhetoric and poetry.[80]

The ability of Buckingham's masque writers to mount responses to the 'open-mouthed' populace alongside elaborate propaganda spectacles, slight ballets, and improvised romps suggests some of the sophistication of political interaction in the period. Like the propaganda poems of the 1628 Parliament both message and medium are the issue, and the exchange of oppositional voices and governmental responses illustrates the range of ideas masques might express and the functions they could serve. Crucially, Buckingham's propaganda campaigns and his use of the masque provide another context of reading *The Gypsies Metamorphosed*, not as the ironic masterpiece of a disenchanted poet, nor as the myopic fiction of an ignorant elite, but as the appropriation of images, discourses, and forms that, while they also appealed to the elite, had popular and even oppositional resonances. In this context, although of an earlier date, the association in *The Gypsies Metamorphosed* of Buckingham with the Devil can be associated with the libellers' regular depiction of the favourite as satanic or assisted by his mother's witchcraft, while the final cataclysmic fart appears to parody the apocalyptic readings of history by the pro-Palatinate Protestants.[81]

Jonson's arse-metrics: feasting, farting, and the Devil's Arse

In the Burley text Cock Lorel's feast belongs to the masque's festive ethos and the song's emphasis on grotesque hospitality, that 'never the fiend had such a feast' (BUR 697), conjures up the anti-order represented by the gypsies. This upside-down version of the communality, conviviality, and hospitality that the Burley performance manifested in both its fiction and also in its actual function as a progress entertainment, balances the subversive energy of the gypsy gang supported by the inventive humour of the parade of dishes against some of the more disturbing implications of feasting with the Devil. In this sense, it is tempting to stress one aspect of 'Cock Lorel's music': not only the association with popular bawdy balladry but the connection to the 'rough music' or 'harmony of tinging kettles' that accompanied popular inversion rituals. As these carnivalesque rituals were often complicit with more official culture, reasserting communal order in the face of anti-social acts (such as adultery or bastardy) often through parodic versions of the rituals of authority, it is not unreasonable to align Cock Lorel with the 'royal' licence allowed to the gypsies and the authorised inversions of early modern ludic culture.[82] As a carnivalesque moment of inversion, with close relationship to both the impromptu improvised entertainments of the court and the various forms of popular 'customs of mockery or disapprobation' (playlets, skimmington and other riding rituals, libels and ballads, and songs and rough music), Cock Lorel's song absorbs these different energies, cultures, and functions, and encapsulates the different ways in which *Gypsies* operates and can be interpreted. It oscillates between acting as a complex symbol of the function of the masque itself, and acts out the ambivalences of the gypsies and their actions.

At Burley, enveloped in convivial hospitality, it becomes a demonstration of the harmless festivity that the masque claims. At Windsor, particularly given the additional stanzas, the already ambivalent ending of the feast acquires less easily incorporated resonances. The more disturbing aspects of the Cock Lorel ballad that emerge in the second version prompt more concerns about the danger presented by the gypsies to the social structure. Moreover, beyond this, even as the song appropriates the language of popular festivity and translates it into royal festivity, it also then turns that ludic culture back against the elements or uses of popular culture that have been used to criticise the gypsies.

The multiplicity of Cock Lorel's feast is complicated by the increased 'situational' ambivalence of the performances as the song was revised for the Windsor staging. Whereas the final fart had been briefly mentioned at Burley, it is much more graphically invoked at Windsor. At Burley, the bawdy tale provides an origin for the gypsies' gathering-place, the Peak Cavern in Derbyshire, known colloquially as 'The Devil's Arse', and this localisation contributes to the Midlands context for the masque and the construction of a local identity for Buckingham who had been reconnecting with his Leicestershire and Rutland roots in the 1620s as part of a process of creating a local identity and power-base for his family. At Windsor the final fart becomes the origin of tobacco, and echoes James I's well-known dislike of smoking as part of the process that revises and refocuses the masque towards the King.[83] Here the aim is to 'send him good meat and mirth without end' (WIN 817). On one level the inclusion of these stanzas may be seen as part of the anxiety expressed about the gypsies and their entertainments justified by their origin in the royal desire for 'mirth without end', but equally they also challenge the audience to object to their bawdy precisely because they are the products of royal pleasure just like the transgressive and body-oriented entertainments staged by the bedchamber and the royal entourage.[84] The resonances of this become much more awkward in the context of a performance close by a town noted for its Protestantism, and although the song presents a general satirical catalogue of social types (promoters, tailors, sempsters, feathermen, usurers, and so on), some of the verses include other figures that mock either religious enthusiasm (the 'Puritan poached'), or local officialdom ('the mayor of a town', the roasted sheriffs, the constable), and which may have been more uncomfortable in the context of the Windsor performance.[85]

The complexity of the response invoked by Cock Lorel's ballad is encapsulated by the Patrico's double description of the song as 'The tail of the jest' (727) and as 'the farce / Of the grand Devil's Arse' (739–49). 'Jest', in particular, casts the 'history' of the gypsy band as a mock chivalric romance, and endows the events with a gravity which the other meanings of 'jest' as 'idle tale' or 'joke' complicate. So, 'farce' combines the performative dimension of the Cock Lorel ballad with the more widespread meaning of 'a comic tale', but also puns on the 'farce' or force-meat (stuffing) used in cooking.[86] In this sense the 'tale' offered is the mock-heroic stuffing of the Devil, although the whole question of who is the hero of the tale (Cock Lorel for providing the feast, the Devil for eating it), and what is the heroic deed to be celebrated (making the feast, eating the feast, or expelling the fart) are all playfully suggested.[87]

This playfulness and cultivated indeterminacy about the feast has important implications as diabolic feasts were more usually associated with witches' sabbats.[88] While Cock Lorel's feast is nominally associated with the diabolic, it largely owes more to the tradition of the fantastic feast.[89] The baroquely exaggerated grotesquery perhaps recalls Rabelais' *Pantagruel* where the Devil dines off hobgoblins, students, and 'counsellors, mischief-mongers, multipliers of law-suits, such as wrest and pervert right and law', although there were various proverbs including one cited by John Florio which claimed that 'Of three things the devil makes his mess: of lawyers' tongues, of scriveners' fingers, you the third may guess'.[90]

Cock Lorel's banquet has a multi-layered symbolic importance within the masque. The banquet had become one of the central symbols of humanism, providing its vision of intellectual civility and sociability as the cornerstone of society, or in the Ovidian 'banquet of sense' of the philosophical potential of sensory perception and sensuality, but here the feast both breaks manners and also provides an anti-type of philosophical banquet, climaxing in the scatological rather than the intellectual.[91] Yet these carnivalesque inversions cannot simply be seen as anti-authoritarian or liberatory as they are the product of intellectual culture as much as of popular culture. The underlying structure of the feast with its variety of courses alludes to one of the etymologies for satire in the Latin *'satura'*, a heterogeneous stuffing, while the Devil's 'crudities' (WIN 747) rising up his gorge due to the rough coach trip to reach the cavern echoes early modern medicine which attributed humoral imbalance to improperly digested food in the stomach.[92] Both images belong to the culture of learned humour where improper digestion and the failure to assimilate texts were linked. Aspects of Cock Lorel's banquet recall the feast-poems and jokes of the Mermaid Tavern circle and other literary groups, especially the multiple mock-panegyrics attached to Coryat's *Crudities* (1611), also known as the 'Odcombian banquet', which celebrated his travel-narrative as a kind of deliberately rough and undigested text designed to amuse and unsettle in equal measure.[93] At Burley, the more disruptive potential of the feast was kept in check by the intimacy and familiarity of the occasion that allow the feast to be treated as a grotesque extension of hospitality and to remain, largely, comic. Even though this feast is not the *convivum philosophicum* celebrated by humanism and imitated by Jonson and his friends, nonetheless, it retains its festivity and sociability.

Yet, as Leah Marcus remarked, after the promulgation of the 1617 *Book of Sports* any invocation of festivity acquired a more political edge. Thus the Windsor version provokes royal mirth and invokes royal authority ('mirth without end'), but also places much greater and much more explicit emphasis on the final fart, so that the 'tail of the jest' does, indeed, dominate:

> And there he made such a breech with the wind,
> The hole too standing open the while,
> That the scent of the vapour before and behind
> Hath foully perfumed most part of the isle. (WIN 806–9)

The Windsor stanzas continue not only to allude to the foodstuffs disliked by the King but to associate the flatulent odour with tobacco smoked by 'polecat and madam' and 'gallant and clown' and which has infected the nation. The King's opposition to tobacco was famous but it serves as an image of his attempts to regulate the behaviour of his subjects and their disorderly rejection of his paternal advice. So what passes for a festive joke at Burley, when augmented at Windsor, becomes a symbol of the tensions and differences in society. These may be softened by the prayer to 'send him [the King] good meat' (WIN 817) and 'mirth without end' but the expansion to a national stage, and into matters of dispute even if comic and ultimately trivial, provides a much more contested image.

The performative dimension in this part of the masque has important implications, too. The Cock Lorel song not only tells the 'tail of the jest' (WIN 727), it also acts it out and so the final fart becomes a gesture of defiance, a verbal demonstration of disapproval, a showing of its arse to the nation. In staging a fart the Cock Lorel ballad registers the complex resonances of farting as a social and political gesture. The fart, of its nature, is a gesture of emptiness and proverbial for worthlessness, as in the early modern phrase 'not worth fart', but it also can become a highly charged gesture of defiance.[94] In *Poetaster* the fart is linked to critical modes of writing, the 'humours, revels and satires that gird and fart at the time'.[95] Although Jonson combines the fart here with 'humours, revels and satires', three genres of writing that were popular at the time of the play's composition, the fart borders on the uncivil and the unsuitable for discourse. Sometimes this can be comic, as in the Chaucerian antecedents such as *The Miller's Tale* where Alison's fart in Absolon's face is a gesture of deliberate incivility and comic defiance, but in other cases, the fart becomes associated with noise, and especially the politicised noise of plebeian dissent. Cacophony, babble, even collective speech could all be connected in the minds of the early modern elite with social disorder.

Although it is tempting to treat the fart as simply an example of gross humour and to trace its antecedents in the literary grotesque, in fact the contemporary context provides a precise *political* context for the Devil's flatulent eruption. The satirical 'Parliament Fart' depicts the fart let loose by Henry Ludlow during one of the debates in the 1607 Parliament, and the poem rapidly became one of the most popular of the period. Although it largely concerns events and parliamentarians from the 1607, 1610, and 1614 Parliaments the poem seems to have continued to circulate in the early 1620s, possibly because it voices issues – in a witty form – that were raised in the 1621 Parliament, including the liberty of speech. The fart stands for the 'somewhat uncivil' in political discourse and its failure to correspond to the rules of grammar:

> You cannot find out this figure of farting
> Nor what part of speech save and interjection
> This fart canne be in grammatique perfection.[96]

Michelle O'Callaghan has argued that the fart, a disruptive force of nature, is used to figure licentious free speech (it is an 'interjection'), and that the 'Parliament Fart' even cites Horace to articulate a critique of royal service. Jonson not only alludes to this poem in 'On the Famous Voyage' and in *The Alchemist*, but he belonged to the Sireniacs, one of the tavern groups, whose members were closely involved in writing and circulating 'The Parliament Fart'.[97]

The description of Coryat's verbal banquet as 'unsettling' through the dual evocation of the humanist ideal of the serious digestion of texts and foods to produce a balanced body and mind and its opposite 'textual indigestion' offered by the deliberately light, sweet, but indigestible fare, is echoed in Cock Lorel's feast. The fart is a literal sign and symbol of that failure to ingest food and texts, and disrupts both good manners and good reading, but it is neither simply dismissed nor solely treated as humorous interruption. Like the fart in the 'Parliament Fart', it can suggest the licentiousness of free speech, but also in its noisiness it is a matter of unresolved dissonance. The point is to produce an unsettling mixture which prevents any reductive ascription of meaning or significance. This ambivalence is echoed in the generic uncertainties of the poem (both 'gest' and 'jest'), and in what Michelle O'Callaghan characterises in the 'Parliament Fart' as ludic transpositions.[98] Where mock-heroic translates the unimportant through the frame of epic, the 'Parliament Fart' recasts the familiar through the solemn, and 'Cock Lorel's Feast' both transforms the familiar (food and farting) into solemnity and also operates through the frame of mock-heroic. This pluralised ballad creates unstable meanings that can be enjoyed without ever being reduced, unsettling and disturbing in suggestive and elusive ways.

Although the dissonance of the fart can be used to destabilise meanings and offer a subversive potential without ever quite becoming subversion, the literary heritage of the fart, however, suggests that such dissonance can become more than simply critical. Probably the best-known fart in the literary canon occurs in Chaucer's *The Summoner's Tale* where Thomas farts in Friar John's hand as an expression of his anger at the friar's financial trickery. Famously, Thomas promised the friar a hugely valuable gift as long as he divided it equally amongst his brethren presenting a tricky issue in 'ars-metricke' as to how 'every man shold have yliche his part / As the soun or savour of a fart' (*The Summoner's Tale*, 2219, 2222–3). Thomas' question has considerable political resonance as the idea of division to 'every man ylike' is presented by the local lord who the Friar has consulted as 'an inpossible, it may not be' (*The Summoner's Tale*, 2227–8) and has been construed as an image for the political claims of the 1381 Peasants' Revolt for a fairer share in material wealth.[99] Indeed, the fart has been associated with the political valencies of noise in other Chaucerian texts, such as *The House of Fame*, where dissonance was used as a way of figuring rebellious demands as uncivilised, unreasoned, and unreasonable.[100] Indeed, some early modern elite histories even referred to rebellions, such as the 1381 Peasants' Revolt, as 'The Noise'.[101]

As the occasion and circulation of the 'Parliament Fart' implies, however, farting is not simply a plebeian gesture, nor is it simply non-verbal noise, signifying disorder and rebellion. It is – literally and metaphorically – an act and gesture shared by popular and elite bodies and cultures and, although it carries different meanings in plebeian and patrician uses, the fart occupies a complex social and political space, both within and beyond discourse. Jonson's own earlier uses in *Poetaster* and in *Every Man In His Humour* confer more literary associations on the fart, as in 'On the Famous Voyage' where the ghostly farts become part of the mock-heroic machinery, but the use of the fart, especially in *Every Man In His Humour*, has particular relevance to the *Gypsies*. Indeed, in *Every Man In His Humour* a fart is an ultimate and apt literary judgement. As part of the play's final distribution of justice Matheo is arraigned by Doctor Clement for his literary incontinence, his endless and meaningless writing that is largely culled from other writers. Matheo is exposed when Clement challenges him at poetic extemporisation, which Matheo cannot match, and the justice demonstrates his own poetic skills though his mock-heroic verses that describe Jove's 'podex, white as ivory' producing a thunderous fart (*Every Man In His Humour* (Q), 5.3.219–22). The overblown but learned description of Jove's naked arse and the divine fart aptly summarises Matheo's poetry. As Clement says, issuing his challenge: 'There's for you, sir' (5.3.223).[102] Intriguingly, in the folio version, the apparently performed fart has vanished (F: 5.5.13).

Clement's poetic fart is, like the equivalent eruption in *Gypsies*, both a sophisticated literary joke in its own right, a gesture of defiant denigration, and a damning judgement of other writing. In *Gypsies* the target is not improper literary imitation but partly the gullibility of the clowns and mainly the kind of ballads and popular poetry they enjoy. The target of the attack is not so much the clowns themselves but the kind of unintelligent and contradictory Puritanism they are made to represent, enjoying salacious ballads as much as pious tracts. Moreover, although it is not explicit in the text, the inference is that this poetry includes not only salty ballads but political libels. Indeed, the performance of the Cock Lorel ballad suggests exactly these connections as it echoes the kind of impromptu and scurrilous performance of libels that we know took place in alehouses and other public venues.

Libels both invoked and generated performances. In many cases the simple poetic metres and stanzaic structures of the libels recalled oral poetic forms and, in particular, the four-stress largely octosyllabic line of libels like the 'Parliament Fart' were designed to encourage improvisation. Developing from the studies of Adam Fox on ballads and libels as texts of 'live voices' that were to be absorbed and reinvigorated in the act of reading and repetition, Michelle O'Callaghan has suggested that the 'Parliament Fart' provided for continuous revision and adaptation, a process that is equally observable in the many versions of the Cock Lorel ballad across manuscript and print in the seventeenth century.[103] Although Cock Lorel uses a more complex form (its lines are predominantly pentameter) the stanzaic form and the catalogue-like nature of the material lends itself to both anthologisation and adaptation. Indeed, the jaunty rhythm and steady rhyme made it both memorable and adaptable.[104]

Much of *Gypsies* uses exactly the kind of short lines (octosyllables, Skeltonic metres) associated with popular verse and this song, in particular, echoes the performances associated with ballads and scurrilous verse. Many broadside ballads were printed without music and partly due to this evidential loss and the irrecoverability of earlier performances, the musical dimension of ballads has been underestimated by the predominantly textually oriented historians and literary critics who have investigated balladeering. More recently, Christopher Marsh has stressed how particular tunes, through their constant recycling, gained specific associations as suitable for godly, bawdy, festive, or other material, while prior knowledge of earlier uses of the tune may have influenced reception and the decoding of subliminal meanings.[105] Thus, the anti-Catholic ballad of the mid-1620s, 'A New Year's Gift for the Pope', which attacks the Spanish match, was sung to 'Thomas you cannot', a tune associated with male sexual failure.[106]

Unfortunately, for *Gypsies*, the evidence about music and performance is difficult to assess as the tune for Cock Lorel has not survived in any of the manuscript copies, and although some of the later seventeenth-century printed versions provide a tune known as 'An Old Man is a Bed

Full of Bones', which may possibly have predated the masque, there is no immediately obvious connection between the few words of that ballad and the Devil's feast.[107] Moreover, while the accounts tell us of payments for fiddlers and a taborer and the text mentions a bagpipe-player, very little is known of the music for this masque.[108] These forces do, however, suggest the kinds of music associated with popular ballads and with the sung versions of libels. Indeed, the most heavily documented instance of sung libel, the Staines fiddlers of 1627 who were tried in Star Chamber for seditious libel, demonstrates the association with fiddle-players and the lowest social orders and situations such as the alehouse, and other evidence suggests that those labelled as fiddlers were also adepts at tabor and pipe.[109] The Staines fiddlers are particularly interesting because they were prosecuted for singing two libels, 'so lewde and unfit to be hearde' that included 'Come hear Lady Muses' or 'The Clean Contrary Way' against Buckingham.[110]

The case of the Staines fiddlers has been studied by Alastair Bellany and his account brings out not only the authorities' concern about such libels and the lengths to which prosecutions went, but also the complexity of the meanings that libels could generate, especially in their performed versions. In particular Bellany's analysis confirms the cultural contest between the authorities and those who took a more sceptical view of Buckingham's abilities and just how much the struggle to appropriate words, music, and performance practice permeated society. The text of the libel, which uses refrain 'the clean contrary way' to reverse all its – seemingly – positive statements about Buckingham is rooted in precisely this circulation and appropriation of meaning. Thus the opening stanza offers:

> Come heare, Lady Muses, and help mee to sing,
>   Come love mee wheras I lay
> Of a Duke that deserves to bee made a King
>   The cleane contrary way
>   O the cleane contrary way.

The 'delayed comic inversion' that Bellany traces is accentuated by the inversion implicit in the refrain itself which contains its own reversal. Not only does the refrain invert the previous lines ('clean' meaning 'absolute'), but implicitly Buckingham's power has nothing 'cleane' about it, 'dirty' as the 'contrary way' suggesting the sexual activity that has promoted Buckingham's power. This may provide one of the reasons why the Earl of Manchester regarded the poem as 'lewde' but, interestingly, the case was also concerned with the form of the text and Heath, the Attorney General, called the libels 'scandalous for the matter' but also 'base and barbarous' in 'their forme'. Part of the baseness derives from the performance by lower-class musicians in public and lower-class venues, but the 'form' suggests that part of the potency lay in the representation of Buckingham in a potentially lower-class genre, the ballad or song. Behind the concern with social decorum lies an equal awareness of generic and representational suitability that implies a politics of form in operation whereby certain forms accrued political meanings and their use or appropriation becomes part of the meaning of the text. Buckingham is demeaned by almost every aspect, then, of this occasion, by the performance by fiddlers in public and plebeian venues, by the text, by the music, and by the choice of form, popular song.

The Staines fiddlers establish how struggles for control of representations could include form, performance style, and venue as much as content. Significantly, the punishment meted out to the musicians illustrates exactly this process as they were not only whipped and pilloried (as well as fined an impossible amount) but they were also paraded in their home towns of Staines and Ware so that the court's judgement might 'spread it selfe from Ware into the North and through Staines come to them in the west'. Most pointedly, as their song had invoked the 'contrary way' they were made to ride from Westminster to Cheapside 'the clean contrary way that is with theire faces to the horses tayle'. Not only does the official punishment echo the types of popular shaming ritual whose language and form had also been used to attack Buckingham, but the court 'appropriated the inversionary energy of the lyric to counter it'.[111]

This economy of inversion, first by the libellers and then by the court, finds its echo in Corbett's writings for Buckingham, in Buckingham's masque of Truth, and in the use of popular forms in *Gypsies*. Indeed, the use of popular elements in *Gypsies*, as Chamberlain's letter implies, appeals to a festive culture shared by the elite and wider populace even if the impromptu entertainments and playfully grotesque feasts of the aristocracy and the morrises and popular ballads and songs of the clowns take on slightly different forms and are inflected in slightly different ways. In this sense, the popular cultural elements in *Gypsies* provide a 'point of contact', bringing together elite and plebeian, but rather than this contact being the route to social harmony, the use of these elements becomes part of an elite appropriation of the popular world, not simply to control those forces and regulate them, but to turn the language of plebeian dissent back against the critics and libellers. What emerges, instead, is a highly contested culture in which the reappropriation of the language of the libellers is turned against them, so that the scatological and cacophonous attacks on the court, and especially the Villiers tribe, is returned at them in a gesture of equal defiance. The two great gestures of plebeian rejection of elite order – the baring of the buttocks and the fart – are offered to an elite audience not as a gesture of defiance, nor to become simply the source of humour, but as a response: 'the taste of the court, / For the court's own mouth' is to offer 'the town' a pair of dropped hose and a cataclysmic fart.

'All ensigns of a war are not yet dead': the masque and the politics of the 1620s

The fart that ends Cock Lorel's ballad resurfaces in many ways in the 1620s, not only in the large number of recycled copies of the ballad that circulated, but also in Jonson's own writings. In his 'Execration' (c.1624), among the places to which Jonson wishes Vulcan had confined his fiery activity is the 'Devil's Arse' where, assisted by a friar, the Devil 'did guns beget' ('Execration', 202). Jonson refers to the 1624 engraving of the Devil swallowing Jesuits and shitting soldiers, while a friar reads James I's proclamation banishing the Jesuits which is pinned to a pillar.[112] In this instance the Devil's fart no longer simply perfumes or reshapes the land, it becomes the 'petards and grenades' that do 'Blow up, and ruin, mine and countermine' ('Execration, 205–6), and bring Europe to religiously inspired massacres and warfare.

This concern with the possibility of continental warfare and the domestic tensions created by the ramifications of the Palatinate crisis and the dominance of Buckingham and his kin can be traced, too, in Jonson's 'Epistle to a friend, to Persuade him to the Wars' which is riven by the poet's disillusion as he finds himself 'hoarse with praising' (*The Underwood*, 15.151). Indeed, throughout the 1620s, Jonson's political and aesthetic positions seem to have translated themselves, perhaps in response to the highly complex and fluid situation provoked by the Palatinate crisis, the Spanish and then French matches, the omnipresence of Buckingham, and the new monarch. While some of his writings in 1619–20 share concerns with pro-Palatinate writers, his 'Speech Out of Horace' (c.1626) is more militant still, and his aesthetic position also shifted with closer contacts to Spenserian poets, such as Michael Drayton, with whom he had little in common in the 1610s.

To couch these issues, however, solely in terms of factional and court politics is to underestimate the extent of the engagement of the wider populace, in a variety of ways, with politics and political culture. The difficulties Jonson encountered, and the palpable sense of effort expended to maintain an equilibrium, come not simply from court faction and politics but from how to accommodate the popular and oppositional political voices. As the Prologue to the Windsor versions shows, the question lies in how to incorporate the 'boldness' (WIN, Prologue, 19) of an increasingly fraught debate. In *Gypsies* Jonson succeeded by translating libels into laughter – though even there it is marked by darker undertones – but by 1623 there can be no such reconciliation. Jonson may translate this into an issue of the incivility of popular discourse (he call their verses 'tumultuous' (*Neptune's Triumph*, 114)) but the problem is a broader response to the whole idea of a civil society that might debate politics. This goes to the heart of the politics of the court masque, responding not only to the stress of factional politics within the court, but also to the contradictions between the court and the wider nation. Indeed, it is often the relations to the world outside that power these issues. *The Gypsies Metamorphosed* frequently invokes the idea of the 'loyal' or the 'royal' nation (BUR 172; WIN 169) and dramatises the question of who might be included in that body. The 'royal nation' may have sung that they were 'one man's all', ambiguously either to James or Buckingham, but as *Gypsies* shows, masques are far from 'one man's all', rather they belong to and need to be read as part of a public political culture of civil and uncivil discourses.

6
"'Tis for kings, / Not for their subjects, to have such rare things': *The Triumph of Peace* and Civil Culture

Writing of the Civil War the Earl of Clarendon puzzled how 'a small discernible cloud' that 'arose in the north' could have disrupted the 'blessed conjuncture' of the Caroline peace with 'such a storm that never gave over raging . . . until it had rooted up the greatest and tallest cedars of the three nations'.[1] Others were less surprised: as early as 1626 the Earl of Arundel had reportedly questioned whether Charles could avoid seeing his 'house overturned'.[2] Indeed, by the late 1620s Charles' early bellicosity collapsed in a humiliating withdrawal from European warfare and concluded in a series of political and personal crises including the suspension of Parliament in 1629.

Clarendon's 'blessed conjuncture' has seemed more 'contested, controversial and fragile' to some recent historians.[3] This more conflicted 1630s can be discerned in James Shirley's *The Triumph of Peace*, staged on 3 February in the Banqueting House at Whitehall and again on 13 February 1634 at the Merchant Taylors' Hall. Deprived of the institutional arena for debate that might have been provided by Parliament, a whole range of political actions and expressions were displaced into other political and cultural fora. Shirley's masque, indeed, complicates the consensual ideology attributed to Caroline political culture with more controversial content.[4]

The Triumph of Peace responds directly to the reinstitution of the regular Twelfth Night and Shrovetide masques in Jonson's *Love's Triumph Through Callipolis* and *Chloridia* in 1631. Prefaced by poetic defences and printed in high-quality quartos recalling Jonson's earlier attempts to establish the primacy of his masque-poetics, these masques announced the royal return to large-scale masquing alongside the concerted attempt of royal advisers to re-establish royal authority after the setbacks of the late 1620s.[5] The nostalgia that suffuses these productions, then, embodies a strategic recreation of an earlier masquing culture rather than creative exhaustion.[6] Indeed, throughout the early 1630s a sequence of events to engage aristocracy and populace with the ceremonial aspects of monarchy sought to establish a new and persuasive monarchical image rooted in an iconography of married monarchy and personal rule over both self and nation sheltered by pacifism and isolation. As with the 1633 Scottish coronation, such ceremonial re-inauguration carried risks: the public clarification of key themes and ideas in the Caroline regime also brought sharpened focus on the points of conflict.

Planning for *The Triumph of Peace* had begun in late 1633 to mark the birth of James, Duke of York, although accounts differ as to whether the King or the four Inns of Court were the instigators.[7] Preparations collided, however, with the publication of William Prynne's *Histriomastix*.[8] Prynne's text – or rather his position as barrister at Lincoln's Inn – associated the lawyers not only with anti-theatrical polemics widely understood by many contemporaries as a direct attack on Queen Henrietta Maria but also with 'disobedience to the King, disobedience to the state, and a general dislike unto all government'.[9] Despite loyal, conciliatory, and celebratory origins, as well as being 'so well performed and so well liked' by the monarchs, *The Triumph of Peace* was, in almost all aspects, riven with dissent and tension.[10]

Interpreting *The Triumph of Peace* with its palimpsest of purposes and multiple transactions presents particular problems. Complicated by a collective commissioning process and its effective co-production by the court and the legal colleges, an unusually rich but not always coherent archive attests its commission, preparation, and reception.[11] Thus Bulstrode Whitelocke's *three* accounts of his central role in the creation of this masque, for example, depict public harmony but reveal private disputes, each narrative highlighting slightly different points of controversy.[12] In his unpublished and near contemporaneous manuscript *Diary* Whitelocke records sharp disputes with Sir Henry Vane, the comptroller of the household, that necessitated the Lord Chamberlain's intervention.[13] The longer 'Annales' amplifies the diary's account of the fractious tussle over who would manage all aspects of the masque detailing Vane's provocative and 'scornful slighting way of expressing himself', and his 'great pride as parts'.[14] In contrast, although the *Memorials of the English Affairs* (1682) places the masque alongside the reissue of *The Book of Sports* which gave 'great distast' to many, Whitelocke is more concerned to evoke 'the outward and visible splendid testimony' of legal loyalism.[15] This printed version omits any mention of actual disputes, and substitutes his famous claim that Shirley's antimasques were means by which 'an Information was covertly given to the King, of the unfitness and ridiculousness of these Projects against the Law'.[16]

Although critics and historians have expressed some scepticism about the rather obvious nature of the 'covertly given' message, recent interpretations have recognised that, even if designed to affirm the lawyers' loyalty, Shirley's masque also articulates differences between proper and improper monopolies.[17] This chapter expands this interpretation and draws on Whitelocke's *Diary* and the 'Annales' to explore how key aspects of the performance, design, and main fiction of *The Triumph of Peace* embodied a collective and civic culture antithetical to court culture. Concentration on Shirley's antimasques as the main vehicle of critique has obscured how masque and procession and were differentiated from court culture and politics in fundamental ways. Equally, Whitelocke's printed *Memorials*, which echoes the public evocations of consensus found in many Caroline texts, contrasts with the deep disagreements evidenced in his unpublished diary and in other contemporaneous documents, thus illuminating the more fraught transactions and fissiparous climate of Caroline masque-making.

Key aspects of *The Triumph of Peace* dispute the premises of the re-launch of Charles I's rule.[18] As John Peacock has shown, Aurelian Townshend's *Albion's Triumph* (1632) generates a new imperial imagery for Charles I rooted in moral rather than military triumph, making its 'triumphant' Peace a product of 'self-mastery' and good governance.[19] Shirley's *The Triumph of Peace* rejects this royal reading of the origins and nature of Peace, and reasserts the importance of military engagement, its civic and collective notion of activist pacifism at odds with Townshend's personalised emphasis. *The Triumph of Peace* questions how peace might be achieved, differs over the nature of that peace, accentuates the role of law in peace-making, and articulates a markedly Protestant reading of the road to peace. The elaborate procession enacts a contest over space and legal rights that is then expounded in the text.[20] The appropriation of processional routes associated with civic ritual, and the King's own processional response before the second performance, apparently embody reciprocity and a balance of jurisdictions, but they also assert the rights of the city and the alignment of the lawyers with them.[21]

Where earlier Jacobean masques appropriated and absorbed languages from beyond the court, utilising the nostalgic recreation of the Jonsonian masque, Shirley places the lawyers as purveyors of appropriately voiced counsel against the rougher voices of criticism. It is no coincidence that this masque attracted such extensive contemporary commentary, and prompted such a widespread dissemination of the text and a range of secondary texts. These reveal the gravity of the issues involved, illuminating how masques might reach beyond Whitehall and inform political debate. *The Triumph of Peace* speaks out against the privatised sense of virtue and questions royal pacifism, finding instead an activist and militant pacifism rooted in collective and civic institutions.

'There are two masques in hand': dates and occasions

The claim that *The Triumph of Peace* was 'for the variety of the shows, and richness of the habits, the most magnificent that hath been brought to Court in our time' (782–4) is borne out by the occasion. The massive pre-performance procession in which the masquers progressed from Hatton House at Ely Place (the rehearsal rooms) to the Whitehall Tiltyard, was carefully recounted in a masque-book which may itself have been printed in as many as three thousand copies.[22] The masque-text shows the elaboration and comic facility of the antimasques, envisaging a gracefully executed masque filled with magical scenic effects, supported by substantial musical forces.[23] Afterwards, paratextual commentaries in poems, pamphlets, and a ballad, supplemented the knowledge of the event, and the masque is the subject of widespread commentary in provincial newsletters, even appearing on a Cambridgeshire tombstone.[24]

The Triumph of Peace opened with twelve antimasques. The first of these, presented by Opinion and Confidence, and conjured up by Fancy and his companions Laughter and Jollity in the search for amusing and innovative entertainment to satisfy the company (which includes Opinion's wife, Lady Novelty, and Admiration), expresses the benefits of peace, such as 'good fellowship' (296).[25] As the numerous danced antimasques interspersed with the presenters' commentary progress, the ill-effects of peace seen in the excessive latitude given to Fancy, manifest themselves. The grotesque antimasques, part drawn 'out of Rabelais' (370), provided a brilliant conspectus of the types of folly, including nymphs and satyrs, a troupe of dancing birds led by an owl, fabulous dotterels and their would-be catchers, and a 'Fantastic adventurer' (453), or knight, who tilts at a windmill. The most remarkable depicts six projectors with bizarrely improbable projects, such as a jockey with a mechanical bridle that harnesses his horse's breath to cool the beast and so prolong its freshness, or the scuba-diving 'water-rat' who proposes to walk underwater using bellows (370–5). Each projector dances to express his nature and was attired in wonderfully eccentric and symbolic costumes: the 'scholastic' projector who plans to boil beef using a lamp wore 'a furnace on his head' (52).[26]

These fantastical projectors with their grotesque dances and outlandish proposals threaten to continue unabated until 'strains' of celestial music interrupt and 'Fancy and the rest go off fearfully' (483). As the masque of the Hours, Peace, Law and Justice descend from the clouds in golden chariots, their musical dialogues celebrate the benefits of Peace, famously insisting that true peace is defined when Law and Peace 'flourish but together' and 'The world shall give prerogative to neither' (540–1). Shirley's dramatisation of the classical myth of the return of the Golden Age and the goddess Astraea, here named as Justice, echoes both Ovidian and Virgilian accounts: this new golden world is more perfect than its classical antecedent. Here, Astraea is blind, and therefore impartial, due to the virtue of the monarchs. The masque then turns to praise Charles and Henrietta Maria in a series of large-scale musical odes, and the masquers, the Sons of Peace, appear in their 'theatre' (604) or bower, introduced by Genius, to dance their entry.

Before the revels can proceed the masque is interrupted by the entry of the masque-makers, craftsmen responsible for the machinery, scenery, and props, accompanied by a 'great noise and confusion of voices' (669).[27] These workmen, who had hoped to see the performance accompanied by their wives, have been prevented by the recently introduced and more stringent regulations to exclude unsuitable spectators from court, and they fight their way into the hall and tumble onto the stage. Aware they are in the wrong place at the wrong time, and in danger of being jeered at, their leader, a tailor, proposes they should pretend to be another antimasque and so they 'dance a figary themselves' (706) to persuade the audience that they really are part of the masque and so escape. The delayed revels were finally danced, and the masquers were encouraged in song to 'clear [their] manly faces' (722). Then a final scene change offered 'a plain champaign' over which, accompanied by a 'great vapour' that enveloped the scene, Amphiluche, 'that glimpse of light' that warns of daybreak appears (731–45), and the masquers are called away by a chorus of 'other voices' (758) as Amphiluche re-ascends and the scene 'closeth' (781).

Even amidst the widespread praise that greeted *The Triumph of Peace*, contemporary reports suggest some unease about the opulent scale of the production. Several commentators noted the unfortunate contrast between a cash-strapped crown and the wealthy lawyers.[28] Among the positive contemporary reporters, the lawyer and masquer Justinian Pagitt commented:

> I have sent you a book of our Masque which was presented on munday last with much applause and commendation from the K and Queene and all the spectators . . . And [the King] being much pleased and taken with the sight hath sent us to ride againe on Tuesday next to Merchant Taylors' Hall in the same manner as we rode to Whitehall. Sir Henry Vane, and other great travellers say they never saw such a sight in any part of the world.[29]

While Pagitt conjures an image of cultural harmony in the Caroline polity and the interplay of gifts freely given and graciously received, other evidence presents a more equivocal consensus. Sir Henry Vane, as Whitelocke's *Diary* shows, had in fact obstructed the masque's creation and first performance. The second performance at Merchant Taylors' Hall on 13 February, attributed to royal 'applause and commendation', was coloured by the after-effects of serious confrontations between the mayor and the King.[30] Despite the subtle oscillations of dispute and conciliation in the creative process and the rituals of honour and deference implied in the 'royal negotiation' over the second staging, these manoeuvrings cannot disguise the disputes about belief and, ultimately, principle which underpinned *both* stagings of this masque.

The most controversial aspect of this masque was, undoubtedly, its proposed initial performance date which enmeshed the masque in three interwoven religious conflicts that had emerged in the late 1620s: the promulgation of *The Book of Sports*, sabbatarian observance, and the elaboration of celebratory rituals on key feast days. Several sources show that although *The Triumph of Peace* was staged at Whitehall on 3 February 1634 it had originally been scheduled for 2 February. The Dorchester diarist William Whiteway reported that

> This masque should have been danced on Candlemas day which was Sunday, to countenance the King's book, but at the request of the Gentlemen of the Inns of Court, as it was thought, it was put off till Monday.[31]

Neither Whitelocke's published account nor the *Diary* mention this changed date, although both attribute the masque to a refutation of

Prynne's views, furnishing – especially in the *Memorials* – an impression of loyalty and service balanced by appropriate criticism.[32] In contrast, Whiteway situates *The Triumph of Peace* against not only the controversial questions of *The Book of Sports* and sabbatarian observance but also draws attention to its connection to one of the 'hotspots' of the Caroline church calendar, Candlemas Day, the 'purification', dedicated to the Virgin Mary.[33] Exacerbated by the Queen's intensive involvement in Marian cults, the reissue of *The Book of Sports* (1633), and the Laudian insistence on the ritual calendar, such festal dates focused Protestant concerns over the direction of Anglican worship.[34] Erica Veevers has pointed out the connections between William Davenant's *Luminalia* (1637) and Laud's belated attempts to regulate the newly confident Catholic community around Henrietta Maria, drawing attention, in particular, to the use of light imagery. Parallel images, used in an entirely different fashion, can also be traced in the earlier *The Triumph of Peace*.[35] Indeed, some later commentators recognised the religious resonance of Shirley's masque: one noted how 'this month may be said to have had two Candlemas nights'.[36]

The original performance date was doubly marked as a feast day and as a Sunday. In *Histriomastix*, Prynne classified Candlemas as 'one of these prophane abominations' created when 'Pagan holy-dayes were metamorphosed into Christian' and specifically associated its celebration with 'Stage-Playes, Masques and all other Ethicke sports'.[37] Whiteway's *Diary*, indeed, clearly recognises that the original date raised the question of sabbatarian observance by noting that at some point a Sunday performance designed to conform with *The Book of Sports* ('countenance the king's book') had been agreed.[38] Given that the masque had, at least in part, been designed 'to manifest the difference of their [the Inns'] opinion from Mr Prynne's new learning', the acceptance of a Sunday performance, castigated in *Histriomastix* as an idolatrous replacement of proper worship, would indeed 'countenance' *The Book of Sports*.[39] But the masque may also, in its use of Candlemas imagery, seek to differentiate the Inns from Prynne's earlier attacks on John Cosin's *Private Devotions* (1628) for their Marian content, paying particular attention to the 'popish' and even 'pagan' practice of lighting candles 'on Candlemas Day as if the God of light had need of light and tapers to behold his blind and dark devotions'.[40]

Although for others of strict views, this feast was tainted with irredeemably popish ceremonial, John Donne, who preached two Candlemas sermons during his clerical years, argued that such feasts may be 'good in the Institution' but might 'grow ill in their practice'.[41] The use of Candlemas in *The Triumph of Peace* not only amended the 'practice' of the feast, but also accentuated significant aspects of Candlemas that were amenable to a more radical interpretation and its liturgical texts highlighted the role of law.[42] Alongside the feast's purificatory and regenerative associations, and the advocacy of communal unity and charity, the lessons for the day commanded observance of the law and the importance of justice: 'order the world according to equity and righteousness, and execute judgement with an upright heart.'[43] Such ideas, consonant with the masque's fiction and its legal auspices, assert the importance of righteousness and divine wisdom in judgement. Drawn from The Wisdom of Solomon, a text closely associated with the King's father, the lesson advances the role of divinely guided justice among 'the children of men', giving a religious inflection to a central Caroline iconographic trope of the monarchs as parents of the nation.[44] The Wisdom of Solomon furthermore presents the centrality of a divinely inspired justice and the transitoriness of the human ('the thoughts of mortal men are miserable, and our devices are but uncertain'), and crucially Wisdom, 12.14, sets the judgements of the righteous above 'king or tyrant'. [45]

The sensitivity of this day cannot be overstated. Having been chosen by Charles I for his coronation (2 February 1626), the feast was marked by particularly elaborate ceremonial in the royal chapel.[46] In 1634, the selection of Candlemas Day would have combined the debates about church ceremonial with earlier controversies about the coronation date and oath when questions were raised as to how far the King was bound to obey pre-existing laws or how far it was an oath only to God. The concern that the coronation and its surrounding ceremonial had provoked rankled enough in some circles for it to be revived at Laud's trial in 1644, and even in 1634 in the context of a legal entertainment, with its precise discussion of rights and responsibilities, its invocation was pointed if not provocative.[47] The choice of such a date can reasonably be seen as challenging the King on the very day he had chosen to mark his purified and sacralised sense of monarchy with a very different interpretation of the rights of monarchy in relation to the law.[48]

The controversial potential in Candlemas is evident in the 1626, 1628, and 1637 debates over the feast. Prynne's associate, Henry Burton, complained during a Gunpowder Day sermon in 1636 that its 'capers and candles' hindered spiritual illumination bringing 'spiritual darkness upon men's souls, by shutting out the ancient morning prayers', while Donne explicated the feast as less about the ritualistic candlelight than concerned with the personal light of witness: 'Let your light shine forth before man'.[49] Donne's emphasis upon public witness contrasts Catholic candles and Protestant torches: 'as your lights are Torches, and not pretty Candles, and your Torches better than other Torches so he may be a larger example to others'.[50] Not only does the language of light suffuse *The Triumph of Peace*, the torchlit journey from Holborn to the Banqueting House acquires fresh, and potentially less conformable, significances. The torchbearers offer a public and communal witness of Protestant faith excelling the privatised and superstitious devotions of Catholicism.

The public witness found in Candlemas imagery is invoked throughout Shirley's masque but especially when Genius, here cast as a winged 'angelical person', presents the masquers after 'The Scene is changed' to reveal the masquers 'sitting on the ascent of an hill' (603). Genius summons the 'clearest light' (634), treasured by those 'That love good for itself' (637):

> No foreign persons I make known
> But here present you with your own,
> The children of your reign, not blood;
> Of age, when they are understood,
> Not seen by faction or owl's sight,
> Whose trouble is the clearest light . . . (630–5)[51]

Against the court masque's instant illuminations, Genius outlines a different, spiritual enlightenment in which those who see aright, in 'the clearest light' (635), recognise the masquers as the true and manly children of the reign, something 'not seen by faction or owl's sight' (634).[52] The speech not only establishes those who fail to see the virtue of the young lawyers (by implication the very courtiers who criticised their masque) as afflicted by false forms of vision, but their 'trouble' with 'clearest light' suggests a wider spiritual ignorance. The moment differs from the illuminated masque-landscapes of 'bright and glorious palace' or 'glorious bower' often revealed at this highpoint of scenic transformation.[53] Such 'scene[s] of light' embody the royal wisdom and power at the heart of the masque, but Shirley's 'delicious arbour' (604), introduced by a Genius who is not simply a figuration of national place, but also a symbol of the masque-values and their origin in the Inns of Court, offers 'gracious but not set form' (611).[54] Usually Genius carried either a branch or sometimes a cornucopia, but here the 'white staff' marks his role in marshaling the masque, implying its orderliness even without following 'set form'.[55]

The scene with its 'sky beyond' (609) suggests enlightenment glimpsed but not yet achieved.[56] Thus the masque's closing section moderates between the different readings of light with the appearance of 'the figure that ends it all', Amphiluche ('morning twilight').[57] Enlarging upon biblical tropes that associated Christ with spiritual enlightenment, Protestant writers had accentuated the apocalyptic and revelatory implications of the image, especially by stressing the significance of the woman clothed in light and then exiled to the wilderness as a figure for the tribulations of the Protestant reformation.[58] Sceptics about the Caroline policy towards the church were already using this trope and its more radical implications to represent their alienation from the Laudian regime. Dawn could easily come to stand for the Protestant hope of a new reformation that would overthrow the false reformation (as they saw it) enacted by Laud. Spenserian poets such as Phineas Fletcher proclaimed: 'Tomorrow shall ye feast in pastures new, / And with the rising sun banquet on pearled dew'.[59]

Shirley's dawn begins in a strikingly martial vein: her 'unwelcome light' will 'invade' Night's sphere, 'Proclaiming wars / To Cynthia'. Amphiluche's language conflicts with the peaceful and magical atmosphere invoked in the preceding scene-change (731–8), but her militancy is then softened by 'other voices' who, singing, summon the masquers from the revels so that conflict is avoided as the masquers are urged to 'Retire, retire to your own place' (775). Besides gracefully signalling the masque's end, the final song urges retreat rather than engagement. It turns the 'active sports' (766) into the accompaniments of night and the masque-world to be superseded by prayers that the monarchs' 'story' will be filled with 'the glory / Of great and good' (778–9). This invocation of a continued peace and a retirement to 'own place' modifies the possible apocalyptic implication of the light and dawn, although it does not entirely erase their possible existence. Shirley's choice of the figure of Amphiluche is striking here: she is not goddess of the dawn (Aurora), but rather the 'glimpses of light' hinting that dawn is about to arrive.[60]

At first glance the choice of such a controversial feast as Candlemas seems explosive, yet the dual nature of the religious texts for the feast balances ideas of regeneration and purification. Regeneration implies the reconciliation of grievances and difficulties in the creation of a new order; purification retains the implicit hope for radical change that might satisfy the more radical members of the legal community.[61]

Donne's Candlemas sermon reconfigures the controversial feast, so that its potentially idolatrous forms are redirected in a more correct (Protestant) form. Shirley undertakes the same with the masque, eschewing the more radical calls for the reformation of the masque seen in the 1630s, but instead reshaping it to offer a better tool of public witness. As the sermon moves from individual reformation to the collective representation of 'improvement', so that 'your lights are Torches . . . and your Torches better than other Torches', so the masque looks towards collective and public culture.[62] This spectrum of meanings, and the balanced use of the double-aspected feast, poises the masque between the court and the Inns of Court, but also allows the occasion with its mixture of royal and other meanings to articulate a powerful critique of the Caroline polity without producing conflict. Candlemas, as the occasion, becomes not only the subject of the masque but a demonstration of its means. It is not too far-fetched to suggest that the antimasque enacts purification and the masque presents regeneration.[63]

It is not that this masque starts in controversy and ends in consensus, or simply follows the post-hoc recasting of conflict into consensus when recalling the engagement in earlier disputes has become inopportune. Instead, the masque suggests that consensus is neither straightforward nor stable. Shirley inflects the Caroline trope of 'halcyon days' to present security and stability, surrounded by threat, but also as fragile and temporary as a nest built on waves and in the lull between storms. This Candlemas consensus achieves a delicate balance between the lawyers and the court, but by employing language and terms already espoused by the court, creates a space for a different view of the culture of peace. These emerge in the vision of chivalry presented in the masque.

Pacific pursuits and civic chivalry: the first performance

The recasting of the light imagery associated with Candlemas Day created an alternate, more clearly Protestant version of the feast that permeates *The Triumph of Peace*. Such radical interventions and the potential for conflict enshrined in the date of the masque show how, in a highly reflexive masquing tradition, inflections of small aspects of form, structure, topic, and even performance style, redirect emphases and meanings. This intensified intertextuality, heightened by the circumstances of this particular production, allows *The Triumph of Peace* to differentiate itself from the court and its entertainments. Commenting directly on the King's most recent masque, Townshend's

Albion's Triumph (1632), the 'triumphal' element responds to the royal masque, but the paradox of its formation – a military celebration of peace – offers a complex understanding of the nature of peace and how it might be achieved.

In 1632 Townshend had closed his masque with a vision of Innocency, Justice, Religion, Affection to the Country, and Concord each offering 'freely to impart / Such favours as we can afford' so that Plenty may 'Proteus-like appear / Varying your pleasures every year'.[64] The stress on a nation 'fruitful every way' is demonstrated in the olive garlands and palm leaves that the 'deities' carry to replace the 'bay' of victory.[65] The vision of ultimate and surpassing plenitude is not so much the Golden Age restored as reconceptualised. It culminates in the 'Valediction' to the royal couple 'Hymens Twin the MARY-CHARLES' whose virtue ensures that the island becomes 'the Halcions nest'.[66] Although this key image of Caroline peace was frequently used, even courtiers like Thomas Carew allowed its ambivalence to sound.[67] In his case, the image conveys the poetic and political emasculation of the country; in Shirley's case, the image marks a different, more military response to the fragile peace.

The moral rather than military triumph offered in *Albion's Triumph*, the vision of plenty created by royal bounty and, particularly, the personalised virtue eulogised in the masque are modified or corrected throughout *The Triumph of Peace*. In contrast to the proscenium arch for *Albion's Triumph*, which had been dominated by the royal coat-of-arms and the imperial crown, *The Triumph of Peace* proscenium design stresses another dimension to the pacific rhetoric that dominates the Caroline period. Shirley's description includes not only a sharp-sighted eye and a yoke (symbol of agriculture), but identifies the two flanking figures that stood on pedestals as Minos and Numa (lines 132–49).[68] Renowned as law-givers and peace-bringers both men were, significantly, also warriors. Numa's reign was, in some classical sources, seen as a breathing space and preparation for war. Indeed, Plutarch's *Moralia* even employs the image of the halcyon to evoke the temporary peace of his reign. Numa's peace allowed development for conflict and, especially, for the training of the young in war: 'the people trained, like an athlete, for forty-three years, in order to produce a force capable of confronting its later adversaries'.[69] Roman sources argued that Numa's reign resulted in four hundred and eighty years of military conquest, so that although the masque apparently conforms with royal idealisations of peace, its allusion to Numa's Golden Age reign as the training period before war colours its central conceit.

The process of differentiation extends to the scenography. In particular, the main set, the forum or piazza of peace, depicts a public collective space, employed both as a 'place of negotiation, or marchandising', as well as to dispense justice.[70] Interestingly, the sources of Jones' designs have been traced to several engravings by Jacques Callot, and the overall effect is one of 'Italianate vernacular quality' reshaped by an austere classicism.[71] These differences between the settings of the masques may reflect the linkage between genre and class in early modern thought as vernacular and lower classical orders were deemed suitable for the gentry, but these designs also create spaces for *The Triumph of Peace* differentiated from the palatial spaces of the Caroline masque and outline a distinctive identity for the Inns of Court.

This austere vernacular style contrasts with the designs for *Albion's Triumph* where a Roman atrium and amphitheatre, like many of the King's masques of the period, echo Augustan rather than republican Rome. The contrast between the atrium and the 'piazza or forum' extends to their uses as the atrium represents the central space of a royal palace. Its design alludes to aristocratic collecting practices, and its ranges of statues echo the depictions of Arundel's statuary gallery, while the frieze is based on marbles copied from the earl's collection.[72] This contrast between the two masques continues in the final settings, for where the main masque in *Albion's Triumph* had been framed by the prospect of London dominated by Whitehall Palace, *The Triumph of Peace* was set on the 'ascent of a hill cut out like the degrees of a theatre' and surrounded by 'a delicious arbour' (lines 603–4), perhaps to recall the vision of the Heroes offered in Middleton's earlier *Inner Temple Masque* (1619), rather than the imperial temple and grove conjured up in *Albion's Triumph*.[73]

The arbour in *The Triumph of Peace* modifies the pastoral language often associated with the monarchy. In *Albion's Triumph* the return of Peace was marked by unsurpassed Plenty, but in *The Triumph of Peace* the titular deity requires the operations of Law and Justice to 'flourish' (540) and create 'the paradise of love' (596) around the King and Queen. Although the masque echoes the image of the 'olive' that 'at once bloom and bear' from the royal masque, the plenty offered in Shirley's masque is less exuberant and all-encompassing and, crucially, based on the co-operation of the three deities. In contrast to the olive that magically both blooms and fruits 'at once', this plenty is associated with images of labour:

> Irene enters like a perfum'd spring,
> Eunomia ripens every thing,
> And in the golden harvest leaves
> To every sickle his own sheaves. (541–4)

This new age, based upon the 'sickle' and just distribution ('his own sheaves'), counters the unforced plenty of the royal masques which draw, in part, on Ovidian versions of the Golden Age where law was unnecessary (and, indeed, associated with the Iron Age). Although the masque alludes to other depictions of the Golden Age, and the title page quotes Virgil's *Eclogues*, the overarching conception is a georgic one: the proscenium is graced by a 'golden yoke'.[74]

This yoke carries further symbolic associations. Linked to the Hours as agricultural deities, the yoke also alludes to the February performance date which was widely associated with ploughing. So in Spenser's 'Mutabilitie' 'cold February' is characterised with austerity and fast (symbolised by his astrological sign Pisces) and

> yet had he by his side
> His plough and harnesse fit to till the ground
> And tooles to prune the trees, before the pride
> Of hasting Prime did make them burgein round.[75]

The relation of February not simply to labour but to the work of regulation appears to be echoed in the masque's view of Peace as 'wild' without Law. Although Shirley's peace recalls Caroline idealisation of royal reform, it is attached to Law rather than royal will.

Shirley's emphasis upon natural justice imagined in the eternal spring found at the return to the Golden Age when spring and harvest will co-exist continually ('at once bloom and bear'), is enacted as Irene (spring) and Eunomia (autumn) sing together. Shirley's version, however, draws upon the associations of Autumn, and particularly harvest and September, with justice. Indeed, the 'mutabilitie cantos' at the end of *The Faerie Queene*, which share a common source with Shirley's text in Ovid's *Fasti*, are one of the classic expressions of this idea:

> Next him, September marched eeke on foote;
> Yet was he heavy laden with the spoyle

> Of haruests riches, which he made his boot,
> And him enricht with bounty of the soyle:
> In his one hand, as fit for haruests toyle,
> He held a knife-hook; and in th'other hand
> A paire of weights, with which he did assoyle
> Both more and lesse, where it in doubt did stand,
> And equall gaue to each as Iustice duly scann'd.
> (*The Faerie Queene*, 7.7.38)

In this stanza the second half of the month is linked to Libra, and the 'paire of weights' suggests Justice's scales. This develops the point begun in the preceding stanza where Spenser had associated August with Virgo (another version of Astraea/Justice), and the 'eares of corne' with which she was crowned make her a symbol of fruitfulness. The labour of harvest (the 'knife-hook') leads to the 'equall' distribution.[76]

Shirley's reworking of this common association of Justice with harvest and just distribution lacks the automatic plenitude of royal pastoral, but it also eschews the more radical possibilities of the return of the absent god which might have recalled the apocalyptic harvest of Revelations.[77] Nonetheless, the emphasis upon the role of labour in the production of plenty echoes the later intervention of the masque-makers. In *The Triumph of Peace* the appearance of Justice, Law, and Peace are still attributed to 'Themis' and 'Jove', figures for the King and Queen, but the masque advances a view of co-operation and labour to maintain 'The paradise of love' that differentiates it from Townshend's mystical bounty. Even if the presence of the monarchs allows Dice to regain her sight, the benefits of peace do not magically arrive through the personal virtue of the sovereigns; it is a collective work maintained 'but together'.

The interplay here between genres as a way of answering the royal interpretation of peace suggests the nuanced responsiveness of the text to royal ideology. Both Inns of Court and court might agree on peace, on its subsequent prosperity, but *The Triumph of Peace* traces a very different disposition within peace which argues for the primacy of law and the just distribution of plenitude. The neatness of the dialogue stems from how the response is delivered – precisely – in a tactful manner that utilises the vocabulary and imagery of the court but re-inflected to new ends.

This nuanced difference between the monarch and masquers continues in the revelation of the masquers which appropriates the Roman history used by the court to advance a different view of the purpose of military preparation. Most forcefully expressed in the explicatory speech offered by Genius at the appearance of the masquers, Shirley hints that, like the children of Numa in Roman mythology, these young men – conspicuously 'Of age' – might seek a more active and military future. The divergence from Caroline court masques continues with the conspicuously weaponless sons of Peace, Law, and Justice, located as 'children' of the King's 'reign', who are not, as the verses insist, comparable to aristocratic infant masquers often found in Caroline masques. As Barbara Ravelhofer has pointed out, aristocratic child dancers, used as symbols of the reformative prospects of Caroline culture, enacted the royal couple's role as national parents.[78] Significantly, although Shirley pays homage to the parental rhetoric of royal masques, the Inns of Court masquers are 'Of age'. The masque rejects the 'faction or owl's sight' that fails to see, and certainly does not 'understand', their 'virtue'. While they have 'no form, no sun, no shade' (639) except that offered by the King, locating their virtue within Caroline ideology, the speech equally distances itself. Unlike in other masques Genius offers 'no foreign persons', stressing the Englishness of the sons of Peace against the classical and other deities who danced in earlier Caroline masques, while the resolutely domestic setting contrasted with their exotic locations. Moreover, the intensely religious language of the speech – the masquers will 'tower to Heaven' – echoes the sacralism surrounding the Caroline monarchy, but carefully distinguishes obedience to the monarch from divine command: monarchy is only obeyed 'next' the 'blessedness' of heaven (642). So while the masquers offer 'joyful tribute', the festivities are balanced by a nuanced awareness of the difference between the 'children' of the 'reign' and the parent-king.

Although military preparedness remained a major element of royal policy in the 1630s with the strengthening of local militias, the development of the royal chivalric cult of the Order of the Garter had also reduced some of the actively military elements in Caroline court culture.[79] As is well known Charles reshaped the Garter rituals to emphasis their devotional aspects and augmented the ceremonial aspects of the installations and feasts; they were also removed to Windsor Castle from London.[80] Under Charles, the Garter came to symbolise 'manliness and chivalry, chastity, piety, and self-regulation, honour and hierarchy, order and propriety', values echoed in *Albion's Triumph*.[81] Interestingly, Elias Ashmole commented on the augmented Garter ceremonial in terms of the Roman triumph:

> We think it not amiss in speaking of processions to divide them into military, civil and ecclesiastical: under the military may be best

comprehended Triumphs, and transactions of the Roman knights; under the civil, the pompous entries of cavalcades of Princes, into or through any great city; and the ecclesiastical are those so generally called wherein the Church proceeds upon a solemn account of supplication or thanksgiving . . .[82]

Caroline Garter ceremonial presents a fusion of 'secular and ecclesiastical triumph' and blends restrained militarism, religiosity and order. In *Albion's Triumph*, its personalised and even privatised virtue is self-mastery rather than military engagement.

Military activity was not solely the preserve of the aristocracy and the 'Directive' added to the reissued *Book of Sports* (October 1633) included 'manlike and lawfull Exercises' among the more peaceful country sports also to be encouraged.[83] Cities such as London had seen a marked development of civic military training focused on the Artillery Garden (near Moorfields) where 'young scholars and other youth . . . of their own warlike dispositions . . . practiced all the points of war which they had seen their elders teach'.[84] On a practical level these urban companies which appeared across England provided basic military training, but on another level they also propagated the figure of the Christian solider defined by both the 'spiritual arms' borne against the 'enemies of your salvation' and the 'material arms' carried against foreign foes, and for whom 'good' or 'virtue' were the defining characteristics of chivalry rather than birth and honour.[85] These values were inculcated through regular musters, often accompanied by a sermon, and many of these tracts espoused a militant version of Protestantism, including support for Elizabeth of Bohemia and intervention in the continental wars of religion.[86] Considerable evidence exists of a strain of 'civic chivalry' which celebrated the heroic qualities of those usually excluded from aristocratic honour and heroism.

Whereas the royal cult of St George and the Garter stressed piety and self-control, the exercises practised by the citizen-soldiers were more clearly a preparation for war.[87] In 1638 the Artillery Company staged William Barriffe's *Mars His Triumph*, an entertainment for which the only analogy is the modern military tattoo, in which a confrontation of Christian and Saracen troops was staged, accompanied by drums, music, and speeches.[88] Barriffe's text, which was addressed to the aldermen and 'the choice and best affected Citizens', recalls Roman military history, attributing their world-domination to military training and drawing the lesson that 'by neglecting discipline and the

Art Military, suffered it self to be crushed and over-trodden by every barbarous nation'.[89] Although dealing with the fall of Rome rather than with the beginning of its power as marked by Pompilius Numa's reign, *Mars His Triumph* suggests that the cost of peace is military preparedness.

Indeed, in a slightly earlier civic military text addressed to Sir Hugh Hammersley, Lord Mayor and 'Colonel of the Artillery Garden', Dekker had saluted the mayor and city sheriffs as 'praetor' and 'consul' and celebrated the involvement of the Artillery Garden militia in the 'praesentation of your triumphs on the day of your lordships' inauguration'.[90] Dekker's writing suggests the subtext that might lie behind the civic militarism of *The Triumph of Peace* when he compares Rome and London as equal for the 'fame' of their sons 'decked with bays', and questions:

> But, above the rest, why should not I,
> The fames sing of our twice *Decemviri*,
> Our twenty City Captains . . . [91]

The evocation of a City-led national force modelled on Roman forms with a distinctly militant Protestant character illustrates the culture Shirley's masque draws upon: civic, collective, nationalist, and Protestant. Dekker's enthusiasm for a national defence force was matched by many in the 1630s, and the opening of Genius' speech that offers 'No foreign persons' may echo these interests in English military training against the employment of foreign mercenaries. Such views may not have been entirely welcome to the Caroline authorities, for although the early years of the reign had seen the development of the City and provincial militia companies, during the 1630s the membership declined, in part discouraged by the Crown's attempts to control the companies by asserting its right to nominate officers, as occurred in January 1634.[92]

Although these martial elements are most manifest in the procession (see below, pp. 197–9), at one stage military display was supposed to occupy a larger place in whole occasion. Certainly, George Garrard described the original plan for entertainment as 'a Masque and Barriers' which would have echoed the kind of entertainments last seen under Prince Henry and recalled the early, more martial hopes for Charles when Prince of Wales.[93] Some observers also noted not simply the glorious show but also the more belligerent elements, and Arundel, the Earl Marshall, praised the participants as 'brave cavallata'.[94]

One contemporary poem clearly relishes the military implications of *The Triumph of Peace*. 'Now did heaven's charioteer' enlarges on more militant elements of the processional triumph, depicted as the recreation of a lost heroic age:

> I was confident
> When first I saw this goodly regiment,
> All the glistering of this comely train,
> The silver age was now returned again . . . [95]

Rather than invoking the 'golden age' usually proposed in court masques, the poem's 'the silver age', puns not only on their predominantly silver costumes, but also suggests that the masquers may reverse the degeneration of the ages. The poem then rehearses a range of possible heroic comparisons, from the Greeks at the Olympic Games, to the Trojans, and culminates with the masquers as 'The flower of gentry, hope of chivalry'. Moving the locus of chivalric values away from court the writer concludes:

> These are the sons of Charles's peaceful reign,
> Whom yet if war's rude accents shall constrain
> To put on arms will quickly understand
> The laws of arms as well as of the land,
> And be as valiant in the midst of fight
> As they seemed glorious in the masque of night.

The poet has rewritten the Caroline images of national parenthood and peace, so that these sons are ready to fight 'if . . . constrained', making good the promises of martial virtue. The linkage of 'fight / night' points up the contrast between the promise of virtue in the nocturnal revels, perhaps glancing at the kind of heroism celebrated in the courteous chivalry of Caroline court masques such as *Albion's Triumph* and Carew's *Coelum Britannicum* (1634). Against the critics of civic chivalry the anonymous poet suggests how 'If war's rude accents . . . constrain', their preference for proper military action rather than the courtier's manners and images of warfare will help these would-be warriors be true 'sons' of the 'peaceful reign' as they will 'quickly understand' the needs of conflict. The poem offers a subtle rebuke to the requirements of courtesy and reconciliation, admitting that neither may be effective when 'rude war' intervenes.[96] The poem returns, too, to the heart of the debate over the nature of the Caroline peace embodied in the contemporary proverb: 'he who desires peace must prepare for war.'[97]

'Now did heaven's charioteer' provides evidence of how contemporary opinion beyond the masque's original community recognised some of the more sceptical elements of the text. Employing the self-same language of light ('glorious') found in *The Triumph of Peace*, the poem implies the distance between night-time visions of heroism and its actual achievement. This sense of distance and difficulty – the troubling of the smooth forms of the masque – can also be found beneath the adulatory surface of the commendations of the masque in contemporary newsletters. For example, there are some indications that the differences between courtiers and lawyers may have been more apparent to the contemporary audience as several contemporary documents hint at tensions around the danced elements. Thus when the courtier William Crofts wrote to the Earl of Newcastle of the 'great expectation' of 'a horse masque and a foot masque', he sneered how 'opinions [are] much divided which will prove the best', preferring the horse 'masque' as 'I think their horses will dance under them much better than they can when they are on their own legs.'[98] Among the lawyers, Thomas Coke wrote to his brother Sir John, that

> The emulation that will be between the Inns of Court men and the courtiers you may easily imagine. But my fear is that we shall give them just cause of jeering by reason of our weak performance. The four selected in our House . . . have not been at the dancing school above half a year, and can scarce dance one dance to any purpose, nor ever see any dance or mask at Court, neither know what belongs to it.[99]

Coke's letter, striking for its sense of the cultural difference between the court and the lawyers, echoes contemporary views declining festive culture at the Inns of Court. Although dancing lessons still formed an important part of the lawyer's extra-curricular activity, there are signs that during the 1620s, the all-male dancing which had characterised the legal communities was less practised.[100] Certainly, it took weeks of rehearsal to bring the dancers up to standard, and beyond the practical concern Coke conveys palpable social anxiety: competitive 'emulation' soon leads to 'jeering'.[101] Even, then, in the moments of reconciliation, such as when lawyers and courtiers combine in the revels (716–30), differences of class and perhaps performance would have remained clear, not only differentiating lawyers and courtiers, but also symbolising their distance.

The first staging of *The Triumph of Peace* shows how behind reconciliation and apparent consensus – at all levels of the performance including the process of its production – lie more disputatious situations. Shirley, with great dexterity, rewrites central parts of Caroline court myth and the understandings they represent, challenging the assumptions of the Caroline polity. This is most marked in the eruption of the workmen onto the stage, summoned by the Painter's injunction to his fellow scenery-makers to 'challenge a privilege' (694). His language not only returns to the economic questions of the projectors and monopolies in the antimasques, but also reshapes the whole masque (674–715), by insisting on the role of workmen in its creation. This 'new device' (709), produced by the craftsmen themselves, restates the right of the lower orders to be heard in comic but crucial legal terms: 'we are Christians in these clothes, and the King's subjects' (700–1).

'Not without some disgrace and distast to the citizens': the second performance, politeness and processions

If the first performance of *The Triumph of Peace* is strikingly explicit about the role of the city craftsmen in creating the masque and their grasp of their rights, the second staging of the masque at the Merchant Taylors' Hall on 13 February 1634 highlights issues about how monarchy and citizens interact, and also about the public presentation of the monarchs to the populace and the role of ceremony.

On one level, the citizens' decision to 'dance a figary' to get themselves offstage without being the object for further mirth (702–3, 705–6) rehearses some of the anxieties around the masque's performance expressed by the commentators on the lawyers' dancing skills.[102] Their dance instances the ways in which the lower classes, in fact, hold the labour and skill necessary 'in the works' (686) to understand how the masque should operate: 'the Masquers will do no feats as long as we are here' (705). In this sense they truly are 'a piece of the plot' (706). Their ordered and rational behaviour challenges the whole basis of the masque's hierarchies and exclusions and, as they dance their exit, they are supported by the musicians, the other great masque artisans, who fold them into the harmonic structures of the songs. Here, the mechanic forces underpinning the performance clearly shape the masque vision as much as the masquers, and their intuitive recognition of the need for a dance ('And the musicians but knew our mind now . . . Hark they are at it', 711–13) rescues the situation and restores order.

Unlike the silent 'dancing spirits of the pits' in the *Masque at Coleorton* (1618) or builders of *The Entertainment at Bolsover* (1634), these articulate lower orders are able to claim their legal rights of ownership ('privilege') and of freeborn men ('Christian's', 'King's subjects').[103] The contrast between the depiction of 'a great noise and confusion of voices within' (669), the offstage disorder that heralded their arrival, and their onstage appearance 'in these clothes', means their utterances cannot be typed as indecorous or as the unruly noisiness associated with dissent and libel.[104] Indeed, this aspect of Shirley's script must have seemed prescient given the disputes that arose with the City over the second performance which was mounted in the aftermath of the dispute between the soap-boilers and laundresses, who had been displaced by a new patented soap-making company. During this bitter disagreement, opponents of royal policy were cast as mere noise-makers and rebels.[105]

Although the second performance of *The Triumph of Peace* was rapturously received, like the first performance it was shadowed with controversy. On the surface it was preceded by polite coercion, deference, and even negotiation. Finet's diary places the impetus for the repeat with the King and Queen but Whitelocke reports 'an Intimation being given to the Lord Mayor of London' he complied with the hint and issued an invitation.[106] Considerable money and effort were expended, Shirley added a new speech, the procession from the Inns was repeated, and several elaborate feasts were prepared. Whitelocke claims 'this gave great contentment to their Majesties and no less to the citizens, especially the younger sort of them', and for the Court of Aldermen the royal visit demonstrated the 'extraordinary love and favour' of the Crown towards the City.[107]

The Aldermen's comments, however, were an expression of relief at this favour at 'this tyme when as many questions and great suits are depending between his Majesty and this city'. The harmony of this occasion barely covered the 'many questions and great suits' between City and King, and which would have been known to many participants and spectators of the second staging.[108] William Whiteway supplies more detail:

> This maske cost the actors 17000 pound and did so please the King, that he invited himselfe, the Queene and the Maskers to sup at the Lord Maiorrs, Sir Ralph freeman the 13 february. Where the Lord Maior spent 3000s to entertaine them, in pulling downe diverses houses between his house and Marchan-tailors Hall, and making a gallery for the King to pass through. The Kinge invited himselfe to the Lord Maiors, to make them amends, for the sharpe words he had lately given him, calling him old foole, for speaking in behalfe of the Sopeboilers and Laundresses of London. Which troubled him so that

he kept his bed a whole moneth after it, and was like to dy, had not the Kings message revived him.[109]

In fact, as George Garrard makes clear, the Mayor was summoned to the 'board' of the Privy Council where his brother-in-law, the Lord Privy Seal, 'very sharply' gave him a 'shrewd reprimand for his pusillanimity being afraid of a troop of women that clamourously petitioned against the new soap'. One of the 'poor women out of Southwark' was summoned and dressed down, some workers were charged in Star Chamber and imprisoned, and these 'disordered clamours' from 'insolent and contemptuous persons' were forbidden.[110]

This tense climate provides an interesting counterpoint to Whitelocke's silence on the soapmakers' dispute, while the uncomfortable negotiations illustrate how the Caroline rhetorics of reconciliation and consensus impelled individuals towards agreement that often masked unresolved disputes. Written from the standpoint of the master of ceremonies at court, Finet stresses the ceremonial surrounding the masque and the deference expected and, in effect, exacted from the City.[111] In fact, these demonstrations of civic 'loyalty' required the presentation of two purses containing £1,000 each of gold. Finet reports that 'this golden way being disliked' the King intimated via the Lord Chamberlain that he would prefer a specific diamond. This second choice of gift, a 26 carat diamond costing £4,000, outweighing the total cost of the whole masque to the Inns of Court, must be added to the £5,300 spent on the preparations for the masque by the City.[112] Significantly, however, although Finet concludes his narrative with a 'resolution' that echoes Caroline images of harmony he notes that the King's first refusal of the gift was a 'disgrace' to the citizens – presumably as they had failed to anticipate the royal desires – and that the new gift only delivered days later caused them 'some distaste'.[113]

In these circumstances of coercion by the Crown, it is somewhat surprising to discover that the second staging of *The Triumph of Peace* occasioned one of the major appearances of the King and Queen in public. On this civic occasion, the King and Queen appeared in 'an open chariot' in 'the full aspect' of the aldermen, their wives and 'many others of the Chiefe Citizens men and women'.[114] Indeed, the additional ceremony for the occasion included the King and Queen's entry into the City where they were greeted at Temple Bar by the 'captains of the city' and two hundred soldiers from the Artillery Garden, as well as the public walkway between the venue for the masque and the dinner.[115] Peter Heylyn's *Observations on the history of the reign of King Charles*

(1656) notes this was 'the first act of popularity which the King did all his reign, so it begat a high degree of affection towards him in the hearts of the citizens'.[116]

Heylyn's optimistic reading of the royal procession to the Lord Mayor's masque and feast illustrates how concern had developed about the failure of the Stuart monarchs to present themselves. The politics of public presentation had been a key issue in the 1633 progress to Scotland and Cavendish and Jonson's *Entertainment at Welbeck* can be seen as the advancement of an argument in favour of a return to an 'Elizabethan' popular monarchy.[117] Indeed, Cavendish's writings are filled with concerns over royal presentation and, writing to Prince Charles in 1638, he noted 'what preserves you Kings more than ceremony . . . for in all triumphs whatsoever or public showing yourself, you cannot put upon you too much king'.[118] Most discussions of Caroline royal journeys notice the abandonment of the public progress and its replacement with travel in closed coaches.[119] Momentarily, here in the capital, the King seems to have recognised the importance of creating public theatrical displays, although it is interesting to note that his gesture had been provoked by the actions of the Inns of Court.

The triumph was a contested form. It was not exclusively the property of the court, and as *Troia Nova Triumphans* (1611), *The Triumphs of Truth* (1613), or *The Triumphs of Honour and Industry* (1617) show, the triumphal form was much used in civic ritual. These collective civic events embodied city values that included civic participation, self-governance, and the public good, while their processional routes staked out areas of jurisdiction and authority. Their authority within political culture allows differentiation from court values but also serves to recall the orderliness of the city: the views they articulate are not simply the 'great noise and confusion of voices' from the clamorous lower orders. Despite this, in the 1630s there were factors that bound the triumph more closely to the court such as the purchase of Mantegna's *Triumphs of Caesar* which had just arrived in England.[120] As well as offering a graceful homage to the King's new acquisition, the title of the masque echoes other court events, notably *Love's Triumph Through Callipolis* (1631) and *Albion's Triumph* (1632), and the choice of triumphal form not only 'summed up' the court vogue, but 'fell into line' with royal iconography.[121]

Yet *Albion's Triumph* also contained one of the most directly critical moments of the Caroline masque, Townshend's figures of Publius and Platonicus debate the significance of the triumph and 'insinuate a scepticism about whether the images really do correspond to the values they are supposed to embody'.[122] For Platonicus the materials of the triumph are irrelevant, mere bodies that convey more significant souls:

> PUBLIUS: Albanactus Caesar from his sumptuous palace, through the high-streets of Albipolis rid triumphing, on a chariot made –
> PLATONICUS: Of wood, perhaps gilt, perhaps gold. But I will save you all those charges if you will go on to the persons and let the pageants alone.[123]

Momentarily, Platonicus sounds like the mountebank of Buckingham's running masque, offering economical means to hold court entertainments, but as his name suggests, he concentrates not on the material but on the ideal, and in dismissing the triumphal carcass he reveals the gap between what Martin Butler neatly describes as 'inner qualities' and 'strategic representations': the chariot is maybe 'Of wood, perhaps guilt, perhaps gold'.[124]

Platonicus may mean to dismiss the material dimension of triumphs but, in so doing, he effectively draws attention not just to the disjuncture between representation and its vehicle, and also to two of the fundamental elements of the triumph – cost and scale – that made triumphal form so double edged for the Caroline court. Triumphs were designed to be a display of material and physical conquest, of brute military force, of the destiny of Rome, and of the general or later emperor. Townshend may have sought to suggest that personalised and moral triumphs outstripped the physical form, but the speech also reveals the importance of 'Charges', the presentation of royal magnificence through the cost of the masque.

Although the Venetian ambassador (among others) attributed the King and Queen's 'particular gratification' at the masque to the procession, the triumph of the *Triumph of Peace*, the procession to Whitehall from Hatton House contrasted with the King's pasteboard procession.[125] All the accounts stress the scale and effect of this procession, and the Venetian ambassador noted the 'numerous, stately and glittering cavalcade' that 'by their dresses, liveries and devices, attracted a great crowd, exciting the curiosity and applause of all the people'.[126] The procession involved just under nine hundred people, including actors in their antimasque costumes, masquers, musicians, three hundred torchbearers and servants, and two hundred halberdiers.[127] At its first iteration the wall of the Tiltyard was breached to allow its passage and for the second masque performance the Lord Mayor was commanded to clean and order the streets, especially Aldersgate, to facilitate the passage of the parade.

The procession echoes that associated with Chapman's earlier *The Memorable Masque* (1613) staged by the Middle Temple and Lincoln's Inn. On that occasion, fifty footmen preceded an antimasque of baboons, the musicians, actors dressed as Indian priests, each mounted masquer accompanied by a torch-bearer, and followed by the three chariots and two hundred halberdiers.[128] But in contrast to these individual and 'fantastical' elements, Whitelocke's *Memorials* stresses not only that the triumphal chariots were carefully reconstructed after Roman antique models gleaned from 'some old Prints and Pictures extant of them', but that the whole organisational structure and ordering of the procession embodied collective rather than individual celebration.[129] Crucially, the position of each Inn's 'chariot' was decided by lot and each Inn supplied an equal number of gentlemen riders and masquers. Even within the chariots, Whitelocke stresses that the chariots' 'seats . . . were made of an Oval form in the back end of the chariot, so that there was no precedence in them, and that the faces of all that sate in it might be seen together'. Although the procession did not have the ceremonial heritage of City processions or comparable continental examples, such as the ducal processions in Venice, the purpose remained to embody the order and magnificence of the Inns. Indeed, the 'manner of the progression', which possibly encapsulates an early stage of the planning for the procession, stressed hierarchy (antimasque over masque, the gentlemen participants), and order (the central role of the Marshall). The procession was concluded by the Marshalls of London and their halberdiers, lending not only a suitably military air to the occasion, but also linking the Inns to the civic order.

In the event, according to Whitelocke, the Marshall headed the procession along with his men to enforce order, but it is interesting to note that some of the contemporary commentary afforded Thomas Dayrell a key military role.[130] Francis Lenton's *Inns of Court Annagramatist* (1634), issued to capitalise on the occasion and no doubt increase sales by naming and celebrating as many of the participants as possible, described him as the 'Martial Leader' and attributing his subsequent knighthood to the King's recognition of his 'Martiall spright'.[131] The knighthood is seen not solely in chivalric terms: '*Miles*, both knight and souldier signifies.'[132] While Lenton's work was undoubtedly opportunistic, his emphasis on the military aspect of the triumph does suggest how some contemporary witnesses viewed the occasion and seems carefully to distinguish between the 'knight' and the 'soldier', stressing that Dayrell's title was not simple ceremonial or chivalric in the terms of the reformed Garter, but attached to a proper military role.

The emphasis on loyal militarism pervades almost all aspects of *The Triumph of Peace*. Thus, the strict marshalling of the parade for the second performance was designed to manifest civic good governance, as the unruly and unsuitable were excluded, and those citizens permitted to watch were enjoined to good behaviour.[133] En route to the performance the monarchs were met 'at their entrance into the Lord Mayor's liberty at Temple Bar' by twenty 'captains of the city' and two hundred citizen-soldiers of the Artillery Garden, and the whole parade route was further protected by the presence of the citizen-householders who had been ordered to stand before their own doors armed with halberds as a symbol of the city's good order.[134]

Temple Bar was an obvious point to mark the boundaries and different but mutually supportive powers of city and monarch. As one of the standard stopping points for coronation entries, James I's entry had been marked by the Temple of Janus where the King had seen Peace accompanied by Wealth and Liberty triumphant over War and been addressed by the Genius Urbis.[135] The physical gate that stood at Temple Bar may not have been especially impressive and certainly in 1636–7 Charles sought to have the old gate replaced by a triumphal arch modelled on the Arch of Constantine as part of his planned triumphal route towards St Paul's.[136] This lack of physical structure may well have accentuated the significance of the collective and civic culture, less concerned to build temporary triumphal arches and symbols of peace, but then actively engaged in using peace as preparative for war. The good order of the City, represented by its very palpable military presence and populace, reinforces the symbolism of the place that marks the boundaries of mutual duties and powers but also reminds the entering monarch of the difference and independence of the City.

The awareness of both the use of the triumph motif and the military emphasis of the text can be seen in the two-sheet, black-letter broadside *The Honor of the Inns of Court Gentlemen*, probably written by Martin Parker, and most likely published after the first performance (Illustrations 6.1 and 6.2).[137] Parker's ballad stresses the central role given to the procession and especially the chariots:

> But that which admiration
>   exacts from all men,
>   that saw or heard of it,
> Was the Charets
> Which is a fashion
>   for mighty Princes and Conquerors most fit,
> The glory of this nation exceedeth all report.

Illustration 6.1 *The Honour of the Inns of Court Gentlemen* (1634) (Crawford Collection, National Library of Scotland)

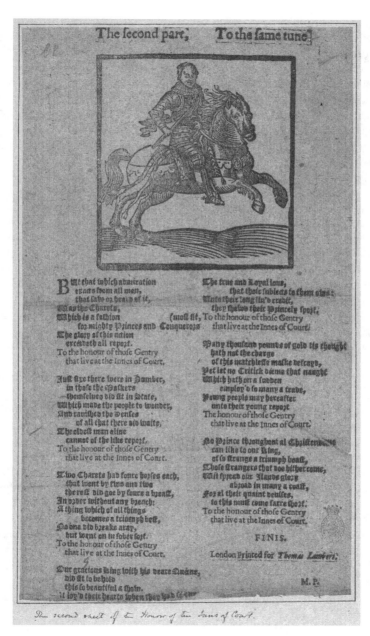

Illustration 6.2 The Honour of the Inns of Court Gentlemen, The second part (1634) (Crawford Collection, National Library of Scotland)

Parker continues by describing the six chariots, and comments on the good order of the procession 'which of all things / becomes a triumph best'. Although Parker's text only provides a sketchy description of the procession, mentioning key elements such as the 'various crew of Anticks' in general terms, and highlighting the 'wonderful content' generated among the spectators, he also provides a jingoist assertion of the superiority of this triumph, and so the kingdom, over all other nations: 'Those strangers that doe hither come, / Will spread our Ilands glory / abroad in many a coast'.[138] The constantly reiterated refrain lauds the 'the honor of those gentry / that live at the Innes of Court', perhaps responding to the anxieties about the masque expressed in some court circles, and Parker also gives the wonderful justification of the masque against its critics that the masque was a job-creation scheme.[139]

The exact stance taken in this ballad towards the masque is contradictory. On one hand Parker's text clearly notices the use of triumphal devices, normally the prerogative of monarchs and emperors, but rather than simply stressing the usage by the Inns of Court seems to deflect some of the critical implications through nationalism. Also the ballad celebrates 'The true and Loyal loue' of the 'subjects' towards their monarchs, and so the emphasis upon the 'gentry' may suggest a defensive element in the text. Indeed, the pictorial elements of the broadside bear no resemblance to the actual procession and instead recycle earlier woodcuts of a royal progress and an equestrian portrait (for *The second part*) broadly based on portraits of the earl marshal.[140] Although the woodcuts may have been chosen less for their appropriateness than their availability and condition, the ballad tune suggested is 'our noble king in Progresse', and might be part of an attempt to corral an event widely seen as highly charged back into acceptable bounds and models and to translate the event as an expression of loyalty.[141]

Parker was not the only commentator who recognised the critical implications of some of the masque had not gone unnoticed. Shirley – for reasons that are unclear – altered the text of the masque, changes that in all probability can be linked to the second performance. Copies of Q3 contain an additional sheet that provides an eighteen-line speech for Genius which most likely replaced lines 630–47.[142] So, a series of lines which highlighted the more pointed nature of the Sons of Peace, and saluted their Englishness, are excised in favour of rather more bland fare that describes the masquers as

> Happy in their ambition to wait
> And pay their second duty to your state
> Acknowledging no triumph but in you . . . (799–801)

In these ultra-loyalist lines not only are the masquers constrained by the 'their ambition to wait', a combination of service and delay, but submission to the monarch is accentuated; any sense of their possible military associations is platonised as the 'honour' given them of the double performance rather than military engagement 'is so new / And active in their *souls*' (802–3; my italics). Indeed, in contradiction to the just distribution stressed in the main masque this replacement speech has the monarchs as the receivers of greater reward: 'Which shows you nearest Heaven, that can let fall / Unequal, yet a perfect bliss to all' (807–8).

The sensitivity of the issues raised by *The Triumph of Peace* is perhaps registered in the Q3 insertion which excises the more uncomfortable and assertive version of the 'sons of Peace'. In the earlier version the masquers had retained agency, which they would employ to 'wish no blessedness but to you' (643), but in Q3 they are reduced to 'Happy' dependants on the royal will, 'Acknowledging no triumph but in you' (801). The suggestion there can be 'no triumph' except for that sanctioned by or created for the monarch seems to undo the claims to cultural authority that *The Triumph of Peace*, as a triumph above all else, sustained. 'No triumph' appears to claim that the only proper triumph must be royal.

1634, 1643, 1682: the afterlives of *The Triumph of Peace*

Both the procession with its multitude of spectators and the ballad with its proposed mass audience illustrate how masques – or at least the idea of the masque – could reach far beyond the court, albeit in modified and mediated forms. Parker was a commercially astute hack writer, and his black-letter ballad could reach the widest possible audience, either through direct reading or through posting on tavern walls.[143] The two-part ballad seeks to double the audience and the whole endeavour suggests Parker was responding to the printing community's anticipation of heightened demand for texts linked to *The Triumph of Peace*. This partnership of text publication, or of descriptive news pamphlets, and ballads shows how masques permeated beyond the world of expensive quarto printings. Scholars have long exploited such materials to supplement information about specific occasions and, as in the case of *The King of Denmark's Welcome* (1606) [STC 5194] and *The Most Royall and Honourable Entertainment of the famous and renowned King Christian of Denmark* (1606) [STC 21088], news pamphlets provide much contextual and even textual details missing from authorial or patronal texts. Less thought has been devoted to their original uses, while the tradition of 'event ballads' has been neglected, probably because as in the case of *A ballad of the Kinges goinge to the*

Parliament (1604) and *A Ballad of the Kinges Royall Rydyng to his high Cession of parliament accompanied with his nobility on Monday 19 Marchii 1603* no examples are extant.[144] Although many of these supplementary productions were likely to have been produced by entrepreneurial printers, the wider range of tracts and ballads suggests how elements of masque occasions could be transmitted to wider audiences. If prints and woodcuts were, clearly, aimed at affluent buyers, ballad productions such as the *Excellent New Ballad showing the petigree if our Royal King James the first of that name of England* (1603) also helped inform wider audiences about – in this case – their new rulers.[145]

The survival of numerous documents, public and print narratives, manuscript poetry, and black-letter ballads evidences the range of media through which *The Triumph of Peace*, in various forms, reached its audience after its performances. Interestingly, a number of these supplementary texts and commentaries seek to limit some of the more awkward implications of the masque, revealing an anxiety about the state of the country at odds with several of the more assured Caroline invocations of peace and prosperity. Thus, as with many of the masques examined in this study, news of *The Triumph of Peace* penetrated the provincial circles of gentry and governors who ruled on behalf of the Crown. Indeed, two contrasting commentaries on *The Triumph of Peace* illuminate the unresolved tensions generated by its performances and exposed some of the weakness of the Crown. Both note the evident cost and the vast scale of the undertaking and the contrast between an insolvent monarch unable to stage the requisite pageantry and the wealth of the gentry lawyers, a major component of England's parliamentary class, but draw different conclusions. George Garrard's letter to Wentworth in Ireland, a courtier's response, links the lawyers' opulence with the requirement for greater submission:

> Oh that they would once give over these Things, or lay them aside for a Time, and bend all their Endeavours to make the King Rich! For it gives me no Satisfaction, who am but a looker on, to see a rich Commonwealth, a rich People, and the Crown poor. God direct them to remedy this quickly.[146]

Garrard's letter provides an interesting gloss on the Caroline imagery of plenty belonging to the people and destabilising the Crown, so that the masque critiques legal over-mightiness rather than court extravagance. It also articulates more of the tensions that underpinned the Caroline polity, and suggests an awareness of the fragility of monarchy.

In contrast, another response produced at a distance from the court concentrated on the same features of the occasion but reached very different conclusions:

> The vulgar did much rejoice, saying that it showed the honour of the kingdom, and that it would much ingratiate the Inns of Court with the king and court [but] men of judgement [feared that] the courtiers would be apt to scoff at the gentlemen, of which scoffs may be bred ill blood. [He] wished a greater gravity and moderation in them than to give way to the spending of so great sums of money which might have been reserved for better uses ... neither did the condition of the present time befit such shows of magnificence, our neighbour countries being all in combustion about us and his Majesty's only sister and her children wanting money to keep and preserve their country from the spoil of their enemy.[147]

It is particularly interesting, then, that while the courtier saw the threat to an impoverished king in the wealth of the lawyers, William Drake of Shardloes noted that the expense of the masque reflected poorly in the context of the failure to restore the Palatinate and the ongoing conflicts of the Thirty Years War. It is not entirely clear where Drake locates the blame for this failure, although both lawyers and Crown seem at fault, but shows awareness of 'all in combustion around us'. This echo of the Caroline trope of 'war is all the world about' does not lead to celebration of England's pacified bliss, but ushers in a lament about the state of the country and also of England's co-religionists. This linkage to the issue of the Palatinate and religious conflict in Europe not only illuminates the connections between local, national, and international events and their perception, it also places the nature of the Caroline peace back at the centre of *The Triumph of Peace*. Drake is quite clear about the waste in 'spending so great sums of money that might have been reserved for better uses', and suggests how the wealth and power of an important part of the political classes might have been deployed if greater agreement – the 'gravity and moderation' evoked in his letter and envisaged by the masque – could have been achieved between monarch and his subjects.

If the positive public responses to *The Triumph of Peace* – whether from monarch, lawyers, or spectators – confirm our sense of a polity committed to consensus and reconciliation, the private documents reveal a far more conflicted creative process, and aspects of the masque can be seen as far more critical and less constrained by considerations of tact. The responses from Garrard and Sir William Drake, occupying very different positions in the political world, both illustrate contemporary awareness of the fragility of any consensus, but also of the intractable issues facing the Caroline state. Drake, in particular, embodies views from outside the court and even outside London, illustrating how masques might operate in a wider political culture, and links the masque to the issue of foreign policy in a critical fashion.

The Triumph of Peace is, however, unusual in having a more sustained afterlife than many masques that illuminates its potential political impact. The most detailed and striking post-performance text occurs in *The Tragedy of the Cruel War* (1643), which rewrites parts of the antimasque from *The Triumph of Peace* to critique cavalier cruelty.[148] Accentuating the darker side of the antimasque figures of Confidence, Opinion, Admiration, Jollity, and Laughter, *The Tragedy of the Cruel War* depicts vicious cavaliers governed by the unstable and voracious 'Fancy', and a brutalised country scarred by 'the effects of war and corruption', where 'the fashion is now to pillage plunder (110, 136). The only profitable monopolist is the 'iron projector who foresaw these wars and got a patent for the ordnance under pretence of pots for plumbroth' (145–6). Unsubtle but effective, *The Tragedy of the Cruel War* employs masque form to generate antithetical meanings: the royalists, linked to antimasque figures, are a dangerously disorderly inversion of the norms of the masque, while the masque, which would usually embody the imposition of order, is replaced by a 'prophecy' of their defeat which they themselves seek. The prophecy, a form much associated with radical Puritan and millenarian thinking, follows the text of Shirley's songs 1, 2, and 3 (491–540) from *The Triumph of Peace*, but traces the re-establishment of peace to a jointly conceived and negotiated peace of King and Parliament: 'We cannot but flourish together' (*The Tragedy of the Cruel War*, 212–13). This generic transformation where masque becomes tragedy, and ode becomes prophecy suggests how inverted the world has become, while the blurred line between antimasque and masque – indeed there is no solution through a vision of royal or legal order – reinforces the sense of a dark and arbitrary world.[149]

The Tragedy of the Cruel War requires a sophisticated understanding of masque conventions and not just the knowledge of this specific masque that might have survived due to the multiple editions available. Susan Wiseman has concluded that its existence 'suggests a particular understanding of court culture, and its existence is evidence for a widespread apprehension, not simply a court knowledge, that the masque as a form was implicated in political debate and criticism'.[150] In this case, the choice of the vehicle may even suggest that the problems the 1634 masque sought to articulate were recognised and the connection between its tensions and current open warfare are voiced in Opinion's rejection of 'the Parliament, and Law, reason and conscience' (81). It is interesting that the passage selected to conclude the prophecy in *The Tragedy of the Cruel War* from *The Triumph of Peace* highlights the balance of powers: 'The world shall give / Prerogative to neither' (*Cruel War*, 212–13; *The Triumph of Peace*, 539–40).

Although *The Tragedy of the Cruel War* closes with Shirley's line 'We cannot but flourish together' (214), the exact political position of the tract is hard to ascertain as the speakers oscillate between acting as cavaliers and revelling in their destruction, although this later turns to criticism, as Fancy entices the cavaliers into a desolate wilderness suited to their savagery. This may well fit with Fancy and Opinion's changeableness, but it complicates any stable argument in the tract. Nonetheless, Opinion voices the prophecy of 'the glorious night' (the Parliament time) when peace will be promulgated (*Cruel War*, 179), and contrasts the 'new' world of the cavaliers which has deceived the King and Queen, against the 'starry and aged sphere' (181) which offers, by implication, proper guidance. The aim of Irene is 'To procure a right understanding between King and Parliament' (*Cruel War*, 187, note f). *The Tragedy of the Cruel War* centres on the most politically explosive lines of *The Triumph of Peace* and provides a bleak vision of the failure of 'right understanding' and by turning masque into prophecy suggests the prescience of the 1634 text as an intervention in the political debates of 1643. For all its roughness, it also implies an audience capable of understanding masque conventions, or at the very least, the concept of the masque as a way of communicating political ideas.

That *The Triumph of Peace* continued to feature in the post-civil war narratives exemplifies its impact and its political engagement. Thus Hammon L'Estrange connects the institution of *The Book of Sports*, which he regards as one of the most misguided and unpopular pieces of Caroline legislation, with masquing and attributes the practice of Sunday masques, a violation of strict sabbatarian beliefs, to poor counsel.[151] Later Bulstrode Whitelocke's *Memorials* (1682), the prime witness for the inclusion of a covert agenda of counsel in *The Triumph of Peace*, modifies material of earlier date in response to post-Restoration sensitivities.[152] In part, Whitelocke's published narrative coincides with post-Restoration retrospective refashioning of a difficult recent past helped by the symbolic position rapidly acquired by *The Triumph of Peace* in the 'official' narrative of the period that yoked masques to royalism and anti-theatricalism to Puritanism that emerged as early as the 1660s.[153] Interestingly, Whitelocke's *Memorials* concentrated on public events ('English Affairs') and endowed Prynne's prosecution with wider political resonances rooted in personal antipathy and ideological differences.[154] So, while retaining the connection to the dispute over *Histriomastix*, Whitelocke carefully disengages Prynne's diatribe from any direct association with the Queen's pastoral at Somerset House, sometimes seen as the specific target of his criticism, linking it instead with widespread discontent over *The Book of Sports*.[155] In this version, Whitelocke depicts Laud and Heylyn as the Machiavellian villains who stirred up royal displeasure and claims that Laud had been angered by Prynne's anti-Arminianism. The characterisation of Heylyn and Prynne as 'well matched' perhaps represents another post-Restoration accommodation that placed blame on both parties.[156]

It is unsurprising given the severity of the shock occasioned by the civil wars across wide sections of national political culture that Whitelocke's revisions in his multiple narratives illuminate how public history, reshaped in the post-war political climate, disguised the more fissiparous conditions of production. While some kinds and degrees of dissent are allowed and conflict is admitted, Whitelocke's narrative retreats into the discourse of evil counsel misleading a fundamentally virtuous monarch alongside loyal opposition. This post-war silencing, however, also illuminates some of the broader operations of tactful constraint that have often been seen as limiting the masque's capacity for critique.

Tact enables difficult issues to be spoken as much as it constrains their expression. The very statement of conscious tact may itself bind speaker and listener into a situation that allows the articulation of challenging topics. Given this, it also seems worth noting that the very presence of stated tactfulness, the awareness of the need for tact, may equally be the marker of submerged conflicts and the trace of processes of negotiation and dissent. In this context it is worth returning to Fletcher's description of masques as 'tied to the rules of flattery', often cited as evidence of the apolitical or limited nature of the masque, which overlooks Melantius' later preference for the 'dance with arms' over these 'soft and silken wars'.[157] Love as a battle and war as dance are commonplaces often summoned in the poems and masques of the period, but the image of the masque as war by other means, and the implication of indirection that is still potentially hostile and challenging, should make us pause. The image of conflict concealed within the 'soft and silken', which seems to be as much verbal and expressive as material, not only questions the idealised consensus of Caroline culture but suggests the subtle, suave, yet strong ways in which masques articulate difference and even dissent.

Notes

1 Introduction: 'Friends of All Ranks'?

1. John Fletcher, *The Maid's Tragedy*, 1.1.8–11, in *The Dramatic Works of the Beaumont and Fletcher Canon*, ed. F. Bowers, 10 vols. (Cambridge: Cambridge University Press, 1970), 2.29.
2. See my 'The "Running Masque" Recovered? A Masque for the Marquess of Buckingham (c.1619–20)', *English Manuscript Studies*, 8 (2000), 79–135, p. 79.
3. Peter Lake and Steven Pincus (eds.), *The Politics of the Public Sphere in Early Modern England* (Manchester: Manchester University Press, 2007), p. 1. See also I. Atherton and J. Sanders (eds.), *The 1630s: Interdisciplinary Essays on Culture and Politics in the Caroline Era* (Manchester: Manchester University Press, 2006), p. 3, on the 'contested, controversial, and fragile' 1630s.
4. *Love Restored*, 4–5.
5. Glenn Burgess, *Absolute Monarchy and the Stuart Constitution* (New Haven: Yale University Press, 1996), p. 9 (esp. n. 26), and Nicholas Henshall, *The Myth of Absolutism: Change and Continuity in Early Modern European Monarchy* (London: Longman, 1992), pp. 1–5.
6. Stephen Orgel and Roy Strong, *Inigo Jones: The Theatre of the Stuart Court*, 2 vols. (Berkeley: University of California Press, 1973), 1.1, 1.7, 1.11.
7. James VI and I, *Basilicon Doron*, cited in Stephen Orgel, *The Illusion of Power* (Berkeley: University of California Press, 1975), pp. 42–3. James VI and I used this analogy frequently but argued that because the people 'doe gazingly beholde', a monarch must be 'precise in the discharging of his office': see *The Basilicon Doron of King James VI*, ed. James Craigie, 2 vols. (Edinburgh: Scottish Text Society, 1944–50), 1.163. For an interesting development of this perspective, see Stephen Orgel, 'The Royal Theatre and the Role of the King', in *Patronage in the Renaissance*, ed. S. Orgel and G. F. Lytle (Princeton: Princeton University Press, 1981), pp. 261–73.
8. Orgel, *Illusion of Power*, p. 40.
9. The phrase is Stephen Greenblatt's: see 'Invisible Bullets: Renaissance Authority and its Subversion, Henry IV and Henry V', in *Political Shakespeare: New Essays in Cultural Materialism*, ed. J. Dollimore and A. Sinfield (Manchester: Manchester University Press, 1985), p. 45. On Burkhardt, see David Norbrook, *Poetry and Politics in the English Renaissance*, revised edition (Oxford: Oxford University Press, 2002), p. 4.
10. Martin Butler, 'Politics and the Masque: *The Triumph of Peace*', *The Seventeenth Century*, 2 (1987), 117–41, p. 118.
11. K. Sharpe, 'Parliamentary History 1603–1629: In or Out of Perspective', in *Faction and Parliament: Essays on Early Stuart History*, ed. K. Sharpe (Oxford: Clarendon Press, 1978), pp. 1–42, p. 5. On the historiography of James VI and I, see Jenny Wormald, 'James VI and I: Two Kings or One?', *History*, 68 (1983), 187–209.
12. The core of the revisionist case was that the causes of the civil war were short-term and contingent, with few real ideological divisions in earlier

decades, but that the British state was dysfunctional fiscally and afflicted by religious tensions. Parliament was regarded as less effective, certainly less innovative, and much less active in seeking power or to curb royal power; the court was seen as more political, more effective and innovative. For a more elegant summary, see Ronald Hutton, *Debates in Stuart History* (Basingstoke: Palgrave Macmillan, 2004), p. 16.
13. Martin Butler, 'Courtly Negotiations', in *The Politics of the Stuart Court Masque*, ed. David Bevington and Peter Holbrook (Cambridge: Cambridge University Press, 1998), pp. 20–40, p. 27.
14. Butler, 'Courtly Negotiations', p. 27.
15. Jonson makes this distinction in *Hymenaei*, 5–20. The fullest discussion of this distinction is given in D. J. Gordon, 'Poet and Architect: The Intellectual Setting of the Quarrel between Ben Jonson and Inigo Jones', *Journal of the Warburg and Courtauld Institutes*, 12 (1949), 152–78, reprinted in *The Renaissance Imagination: Essays and Lectures by D. J. Gordon*, ed. S. Orgel (Berkeley: University of California Press, 1975), pp. 77–101, p. 79.
16. Butler, 'Politics and the Masque: *The Triumph of Peace*', p. 113.
17. Butler, 'Politics and the Masque: *The Triumph of Peace*', p. 118, and Butler, 'Courtly Negotiations', p. 28.
18. Martin Butler, 'Ben Jonson and the Limits of Courtly Panegyric', in *Culture and Politics in Early Stuart England*, ed. K. Sharpe and P. Lake (Basingstoke: Macmillan, 1994), pp. 91–115, p. 92. Pliny's phrase (*'laudando praecipere, when by telling men what they are, they represent to them what they should be'*) is cited in Bacon, 'Of Praise', in *Essays* (1625), in *Francis Bacon*, ed. B. Vickers (Oxford: Oxford University Press, 1996), p. 443.
19. Kevin Sharpe, *Criticism and Compliment: The Politics of Literature in the England of Charles I* (Cambridge: Cambridge University Press, 1987); Richard Cust and Ann Hughes, 'Introduction: After Revisionism', in *Conflict in Early Stuart England: Studies in Religion and Politics 1603–1642*, ed. Cust and Hughes (Harlow: Longman, 1989), p. 4.
20. Thomas Scott, *Vox Regis* (1624), sig. E1v.
21. 'Courtly negotiations' were first named such by Cedric Brown, 'Courtesies of Place and Arts of Diplomacy in Ben Jonson's Last Two Entertainments for Royalty', *The Seventeenth Century*, 9 (1994), 147–71, p. 147.
22. Richard Cust, 'The "Public Man" in Late Tudor and Early Stuart England', in *The Politics of the Public Sphere*, pp. 116–143, esp. pp. 130–1.
23. John Guy, 'The Rhetoric of Counsel in Early Modern England', in *Tudor Political Culture*, ed. Dale Hoak (Cambridge: Cambridge University Press, 1995), pp. 292–310, p. 294.
24. Cust, 'The "Public Man"', pp. 130–1; Guy, 'The Rhetoric of Counsel', p. 299.
25. David Colclough, *Freedom of Speech in Early Stuart England* (Cambridge: Cambridge University Press, 2005), pp. 3–6, 120.
26. Bacon, 'Of Counsel', from *Essays* (1625) in *Francis Bacon*, p. 381.
27. David Colclough, '*Parrhesia*: The Rhetoric of Free Speech in Early Modern England', *Rhetorica*, 17 (1999), 177–212, p. 207; Joad Raymond, 'Perfect Speech: The Public Sphere and Communication in Seventeenth-Century England', in *Spheres of Influence: Intellectual and Cultural Publics from Shakespeare to Habermas*, ed. Willy Maley and Alex Benchimol (Frankfurt: Peter Lang, 2006), pp. 43–69, p. 57, who both stress the shift towards ideas of propriety. Debora

Shuger connects civility with reticence in an essay that makes a strong case for censorship as a function of 'civil harmony': see 'Civility and Censorship in Early Modern England', in *Censorship and Silencing: Practices of Cultural Regulation*, ed. Robert C. Post (Los Angeles: Getty Research Institute for the History of Art and the Humanities, 1998), pp. 89–110.

28. Markku Peltonen, *Rhetoric, Politics and Popularity in Pre-Revolutionary England* (Cambridge: Cambridge University Press, 2013), pp. 6 and 63. Peltonen is quoting Ethan Shagan's view in *Popular Politics and the English Reformation* (Cambridge: Cambridge University Press, 2003).
29. Erasmus considered *The Praise of Folly* as the equivalent, if an oblique version, of his *Education of a Christian Prince*: see Douglas Duncan, *Ben Jonson and the Lucianic Tradition* (Cambridge: Cambridge University Press, 1979), pp. 37–8; on 'bitter medicine' and free speech, see Michelle O'Callaghan, *The English Wits: Literature and Sociability in Early Modern England* (Cambridge: Cambridge University Press, 2007), pp. 7 and 41.
30. Duncan, *Ben Jonson and the Lucianic Tradition*, p. 228, suggests only limited connections between masques and the Lucianic tradition. On Jonson's wider links with this culture and the connection of his emphasis on 'judgement' and 'wit' to humanist dialectics between *jocus* and *serium*, see O'Callaghan, *The English Wits*, esp. p. 50.
31. Most of the Lucianic references in the masques are passing allusions to the *Dialogues of the Gods* (for example, *Haddington*, *Oberon*).
32. Julie Sanders, *Ben Jonson's Theatrical Republics* (Basingstoke: Palgrave Macmillan, 1998), p. 2. Sanders provides an important qualification of the term 'radical' linking it to usage in the 1620s where it broadly means disagreement with current policies and shades into scepticism about monarchy and the extent and use of its powers.
33. Jonson, 'Informations to William Drummond of Hawthornden', 293, recounts how Jonson composed his poems initially in prose 'for so his master Camden had learned him'.
34. Martin Butler and David Lindley, 'Restoring Astraea: Jonson's Masque for the Fall of Somerset', *English Literary History*, 61 (1994), 807–82, p. 820.
35. Clare McManus, *Women on the Renaissance Stage: Anna of Denmark and Female Masquing in the Stuart Court 1590–1619* (Manchester: Manchester University Press, 2002), p. 18; Butler, 'Courtly Negotiations', pp. 33–6, highlights the tensions between the King's pacific policies and the militarism of Prince Charles.
36. *Pleasure Reconciled to Virtue*, 305–6.
37. Title page for *Hymenaei: or The solemnities of masque, and barriers magnificently performed on the eleventh, and twelfth nights, from Christmas; at court* (1606).
38. 'An Epistle to a Friend, to Persuade Him to the Wars', 151; 'An Execration Upon Vulcan', 155; 'An Epistle Answering to One that Asked to be Sealed of the Tribe of Ben', 51–3.
39. *Every Man In His Humour* (F) paraphrases Florus, *De Qualitate Vitae*, 'Consuls are made annually . . . only a king or poet is not born every year' (5.5.32).
40. Sanders, *Ben Jonson's Theatrical Republics*, pp. 3, 8, 67.
41. Cust, 'The "Public Man"', p. 123.
42. Cust, 'The "Public Man"', p. 116. Malcolm Smuts provides a parallel description of Jonson as an ethical republican who 'sees governance as ideally an

exercise of human virtue in the service of the public good' ('The Court', in *Ben Jonson in Context*, ed. Julie Sanders (Cambridge: Cambridge University Press, 2010), p. 150).
43. 'To Sir Robert Wroth', 10. Julie Sanders sees similar issues at work in *Bartholomew Fair* (1614), with its rapid transposition between public stage and court 'pushing at the possibilities of what could be said or done before the king' (*Ben Jonson's Theatrical Republics*, p. 100).
44. See 'Introduction' to *Culture and Politics in Early Stuart England*, ed. Sharpe and Lake, pp. 1–20, for a subtle survey of the revisionist assault on 'principle-centred' accounts of early modern political change and conflict.
45. See Derek Hirst, 'Court, Country, and Politics before 1629', in *Faction and Parliament*, ed. Sharpe, pp. 105–37 (esp. p. 128), and also his 'Revisionism Revised: The Place of Principle', *Past and Present*, 92 (1981), 79–99. The 'cultural turn' that brought critical and historical studies closer together fostered interest in the 'commonwealth of meanings' but treated it not as 'the language of party' or 'representations of rival programs' but rather an ideal 'for the whole commonwealth', so that the possibility of ideological differentiation became almost a linguistic impossibility: see Kevin Sharpe and Steven Zwicker (eds.), *The Politics of Discourse: the Literature and History of Seventeenth-Century England* (Berkeley: University of California Press, 1987), p. 6 (see pp. 1–6 throughout).
46. Malcolm Smuts, 'Cultural Diversity and Cultural Change at the Court of James I', in *The Mental World of the Jacobean Court*, ed. Linda Levy Peck (Cambridge: Cambridge University Press, 1991), pp. 103–4.
47. Tom Cogswell, Richard Cust, and Peter Lake, 'Revisionism and its Legacies: The Work of Conrad Russell', in *Politics, Religion and Popularity: Early Stuart Essays in Honour of Conrad Russell*, ed. Cust, Cogswell, and Lake (Cambridge: Cambridge University Press, 2002), pp. 10–11.
48. Alastair Bellany, *The Politics of Court Scandal in Early Modern England: News Culture and the Overbury Affair, 1603–1660* (Cambridge: Cambridge University Press, 2002), p. 23; Peter Lake, 'Retrospective: Wentworth's Political World in Revisionist and Post-Revisionist Perspective', in *The Political World of Thomas Wentworth, Earl of Strafford, 1621–1641*, ed. J. F. Merritt (Cambridge: Cambridge University Press, 1996), p. 259. Lake and Sharpe's 'Introduction' to *Culture and Politics in Early Stuart England* lists verbal and visual sources, both high and low cultural forms including classical translations, portraits, palaces, patterns of display, chivalric ceremony, religious ritual, cheap pamphlets, verses, libels, and – of course – plays and masques, as political (p. 6).
49. Richard Cust, 'Politics and the Electorate in the 1620s', in *Conflict in Early Stuart England*, ed. Cust and Hughes, pp. 134–67, esp. pp. 154, 162, shows the interconnection of national and local issues often couched in terms of contest and opposition.
50. Mark Goldie, 'The Unacknowledged Republic: Officeholding in Early Modern England', in *The Politics of the Excluded, c.1500–1850*, ed. T. Harris (Basingstoke: Palgrave Macmillan, 2001), pp. 153–94, esp. pp. 180–2.
51. Lake, 'Retrospective', p. 273 illustrates how key ideas such as court and country, local and national, can acquire divergent meanings depending on specific circumstances of deployment.

52. Joad Raymond, 'Describing Popularity in Early Modern England', *The Huntingdon Library Quarterly*, 67 (2004), 101–30, p. 103, notes Bellany's use of 'ethnography', or 'overlapping and overlaid descriptions that elicit deep, short-term meanings' combined with accounts of 'longer term historical significance'.
53. Lake, 'Retrospective', p. 277; Cust and Hughes, 'Introduction: After Revisionism', pp. 19–21.
54. Cust and Hughes, 'Introduction: After Revisionism', p. 17. John Pory, the newsletter writer who proposed a monopoly of printed news to the king in 1621, justified his project as a control mechanism which would 'establish a speedy and reddy way wherby to disperse into the veynes of the whole body of a state such matter as may best temper it and be most agreeable to the disposition of the head and the principale members' (cited by Fritz Levy, 'The Decorum of News', in *News, Newspapers and Society in Early Modern Britain*, ed. Joad Raymond (London: Frank Cass, 1989), p. 28).
55. See the discussion of the Caroline trope of 'halcyon days' in Chapter 6 (pp. 183–4).
56. Stephen Orgel comments that 'The print revolution . . . was in fact a reading revolution, a revolution not of technology but of dissemination and reception'; see 'Afterword: Records of Culture', in *Books and Readers in Early Modern England: Material Studies*, ed. J. Anderson and E. Sauer (Philadelphia: University of Pennsylvania Press, 2002), p. 282, and Roger Darnton, '"What is the History of Books?" Revisited', *Modern Intellectual History*, 4 (2007), 495–508.
57. Thomas Cogswell, 'Underground Verse and the Transformation of Early Stuart Political Culture', in *Political Culture and Cultural Politics in Early Modern England*, ed. Susan D. Amussen and Mark Kishlansky (Manchester: Manchester University Press, 1995), pp. 277–300, esp. pp. 293–5.
58. Shuger, 'Civility and Censorship', p. 94.
59. David Norbrook, '*Areopagitica*, Censorship, and the Early Modern Political Sphere', in *British Literature, 1640–1789: A Critical Reader*, ed. Robert DeMaria (Oxford: Blackwell Publishers, 1999), pp. 13–39, p. 16.
60. Cust, 'News and Politics', p. 89. Cust stresses the scatological and pornographic elements in news culture, but also – more crucially – its capacity to disrupt the divisions between popular and elite culture: 'Here . . . the literate and the illiterate shared the same medium' (p. 69).
61. Cust, 'News and Politics', p. 89; Cogswell, 'Underground Verse', discusses the 'visceral' impact of much of this literature (p. 279).
62. Thomas Cogswell, 'Underground Verse', p. 286; Matthew Pattenson, *The Image of Both Churches* (1623), cited in Peltonen, *Rhetoric, Politics and Popularity*, p. 5.
63. William Laud, *Works*, ed. Philip Bliss, 7 vols. (Oxford: Oxford University Press, 1847–60), 7.371.
64. For example, the Derbyshire miners studied in Andy Wood, *The Politics of Social Conflict: the Peak Country, 1520–1770* (Cambridge: Cambridge University Press, 1999).
65. O'Callaghan, *The English Wits*, pp. 35–59, and Colclough, *Freedom of Speech*, pp. 238–48, trace Jonson's links with the Inns of Court and political figures such as John Hoskyns and Richard Martin.
66. For an enlightening discussion, see Barbara D. Palmer, 'Court and Country: The Masque as Sociopolitical Subtext', *Medieval and Renaissance Drama in England*, 7 (1995), 338–54.

67. James Knowles, 'Songs of Baser Alloy: Jonson's *Gypsies Metamorphosed* and the Circulation of Manuscript Libels', *Huntington Library Quarterly*, 69 (2006), 53–176.
68. Lake and Pincus, 'Rethinking the Public Sphere in Early Modern England', p. 6.
69. Norbrook, '*Areopagitica*, Censorship, and the Early Modern Public Sphere', p. 20, makes a parallel suggestion with periods of intense political debate around parliaments, and 'unparliamentary' periods of 'bodily submission' akin to those seen by revisionist historians and the New Historicists.
70. Pauline Croft, 'The Reputation of Robert Cecil: Libels, Political Opinion and Popular Awareness in the Early Seventeenth Century', *Transactions of the Royal Historical Society*, 6th ser., 1 (1991), 43–69.
71. Lake and Pincus, 'Rethinking the Public Sphere in Early Modern England', p. 19.
72. Lake and Pincus, 'Rethinking the Public Sphere in Early Modern England', p. 5 (n.23).
73. Kevin Sharpe, 'Parliamentary History 1603–1629', p. 36, argues that the main foreign policy debates reflected personal rivalries at court. Sharpe's argument places the initiative firmly with the court and Privy Council, but in so doing suggests that major political issues can be traced in the factions that danced in masques.
74. Richard Dutton, *Licensing, Censorship and Authorship in Early Modern England* (New York: Palgrave Macmillan, 2000), p. 81.
75. Sanders and Atherton, 'Introducing the 1630s', in *The 1630s: Interdisciplinary Essays on Culture and Politics in the Caroline Era*, suggest that cultural activity resonated with the politics displaced by the absence of parliaments (p. 9).
76. Jonathan Goldberg, *James I and the Politics of Literature* (Baltimore: Johns Hopkins University Press, 1983), pp. 56–65, esp. p. 62.
77. David Lindley, 'Introduction', in *The Court Masque*, ed. Lindley (Manchester: Manchester University Press, 1984), p. 4.
78. Colclough, *Freedom of Speech*, p. 249.
79. François de Lauze, *Apologie de la Danse* (Paris: no publisher, 1623), sig. B4r. This tract was known in England at the time and a version of it by Buckingham's French dancing master Barthélemy de Montagut was dedicated to him: see Montagut, *Louange de la Danse*, ed. B. Ravelhofer (Cambridge: RTM Publications, 2000).
80. Bellany, *The Politics of Court Scandal in Early Modern England*, p. 23.
81. Raymond, 'Perfect Speech', p. 46, provides a list of elements of the early modern public sphere that diverge from the Habermasian view, including the prevalence of hierarchy and hierarchal behaviours and spaces, censorship, and so on.
82. It is interesting that Heywood, who commented 'I have forborne to spend much paper on needelesse and Impertinent deciphering' (*Londons ius honorarium*, sig. C4v) is typed as a popular writer, while Jonson is treated – uniformly – as elitist: see Tracey Hill, *Pageantry and Power: A Cultural History of the Early Modern Lord Mayor's Show, 1585–1639* (Manchester: Manchester University Press, 2010), p. 173.
83. I have retained the italics used for Jonson's technical terminology: see *Ben Jon: His Part of King James his Royall and Magnificent Entertainment through his Honorable Cittie of London* (London: Edward Blount, 1604), sig. B2v.
84. 'Truchman' (interpreter) derives from the same word as 'dragoman' and was associated most frequently with puppet shows where a presenter filled in the action (as with Leatherhead in *Bartholomew Fair* or Medlay in *Tale of a Tub*). Jonson described the tongue as the 'truchman' of the mind in *Art of Poetry*, 157.

85. D. J. Gordon, 'Roles and Mysteries', in *The Renaissance Imagination*, pp. 3–23, esp. pp. 17–21, modifies heavily Neoplatonic interpretations of masque 'mysteries', especially the hermetic visual tradition outlined in Ernst Gombrich's essay 'Icones Symbolicae: The Visual Image in Neo-Platonic Thought', *Journal of the Warburg and Courtauld Institutes*, 11 (1948), 163–92.
86. *The Magnificent Entertainment*, 65–7, in *The Dramatic Works of Thomas Dekker*, ed. F. Bowers, 8 vols. (Cambridge: Cambridge University Press, 1955), vol. 2; Hill, *Pageantry and Power*, pp. 171–6 outlines the potential for different audience responses to differing aspects of the Lord Mayor's show.
87. Here 'profess' perhaps carries some of its Latinate implications of the recognition of skill and even religious vocation.
88. Andrew Gurr, *Playgoing in Shakespeare's London* (Cambridge: Cambridge University Press, 1987), p. 121, suggests Dekker and Jonson shared this use of print.
89. Sanders, *Ben Jonson's Theatrical Republics*, p. 96.
90. Sanders, *Ben Jonson's Theatrical Republics*, p. 124.
91. The classic study is Richard C. Newton, 'Jonson and the (Re-)Invention of the Book', in *Classic and Cavalier: Essays on Jonson and the Sons of Ben*, ed. C. Summers and Ted-Larry Pebworth (Pittsburgh: University of Pittsburgh Press, 1982), pp. 31–55, but see also Martin Butler, 'Jonson's Folio and the Politics of Patronage', *Criticism*, 35 (1993), 377–90, and Timothy Murray 'From Foul Sheets to Legitimate Model: Antitheater, Text, Ben Jonson', *New Literary History*, 14 (1983), 641–64, for important modifications.
92. Gurr, *Playgoing in Shakespeare's London*, p. 102, notes that 'spectator' implied a singular viewer against the more common and collective 'audience' or 'auditory', so Jonson's prefatory epistle, in addressing 'spectators', emphasises the verbal more than the visual but retains the collective experience in both terms.
93. Aby Warburg, 'The Theatrical Costumes for the Intermedi of 1589', in *The Renewal of Pagan Antiquity: Contributions to the Cultural History of the European Renaissance*, ed. and trans. David Britt and Kurt W. Foster (Los Angeles: Getty Research Institute, 1999), pp. 349–401, pp. 365, 368.
94. Butler, 'Courtly Negotiations', pp. 22–3. For an interesting critique of the 'unrealistic panoptic eye' adopted by historians, the complexities of viewing perspective within Jacobean court performance spaces, and the more active engagement of spectators, see Ross Parry, 'The Careful Watchman: James I, Didacticism and the Perspectival Organisation of Space', in *Disziplinierung im Alltag des Mittelalters und der frühen Neuzeit*, ed. Gerhard Jaritz (Vienna: Der Österreichischen Akademie der Wissenschaften, 1999), pp. 275–97, esp. p. 292.
95. At least three masques may have been staged in the Hall at Whitehall (*Hymenaei*, *Love Freed*, *News*) and we know *The Memorable Masque* was staged there; in 1603 all the masques were staged in the Hall at Hampton Court, and both Anna of Denmark and Henrietta Maria made use of Somerset House for their entertainments.
96. For the 1621 inscription and purposes of the building: see David Howarth, *Images of Rule: Art and Politics in the English Renaissance, 1485–1649* (Basingstoke: Macmillan, 1997), pp. 34–8, and Chris Kyle, 'Parliament and the Palace of Westminster: An Exploration of Public Space in the Early Seventeenth Century', *Parliamentary History*, 21 (2002), 85–98, pp. 88, 90, 97.
97. Anthony Milton, *Laudian and Royalist Polemic in Seventeenth-Century England: The Career and Writings of Peter Heylyn* (Manchester: Manchester University

Press, 2007), p. 42, citing Sir Gervase Clifton's description of clergy debates as 'civill warres among the Clergy, whose poems are their pikes'.

2 'Vizarded impudence': Challenging the *regnum Cecilianum*

1. Martin Butler, 'Ben Jonson and the Limits of Courtly Panegyric', in *Culture and Politics in Early Stuart England*, ed. Kevin Sharpe and Peter Lake (Basingstoke: Macmillan, 1999), pp. 91–115, pp. 101–3.
2. These were the sisters Frances and Catherine Howard: see Clare McManus, *Women on the Renaissance Stage: Anna of Denmark and Female Masquing in the Stuart Court (1590–1619)* (Manchester: Manchester University Press, 2002), pp. 18–20 and 58–9.
3. Butler, 'Ben Jonson and the Limits of Courtly Panegyric', p. 103. For the significance of the Jacobean Scots, see Martin Butler, 'Sir Francis Stewart: Jonson's Overlooked Patron', *Ben Jonson Journal*, 2 (1995), 101–27 and my 'Jonson in Scotland', in *Shakespeare, Marlowe, Jonson: New Directions in Biography*, ed. T. Kozuka, and J. R. Mulryne (Aldershot: Ashgate, 2006), pp. 259–77.
4. Peter Lake and Steve Pincus, 'Rethinking the Public Sphere in Early Modern England', in *The Politics of the Public Sphere in Early Modern England*, ed. Lake and Pincus (Manchester: Manchester University Press), pp. 1–30, p. 8. See Pauline Croft (ed.), *A collection of several speeches and treatises of the late Lord Treasurer Cecil, and of several observations of the Lords of the Council given to King James concerning his estate and revenue in the years 1608, 1609 and 1610* (London: Royal Historical Society, 1987) [Camden Miscellany, 29], 273–318, esp. p. 352 on this period as 'crucial . . . for focussing national attention on high politics' through popular forms.
5. For a general summary of Cecil's career, see P. Croft, 'Robert Cecil, first earl of Salisbury (1563–1612)', *ODNB*, electronic edition, www.oxforddnb.com/?/4890, accessed 5 December 2006.
6. Florio defines 'Mascarata' as a 'maske, a masking' and 'mascarare' as to 'maske, to mum, to cloke': see *Queen Annas New World of Words* (1611), sig. 2Cv.
7. The masque cost as little as £280: see National Archives, SP39/4, no. 68, Signet Office, King's Bills, 28 March 1614–22 March 1615. I am grateful to Dr Karen Britland for drawing my attention to this document.
8. Stephen Orgel (ed.), *The Complete Masques* (New Haven: Yale University Press, 1969) and David Lindley (ed.), *Court Masques: Jacobean and Caroline Entertainments, 1605–1640* (Oxford: Oxford University Press) both gloss this as meaning the King's Men, the theatre company, but in the sequence *Irish Masque, Mercury Vindicated*, and *The Golden Age Restored* parallel phrases always refer to members of the household: the printed text of the latter lists 'Lords, and Gentlemen the King's Servants' as performers on the title page, and Chamberlain's letter on *The Irish Masque* names 'gentlemen of his own servants that are good dancers' as the masquers (National Archives, SP14/75/33, 3 December 1613). The King's Men were enrolled as *grooms* of the chamber in 1603.
9. National Archives, A03/908. Other documents link the masque to the King and the payments are through the Exchequer rather than Prince Henry's

household. It is possible that the A03/908 reference may even simply be an error or just a confusion with the cancelled joint masque planned by the Queen and Prince Henry (*Ben Jonson*, 10.131, *HMC Downshire*, 3.181).
10. It appears as 'LOVE RESTORED, / In a Masque at Court, by Gentlemen the / KINGS *Seruants*' in the *The workes of Benjamin Jonson* (1616), sig. 4O3.
11. Leah S. Marcus, *The Politics of Mirth* (Chicago: University of Chicago Press, 1986), p. 31. For Marcus, *Love Restored* creates a 'nobler' version of the country sports that embody communal solidarity and unpick the isolated individualism that threatens social cohesion with miserliness and isolation (p. 33).
12. 'Speech to Parliament', 21 March 1610, in *King James VI and I: Political Writings*, ed. J. Sommerville (Cambridge: Cambridge University Press, 1994), p. 193.
13. It still rankled in 1610: see *King James VI and I: Political Writings*, p. 196.
14. Timothy Wilks, '"Forbear the Heat and Haste of Building": Rivalries among the Designers at Prince Henry's Court, 1610–12', *Court Historian*, 6 (2001), 49–65, p. 54. The Prince's desire to edify his homes placed considerable strain not only on his finances but on relations with Cecil as the Prince refused to pay the full cost of expensive works at Richmond Palace undertaken by the King's Works. It had also been reported in 1610 that the Prince did not wish to see wardship abolished (part of the Great Contract) because he coveted the profitable office of Master; Cecil was Master of the Wards: see Elizabeth Read Foster (ed.), *Proceedings in Parliament 1610*, 2 vols. (New Haven: Yale University Press, 1966), 2.59.
15. Croft, *A collection*, pp. 258–9, summarises the financial problems attending on Henry's creation and his lavish expenditure. The Cleves–Jülich crisis (1609) concerned the succession in the united Duchy of Cleves, Jülich and Berg (largely modern North Rhine Westphalia and part of the Dutch province of Gelderland); James VI and I sent troops to support a Protestant succession.
16. E. Lindquist, 'The Failure of the Great Contract', *Journal of Modern History*, 57 (1985), 617–51, p. 625; P. Croft, 'Robert Cecil, first earl of Salisbury (1563–1612)', *ODNB*, electronic edition, www.oxforddnb.com/4890, accessed 5 December 2006, calculates the income from impositions.
17. Croft, *A collection*, p. 255.
18. The sums set for these were £600,000 and £200,000 respectively. P. Croft, 'Robert Cecil, first earl of Salisbury (1563–1612)', *ODNB*, electronic edition, www.oxforddnb.com/?/4890, accessed 5 December 2006, stresses Cecil's isolation.
19. Neil Cuddy, 'The Real Attempted "Tudor Revolution in Government": Salisbury's 1610 Great Contract', in *Authority and Consent in Tudor England: Essays Presented to C. S. L. Davies*, ed. G. W. Bernard and S. J. Gunn (Aldershot: Ashgate, 2002), pp. 249–70, pp. 249, 254, 263–4.
20. Cuddy, 'The Real Attempted "Tudor Revolution in Government"', p. 253.
21. Cecil's pithy phrase as given in Croft, *A collection*, p. 257; Prince Henry's concerns are cited in Butler, 'Ben Jonson and the Limits of Courtly Panegyric', p. 103.
22. Cited in S. R. Gardiner (ed.), *Parliamentary Debates in 1610* (London: Camden Society Publications, 81, 1862), pp. 11, 47.

23. *King James VI and I: Political Writings*, p. 197.
24. In 1610 he wrote: 'I hope you will consider that what I have given, hath been given amongst you; and so what comes in from you, goes out again amongst you. But it may be thought I have given much amongst Scottishmen': 'Speech to Parliament', 21 March 1610, in *King James VI and I: Political Writings*, pp. 179–203, p. 197.
25. James I to Robert Cecil, 6 December 1610, HMC *Salisbury*, 21.265.
26. *Journals of the House of Commons, 1547–1607* (1803), 1.333. Le Fèvre de la Boderie describes how Piggott called the Scots 'les plus babarres, et méchantes gens du monde': see *Ambassades*, 5 vols. (1750), 2.87.
27. John Orrell, 'The London Stage in the Florentine Correspondence, 1604–1618', *Theatre Research International*, 3 (1978), 157–76, p. 162. I am grateful to Dr Lucy Munro for this reference.
28. See *Early Stuart Libels: An Edition of Poetry from Manuscript Sources*, ed. Alastair Bellany and Andrew McRae, Early Modern Literary Studies, Text Series I (2005) (http://purl.oclc.org/emls/texts/libels), E5. This electronic edition is abbreviated to *Early Stuart Libels*.
29. *Early Stuart Libels*, E1.
30. See *Early Stuart Libels*, E5 (introduction).
31. N. Cuddy, 'The Revival of the Entourage: The Bedchamber of James I, 1603–1625', in *The English Court: From the Wars of the Roses to the Civil Wars*, ed. David Starkey (London: Longman, 1987), pp. 173–225 and Cuddy, 'Anglo-Scottish Union and the Court of James I, 1603–1625', *Transactions of the Royal Historical Society*, 39 (1989), 107–24.
32. *HMC Portland*, 9.113.
33. See Cuddy, 'The Revival of the Entourage', p. 198, note 65, and 'The Real Attempted "Tudor Revolution in Government"', p. 263. George Home, Earl of Dunbar, was briefly Chancellor of the Exchequer of England (1603–6), but his main function was to improve Scottish law and order, mainly through his role on the border commission. He was a close ally of Robert Cecil and his second daughter married Elizabeth, daughter of Theophilus Howard (another Cecil associate): see M. Lee, 'Home, George, earl of Dunbar (d. 1611)', *ODNB*, electronic edition, www.oxforddnb.com/view/printable/13642, accessed 12 December 2006.
34. Cuddy, 'The Revival of the Entourage', p. 198, note 65.
35. Foster (ed.), *Proceedings in Parliament 1610*, 2.344–5. The leaky cistern metaphor was common: compare 'a silver stream out of the country into the royal cistern, if it shall daily run out thence by private cocks' (Cuddy, 'The Real Attempted "Tudor Revolution in Government"', note 27).
36. Foster (ed.), *Proceedings in Parliament 1610*, 2.245n. In another report la Boderie wrote that 'comme les pleintes de Parlement ont esté pour la plupart fondées sur les dons que leur faisoit le Roy, ilz ont tellement bridé' (National Archives, PRO31/3/41 cited in Cuddy, 'The Real Attempted "Tudor Revolution in Government"', p. 268, note 49).
37. *HMC Downshire*, 3.315 and *Chamberlain Letters*, 1.356 (from National Archives, SP 14/69/67).
38. HMC *Salisbury*, 21.260–2. Found in Cecil's papers, the libel can tentatively be dated to November 1610.

220 Notes

39. This contrasts with John Donne's assessment (see letter cited below, pp. 37–8) that 'in the chiefest businesses between the Nations . . . [Cecil] was a very good patriot'.
40. Pauline Croft, 'Robert Cecil and the Early Jacobean Court', in *The Mental World of the Jacobean Court*, ed. Linda Levy Peck (Cambridge: Cambridge University Press, 1991), pp. 134–47, p. 144; 'Robert Cecil, first earl of Salisbury (1563–1612)', *ODNB*, electronic edition, www.oxforddnb.com/?/4890, accessed 5 December 2006; Cuddy, 'The Real Attempted "Tudor Revolution in Government"', p. 250.
41. Croft, 'Robert Cecil and the Early Jacobean Court', p. 144.
42. Croft, *A collection*, pp. 304–5.
43. AO3/908, lists 'the Princes Mask performed by Gentlemen of his Highness'.
44. *Chamberlain Letters*, 1.328.
45. These features are emphasised in Martin Butler's fine, brief reading of this masque: see Butler, 'Ben Jonson and the Limits of Courtly Panegyric'.
46. See note 9 above.
47. *Chamberlain Letters*, 1.328.
48. Livingston is a common name but the only other prominent Scottish family of that name connected to the Jacobean court, the Livingston earls of Linlithgow, appear not to have had a son called James: see G. E, Cokayne, *The Complete Peerage*, ed. V. Gibbs, 13 vols. (London: The St Catherine Press, 1910–59), 8.27 and *The Scots Peerage Containing an Historical and Genealogical Account of the Nobility of that Kingdom*, ed. J. Balfour Paul, 9 vols. (Edinburgh: David Douglas, 1904–14), 5.445. A John Livingston is listed in the 1605 household list as receiving £100, among the other bedchamber staff: HMC *Salisbury*, 24.62.
49. See HMC *Salisbury*, 21.253, 21.343.
50. Livingston, created a baronet (of Kinnaird, Fife) in 1627, died in 1628. He had married Jane Sproxtoune, and their son James became first Viscount of Newburgh, marrying the widowed Lady D'Aubigny in 1648: see Cokayne, *The Complete Peerage*, 9.511–14.
51. He danced in *The Irish Masque* (one of the 'high dancers', see *Chamberlain Letters*, 1.496), *Pleasure Reconciled to Virtue*, and *For the Honour of Wales*, *The Masque of the Twelve Months* (1619), and possibly *Love's Triumph* (1631): see James Knowles, 'The "Running Masque" Recovered? A Masque for the Marquess of Buckingham (c.1619–20)', *English Manuscript Studies*, 8 (2000), 79–135, p. 125 and note 138. The Abraham Abercromby linked to Prince Henry is listed as a 'sadler' (*CSPD, 1603–1610*, p. 430), although a pension of £80 was paid to one George Abercromby in March 1612 (*HMC Salisbury*, 21.350).
52. *Chamberlain Letters*, 1.497. He is usually referred to as 'Sir Henry' although he is not listed in official records as a knight. His father, Sir William I, was MP for Dunheved (Launceston), probably through the patronage of the Killigrews and Cecils. His brother-in-law had been William, Lord Burghley's secretary: see P. W. Hasler, *The House of Commons, 1558–1603, Members A–C* (London: Published for the History of Parliament Trust by HMSO, 1981), 1.475–6. Sir William, as well as being a teller of the Exchequer (*CSPD, 1603–1610*, p. 553), supplied Cecil with stone for his building projects (*HMC Salisbury*, 20.262).

53. Carleton to Chamberlain, 15 January 1604, in *Dudley Carleton to John Chamberlain, 1603–1624*, ed. M. Lee (New Brunswick, NJ: Rutgers University Press, 1973), p. 59. Interestingly, the £280 paid to finance this masque was handed over to Meredith Morgan who had been a servant of the Earl of Dunbar (see above note 9).
54. It is intriguing, therefore, to note the absence of any mention of Robert Carr. Carr may have been too divisive a figure, not just for his rapid rise, but because he had opposed the Great Contract and may even have propagated the rumour that the Commons had planned to petition for the removal of the Scots in late 1610: see A. J. Bellany, *The Politics of Court Scandal in Early Modern England: News Culture and the Overbury Affair, 1603–1660* (Cambridge: Cambridge University Press, 2002), pp. 38–9, for a succinct summary of this evidence.
55. *HMC Salisbury*, 16.388–9. As early as 1604 Roger Wilbraham believed the recent masques had cost £2,000 or £3,000, giving the total bill for 'apparells, rare musicke, fine songs, and jewels most riche' at £20,000, and that the whole had cost the Queen £100,000: see *The Journal of Roger Wilbraham, 1593–1616*, ed. H. S. Scott (Camden Society Miscellany, 10, London, 1902), p. 66.
56. It should be noted that the declared accounts for the masque do not include any costume costs.
57. *ES*, 4.177, and John H. Astington, *English Court Theatre, 1558–1642* (Cambridge: Cambridge University Press, 1999), p. 245. It is hard to calculate the cost of these specific plays but overall for the six months October 1611 to March 1612, the plays cost a total of £140 (*ES* 4.177). For gifts, see *Chamberlain Letters*, 1.327–8. £200 apiece was given to each of Prince Henry and the Duke of York's 'followers'.
58. R. Malcolm Smuts, 'Art and the Material Culture of Majesty in Early Stuart England', in *The Stuart Court and Europe: Essays in Politics and Political Culture*, ed. Smuts (Cambridge: Cambridge University Press, 1996), pp. 86–112, pp. 90–3.
59. 'Strife' here is 'competition, emulation; an effort of exertion of rivalry' (*OED*, 'strife', 3).
60. See David Norbrook, 'The Reformation of the Masque', in *The Court Masque*, ed. David Lindley (Manchester: Manchester University Press, 1984), pp. 94–110.
61. Douglas Duncan, *Ben Jonson and the Lucianic Tradition* (Cambridge: Cambridge University Press, 1979), p. 228, argues that the antimasques 'built up and exploited quite openly the same tensions and oppositions which underlay the ironic comedies: between "low" actuality and "high" ideals, coarseness and delicacy, energy and order, wit and judgement, sense and understanding'.
62. Cuddy, 'The Real Attempted "Tudor Revolution in Government"', p. 257.
63. *HMC Salisbury*, 21.320–3.
64. *King James VI and I: Political Writings*, pp. 180, 189–90.
65. *King James VI and I: Political Writings*, p. 183.
66. See *OED*, 'rail', *v.*4, 1a; *The Poems of James VI of Scotland*, ed. James Craigie, 2 vols. (Edinburgh: Scottish Text Society, 1955–8), 2.182–91, lines 22–3.
67. Cecil found himself back in favour due to his key role in the marriage negotiations for Prince Henry (see Croft, 'Cecil, Robert'), but not before the King had accused his minister of being 'a little blinded with self-love of your own counsel' (*Letters of King James VI and I*, ed. G. P. V. Akrigg (Berkeley:

University of California Press, 1984), pp. 316–17). On exact events in 1611-12, see Pauline Croft, 'The Catholic Gentry, the Earl of Salisbury and the Baronets of 1611', in *Conformity and Orthodoxy in the English Church, c.1560–1660*, ed. Peter Lake and Michael Questier (Woodbridge: Boydell Press, 2000), pp. 262–81, p. 267.
68. Pauline Croft, 'The Reputation of Robert Cecil: Libels, Political Opinion and Popular Awareness in the Early Seventeenth Century', *Transactions of the Royal Historical Society*, 6th ser., 1 (1991), 43–69.
69. Croft, 'Reputation', p. 47; the poems are 'The Old Cecilian Fox', 'Here Robin rousteth in his last nest', 'At Hatfield near Hertford there lies a coffin', and 'The devil now hath fetched the ape': see *Early Stuart Libels*, D7, D17, D18, D8.
70. 'Here lieth Robin Crooked backed, unjustly reckoned', *Early Stuart Libels*, D4.
71. *Early Stuart Libels*, D1. The poem is often attributed to Ralegh: see *The Poems of Sir Walter Ralegh: A Historical Edition*, ed. M. Rudick (Tempe, Arizona: Arizona Center for Medieval and Renaissance Studies, 1999), lxvi.
72. A. McRae, *Literature, Satire and the Early Stuart State* (Cambridge: Cambridge University Press, 2004), p. 61. McRae's analysis of this poem, in particular, emphasises the public stigma of venereal disease and the sense of divine retribution associated with syphilitic deaths.
73. John Manningham repeated common gossip when he claimed 'Sir Robert Cecil followed the Earl of Essex's death not with a good mind': Manningham, *Diary*, pp. 235–6, cited in Bellany, *Politics of Court Scandal*, p. 41.
74. *Early Stuart Libels*, D16, also cited in its original context in *Newsletters from the Archpresbyterate of George Birkhead*, ed. M. C. Questier (Camden Society Publications, 5th Ser., 12, 1998), p. 193.
75. Richard Dutton, *Ben Jonson, 'Volpone' and the Gunpowder Plot* (Cambridge: Cambridge University Press, 2008), explores the connections of these fox images to *Volpone*.
76. Pauline Croft, 'Libels, Popular Literacy and Public Opinion in Early Modern England', *Historical Research*, 68 (1995), 266–85, pp. 270 and 284.
77. *Chamberlain Letters*, 1.362–5.
78. On this 'tactic', see Croft, *A collection*, p. 253.
79. Robert Cecil, *An answer to certain scandalous papers scattered abroad under colour of a Catholic commission* (1606), sigs. B1, E4.
80. Croft, *A collection*, pp. 252–3.
81. In 1601 Cecil used the threat of libels to bring Parliament into line: see Sir Simonds d'Ewes, *Journals of All the Parliaments during the reign of Queen Elizabeth* (1682), p. 684, cited in Croft, 'Libels, Popular Literacy and Public Opinion', p. 283. Cecil's tract differentiated between the treacherous plotters and the majority of loyal Catholics.
82. Benjamin Norton to Thomas More, 9 July 1612, in *Newsletters From The Archpresbyterate of George Birkhead*, p. 172.
83. Letter to 'Sir H.G.', from Spa, 26 July 1612, in John Donne, Jr., *Letters to Several Persons of Honour* (1651), sigs. N–N2v.
84. *Newsletters From The Archpresbyterate of George Birkhead*, p. 172.
85. Debora Shuger, 'Civility and Censorship', in *Censorship and Silencing: Practices of Cultural Regulation*, ed. Robert C. Post (Los Angeles: Getty Research Institute for the History of Art and the Humanities, 1998), p. 101, argues that legal restrictions to enforce civility were about maintaining the

necessary 'civil harmony' and trust which individually directed slander and libel threatened to undermine.
86. Presumably, in the emphasis upon memory, the inference is that epigram and epitaphs are among the familiar and effective types Donne recognises.
87. See Michelle O'Callaghan, *The English Wits: Literature and Sociability in Early Modern England* (Cambridge: Cambridge University Press, 2007), pp. 89–96 on this poem.
88. David Colclough, *Freedom of Speech in Early Stuart England* (Cambridge: Cambridge University Press, 2005), pp. 248–9.
89. Such as 'Little Cecil trips up and down', SP12/278/23 cited in Croft, 'Reputation', p. 47.
90. 'Advance, advance my ill disposed muse' (*Early Stuart Libels*, D2) had been circulated by a servant of the Earl of Arundel: Cecil's relations with the Howards were variable and after his death Northampton, in particular, denounced him: see Croft, 'Reputation', p. 63.
91. Croft, *A collection*, p. 253; poems in praise of Cecil also appeared such as Benjamin Hinton's 'Upon the Death of Robert Cecil, in Queen Elizabeth's Reign Lord Treasurer and Master of the Wards and Liveries': see W. R. Morfill (ed.), *Ballads From Manuscripts*, 2 vols. (London: Ballad Society, 1873), 2.297.
92. *Early Stuart Libels*, D1, D7, D12, D18.
93. Butler, 'Ben Jonson and the Limits of Courtly Panegyric', p. 102, notes the connections to the baronetcies. During 1611 these new titles were marketed with the expectation of raising over £100,000: see Croft, 'The Catholic Gentry', p. 263.
94. Antonio Carer to the Doge and Senate of Venice, 6 May 1609, in *CSPV, 1607–10*, 11.269. He writes: 'Hard by the Court, the Earl of Salisbury has built two great galleries, decorated, especially outside, with much carving and sculpture. Inside each of these galleries, on either hand, are rows of shops for the sale of all kinds of goods . . . Last week he took the King, the Queen, and the Princes to see them. He has fitted up one of the shops very beautifully, and over it ran the words: "All other places give for money, here all is given for love". To the King he gave a Cabinet, to the Queen a silver plaque of the Annunciation worth, they say, four thousand crowns. To the Prince he gave a horse's trappings of great value, nor was there any one of the Suite who did not receive at the very least a gold ring. The King named the place Britain's Burse.'
95. John Stow, *Survey of London*, ed. A. Munday (1618), sigs. 3H3v–3H4r.
96. Indeed, by 1611 Jonson had already provided a more cynical interpretation of the Burse entertainment in *The Silent Woman, Or Epicene* where the 'rich entertainment' offered by Mrs Otter at her china shop (a substance Jonson's text strongly associated the New Exchange) equated with prostitution.
97. *Ben Jon: His Part of King James his Royall and Magnificent Entertainment through his Honorable Cittie of London* (1604), cited in A. H. Gilbert, *The Symbolic Persons in the Masques of Ben Jonson* (Durham, NC: Duke University Press, 1948), p. 199.
98. *Love Restored*, 187–90, cites Lucian's dialogue *Timon*, 20, where the deformed money god reveals how he is lame, blind, and incapable when sent by Zeus (to give money), yet flies away more rapidly when leaving: *Lucian of Samosata*, ed. and trans. A. M. Harmon, 8 vols. (Cambridge, MA: Harvard University Press, 1915–67), 2.349.

224 *Notes*

99. Matthew 6:24 and Luke 16:13 both contain the injunction that God and Mammon cannot be served simultaneously.
100. Edmund Spenser, *The Faerie Queene*, ed. A. C. Hamilton, text edited by Hiroshi Yamashita and Toshiyuki Suzuki (Harlow: Longman, 2001), 2.7.3–4.
101. Spenser, *The Faerie Queene*, 6.10.1–25, esp. 23 which stresses 'Civility' as the crowning virtue of the Graces' dance.
102. McRae, *Literature, Satire and the Early Stuart State*, p. 62.
103. *Letters of King James VI and I*, pp. 316–17.
104. Richard Dutton, *Ben Jonson: To the First Folio* (Cambridge: Cambridge University Press, 1983), pp. 144–53, argues that 'the diffuse and discreet' allusions throughout the poems and plays make it hard to formulate a coherent Jonsonian view of Cecil (esp. p. 153), but more recently he has argued that 'political/religious resentment' underlay their fraught relations: see Dutton, *Ben Jonson, 'Volpone' and the Gunpowder Plot*, pp. 127–32 (esp. p. 128). On the criticism in the epigrams, see R. Wiltenberg, '"What need hast thou of me? or my Muse?": Jonson and Cecil, Politician and Poet', in *The Muses Common-Weale*, ed. C. J. Summers and T. L. Pebworth (Columbia: University of Missouri Press, 1988), pp. 34–47, p. 46, which discusses the Cecil poems as explorations of the 'limits' of the political and poetic worlds, exemplifying the difficult 'tension between accommodation to courtly realities and resistance to subservient clientage'. See also my 'Unprofitable Lovers: Cecil, Jonson and the Negotiation of Patronage', in *The Early Cecils: Patronage, Politics and Culture*, ed. Pauline Croft (New Haven and London: Yale University Press/Paul Mellon Studies in British Art, 2001), pp. 181–95.
105. *Early Stuart Libels*, D19 ('Passer-by know here is interred'); Jonson's comments are in 'Conversations with Drummond', lines 297–8.
106. Here *Love Restored* follows the Timon story which castigates his ungrateful followers for the failure to support their former patron. On the incivility of personal satire, see Shuger, 'Civility and Censorship', pp. 96–7.
107. For confidence, see *OED*, 6 ('confiding of private matters'), and 8 ('trustworthiness'). A legal definition of 'confidence' as 'trust' is also available. 'Reality', *OED*, 4a, 'sincere devotion, loyalty', citing this passage.
108. There is also a curious doubleness to the masque's argument in that Cecil seems to be simultaneously accused of meanness and profligacy, although these accusations echo the libels which circulated in late 1612.
109. Erasmus, 'Letter to Martin Dorp', in *The Praise of Folly*, cited by O'Callaghan, *The English Wits*, p. 7.
110. Glenn Burgess, *Absolute Monarchy and the Stuart Constitution* (New Haven: Yale University Press, 1996), pp. 40–3; Colclough, *Freedom of Speech in Early Stuart England*, p. 158.
111. Petition drawn up by Sir Edwin Sandys, May 1610, cited in Colclough, *Freedom of Speech in Early Stuart England*, pp. 157–8.
112. Foster (ed.), *Proceedings in Parliament 1610*, 2.192.
113. Quentin Skinner, 'John Milton and the Politics of Slavery', *Prose Studies: History, Theory, Criticism*, 23 (2000), 1–22, pp. 2 and 4.
114. Foster (ed.), *Proceedings in Parliament 1610*, 2.83.
115. Daryl W. Palmer, *Writing Russia in the Age of Shakespeare* (Aldershot: Ashgate, 2004), pp. 207–8. Palmer also makes an interesting link between

Russian rulers and their penchant for 'pederasty' and the rise of Carr (see pp. 206–10).
116. Foster (ed.), *Proceedings in Parliament 1610*, 2.195–6. In 1628, Dudley Digges contrasted Muscovite frailty caused by tyranny with freeborn English strength: cited by Skinner, 'John Milton and the Politics of Slavery', p. 5.
117. *Chamberlain Letters*, 1.301.
118. *OED*, 'spout' (v.), I.3; and 'murmurer'. Interestingly, 'to murmur' had a much stronger critical edge in early modern Scots where it was associated with accusations, especially if directed against a judge: see *OED*, 'murmur' (v.), b.
119. See also *OED*, 'boisterous', 9b.
120. Marcus, *The Politics of Mirth*, p. 34.
121. Debora Shuger, 'Irishmen, Aristocrats, and Other White Barbarians', *Renaissance Quarterly*, 50 (1997), 494–525, considers how the English aristocracy and their propensity for violence are as much targets of the civilising process as any 'other'; Jennifer Richards, 'Introduction' to *Early Modern Civil Discourses* (Basingstoke: Palgrave Macmillan, 2003), pp. 6–7, suggests that this doubleness also unpicks the uncivil/civil binary. Both seem crucial possibilities in the light of the violence that surrounded Anglo-Scots relations 1610–12 (see above, pp. 26–8) and the incorporation of dissenting voices.
122. Spenser, *Faerie Queene*, 6.10.23.
123. A. Ribeiro, 'Sir John Roe: Ben Jonson's Friend', *Review of English Studies*, 24 (1973), 153–64.
124. *The Poems of John Donne*, ed. H. C. Grierson, 2 vols. (Oxford: Oxford University Press, 1912), 1.414–5.
125. This strategic use of 'outsider' status aligns Jonson with the 'public men', the new political class, that emerged during the Jacobean period, representing themselves as the voice of the 'common weal': see Richard Cust, 'The "Public Man" in Late Tudor and Early Stuart England', in *The Politics of the Public Sphere in Early Modern England*, ed. Lake and Pincus, pp. 116–43.

3 Crack Kisses Not Staves: Sexual Politics and Court Masques in 1613–14

1. For Stone and Hill, see Joad Raymond, 'Describing Popularity in Early Modern England', *Huntingdon Library Quarterly*, 67 (2004), 101–30, p. 101; David Underdown, *A Freeborn People: Politics and the Nation in Seventeenth-Century England* (Oxford: Clarendon Press, 1996), p. 33; Alastair Bellany, *The Politics of Court Scandal in Early Modern England: News Culture and the Overbury Affair, 1603–1660* (Cambridge: Cambridge University Press, 2002).
2. Joad Raymond, *Pamphlets and Pamphleteering in Early Modern Britain* (Cambridge: Cambridge University Press, 2003), pp. 127–8, illustrates civil war recycling of this material.
3. Roger Darnton comments on the ways in which libels sap legitimacy due to the intensively personal nature of political culture: see *The Literary Underground of the Ancien Regime*, cited in Debora Shuger, 'Civility and Censorship', in *Censorship and Silencing: Practices of Cultural Regulation*, ed. Robert C. Post (Los Angeles: Getty Research Institute for the History of Art and the Humanities, 1998), p. 96.

4. On the 'anaesthetic of official propaganda' in Irish affairs, see David Lindley, 'Embarrassing Ben: The Masques for Frances Howard', in *Renaissance Historicism: Selections from ELR*, ed. Arthur F. Kinney and Dan S. Collins (Amherst: University of Massachusetts Press, 1987), pp. 248–64, esp. pp. 259–60.
5. *HMC Downshire*, 4.285, 286
6. Finet dated the play to 2 February but there are good reasons for accepting 3 February 1614: see Samuel Daniel, *Hymen's Triumph*, ed. John Pitcher (Oxford: Oxford University Press [Malone Society Reprints], 1994), p. vii.
7. Samuel Calvert to William Trumbull, 14 December 1613, in *HMC Downshire*, 4.267.
8. The events surrounding the marriage can be traced back to the rise of Carr and include: the period of his close relations with Sir Thomas Overbury; the ditching of Overbury; the affair between Carr and the Countess of Essex (probably begun in 1611 or 1612); the Essex nullity and divorce (formally ended 25 September 1613); the death of Overbury (September 1613); the Carr–Howard marriage (26 December 1613); the trials of the Earl and Countess of Somerset and their accomplices and the revelation of the adulterous affair between Robert Carr and Frances Howard; and the sequence of punishments meted out to those involved.
9. Bellany, *The Politics of Court Scandal in Early Modern England*, pp. 36–50, 62.
10. CUL, MS Dd.3.63, fol. 44, cited in David Lindley, *The Trials of Frances Howard: Fact and Fiction at the Court of King James* (London: Routledge, 1993), p. 85. Sir Roger Wilbraham summarised the Howard gains as Suffolk became Lord Treasurer, 'his son-in-law, the Earl of Somerset, Lord High Chamberlain and the most potent favourite in my time . . . the Chancellor of Exchequer and many other officers placed by his means and his son in law Somerset's, that great favourite' (*The Journal of Sir Roger Wilbraham*, ed. H. S. Scott, Camden Miscellany, 10 (1902), p. 115).
11. *The Irish Masque at Court*, line 166.
12. John Orrell, 'The London Court Stage in the Savoy Correspondence, 1613–75', *Theatre Research International*, 4 (1979), 79–94, pp. 81–2. Sir John Throckmorton described the procession as made up of most of the court: letter to William Trumbull, 11 January 1614, *HMC Downshire*, 4.286.
13. Bellany, *The Politics of Court Scandal*, p. 250.
14. David Lindley's important study considers Frances Howard concentrates on these libels as exemplifying the subordinate position of women under early modern patriarchy and the collusion of many modern historians and literary critics with the misogynistic commentary of earlier centuries: see *The Trials of Frances Howard*, esp. pp. 123–44.
15. R. Niccols, *Sir Thomas Overbury's Vision* (1616), sig. A3r. The marginal note glosses 'forum' as 'Guild hall'.
16. Niccols' tract equates the poison of the murder with the poison of ignorant discussion which damages the body politic ('every common drudge / Assumed the person of an awful judge') and depicts the scandal as vocal strain and diminishing control ('But from the reach of voice too far compelled / That beast of many heads I there beheld' (sigs. A3r-v).
17. 'Uncouth' literally means unknown (*OED*, 'uncouth', 4), conveying just how strange and distasteful those discoveries had been.

18. *The Journal of Sir Roger Wilbraham*, p. 115.
19. George Calvert to Sir Thomas Edmondes, 1 August 1612, cited in Thomas Birch, *The Court and Times of James the First*, 2 vols. (London: H. Colburn, 1849), vol. 1, p. 191.
20. In what follows I have drawn on Linda Levy Peck's 'Monopolizing Favour: Structures of Power in the Early Seventeenth-Century English Court', in *The World of the Favourite*, ed. John H. Elliott and L. W. B. Brockliss (New Haven: Yale University Press, 1999), pp. 54–70.
21. Neil Cuddy, 'The Revival of the Entourage: The Bedchamber of James I, 1603–1625', in *The English Court: From the Wars of the Roses to the Civil War*, ed. David Starkey (London: Longman, 1987), pp. 173–225, p. 208, and Peck, 'Monopolizing Favour', p. 58.
22. Cited in Peck, 'Monopolizing Favour', p. 59 and Peter R. Seddon 'Robert Carr, Earl of Somerset', *Medieval and Renaissance Studies*, 14 (1970), 48–68, p. 51. Ferdinand de Boisschot, the agent of Isabella and Ferdinand in London, described Carr as a 'privado': see W. Schrickx, *Foreign Envoys and Travelling Players in the Age of Shakespeare* (Gent: Rijksuniversiteit te Gent, 1986), p. 325.
23. Peck, 'Monopolizing Favour', p. 59 and A. R. Braunmuller, 'Robert Carr, Earl of Somerset, as Collector and Patron', in *The Mental World of the Jacobean Court*, ed. Linda Levy Peck (Cambridge: Cambridge University Press, 1991), pp. 230–50, pp. 230–2 (esp. p. 230). Carr's paintings are discussed by Timothy Wilks, 'The Picture Collection of Robert Carr, Earl of Somerset (c.1587–1645), Reconsidered', *Journal of the History of Collections*, 1 (1989), 167–77. Writing in 1610 William Cecil advised a fellow nobleman that he should collect Italian art 'to increase your magnificence' (see Braunmuller, 'Robert Carr, Earl of Somerset, as Collector and Patron', p. 231).
24. Cuddy, 'The Revival of the Entourage', p. 181, and 'The Conflicting Loyalties of a "Vulger Counselor": The Third Earl of Southampton, 1597–1624', in *Public Duty and Private Conscience in Seventeenth Century England*, ed. John Morrill, Paul Slack, and Daniel Woolf (Oxford: Oxford University Press, 1993), pp. 121–50, p. 140.
25. *CSPV, 1613–15*, 13.219.
26. Cited in Peck, 'Monopolizing Favour', p. 58, from G. P. V. Akrigg (ed.), *Letters of King James VI & I* (Berkeley: University of California Press, 1984), pp. 335–40.
27. Bodleian Library, Oxford, Tanner MS 75, fol. 265 (1607), cited in Linda Levy Peck, *Northampton: Patronage and Policy at the Court of James I* (London: Allen & Unwin, 1982), p. 30.
28. *The Journal of Sir Roger Wilbraham*, p. 116 and Lisa Jardine and Alan Stewart, *Hostage to Fortune: The Troubled Life of Francis Bacon, 1561–1626* (London: Gollancz, 1998), p. 360.
29. For a useful survey, see Alan Stewart, *Close Readers: Humanism and Sodomy in Early Modern England* (Princeton: Princeton University Press, 1997), pp. 161–87. The role of the favourite and the significance of royal favour were often opaque matters even for contemporaries, but Bellany, *The Politics of Court Scandal*, pp. 28–32, provides a sensitive reading of Carr's relationship with

the King that stresses its emotional dynamics, and the problematic and ultimately unknowable aspects of Carr and the King's relations.
30. Stewart, *Close Readers*, xxvii–xxviii, and Alan Bray, 'Male Homosexuality and the Signs of Male Friendship', *History Workshop Journal*, 29 (1990), 1–19, also in *Queering the Renaissance*, ed. Jonathan Goldberg (Durham, NC: Duke University Press, 1994).
31. Eve Sedgwick, *Between Men: English Literature and Male Homosocial Desire* (New York: Columbia University Press, 1985), pp. 89–90.
32. William A. McClung and Rodney Simard, 'Donne's Somerset Epithalmion and the Erotics of Criticism', *Huntington Library Quarterly*, 50 (1987), 95–106.
33. For the term 'open secret', see Alan Sinfield, *Cultural Politics — Queer Reading* (London: Routledge, 1994), p. 47.
34. See Lindley, *The Trials of Frances Howard*, esp. p. 77.
35. Samuel Calvert to William Trumbull, 14 December 1613, in *HMC Downshire*, 4.267.
36. Lindley, *The Trials of Frances Howard*, pp. 118–19.
37. Lindley, *The Trials of Frances Howard*, pp. 94–5, provides a succinct summary of the ways of interpreting the nullity.
38. *Complete Collection of State Trials*, ed. T. B. Howell (London, 1818), vol. 2, p. 822, cited in Lindley, *The Trials of Frances Howard*, p. 95.
39. Chester R.O., CR63.2.19, fol. 14 (commonplace book of William Davenport), cited by Lindley, *The Trials of Frances Howard*, p. 99.
40. David Lindley, *Thomas Campion* (Leiden: E. J. Brill, 1986), p. 222, citing *State Trials* (1809), vol. 2, p. 816.
41. Lindley, *The Trials of Frances Howard*, p. 71.
42. Peck, 'Monopolizing Favour', p. 70, note 55.
43. See *Early Stuart Libels: An Edition of Poetry from Manuscript Sources*, ed. Alastair Bellany and Andrew McRae, Early Modern Literary Studies, Text Series I (2005) (http://purl.oclc.org/emls/texts/libels), F6. This electronic edition is abbreviated to *Early Stuart Libels*.
44. *Early Stuart Libels*, F4.
45. Harvard MS 686, fol. 13v, cited in James L. Sanderson, 'Poems on an Affair of State: The Marriage of Somerset and Lady Essex', *Review of English Studies*, NS 17 (1966), 57–61.
46. William R. Chetwood, *Memoirs of the Life and Writings of Ben Jonson* (Dublin: W. R. Chetwood, 1756), iv.
47. A similar pun on 'tail' was used by John Holles who noted 'the cat hath found another tail to play with all' when he described the advent of George Villiers as new favourite (see *Letters of John Holles, 1587–1637*, ed. P. R. Seddon (Nottingham: Thoroton Society, 1975), vol. 1, p. 70.
48. See Lindley, *The Trials of Frances Howard*, pp. 139–40 for a similar emphasis in Chapman's *Andromeda Liberata*.
49. Chamberlain to Carleton, 25 November 1613, *Chamberlain Letters*, 1.487.
50. Carr and Overbury apparently labelled her 'Agrippina' in their coded letters: see Anne Somerset, *Unnatural Murder: Poison at the Court of James I* (London: Weidenfeld & Nicolson, 1997), p. 98.
51. See my 'To enlight the darksome night, pale Cinthia doth arise: Anna of Denmark, Elizabeth I and the Images of Royalty', in *Women and Culture*

at the Courts of the Stuart Queens, ed. C. McManus (Basingstoke: Palgrave Macmillan, 2003), pp. 21–48, for one aspect of the Howard attempts to woo Anna through Campion's *Entertainment at Caversham* (27 April 1613).
52. Peck, *Northampton*, pp. 73–4.
53. Lindley, *The Trials of Frances Howard*, p. 84.
54. *HMC Downshire*, 4.231, 235, 237.
55. Lorkin to Puckering, 8 July 1613, in Birch, *Court and Times of James I*, 1.254; and CUL, MS Dd.3.63, fol. 44 cited in Lindley, *The Trials of Frances Howard*, p. 85.
56. Chamberlain to Carleton, 25 November 1613, and Chamberlain to Alice Carleton, 30 December 1613, *Chamberlain Letters*, 1.487 and 496.
57. John More to William Trumbull, 13 November 1613 in *HMC Downshire*, 4.252; *Chamberlain Letters*, 1.487.
58. *HMC Portland*, 9.31 (Holles Letter Book).
59. *HMC Portland*, 9.31. The letter is dated 1613, but both Lindley (*The Trials of Frances Howard*, p. 204, note 17) and Seddon (*Letters of John Holles*, 1.49), agree that it dates from 1614.
60. John Pitcher has pointed out that *Hymen's Triumph* was probably in preparation by mid-1613 mainly intended for celebrations to mark the completion of the rebuilding of Somerset House and its renaming by the Queen, but the text was also adapted to suit the nuptial occasion and Anne's entertainment of her husband: see Daniel, *Hymen's Triumph*, viii–x. Even though the title page of the printed text links the events to the Queen's entertainment of the King, other elements, such as the additional prologue, stress her difference from the King: see p. 86 below and Daniel, *Hymen's Triumph*, pp. xi–xii.
61. C. McManus, *Women on the Renaissance Stage: Anna of Denmark and Female Masquing in the Stuart Court, 1590–1619* (Manchester: Manchester University Press, 2002), pp. 168–9.
62. These manoeuvres are very complex and the Queen's position is not easy to establish. It is possible that in 'being won' to support the marriage, the Queen had surrendered some of her independence, but the process of creating the masque, given the choice of Campion and the delicate balances created in the text, militate against an event that does not, at the very least, accommodate the Queen and her position. The tenor of Northampton's letter – the sheer fear that she would not consent – reveals her power at this juncture, although once the gifts have been accepted the powerful binding reciprocity involved in early modern elite gift-exchanges may have operated. The King's concessions may have attempted to require a reciprocal concession from the Queen.
63. David Stevenson, *Scotland's Last Royal Wedding: The Marriage of James VI and Anne of Denmark* (Edinburgh: John Donald, 1997).
64. Spenser, *The Faerie Queene*, 2.6.2–18, and compare *Early Stuart Libels*, F4 ('From Katherin's docke there launch a pinke'). Campion also synthesises several classical sources, including Catullus' poem on the wedding of Peleus and Thetis that concluded with the Fates prophesying the birth of a son. The masque also reiterates the idea of the marriage of earth and sea in a movement from sea to land that shapes the masque's central transformation: see Lindley, *Thomas Campion*, p. 217.

65. *The Somerset Masque*, in *The Works of Thomas Campion*, ed. W. R. Davis (London: Faber, 1969), pp. 263–84, p. 270. Hereafter, references to this masque are given in parentheses in the text.
66. *The Third Part of the Countess of Pembroke's Ivychurch* (1592), sig. 5v, cited in *The Works of Thomas Campion*, p. 265.
67. The nine musicians may also have been the nine Muses which would increase the female predominance among the masque's mythological actors.
68. McManus, *Women on the Renaissance Stage*, pp. 172–3, provides a detailed exposition of the olive emblem; she also illustrates *Minerva Britanna*, emblem 13.
69. McManus, *Women on the Renaissance Stage*, pp. 171–2. An alternative view of this seaborne imagery would be to associate her not only with Venus but with the sea as a symbol of fertility (through the sea-god Proteus). More pointedly, Bel-Anna commands and controls the seas, while Frances Howard in the libels merely sails upon them, her association with leaky vessels a confirmation of her weakness.
70. See McManus, *Women on the Renaissance Stage*, p. 167.
71. De Boisschot describes the branch as given to Suffolk (see Schrickx, *Foreign Envoys*, p. 327); John Orrell, 'The Agent of Savoy at *The Somerset Masque*', *Review of English Studies*, NS 28 (1977), 302–4, continues the action as the branch 'was carried to the Earl of Pembroke as a sign that he might begin the dances, which he did offering his hand to the queen'.
72. For Frances Howard's role: see Orrell, 'The Agent of Savoy at *The Somerset Masque*', p. 304.
73. *The Works of Thomas Campion*, p. 276.
74. *The Works of Thomas Campion*, pp. 274–5.
75. Lindley, *The Trials of Frances Howard*, pp. 125–6.
76. John Finet, *Finetti Philoxenis* (1656), sig. B7r.
77. Although the surviving financial accounts are unclear as to who paid for the masque, contemporaries were in no doubt the King funded the occasion: see Orrell, 'The London Court Stage in the Savoy Correspondence, 1613–75', p. 82.
78. The masquers were the Duke of Lennox, four earls (Pembroke, Dorset, Salisbury, and Montgomery), four lords (Walden, Scrope, North, and Hay), and three Howard knights (Sir Thomas, Sir Henry, and Sir Charles): see *Somerset Masque*, p. 284.
79. Sir Thomas Monson was an important musical patron as well as chancellor to Queen Anna: see D. Lindley, 'Campion, Thomas (1567–1620)', *ODNB* (Oxford: Oxford University Press), online edition (http://www.oxforddnb.com/view/article/4541, accessed 7 January 2007), and A. Bellany, 'Monson, Sir Thomas, first baronet (1563/4–1641)', *ODNB* (Oxford: Oxford University Press), online edition (http://www.oxforddnb.com/view/article/18990, accessed 7 January 2007).
80. See my 'To enlight the darksome night, pale Cinthia doth arise'.
81. Lindley, *Thomas Campion*, pp. 232–3.
82. See my 'To enlight the darksome night, pale Cinthia doth arise', esp. pp. 28 (and note 37) and 40 (and note 79).
83. McManus, *Women on the Renaissance Stage*, pp. 177–8.
84. John More to William Trumbull in *HMC Downshire*, 4.252.
85. Alan Young, *Tudor and Jacobean Tournaments* (London: George Philip & Son, 1987), p. 184.

86. Chamberlain to Carleton, 5 January 1614, *Chamberlain Letters*, 1.498, mentions murrey and white as the bride's colours and green and yellow for the bridegroom. This is confirmed by the list of tilters in BL MS Harleian 5176 (*Ben Jonson*, 10.538).
87. The Savoyard agent reported that 'Many lords have been invited to a certain tilt, but many of them have refused because they are relatives of the Earl of Essex, and others have excused themselves, not being part of this [Howard] faction': see Lindley, 'Embarrassing Ben', pp. 254–5.
88. The pro-Catholic Howards opposed military intervention and in the emergent debate over a marital partner for Prince Charles they espoused a Spanish match.
89. The printed text in F1616 contains no mention of the specific occasion: we cannot be sure that the text as performed may not have contained more material that was edited out during 1615–16.
90. David Riggs, *Ben Jonson: A Life* (Cambridge, MA: Harvard University Press, 1989), p. 203
91. The libels commented on Carr's good looks, for example, *Early Stuart Libels*, F10.
92. Lindley, *The Trials of Frances Howard*, pp. 116–17.
93. *Chamberlain Letters*, 1.461.
94. Although little survives of Middleton's lost *Masque of Cupids* its plural title suggests it may have responded directly to Jonson's text. It clearly continues the emphasis upon love and desire: see M. T. Jones-Davies and A. J. Hoenselaars, *The Masque of Cupids* in *Thomas Middleton: The Collected Works*, ed. Gary Taylor and John Lavignino (Oxford: Clarendon Press, 2007).
95. *The Works of Thomas Campion*, pp. 275, 267, and 274.
96. Chamberlain to Dudley Carleton, 5 January 1614, cited in *Ben Jonson*, 10.541 (from SP14/86/2).
97. Andrew Murphy, *But the Irish Sea Betwixt Us: Ireland, Colonialism and Renaissance Literature* (Lexington: University of Kentucky Press, 1999), p. 143; Lindley, 'Embarrassing Ben', pp. 248–64, provides a brief, perceptive discussion of the immediate Irish context of this masque. I have drawn heavily on Lindley's article in what follows.
98. Lindley, 'Embarrassing Ben', esp. p. 262.
99. Thus one of the most perceptive studies passes over the 'incriminating aspects of the scandal' to study the Irish contexts in detail: see James M. Smith, 'Effaced History: Facing the Colonial Contexts of Ben Jonson's *Irish Masque at Court*', *English Literary History*, 65 (1998), 297–321.
100. See Thomas Healy, 'Drama, Ireland and the Question of Civility', in *Early Modern Civil Discourses*, ed. Jennifer Richards (Basingstoke: Palgrave Macmillan, 2003), pp. 131–45, p. 131.
101. The masque draws on Tacitean views of colonialism which encouraged a sceptical response to claims of cultural superiority: see Andrew Hadfield, 'Tacitus and the Reform of Ireland in the 1590s', in *Early Modern Civil Discourses*, ed. Richards, pp. 115–30, esp. pp. 116–17.
102. Debora Shuger, 'Irishmen, Aristocrats, and Other White Barbarians', *Renaissance Quarterly*, 50 (1997), 494–525, pp. 494–5.
103. Cited in Jerzy Limon, *The Masque of Stuart Culture* (Newark, NJ: University of Delaware Press, 1990), p. 181.

104. *The Masque of Flowers*, lines 376–84 in *A Book of Masques*, ed. Stanley Wells (Cambridge: Cambridge University Press, 1967).
105. 'Lady Changed to Venus Dove', lines 7–8 (*Early Stuart Libels*, F6).
106. *Proceedings in Parliament 1614 (House of Commons)*, ed. M. Jansson (Philadelphia: American Philosophical Society, 1988), p. 71.
107. R. Dudley Edwards (ed.), 'The Letter-Book of Sir Arthur Chichester, 1612–1614', *Analecta Hibernia*, 8 (1938), nos. 55, 56, and 58. Letter 58 (Chichester and the Council to King James, 26/27 May 1613) describes also 'dissentions' at the Parliament; see also John McCavitt, 'An Unspeakable Parliamentary Fracas: The Irish House of Commons, 1613', *Analecta Hibernia*, 37 (1996), 223–35, p. 231.
108. *CSP (Carew), 1603–1624*, p. 290, cited in Lindley, 'Embarrassing Ben', p. 260.
109. John McCavitt, *Sir Arthur Chichester, Lord Deputy of Ireland, 1605–16* (Belfast: Institute of Irish Studies, 1998), p. 187.
110. The Old English were the largely Catholic Anglo-Irish families who were regarded with distrust by the English government and who often were seen as having assimilated too much into Irish, Gaelic, and Catholic society.
111. P. Coughlan, '"Some Secret Scourge shall by her come unto England": Ireland and Incivility in Spenser', in *Spenser in Ireland: An Interdisciplinary Perspective*, ed. Coughlan (Cork: Cork University Press, 1989), pp. 46–74, pp. 49–50, notes the Spenserian critique of Gaelic transhumance societies as like 'Scythian' mobility; it may be that the final fixing of the masquers in *The Irish Masque* after their journey, and the emphasis upon their employment, counters this reading of Irish over-motility and social instability.
112. B. Rich, *New Description of Ireland* (1610), p. 36, cited in Limon, *The Masque of Stuart Culture*, p. 181; Sir John Davies, *A Discovery of the True Causes Why Ireland was never Entirely Subdued* (1612), cited in Lindley, 'Embarrassing Ben', pp. 257–8. Lindley suggests that this text may well have provided the basis of the fiction of *The Irish Masque*: see 'Embarrassing Ben', p. 258.
113. See Lindley, 'Embarrassing Ben', p. 259.
114. Crucially, the 'other rude music' suggests the link is with the rough music of popular culture. Bagpipes could also represent the northern English and Scots; it could be linked to northern barbarity (rather than any specific ethnic group); it could also represent social and political disharmony, as in the image of the disharmonious consort from 1607 (cited on p. 27); regularly, it could accompany satirical and libellous verse.
115. See Lindley, 'Embarrassing Ben', p. 260, note 19, on the importance of prophecy in the union project.
116. Philip Edwards, *Threshold of a Nation*, p. 13, cited in Lindley, 'Embarrassing Ben', p. 259. Murphy, *But the Irish Sea Betwixt Us*, p. 195, note 21, notes that Jonson's view that the Irish are complicit in the destruction of their own culture has some basis in historical fact as the Irish bards did seek patronage from those who also destroyed Irish social structures.
117. P. Holman, 'The Harp in Stuart England: New Light on William Lawes's Harp Consorts', *Early Music*, 15 (1987), 188–204, pp. 189 and 200.
118. Holman, 'The Harp in Stuart England', p. 195; *HMC Salisbury*, 24.65.
119. L. Hulse, '"Musique which pleaseth myne eare": Robert Cecil's Musical Patronage', in *Patronage, Culture and Power: The Early Cecils*, ed. Pauline Croft (New Haven and London: Yale University Press, 2002), pp. 139–58, p. 143.
120. 'The Letter-Book of Sir Arthur Chichester', no. 55.

121. 'The Letter-Book of Sir Arthur Chichester', no. 60.
122. 'The Letter-Book of Sir Arthur Chichester', no. 58.
123. Campion, *Somerset Masque*, p. 272.
124. Michelle O'Callaghan, '"Now Thou May'st Speak Freely": Entering the Public Sphere in 1614', in *The Crisis of 1614 and the Addled Parliament: Literary and Historical Perspectives*, ed. Steven Clucas and Rosalind Davies (Aldershot: Ashgate, 2003), pp. 63–79.
125. *Proceedings in Parliament 1614 (House of Commons)*, p. 19, and echoed by Sir Julius Caesar, see p. 422.
126. O'Callaghan, 'Entering the Public Sphere in 1614', pp. 65–7.
127. Chapman, *Andromeda Liberata*, cited in Bellany, *The Politics of Court Scandal*, p. 131.
128. Chapman, *Andromeda Liberata* (1614), sig. ¶3r. Chapman also contrasts his poetry of 'Nuptial states' with the desires of 'the one-eared race / Of set-eyed vulgars' (¶3v).
129. See *Early Stuart Libels*, H1 (lines 51–2).
130. *A Free and Offenceless Justification of a lately Published and most maliciously misinterpreted poeme entitled Andromeda Liberata* (London), sig.*4r.
131. Michelle O'Callaghan has argued that the interplay between oral, manuscript, and printed forms implies a sophisticated textual culture in which manuscript forms can parody the kind of licensing required from print material to announce its own independence: see 'Entering the Public Sphere in 1614', p. 67.
132. Winwood to Carleton (28 September 1613), see Bellany, *The Politics of Court Scandal*, p. 134.
133. Bellany, *The Politics of Court Scandal*, p. 134.
134. Finet, *Finetti Philoxeni*, sigs. B6v–B7, describes these manoeuvres in detail.
135. G. P. V. Akrigg, 'The Curious Marginalia of Charles, Second Earl Stanhope', in *John Quincy Adams Memorial Studies*, ed. James G. MacManaway, Giles E. Dawson, and Edwin E. Willoughby (Washington: Folger Shakespeare Library, 1948), pp. 785–801.
136. It is uncertain whether this prologue was performed in 1614 and simply omitted from the manuscript copy presented to the bride, Jean Drummond, Lady Roxburgh, or whether Daniel revised his text in 1615 in the light of subsequent revelations: see *Hymen's Triumph*, ed. Pitcher, ix–x.
137. *Hymen's Triumph*, ed. Pitcher, xi.
138. *Hymen's Triumph* in *The Complete Works in Verse and Prose of Samuel Daniel*, ed. A. B. Grosart, 5 vols. (London: Hazell, Watson and Viney, 1865–96), 3.331. John Peacock, 'Ben Jonson's Masques and Italian Culture', in *Theatre of the English and Italian Renaissance*, ed. J. R. Mulryne and M. Shewring (Basingstoke: Macmillan, 1991), pp. 73–94, provides an important discussion of the divergences between Campion, Daniel, and Jonson over masque theory.
139. Lindley, 'Embarrassing Ben', p. 262.
140. Shuger, 'Irishmen, Aristocrats, and Other White Barbarians', pp. 498, 501.
141. Hadfield, 'Tacitus and the Reform of Ireland', p. 119; Shuger, 'Irishmen, Aristocrats, and Other White Barbarians', p. 504, cites Spenser on England's recent acquisition of manners 'but even the other day'.
142. James regarded the Highlanders as 'barbarous for the most part and yet mixed with some show of civility' and the Islanders as 'all utterly barbarous'

234 Notes

and recommended penal laws against the clan chiefs and the colonisation of the Highlands 'that within short time may reform and civilise the best inclined among them, rooting out or transporting the barbarous and stubborn sort, and planting civility in their rooms': see *The Basilicon Doron of King James VI*, ed. James Craigie, 2 vols. (Edinburgh: Scottish Text Society, 1944–50), 1.70–1 and A. Williamson, 'Scots, Indians and Empire: The Scottish Politics of Civilization, 1519–1609', *Past and Present*, 150 (1996), 46–83.

143. Some of the surrounding documentation for this masque makes this explicit: 'his Maiesty is determined to have a masque this Christmas performed by some gentlemen of his own servants' (National Archives, SP14/75/53).

144. In placing royal favour at the centre of the marriage, Jonson echoes other contemporaries, such as John Donne who praised 'A Court, where all affections do assent / Unto the King's' in countenancing the Carr–Howard match: see 'Eclogue 1613. December 26', lines 77–8 in *The Complete English Poems of John Donne*, ed. A. J. Smith (Harmondsworth: Penguin Books, 1971).

145. Samuel Calvert to William Trumbull, 14 December 1613, *HMC Downshire*, 4.267, in *A Book of Masques*, ed. Wells, pp. 152–3.

146. 28 November 1613, in B. Anderton (ed.), 'Selections from the Delaval Papers in the Public Library, Newcastle-upon-Tyne', in *A Volume of Miscellanea, Publications of the Newcastle-upon-Tyne Records Committee*, 60 (1930, for 1929), p. 138. Other critics were Philip Gawdy who commented on the 'great gifts of plate' but felt 'the masques were very stale': *Letters of Philip Gawdy*, ed. I. H. Jeayes (1906), 175.

4 'No News': *News from the New World* and Textual Culture in the 1620s

1. *Irish Masque at Court*, line 48. On the politics of this masque and the 1621 season, see Martin Butler, 'Jonson's *News From the New World*, the "Running Masque" and the Season of 1619–20', *Medieval and Renaissance Drama in England*, 6 (1993), 153–79. See also P. R. Sellin, 'The Performances of Ben Jonson's *Newes from the New World Discover'd in the Moone*', *English Studies*, 61 (1980), 491–7, and P. R. Sellin, 'The Politics of Ben Jonson's *Newes from the New World Discover'd in the Moone*', *Viator*, 17 (1986), 321–37.

2. The first extant issue dates from 2 December 1620 but the printer Thomas Archer may have produced corantos in London as early as February 1620: see F. Dahl, *A Bibliography of English Corantos and Periodical Newsbooks 1620–1642* (London: Bibliographical Society, 1952), pp. 31 and 49–50.

3. Peter Lake and Steven Pincus (eds.), *The Politics of the Public Sphere in Early Modern England* (Manchester: Manchester University Press, 2007), p. 8.

4. There is a complex series of puns in these lines: this 'no news' meaning it is news of 'no', that is of 'nowhere'; but also neither is it 'news' as novelty since it is 'no news' to the royal audience; nor is it 'news' in the sense used by the Factor, Printer and Chronicler, since it is not for 'delight' but rather a matter of 'belief'.

5. Although critics have tended to connect *News* to the news culture depicted in *The Staple of News* the play focuses more closely on the slightly different

issue of the London-based publication of printed corantos by the Butter and Bourne syndicate: see D. F. McKenzie, 'The Staple of News and the Late Plays', in A Celebration of Ben Jonson, ed. W. Blissett, Julian Patrick, and R. W. Van Fossen (Toronto: University of Toronto Press, 1975), pp. 83–128, where a very hardline attitude towards 'a stupid audience' and the 'gullible populace' is discussed. These may be Jonson's views by 1625–31, but they are not necessarily his position in 1621.

6. Sara Pearl, 'Sounding to Present Occasions: Jonson's Masques of 1620–5', in The Court Masque, ed. D. Lindley (Manchester, 1984), pp. 60–77, esp. pp. 60–1, which also contrasts public approbation for royal policy with private scepticism. See also McKenzie, 'The Staple of News and the Late Plays', p. 118, which sees the attack on news as part dislike of an uneducated audience and part lament for the loss of theatre's primacy in public debate.

7. Julie Sanders, 'Print, Popular Culture, Consumption and Commodification in The Staple of News', in Refashioning Ben Jonson: Gender, Politics, and the Jonsonian Canon, ed. Julie Sanders, Kate Chedgzoy, and Sue Wiseman (Basingstoke: Macmillan, 1998), 183–207, esp. pp. 184–8. Sanders (p. 188) comments especially how news mediates between the different sections of a shared culture that the modern binary of popular/elite tends to obscure.

8. Popularity is associated with demagoguery and conspiracy theories in this period: see Richard Cust, 'Charles I and Popularity', in Politics, Religion and Popularity, ed. Richard Cust, Thomas Cogswell, and Peter Lake (Cambridge: Cambridge University Press, 2002), pp. 235–58.

9. Herford and Simpson regarded News as inaugurating the decline in Jonson's masque-making as the volatees contrasted insufficiently with the 'colourless and perfunctory rudiments' of the main masque (Ben Jonson, 2.311), but Sellin, 'The Politics of Ben Jonson's Newes from the New World Discover'd in the Moone', pp. 331–2, argues greater unity in the masque, suggesting that the news-mongers and volatees embody the same 'fantastical elements' (that are expelled by the main masque). For other comments on News, see Marcus Nevitt, 'Ben Jonson and the Serial Publication of News', in News Networks in Seventeenth-Century Britain and Europe, ed. Joad Raymond (London and New York: Routledge, 2005), pp. 53–68, p. 54.

10. 'Introduction', The Masque of Heroes in Thomas Middleton: The Collected Works, ed. Gary Taylor and John Lavignino, pp. 1320–4; CSPV, 1619–21, p. 490.

11. J. F. Larkin and P. L. Hughes (eds.), Stuart Royal Proclamations: Volume I, Royal Proclamations of King James I, 1603–1625 (Oxford: Clarendon Press, 1973), nos. 208 (1620) and 218 (the 1621 re-statement).

12. Martin Butler, 'Ben Jonson's Pan's Anniversary and the Politics of Early Stuart Pastoral', English Literary Renaissance, 22 (1992), 369–404, p. 381. Writing much later, in June 1628, John Rous encapsulates how all these issues nested together in the popular imagination: 'A secret whispering of some looking towards the lady Elizabeth is fearfull to be thought of, in regarde of both our soveraigne, and also a wrong to her. Our King's proceedings have caused men's minds to be incensed, to rove, and projecte, but as for this, it is likely to be merely the conceite of the multitude . . .', in The Diary of John Rous, ed. M. A. E. Green (1856), p. 19.

13. Richard Cust, 'Prince Charles and the Second Session of the 1621 Parliament', English Historical Review, 122 (2007), 432–7.

14. On Bolton see E. M. Portal, 'The Academ Roial of King James I', *Proceedings of the British Academy*, 7 (1915–16), 189–208, and pp. 157–8 below. William Barlow, *Two Letters or Embassies* (Amsterdam, 1620) commented on the 'multiplicity of books' on 'the troubles in Europe' and declined to send any on 'because it [the news] will bee stale ere it comes into your hands by my meanes' due to the availability of up-to-date news in London: cited in Laurence Hanson, 'English Newsbooks, 1620–41', *The Library*, 4th ser., 18 (1938), 355–84, p. 379.
15. SP14/124/113 cited in Fritz Levy, 'The Decorum of News', in *News Networks in Seventeenth-Century Britain and Europe*, ed. Joad Raymond (London and New York: Routledge, 2005) pp. 12–38, p. 28. Dated c.1621?
16. See *Letters and Life of Francis Bacon*, ed. J. Spedding, 7 vols. (London: Longman and Green, 1874), 7.152.
17. Robert Burton, *The Anatomy of Melancholy*, ed. Thomas C. Faulkner et al., 6 vols. (Oxford: Clarendon Press, 1989–2000), 1.5.
18. Joad Raymond, 'Describing Popularity in Early Modern England', *Huntington Library Quarterly*, 67 (2004), 101–30, p. 11.
19. Timothy Murray, 'From Foul Sheets to Legitimate Model: Antitheater, Text, Ben Jonson', *New Literary History*, 14 (1983), 641–64, p. 657.
20. This probably refers to the semi-annual quarto newsbooks such as the *Mercurius Gallobelgicus*, or the occasional news pamphlet such as *Newes out of Holland* (which commenced publishing in Cologne in 1594).
21. For a helpful typology of early newsbooks and newsletters that usefully differentiates printed periodical news, written news, the occasional news pamphlet, and numbered serials or newspapers, see Stanley Morison, 'The Origins of the Newspaper', in *Selected Essays on the History of Letter-Forms in Manuscript and Print*, ed. David McKitterick (Cambridge: Cambridge University Press, 1980), pp. 325–57, esp. pp. 328–33.
22. The castle is depicted in Theophilus Schewighardt, *Speculum Sophicum Rhodostauroticum* (1618). *Ben Jonson*, 10.670–1, cites a Latin tract that labels the print '*Vide collegium suspensum in libero aere*', also mentioned in *The Fortunate Isles*, 56–9n.
23. A. Griffiths, *The Print in Stuart Britain, 1603–1689* (London: British Museum, 1998), pp. 13–34 and 144–5 and S. O'Connell, *The Popular Print in Britain* (London: British Museum, 1999), pp. 129–34.
24. O'Connell, *The Popular Print*, p. 134 (5.5) and p. 14. See Thomas Raymond, *Autobiography of Thomas Raymond and Memoirs of the Family of Guise of Elmore*, ed. G. Davies (London: Royal Historical Society, 1917), p. 27.
25. 'Execration', lines 201–2. This print is considered in Chapter 5 (p. 157). Anne Lake Prescott, 'The Stuart Masque and Pantagruel's Dreams', *English Literary History*, 51 (1984), 407–30, describes Jonson's knowledge of the prints in *Les Songes Drolatiques*.
26. There are attacks on cheap printers such as John Trundle who printed the serpent ballad (44), as well as a possible attack on Edmund Howes, the chronicler, who continued Stow (20).
27. *OED*, 'fancy', 4a, 6, 7a. The complex overlapping of meanings in this term is apparent in F2's spelling 'Phant'sie' in these lines and F2's spelling 'phantasie' = 'fantasy' in 72.
28. These are two figures from Lucian's *Icaromenippus*, Jonson's source for the moon voyage.

29. T.W., *A Pleasant Satire or Poesie: wherein is discovered the Catholicon of Spayne, and the chiefe leaders of the League* (1595), sig. 2B1r. Compare the idea of 'bitter medicines' discussed in Chapter 1, p. 5.
30. Frank Kermode, 'The Banquet of the Sense', in *Shakespeare, Spenser, Donne* (London: Routledge & Kegan Paul, 1971), pp. 85–6, outlines the traditional hierarchy with sight and hearing as the upper senses.
31. Kevin Sharpe, 'The King's Writ: Royal Authors and Royal Authority in Early Modern England', in *Culture and Politics in Early Stuart England*, ed. Peter Lake and Kevin Sharpe (Basingstoke: Macmillan, 1994), pp. 117–38, p. 124.
32. James VI and I, *The Workes of the Most High and Mighty Prince James* (1616), sigs. a4, c4.
33. *Workes*, sigs. c2, c4v.
34. Cited in Sharpe, 'The King's Writ', p. 125.
35. *OED*, 'Fullness', 3a, where the phrase 'fullness of your grace' is drawn from *The Book of Common Prayer*.
36. They seem to be related to 'Phant'sy' in *Vision of Delight* (lines 49–60). Commentators have compared Jonson's figure to Spenser's 'Fansy', clothed in 'paynted plumes . . . / Like as the sunburnt Indians do aray' (*The Faerie Queene*, 3.12.8). Fansy's vanity and lightness are symbolized by the feathers and the 'windy fan' he carries as 'dancing in delight . . . / in the ydle ayre he mou'd still here and there'. This description could easily apply to the 'hop' that characterizes the volatees' movements.
37. Raymond, 'Describing Popularity', p. 127.
38. *A Meditation Upon the 27, 28, 29 Verses of the XXVII Chapter of St Matthew or a pattern for a King's inauguration* (1620). The third edition of *Basilicon Doron* (STC 14358.5) appeared in 1619.
39. Sharpe, 'The King's Writ', p. 127.
40. Procritus is the Greek form of the Latin title *princeps iuventutis*, leader of the youth, described in Dio's *Roman History*, 6.405, 7.283, and 9.377 (see Orgel (ed.), *The Complete Masques*, 303). Dio Cassius insists that youths should 'turn their minds to horses and arms, and have paid public teachers . . . In this way . . . they will have had both instruction and practice in all that they will themselves be required to do on reaching manhood, and will thus prove more serviceable . . . for every undertaking': see Dio Cassius, *Roman History*, Book 52, Chapter 26, 1, in *The Roman History*, ed. Earnest Cary and Herbert Foster, 9 vols. (Cambridge, MA: Harvard University Press, 1914–27), vol. 6 (1917), p. 141.
41. S. R. Gardiner (ed.), *Letters Illustrating Relations between England and Germany, 1618–19* (1865), p. 140 (Charles, Prince of Wales to Viscount Doncaster, 7 July 1619), and Thomas Cogswell, *The Blessed Revolution: English Politics and the Coming of War, 1621–1624* (Cambridge: Cambridge University Press, 1989), pp. 58–9.
42. Kevin Sharpe, *The Personal Rule of Charles I* (New Haven and London: Yale University Press, 1992), p. 182; John Bingham, *The Tactics of Aelian* (1616), sigs. A2r–v, and Francis Markham, *Five Decades or Epistles of War* (1622), sigs. A2. Barbara Donagan, 'Halcyon Days and the Literature of War: England Military Education Before 1642', *Past and Present*, 147 (1995), 65–100, p. 82, note 57, suggests that the frontispiece to Aelian, which shows Alexander handing his sword to a modern general, depicts Prince Charles.
43. M. B. Young, *Charles I* (Basingstoke: Macmillan, 1997), p. 17, and Cogswell, *The Blessed Revolution*, p. 62, note Charles' continued militancy. Prince Charles

was offered many literary models to emulate from Rollo of Normandy, the Black Prince and Henry V through to Joshua in the early 1620s.
44. Cogswell, *The Blessed Revolution*, p. 63, and *CSVP, 1619–21*, pp. 225, 227.
45. *Chamberlain Letters*, 2.301, Chamberlain to Carleton, 11 March 1620.
46. Butler, 'Jonson's *News from the New World*', pp. 168–9.
47. *CSPV, 1607–1610*, p. 496.
48. *Chamberlain Letters*, 2.298, Chamberlain to Carleton, 1 April 1620.
49. See A. Young, *Tudor and Jacobean Tournaments* (London: George Philip & Son, 1987), pp. 95–6. Charles continued to present a distinctly martial aspect: for the 1621 tilt, see my 'A 1621 Tilt and Its Imprese: Huntington MS. EL 7972', *Huntington Library Quarterly*, 62 (1999), 391–400.
50. He also points out that the occasion even achieved a 'diplomatic triumph' bringing together opponents of Habsburg power on Twelfth Night: see Butler, 'Jonson's *News from the New World*', pp. 167–8.
51. Martin Butler, 'Courtly Negotiations', in *The Politics of the Stuart Court Masque*, ed. David Bevington and Peter Holbrook (Cambridge: Cambridge University Press, 1998), pp. 30–3, provides a fine reading of *Oberon* as a challenge to royal power.
52. Cogswell, *The Blessed Revolution*, pp. 58–9.
53. *CSPV, 1619–21*, cited in Cogswell, *The Blessed Revolution*, p. 58.
54. Stephen Orgel and Roy Strong, *Inigo Jones: The Theatre of the Stuart Court*, 2 vols. (Berkeley: University of California Press, 1973), nos. 119, 120, compare with no. 108 (design for moon headdress). This costume also echoes Prince Henry's heroic classical body-armour in *Oberon*. Orgel and Strong tentatively suggest that OS 120 may 'conceivably' belong to one of the lost masques of 1619 or 1621.
55. *CSPV, 1619–21*, p. 148. The Venetian envoy, Lando, also described the *Meditation* as 'the Christian Prince . . . it praises peace and touches here and there upon the current events in the world' (14 January 1620; p. 128), although earlier he regarded it as the King's manifesto on Bohemia (2 January 1620; p. 101).
56. STC 14381.5 (quarto format), STC 14382 (duodecimo), STC 14383 (Latin translation). The Latin version of *A Meditation* ensured a pan-European audience.
57. *A Meditation*, ¶10v.
58. *A Meditation Upon the 27, 28, 29 Verses of the XXVII Chapter of St Matthew*, sig. G3r.
59. *A Meditation*, sigs. ¶10v–11r, also sig. E1r. James compares Christ's trial in the Praetorium with legal proceedings in Westminster Hall.
60. Later the King instances the proclamation of his titles in Latin, French, and English at the Garter feasts as part of the publication of his claims to France and to the throne: *A Meditation*, sigs. E4r–E5r.
61. Cited by Sharpe, 'The King's Writ', p. 124.
62. *His Majesties Declaration Touching his proceedings in the late Assemblie and Convention of Parliament* (1621) repeats his view that 'the great actions of Kings are done as vpon a stage, obvious to the publike gazing of euery man' (sig. A4r). For his poems as political interventions, see Curtis Perry, '"If Proclamations Will Not Serve": The Late Manuscript Poetry of James I and the Culture of Libel', in *Royal Subjects: Essays on the Writings of James VI*

  and I, ed. M. Fortier and D. Fischlin (Detroit: Wayne State University Press, 2002), pp. 205–32.
63. *His Majesties Declaration*, sig. A3v.
64. For example, in the running masque the performance and auspices are associated with the French, thus tilting the diplomatic nuance of the debate over Palatine intervention: see James Knowles, 'The "Running Masque" Recovered: A Masque for the Marquess of Buckingham (c.1619–20)', *English Manuscript Studies*, 9 (2000), 79–135.
65. Butler, 'Jonson's *News from the New World*', p. 167.
66. It was entered in the Stationers' Register on 4 July 1620, although it has been suggested that the planned performances might have dated from as early as autumn 1619.
67. The King was feasted by the Prince at Denmark House on 11 March 1620 (*Chamberlain Letters*, 2.301), but there is no evidence of a theatrical performance linked to this event.
68. See S. McGee, 'Introduction', *The World Tossed at Tennis* in *Middleton: The Collected Works*, ed. G. Taylor and J. Lavignino (Oxford: Clarendon Press, 2007), p. 1405, and David Nicol, 'The Repertory of Prince Charles's (I) Company, 1608–1625', *Early Theatre*, 9 (2006), 57–72.
69. The interplay between the *Hic Mulier* and *Haec Vir* pamphlets, James VI and I's own proclamation on apparel, and *The Sermon of Apparel* preached by John Williams at the King's behest in 1620 may also be traced in the costume of the moon epicenes (*News*, 249–55).
70. *JCS*, 1.204.
71. *CSPV, 1619–21*, p. 111; National Archives, SC6, Jac. 1, 1684, 1685, 1687.
72. One contemporary reader of *The Masque of Beauty* in 1616 commented 'For I and maybe many others have not been able to understand what he writes without reading what comes after' (Jonson, *The workes*, p. 904, Huntington Library, RB606578).
73. John Peacock, *The Stage Designs of Inigo Jones: The European Context* (Cambridge: Cambridge University Press, 1995), p. 132.
74. In *Love Freed*, the Sphinx, follies, and she-fools are made to 'vanish' (256); in *The Irish Masque at Court*, the old Irish are banished ('begone', 124); in *Mercury Vindicated* the deformed antimasquers 'Vanish with thy insolencies' (140–1); in *Vision of Delight* the antimasquers 'But vanish away' (111).
75. I differ from Orgel (ed.), *Complete Masques*, p. 13, who argues that the antimasque is seen not as the 'antithesis to the world of the revels, but essentially as another aspect of it, a world that can therefore ultimately be accommodated to and even included in the ideals of the main masque'. See also, Anne Lake Prescott, 'The Stuart Masque and Pantagruel's Dreams', *ELH*, 51 (1984), 407–30, p. 416.
76. Orgel, *Complete Masques*, p. 14, sees the masques of the second decade (post-*Oberon*) as offering 'less a single moment of transformation than . . . a gradual process of refinement'.
77. Timothy Raylor, *The Essex House Masque of 1621* (Pittsburgh: Dusquesne University Press, 2000), pp. 54–6.
78. Margery Corbett and Ronald Lightbown, *The Comely Frontispiece: The Emblematic Title-Page in England, 1550–1660* (London: Routledge & Kegan Paul, 1979), pp. 128–35.

79. *Poetaster*, ed. Tom Cain (Manchester: Manchester University Press, 1996).
80. *Ben Jonson*, 1.204–5: 'I have heard from Court that the late Mask was not so approved by the King, as in former Times, and that your Absence was regretted: Such Applause hath true Worth'.
81. Middleton, *Inner Temple Masque*, lines 207 and 7: see Jerzy Limon, '"A Silenc'st Bricke-layer": An Allusion to Ben Jonson in Thomas Middleton's Masque', *Notes and Queries*, NS 41 (1994), 512–13. H. A. Evans, *English Masques: With an Introduction* (London and Glasgow: Blackie & Son, 1897), p. 136, links Jonson's 'woman's poet' to Middleton. A parallel version of this passage in *News* (114–25) reappears in *Timber: Or, Discoveries* (722ff.) and *Ben Jonson*, 11.235–6 argues that this phrase initially applied to Daniel, but later includes Campion and Middleton.
82. Philip Finkelpearl, *John Marston of the Middle Temple: An Elizabethan Dramatist in his Social Setting* (Cambridge, MA: Harvard University Press, 1969), pp. 1–5.
83. David Norbrook, 'The Masque of Truth: Court Entertainments and International Protestant Politics in the Early Stuart Period', *The Seventeenth Century*, 1 (1986), 81–110, p. 82, and James Knowles, 'Introduction', *Inner Temple Masque, or Masque of Heroes*, in Middleton *The Collected Works*, ed. Taylor and Lavignino, pp. 1320–4.
84. The claim that the masque was 'Presented . . . by gentlemen of the . . . ancient and noble house' may have seemed presumptuous, and similar concerns emerged during the staging of *The Triumph of Peace*: see Chapter 6. The claim to the status of 'gentlemen lawyers' was a key part of the civic and political culture of the Inns: see Michelle O'Callaghan, *The English Wits: Literature and Sociability in Early Modern England* (Cambridge: Cambridge University Press, 2007), pp. 17–18.
85. *The Masque of Heroes* had been performed by members of Prince Charles' Men (see Middleton, *The Collected Works*, p. 1324, lines 12–16).
86. Knowles, 'The "Running Masque" Recovered', pp. 91–2, 100.
87. Simon Thurley, *Whitehall Palace: An Architectural History of the Royal Apartments 1240–1698* (New Haven: Yale University Press, 1999), p. 75. Little is known of these apartments but after 1619 the Queen's Presence Chamber was used as a replacement for the Council Chamber (see p. 78).
88. For the 1621 inscription and purposes of the building, see David Howarth, *Images of Rule: Art and Politics in the English Renaissance, 1485–1649* (Basingstoke: Macmillan, 1997), pp. 34–8.
89. These are the missing Twelfth Night quartos; also unprinted was the *Masque of Owls* (1624). Some booksellers' catalogues apparently contain copies of other unknown masque quartos, but these are probably ghosts based on piecemeal sales of folio copies: see Gabriel Heaton, *Writing and Reading Royal Entertainments: From George Gascoigne to Ben Jonson* (Oxford: Oxford University Press, 2010), p. 233.
90. W. W. Greg, *A Bibliography of the English Printed Drama to the Restoration*, 4 vols. (London: Bibliographical Society, 1939–59), 3.559 and 563, characterises *Neptune's Triumph* and *The Fortunate Isles* as 'intended for private distribution' (also applied to *Lovers Made Men*); on the privileged audience, see *Ben Jonson*, 7.625, which suggests the quarto was an acting copy.

91. Richard C. Newton, 'Jonson and the (Re-)Invention of the Book', in *Classic and Cavalier: Essays on Jonson and the Sons of Ben*, ed. C. Summers and Ted-Larry Pebworth (Pittsburgh: University of Pittsburgh Press, 1982), pp. 31–55, p. 36; Martin Butler, 'Jonson's Folio and the Politics of Patronage', *Criticism*, 35 (1993), 377–90, p. 388; Timothy Murray, 'From Foul Sheets to Legitimate Model: Antitheater, Text, Ben Jonson', *New Literary History*, 14 (1983), 641–64, p. 658, and Timothy Murray, *Theatrical Legitimation: Allegories of Genius in Seventeenth-Century England and France* (New York and Oxford: Oxford University Press, 1987), p. 79.
92. See John Jowett, 'Jonson's Authorization of Type in *Sejanus* and Other Early Quartos', *Studies in Bibliography*, 44 (1991), 254–65. For 'publication' as three differentiated actions (performance, scribal publication, and print publication), see Harold Love, *The Culture and Commerce of Texts: Scribal Publication in Seventeenth-Century England* (Amherst: University of Massachusetts Press, 1998), pp. 35–6.
93. See my 'Manuscript Culture and Reading Practices', in *Ben Jonson in Context*, ed. J. Sanders (Cambridge: Cambridge University Press, 2010), 181–91.
94. J. Loewenstein, 'Printing and the "Multitudinous Presse": The Contentious Texts of Jonson's Masques', in *Ben Jonson's 1616 Folio*, ed. J. Brady and W. H. Herendeen (Newark, NJ: University of Delaware Press, 1991), pp. 168–91.
95. Commentators occasionally lament the lack of illustration and the apparent lack of sophistication in the physical representation of masque texts: only *Lord Hay's Masque* (1607) contains the image of a masquer and none have the high-quality engraving found in continental exemplars.
96. Jerzy Limon, *The Masque of Stuart Culture* (Newark, NJ: University of Delaware Press, 1990), pp. 35, 42, 47.
97. Joseph Loewenstein, *Ben Jonson and Possessive Authorship* (Cambridge: Cambridge University Press, 2002), p. 180.
98. *The vision of the 12. goddesses presented in a maske the 8. of Ianuary, at Hampton Court*, ed. Joan Rees, in *A Book of Masques*, ed. S. Wells, lines 194, 201.
99. See John Peacock, 'The Stuart Court Masque and the Theatre of the Greeks', *Journal of the Warburg and Courtauld Institutes*, 56 (1993), 183–208.
100. *Bibliotheca Norfolciana* (1681), p. 17 (269 = 'Ben Johnson's Queen's Masques'); Bacon, inventory (1624) in *Private Libraries in Renaissance England*, ed. R. Ferhrenbach and E. Leedham-Green, 1.84; Yale University, Elizabethan Club, EC 26, see *The Elizabethan Club of Yale and Its Library*, ed. S. Parks and A. Bell (New Haven: Yale University Press, 1986).
101. 'Masques at Court at E Essex marriage. B. Jonson', in F. Taylor, 'The Books and Manuscripts of Scipio Le Squyer, Deputy Chamberlain of the Exchequer (1620–59)', *Bulletin of the John Rylands Library*, 25 (1941), 137–64.
102. Huntington Library, RB62067. This copy came to Huntington via Huth; a Royal Society 'duplicate'. See Linda Levy Peck, 'Uncovering the Arundel Library at the Royal Society: Changing Meanings of Science and the Fate of the Norfolk Donation', *Notes and Records of the Royal Society*, 52 (1998), 3–24.
103. For *Pleasure Reconciled to Virtue*, see Edward Sherburn to Dudley Carleton, 10 January 1618, SP14/95/10, cited in *Ben Jonson*, 10.574, and Nicholas Barker (ed.), *The Devonshire Inheritance: Five Centuries of Collecting at Chatsworth* (Alexandria, VA: Art Services International, 2003), p. 89; and a third copy

posited by Heaton, *Writing and Reading Royal Entertainments*, p. 242. On *Gypsies Metamophosed* and scribal circulation, see my 'Songs of Baser Alloy: Jonson's *Gypsies Metamorphosed* and the Circulation of Manuscript Libels', *Huntington Library Quarterly*, 69 (2006), 53–176.

104. Herbert of Cherbury's book list of 1637 (NLW MS 5298 E, fol. 28v) includes 'Coleum Britanicum a Mask at Whitehall i633' valued at '0-0-8' and 'Loues Triumph through Callipolis. a court Masq – i630', valued at '0-0-6'. Herbert also owned 'The Newe Inne. A Comoedie. Ben Ionson'.

105. A. Townshend, *Albion's Triumph* (1631) [STC 24155a; HN RB 69679], nineteenth-century binding, inscribed; 'I Bridgewater' and 'ex dono Auctori/Townshend', plus further corrections in ?Townshend's hand. Also, A. Townshend, *Antemasques* (n.d.?) [HN RB136016], possibly with corrections in Townshend's hand. Townshend also wrote an 'Elegy on Countess of Bridgewater'.

106. T. Carew, *Coelum Britannicum* (1634) [STC 4619; HN RB97458], with signature of 'I. Bridgewater'. Three other items may be associated with the earl from early pressmark evidence: B. Jonson, *Love's Triumph Through Callipolis* (1630) [STC 14776; HN RB62068], and W. Davenant, *The Temple of Love* (1634) [STC 14719; Harvard 14424.32.15*], and J. Shirley, *The Triumph of Peace* (1634) [STC 22459a; HN RB69432]. The identification of other copies in this library is complicated by later sales and repurchases by the Bridgewaters and by the later owner, Henry E. Huntington.

107. See *Catalogue of the Singuler and Curious Library Originally Formed Between 1610 and 1650 by Sir Robert Gordon* (1816), and also NLS MS3804 (*c.*1743) for *Chloridia* (no. 1307), *Love's Triumph* (no. 1308), *The Temple of Love* (no. 1309), all listed as '4to sewed'; *Entertainment of Charles . . . Edinburgh* (no. 617), *Corona Minerva* (no. 614), *Triumphs of Prince d'Amour* (1635) (no. 764). The latest masque is no. 2140, Shirley's, *Contention for Honour and Riches* (dated 1633, but in fact 1653) and Gordon also owned Jonson's *Works* '2 vols (1616–31)'.

108. *Ben Jonson*, 10.680 ('this coppie'). See also the use of summaries and printed copies discussed in Martin Butler 'Politics and the Masque: *Salmacida Spolia*', in *Literature and the English Civil War*, ed. Thomas Healy and Jonathan Sawday (Cambridge: Cambridge University Press, 1990), p. 69 and note 35.

109. On the Mostyns see: 'Mostyn family (*per.* 1540–1642)' and 'Mostyn, Sir Roger, first baronet (*c.*1624–1690)', *ODNB*, http://www.oxforddnb.com/view/printable/71880 and http://www.oxforddnb.com/view/printable/19415 (accessed 29 August 2007). The Christie's Sale Catalogue (9–10 October 1974) which included the early MS catalogues (listed in HMC, *Fourth Report*), suggests books were at Mostyn by 1650, although the situation is complicated by the absorption of the Mostyn books into the Wynn of Gwydir library. Many were still unbound at the sale: see 1919 Sotheby catalogues, lots 208, 233, 177 (listed as '14 leaves including original final blank, unbound'), 178, 309 (unbound), 34 (unbound), 176.

110. Some Mostyn books end up in Yale Elizabethan Club: *The Inner Temple Masque* is now Yale Beinecke, Ih M584 619 (pencil notes as Mostyn copy; purchased 1943); *The Temple of Love* is now Yale University, Beinecke Library, Ih D272 634T; two of the masques are at the Pforzheimer (*The Maske of Flowers*, *The Fortunate Isles*).

111. Vivienne Larminie, *Wealth, Kinship and Culture: The Seventeenth-Century Newdigates of Arbury and their World* (Woodbridge: Boydell & Brewer, 1995), pp. 201–2.
112. Payments include: Feb. 1632, 'the queens maske' = *Chloridia*; Feb. 1634, 'my wife going to maske'; July 1634: 'a booke of the maske'; Feb. 1635, 'Davennant's maske' = *Triumph of Love*; Jan. 1638, 'the mask book' = *Britannia Triumphans*. This last item may now be Yale University, Beinecke, Ih D272 637. Larminie identifies 'going to see the maskers pass' as referring to *Coelum Britannicum* but it had no procession, and 'a book of the maske' with a masque at Oxford performed by Prince Charles' Men (although the payment was made in London). The family also owned Davenant, *Luminalia* (Princeton, RHT 17th-151); Jonson *Love's Triumph* (Folger, STC 14776); and Townshend, *Tempe Restored*, Yale University, Beinecke Library, Ih T666 631t. Later rebinding by Sir Roger Newdigate, 5th Bart (1719–1806) hampers certainty as to when these entered the collection
113. Hastings copies: two unnamed Lord Mayor's pageants are listed in Huntington Library, Hastings MSS, HAF6.4. Cavendish copies: '2 maske bookes' (23 March 1614) in Chatsworth MS 29, accounts 1608–23. The Cavendish (Chatsworth) collection also contains MS copy of *Pleasure Reconciled to Virtue* (in hand of Ralph Crane) and a copy of *The Masque of Flowers* in a contemporary limp vellum binding (purchased at sale in 1897). Clifford copies: 2 March [?1634]: two mask bookes brought at London, 00-01-00; 30 Nov. [?1634, possibly from York]: 2 mask books, 00-01-00: see Chatsworth, Bolton Abbey Accs, 172 (1633–4). The York bookseller Andrew Foster was selling Jonson's *Works* in 1616 which suggests a sophisticated book-market available there in the early seventeenth century: see J. Barnard and M. Bell, 'The Early Seventeenth Century York Book Trade and John Foster's Inventory of 1616', *Leeds Philosophical and Literary Society, Proceedings*, 24.2 (1994), 17–132.
114. *The Triumph of Peace* (Folger Library, STC 22459b). Interestingly, another Folger copy of this masque is bound as part of a composite volume of Shirley's plays with a seventeenth-century contents list (Folger Library, STC 22459b.2).
115. *The Library of the Earl of Macclesfield Removed from Shirburn Castle, Part Eleven: English Books and Manuscripts* (2008), lot 3941. See comments by Heaton, *Writing and Reading Royal Entertainments*, p. 267, on binding and date of collection.
116. *Christmas His Masque*, *The Vision of Delight*, *Pleasure Reconciled* (and its revised antimasque *For the Honour of Wales*), *News*, and *Pan's Anniversary*.
117. It is worth noting these marginalia are much shorter than those for *Hymenaei*, *Queens*, and *Oberon*.
118. *JCS*, 4.642. More recently, Martin Butler has proposed Jonson had minimal involvement in the printing of *Augurs* (personal communication). Greg, *Bibliography*, 2.563 (no. 411) notes that Herbert only says 'brought to me by Mr Jon.' which could be Jones.
119. Loewenstein, *Ben Jonson and Possessive Authorship*, p. 203.
120. Loewenstein, *Ben Jonson and Possessive Authorship*, pp. 203–4.
121. Heaton, *Writing and Reading Royal Entertainments*, p. 238, points out that many performances were also delayed from their apparent (and printed) Twelfth Night slot by ambassadorial disputes.

244 Notes

122. Limon, *Masque of Stuart Culture*, p. 49.
123. Joad Raymond, *Pamphlets and Pamphleteering in Early Modern Britain* (Cambridge: Cambridge University Press, 2003), p. 138.
124. Loewenstein, *Ben Jonson and Possessive Authorship*, p. 204.
125. Loewenstein, *Ben Jonson and Possessive Authorship*, p. 204.
126. *The Fortunate Isles* represents a significant exception, with eight known exemplars, a figure equivalent to the survival rates for other pre-1616 texts.
127. Loewenstein, *Ben Jonson and Possessive Authorship*, p. 204.
128. W. A. Jackson points out that until the recovery of the sole exemplar of *Time Vindicated*, it appeared that it too had not been printed in quarto: see *The Carl H. Pforzheimer Library: English Literature 1475–1700*, ed. W. A. Jackson, 3 vols. (New York, 1940), 2.568.
129. B. Jonson, *The fortunate isles and their union* (1625) [STC14772; HN RB62052], TP 'I Bridgewater ex Dono. E ____' (cropped) in hand of 1st Earl ? Edmund Scory. The Mostyn copy is the Pforzheimer library text at the Harry Ransom Center, Texas (PFORZ 547 PFZ).
130. BL C33.e.7, bound in contemporary vellum. For a discussion of this volume and complete list of contents, see Heaton, *Writing and Reading Royal Entertainments*, pp. 253–4.
131. They are not, however, bound chronologically, and the internal order of the collection (if any) is hard to discern.
132. Items 5 and 12. He also owned works on the Palatine wedding celebrations (STC 23763; London Guildhall Library).
133. The civic pageants are Dekker, *Troia Nova Triumphans* (1611) and *Britannia's Honour* (1628), Middleton, *Sun in Aries* (1621), *Triumphs of Honour and Virtue* (1622), *Triumphs of the Golden Fleece* (1623), Munday, *Triumphs of Reunited Britannia* (1605), *Himatia Poleos* (1614), *Metropolis Coronata* (1615), *Chryslaneia* (1616), *Sidero-thriambos* (1618), *Triumphs of the Golden Fleece* (1623).
134. It is worth noting that Camden's library also contained occasional texts that marked major national events (such as Prince Henry's installation or the Palatine match): see Richard DeMolen, 'The Library of William Camden', *Proceedings of the American Philosophical Society*, 128 (1984), 326–409.
135. N. K. Kiessling, *The Library of Robert Burton* (Oxford: Oxford Bibliographical Society, 1988), p. 201 (1064).
136. Middleton, *Inner Temple Maske* = Huntington RB62588; 'RB' on title page.
137. Archer's 1656 catalogue (nos. 188, 566) and London's 1657 catalogue of books on sale in Newcastle (incl. *The Triumph of Peace*), see Greg, *Biliography*, 3.1332, 1337 and 3.1300. George Ridpath, *The Stage Condemn'd* (1698), sig. C7v, a stinging critique of Sabbath-breaking masque performances, especially *Britannia Triumphans*, reprints large parts of the masque because it is 'very rare and scarcely to be had'.

5 'Hoarse with Praising': *The Gypsies Metamorphosed* and the Politics of Masquing

1. Chamberlain to Carleton, 27 October 1621 (from NA, SP14/123/62), in *Chamberlain Letters*, 2.404–5.

2. Versions of the 'Cock Lorel' ballad appeared in black-letter broadside format and remained popular into the Restoration: the black-letter broadsheet *A Strange Banquet, or the Devil's Entertainment* (?1642–50) [BL C2.f.2(292)] was reprinted in 1685 (Wing 1012), and again in 1690 (BL Rox.II.445) and sometime between 1684 and1695 (NLS Crawford EB.286).
3. Martin Butler, 'Private and Occasional Drama', in *The Cambridge Companion to Renaissance Drama*, ed A. R. Braunmuller and M. Hattaway (Cambridge: Cambridge University Press, 1990), p. 134, and D. B. J. Randall, *Jonson's Gypsies Unmasked: Background and Theme of 'The Gypsies Metamorphos'd'* (Durham, NC: Duke University Press, 1975).
4. For example, M. Netzloff, '"Counterfeit Egyptians" and Imagined Borders: Jonson's *The Gypsies Metamorphosed*', *English Literary History*, 68 (2001), 763–93.
5. Jonson had been criticised for the invention of *Pleasure Reconciled to Virtue* (1618) and his revised antimasque included material designed to appeal to lighter tastes: see *CWBJ, 5.311–12*.
6. *Return from Parnassus*, 2.1.10 in *Three Parnassus Plays (1598–1601)*, ed J. B. Leishman (London: Nicholson and Watson, 1949). *OED*, 'ballad', 3; 'ballad' could be a more general term for a song, and even a 'ballad of praise' (Puttenham cited in the *OED*), but the association with 'baser alloy' combines suggestions of both class origin and scurrilous content.
7. There is a fascinating parallel in Jonson's own description of his 'adulterate masquings, such as may not go' in 'Execration' (*The Underwood*, 15.43) which compares them with 'pieces of as base alloy'. It is tempting to ask whether Jonson had heard Chamberlain's description of his masque; certainly elements of *Gypsies* are interwoven into 'Execration'.
8. Thomas Cogswell, 'The People's Love: The Duke of Buckingham and Popularity', in *Politics, Religion and Popularity in Early Stuart Britain: Early Stuart Essays in Honour of Conrad Russell*, ed. Thomas Cogswell, Richard Cust, and Peter Lake (Cambridge: Cambridge University Press, 2002), p. 212, dates this change to 1624; *Gypsies* seems to prefigure and predate this strategy.
9. The Palatine crisis impinged on localities directly as first Elizabeth's envoy, Achatius zu Dohna (April/May 1620), and then the Parliament sought fiscal support for the wars (1620/21). The Earl of Huntingdon's speech in favour of rapid action because 'the celerity of war canot stay the formality that soe great a Council as a Parliament will require' illuminates how political information and activity operated beyond parliamentary periods: see Thomas Cogswell, *Home Divisions: Aristocracy, The State and Provincial Conflict* (Manchester: Manchester University Press, 1998), pp. 34–9.
10. J. F. Larkin and P. L. Hughes (eds.), *Stuart Royal Proclamations, Volume 1: Royal Proclamations of King James I, 1603–1625* (Oxford: Oxford University Press, 1973), nos. 208 and 218.
11. B. Gerbier, *A Brief Discourse Concerning the Three Chief Principles of Magnificent Building* (1662), sig. D3v.
12. Butler, 'Private and Occasional Drama', p. 134, and Randall, *Jonson's Gypsies Unmasked*.
13. The Belvoir text probably contained largely the version staged at Burley, but with a series of minor alterations to adapt the text for a different location and host. There is considerable debate as to whether a fortune for the

Countess of Exeter (*Jonson's Masque of Gipsies*, ed. W. W. Greg (London: The British Academy, 1952), p. 146), added 'late' according to internal evidence, was provided for the Burley performance or added at Belvoir.
14. This chapter uses the designations for the three versions at Burley (BUR), Belvoir (BEL), and Windsor (WIN) found in my edition for *CWBJ*.
15. It is worth noting that we are not sure what was staged at Windsor in 1621 is necessarily what we can read in the printed text (F2). The most striking scatological material is preserved only in the Bridgwater manuscript (Huntington Library, MS HM741), which might suggest that F2 offers a bowdlerised text and might also imply that the performance version could have been yet more controversial (see *The Gypsies Metamorphosed* (Windsor), Appendix 2.A and B).
16. Stephen Orgel, 'To Make the Boards Speak: Inigo Jones and the Jonsonian Masque', *Renaissance Drama*, NS 1 (1968), 121–52, p. 144.
17. Martin Butler, 'Jonson's *News From the New World*, the "Running Masque", and the Season of 1619–20', *Medieval and Renaissance Drama in England*, 6 (1993), 153–178, esp. pp. 163–5, and James Knowles, 'The "Running Masque" Recovered: A Masque for the Marquess of Buckingham (*c.*1619–20), *English Manuscript Studies*, 8 (2000), 79–135.
18. Dudley Carleton letter, 4 September 1620, cited by Butler, 'Jonson's *News From the New World*', p. 161.
19. John Nichols, *The Progesses of James I*, 4 vols. (London: John Nichols, 1828), 3.496, 495.
20. The other performers included Sir George Goring, Thomas Badger, and other members of the inner, bedchamber circle: see Nichols, *Progesses of James I*, 3.465. Chamberlain marvelled that 'none had the judgement to see how unfit it was to bring such beastly gear before a Prince'.
21. MS. Rawlinson Poet. 26, fol. 4, reprinted in *The Poems of James VI of Scotland*, ed. James Craigie, 2 vols. (Edinburgh: Scottish Text Society, 1955–8), 2.177.
22. Roger Lockyer, *Buckingham: The Life and Political Career of George Villiers, First Duke of Buckingham, 1592–1628* (London: Longman, 1981), p. 120.
23. BL, MS Harleian, 481, fol. 3. The first entry from the diary of Simonds d'Ewes, dated 7 January 1622, records the performance of *Augurs* on 6 January, and the King's profession of love for Buckingham. The second and third entries, dated 5 May and 14 May 1622, mention the second performance of the masque on 5 May. I am grateful to *CWBJ* for providing a transcription of this passage.
24. Knowles, 'The "Running Masque" Recovered' (NB Hammond's review).
25. The only comparable moments would be the phonic puns on 'shit' in *The Irish Masque at Court* (see Chapter 3, p. 81).
26. Even making allowances for the looser structure seen in other country-house masques, *Gypsies* is striking in its use of a more improvisatory form for some of its major elements (notably the fortune verses which can be added and subtracted depending on the performers available) and in its rapid shifts of tone and mood.
27. This point was first made in *The Complete Masques*, ed. S. Orgel (New Haven: Yale University Press, 1969), p. 499.
28. Martin Butler, '"We are one man's all": Jonson's *The Gypsies Metamorphosed*', *Yearbook of English Studies*, 21 (1991), 253–73.
29. Butler '"We are one man's all"', pp. 255, 257.

30. Butler, '"We are one man's all"', p. 258.
31. The most cogent discussion of the revisions remains Martin Butler, '"We are one man's all"'.
32. Butler, '"We are one man's all"', p. 259, notes that Buckingham does not take part in the fortune telling (after the King's) or in the theft and so the text preserves his dignity. This can only be inferred from the text as the SD simply says 'the gypsies come about them prying', although Buckingham does not take part in the dialogue with the clowns.
33. Butler, '"We are one man's all"', p. 264.
34. These lines are omitted from F2 which may be part of a later revision of this text towards publication in the Caroline period. F2 contains the notorious couplet: 'You'll ha' good luck to horse flesh o'my life, / You ploughed so late with the vicar's wife' (WIN 556–7).
35. Bodleian Library, MS Eng. poet. f.16, fol. 9. F. E. Brightman, *The English Rite* (London: Rivingtons, 1915), 1.174–91, gives the text which includes the supplication 'From all evil and mischief, from sins, from the crafts and assaults of the devil, from the wrath, and from everlasting damnation', and the response 'Good Lord deliver us' (p. 175). There may be an echo here of the Patrico's role as 'hedge priest': in effect, the 'Blessing' creates an anti-religion practised by the gypsies in which the clowns are co-opted celebrants.
36. One of the most popular devotional tracts published in the seventeenth century. Lewis Bayly's *The Practice of Piety* (2nd edition, 1612) went through thirteen editions by 1621. Bayly (d. 1631) was a noted strict Protestant.
37. Butler, '"We are one man's all"', p. 266, also notes this point. I do not agree that the revisions in the clown scenes allow us to see Buckingham as a figure 'who cements the solidarity of society at large'. That misses some of the ambivalence.
38. For example, the reference to the Oxford fairs (WIN 630).
39. In 1628 some inhabitants celebrated the Petition of Right and Richard Montagu, at that time a canon of Windsor and royal chaplain, descended from the castle and personally stamped out their bonfires: see David Underdown, *A Freeborn People: Politics and the Nation in Seventeenth-Century England* (Oxford: Clarendon Press, 1996), pp. 50–1.
40. Raymond South, *Royal Castle, Rebel Town: Puritan Windsor in Civil War and Commonwealth* (Buckingham: Barracuda Books, 1981), p. 17. Compare, 'You ploughed so late with the vicar's wife' (WIN 556–7).
41. Goodman cited in South, *Royal Castle, Rebel Town*, p. 18.
42. Robert Richard Tighe and James Edward Davis, *Annals of Windsor: being a history of the castle and town, with some account of Eton and places adjacent* (London: Longman, Brown, Green, Longman and Roberts, 1858), 2.82–3.
43. Townshend may suggest some satire on county-town officialdom as he apparently holds the 'town's brains' (BUR 592), but a 'cockerel' is a derogatory term for a young man (*OED*); a 'clod' is a 'blockhead' (*OED*, 'clod', 5); and a 'puppy', an 'empty-headed young man'. Howell (1654) describes a young man as 'a shallow-brained puppy' (*OED*).
44. Martin Butler, 'Ben Jonson's *Pan's Anniversary* and the Politics of Early Stuart Pastoral', *English Literary Renaissance*, 22 (1992), 369–404, p. 384.
45. This was obviously a well-known ballad as it is alluded to in *The New Inn*, 4.1.10. 'Whoop' here is a representation of a cry or shout of surprise or

excitement, probably meant to suggest sexual activity (*OED*, 'Whoop', *int.*, b, citing this passage).
46. Chamberlain to Sir Dudley Carleton, 13 January 1621, in *Chamberlain Letters*, 2.333.
47. Alastair Bellany, *The Politics of Court Scandal in Early Modern England: News Culture and the Overbury Affair, 1603–1660* (Cambridge: Cambridge University Press, 2002), pp. 131–5.
48. Susan Wiseman, '"Adam, the Father of all Flesh", Porno-Political Rhetoric and Political Theory In and After the English Civil War', *Prose Studies*, 14 (1991), 134–57, esp. pp. 134 and 144.
49. Cogswell, 'The People's Love', p. 212.
50. January 1623 entry in Sir Simonds d'Ewes, *Diary, 1622–24*, ed. E. Bourcier (Paris: Didier, 1974), pp. 12–13.
51. David Colclough, *Freedom of Speech in Stuart England* (Cambridge: Cambridge University Press, 2005), p. 249.
52. For the sexual satires see my '"To scourge the arse/Jove's marrow so hath wasted": Scurrility and the Subversion of Sodomy', in *Scurrility and Subversion*, ed. T. Kirk and D. Cavanagh (Aldershot: Ashgate, 2000), pp. 74–92; on the wider implications of this culture, see Thomas Cogswell, 'Underground Verse and the Transformation of Early Stuart Political Culture', in *Political Culture and Cultural Politics in Early Modern England*, ed. Susan D. Amussen and Mark A. Kishlansky (Manchester: Manchester University Press, 1996), pp. 277–300.
53. John Chamberlain to Sir Dudley Carleton, 8 February 1617, cited in *Early Stuart Libels*, L1.
54. 'The Warre in Heaven' appears in Austin Texas MS (the source of the text used here) and in BL Add MS 22,603, fols. 33r–34r, Bodleain MSS, Eng Poet c. 50, Rawl Poet 160 and Tanner 306. See also *Early Stuart Libels*, L10.
55. 'Heaven blesse King James our joy', in *Early Stuart Libels*, L10.
56. *Chamberlain Letters*, 2.338.
57. 'Heaven blesse King James our joy', see note 51.
58. Hatfield House, Cecil MSS, 140/125 (in hand of William, second Earl of Salisbury).
59. A 'trental' is a set of thirty requiem masses, and the 'dirge' the opening of the Office of the Dead in the Latin rite. Although both terms could be used more generally and metaphorically in early modern usage, they are probably meant to suggest Catholicism: see *OED*, 'trental', especially the citation from *Motives of the Romish Faith* (1593); also *OED*, 'dirge' 1, notably the passage from *Mother Hubbard's Tale* (1591).
60. See Orgel (ed.), *Complete Masques*, p. 325 (note 205b) for a parallel pun.
61. Dekker, *Lanthorn and Candelight* (1608), sig. H1.
62. Butler, '"We are one man's all"', p. 260.
63. Richard Cust, 'News and Politics in Early Seventeenth-Century England', *Past and Present*, 112 (1986), 60–90, p. 72.
64. Thomas Cogswell, '"Published by Authoritie": Newsletters and the Duke of Buckingham's Expedition to the Ile de Ré', *Huntington Library Quarterly*, 67 (2004), 1–25, pp. 4 and 7.
65. SP14/124/113 cited in Cogswell, '"Published by Authoritie"', p. 7.
66. National Archives (PRO), SP16/524/9 (see *CSPD, Addenda, 1625–49*, p. 129).
67. E. M. Portal, 'The Academ Roial of King James I', *Proceedings of the British Academy*, 7 (1915–16), 189–208.

68. George Eglisham (fl. 1601–42), a physician and client of the Marquess of Hamilton. Although he had received royal favour, Eglisham accused Buckingham of murdering the Marquess of Hamilton and James I. The tract circulated widely in MS, and Eglisham had to flee to the Low Countries to avoid arrest.
69. BL MS Add 12,528 (accounts of Sir Sackville Crowe for George Villers), fol. 15v; Andrew McRae, *Literature, Satire and the Early Stuart State* (Cambridge: Cambridge University Press, 2004), p. 156; Cogswell, 'Underground Verse', p. 281, suggests Corbett's promotions were in part due to his topical poetic facility.
70. 'A Letter to the Duke of Buckingham', in *The Poems of Richard Corbett*, ed. J. A. W. Bennett and H. Trevor-Roper (Oxford: Clarendon Press, 1955), lines 70–1.
71. See n. 7 above. Bacon, who drafted the proclamation, also wrote to Buckingham about the 'general licentious speaking of state matters' on 16 December 1620: see *Letters and Life of Francis Bacon*, ed. J. Spedding, 7 vols. (London: Longman and Green, 1874), 7.152.
72. *The Poems of James VI of Scotland*, 2.182–91, lines 22–3. These poems are discussed in Curtis Perry, '"If Proclamations Will Not Serve": The Late Manuscript Poetry of James I and the Culture of Libel', in *Royal Subjects: Essays on the Writings of James VI and I*, ed. M. Fortier and D. Fischlin (Detroit: Wayne State University Press, 2002), pp. 205–32.
73. Gerbier, *A Brief Discourse Concerning the Three Chief Principles of Magnificent Building*, sig. D3v.
74. Historical Manuscripts Commission, *11th Report, Appendix, Part 1, Manuscripts of Henry Duncan Skrine (Salvetti Correspondence)*, ed. H. B. Tomkins (1887), pp. 94–5 (dated 20 November 1626).
75. *Chamberlain Letters*, 2.279, 282; for 8 January see Gabaleone to the Duke of Savoy, 9/19 January 1619, cited in Butler, 'Jonson's *News From the New World*', pp. 173–4, and Nethersole to Sir Dudley Carleton, 8 January 1620, in *Letters and Documents Illustrating the Relations between England and Germany at the Commencement of the Thirty Years' War*, ed. S. R. Gardiner (London: Camden Society, 1868), pp. 132–3.
76. Thomas Cogswell, *The Blessed Revolution: English Politics and the Coming of War, 1621–1624* (Cambridge: Cambridge University Press, 1989), p. 86.
77. Letter to Joseph Mead, 16 May 1627, cited in Thomas Birch (ed.), *The Court and Times of Charles I*, 2 vols. (London: H. Colburn, 1848), 1.226.
78. The Beast has an 'open mouth' with a thousand tongues and 'Some were of dogs, that barked day and night' (Spenser, *The Faerie Queene*, 6.12.27–33, also 5.12.37–42).
79. Julius Held, *The Oil Sketches of Peter Paul Rubens: A Critical Catalogue*, 2 vols. (Princeton: Princeton University Press, 1983), 1.390–3.
80. The appearance of Mercury prefigures Honthorst's painting of Buckingham as Mercury presenting the Liberal Arts to Charles and Henrietta Maria: J. R. Judson and R. O. Eckhart, *Gerrit van Honthorst, 1592–1656* (Doornspijk: Davaco, 1999).
81. Peter J. Smith, 'Ajax by Any Other Name Would Smell as Sweet: Shakespeare, Harington and Onomastic Scatology', in *Tudor Theatre: Emotion in the Theatre*, ed. André Lascombes (Bern: Lang, 1996), pp. 125–58, p. 133, suggests that Satanic anality, commonplace in medieval theatre, may suggest that the fart is parodic of the breath of life (Genesis 2:7).

82. Randle Cotgrave, cited in Butler, *'Pan's Anniversary'*, p. 384; Martin Ingram, 'Ridings, Rough Music and Mocking Rhymes in Early Modern England', in *Popular Culture in Seventeenth-Century England*, ed. Barry Reay (London: Routledge, 1985), pp. 166–97.
83. In *Witty Apopthegms delivered by King James* (1658) 'His Majesty professed were he to invite the Devil to dinner, he should have three dishes: 1. a pig; 2. a poll of ling and mustard; and a pipe of tobacco for digesture' (W. Gifford (ed.), *The Works of Ben Jonson*, 9 vols. (1816), 7.420, cited in *Ben Jonson*).
84. Smith, 'Ajax by Any Other Name', pp. 133–4, notes Rabelais' *Gargantua* where Lord Suckfizzle describes captains who 'play the lute, crack with their bums, and give little platform leaps' (note 33). Clearly public farting – especially on demand – could be a socially useful skill at court and Camden records one fart-derived name ('Baldwin le Pettour') where the lord gained his title for farting for royal edification.
85. It is difficult to know if Jonson had access to the original poem, *Cock Lorel's Boat*, but the change from ship of fools to feast of folly allows Jonson still to present a catalogue of satirical types, but relate them to one of the key ideas in the masque, hospitality.
86. (1) 'A short comic drama' (*OED*, *n*.2), possibly here 'a comic tale'; (2) 'force-meat, stuffing' (*OED*, *n*.1).
87. This punning continues: 'the tail of the jest' itself invokes the idea of a 'tale' and the end ('tail') of the narrative which also puns on the ultimate outcome of the story in the fart that creates 'The Devil's Arse'.
88. See Robert Rowland, '"Fantasticall and Devilishe Persons": European Witch-Beliefs in Comparative Perspective', in *Early Modern European Witchcraft: Centres and Peripheries*, ed. Bengt Ankarloo and Gustav Heningsen (Oxford: Oxford University Press, 1990), pp. 161–90, esp. p. 166 which cites 'ye cannot be partakers of the Lord's table and of the table of devils' (1 Corinthians, 10),
89. *Ben Jonson* traces possible sources in Raoul de Houdenc's *Songe de Enfer* (*c*.1214–15). It is possible Jonson had access to the poem through Sir Kenelm Digby who donated a MS copy to Oxford in 1634 (Bodleian Library, Digby MS 86), see M. T. Mihm (ed.), *The Songe d'Enfer of Raoul de Houdenc* (Tübingen: Niemeyer, 1984), 30–1, 84.
90. Presumably the 'third' item is sexual: François Rabelais, *Gargantua and Pantagruel*, trans. Thomas Urquhart and P. Le Motteux with an introduction by Terence Cave (London and New York: Everyman's Library, 1994), 629 (Bk. 4, Ch. 46), and in Florio's *Second Fruits* (1591), 12.179. Florio's anecdote is a variation of an English proverb in which 'The devil makes his Christmas pie of lawyers' tongues and clerks' fingers' (Tilley, D258).
91. Frank Kermode, 'The Banquet of Sense', in *Shakespeare, Spenser, Donne: Renaissance Essays* (London: Viking Press, 1971), 84–115.
92. Michel Jeanneret, *A Feast of Words: Banquets and Table Talk in the Renaissance* (Cambridge: Polity Press, 1991), pp. 152–3.
93. Katharine A. Craik, 'Reading *Coryats Crudities* (1611)', *Studies in English Literature, 1500–1900*, 44 (2004), 79–96, esp. p. 82.
94. A variant on 'not worth a farthing' (Tilley, F71).
95. *Poetaster*, 3.4.155–6.
96. *Early Stuart Libels*, C1.
97. 'On the Famous Voyage', lines 108–11, *The Alchemist*, 1.1.1.

98. Michelle O'Callaghan, 'Performing Politics: The Circulation of the Parliament Fart', *Huntingdon Library Quarterly*, 69 (2006), 121–38, p. 127.
99. All quotations are taken from *The Riverside Chaucer*, ed. Larry D. Benson (Oxford: Oxford University Press, 1988).
100. Peter W. Travis, 'Thirteen Ways of Listening to a Fart: Noise in Chaucer's *Summoner's Tale*', *Exemplaria*, 16 (2004), 1–19, p. 6.
101. Andy Wood, "Poore men woll speke one daye": Plebeian Languages of Deference and Defiance in England, c.1520–1640', in *The Politics of the Excluded in England, c.1500–1850*, ed. Tim Harris (Basingstoke: Palgrave Macmillan, 2001), pp. 67–98, p. 88.
102. 'Podex' is usually politely glossed as 'rump' but 'arse' or 'arsehole' were current translations. *OED* 'arse' notes that Jonson's *Poetaster*, 4.7.16 ('Valiant? So is my arse') suggests early modern usage parallel to the modern dismissive use ('my arse').
103. O'Callaghan, 'Performing Politics: The Circulation of the Parliament Fart', pp. 12–13.
104. Variant lines and additional stanzas could be added to refocus the satire or add to the catalogue of abuses it portrayed and the most elaborate version, in the Percy Ballads MS, contains an additional four stanzas, some of considerably increased rudeness.
105. Christopher Marsh, 'The Sound of Print in Early Modern England: The Broadside Ballad as Song', in *The Uses of Script and Print, 1300–1700*, ed. A. Walsham and J. Crick (Cambridge: Cambridge University Press), pp. 171–190, pp. 179–80.
106. Marsh, 'The Sound of Print', p. 185.
107. Claude M. Simpson, *The Broadside Ballad and Its Music*, 2 vols. (New Brunswick, NJ: Rutgers University Press, 1966), 1.129–33. The tune was printed in 1651 but is mentioned in Rowley's *Match Me at Midnight* (1622) and *The Partial Law* (which may date as early as 1615).
108. Nicholas Lanier was paid £200 for his involvement which may point towards the importance of the musical element although Lanier was also a talented painter and scenographic artist.
109. Alastair Bellany, 'Singing Libel in Early Stuart England: The Case of the Staines Fiddlers, 1627', *Huntington Library Quarterly*, 69 (2006), 177–93, pp. 182 and 189.
110. Lord Manchester, cited by Bellany, 'Singing Libel', p. 181.
111. Bellany, 'Singing Libel', p. 183.
112. Published by Claes Janz Visscher; see *Hollstein's Dutch and Flemish Etchings, Engravings, and Woodcuts, ca. 1450–1700*, ed. C. Schuckman and D. De Hoop Scheffer (Roosendaal: Koninklijke Van Poll, 1991), p. 179 (no. 22) and Plate 22.

6 "Tis for kings, / Not for their subjects, to have such rare things': *The Triumph of Peace* and Civil Culture

1. Edward Hyde, *Selections from the History of the Rebellion and the Life of Himself*, ed. G. Huehns and Hugh Trevor-Roper (Oxford: Oxford University, 1978), p. 83.

2. Malcolm Smuts, 'Force, Love and Authority in Caroline Political Culture', in *The 1630s: Interdisciplinary Perspectives*, ed. Ian Atherton and Julie Sanders (Manchester: Manchester University Press, 2006), pp. 28–49, p. 33.
3. Julie Sanders and Ian Atherton, 'Introducing the 1630s: Questions of Parliament, Peace and Pressure Points', in *The 1630s: Interdisciplinary Perspectives*, ed. Atherton and Sanders, p. 3.
4. Philip Finkelpearl, *John Marston of the Middle Temple: An Elizabethan Dramatist in his Social Setting* (Cambridge, MA: Harvard University Press, 1969), pp. 1–5, describes the City lawyers as 'the largest single group of literate and cultured men in London', possessing a distinctive masquing culture which did, at key points, express disquiet with official policy. See also Chapter 4 (p. 116).
5. Smuts, 'Force, Love and Authority', pp. 34–5.
6. They also mark Henrietta Maria's political interventions: see Julie Sanders, 'Caroline Salon Culture and Female Agency: The Countess of Carlisle, Henrietta Maria, and Public Theatre', *Theatre Journal*, 52 (2000), 449–64, and Karen Britland, '"All emulation cease, and jars": Political Possibilities in *Chloridia*, Queen Henrietta Maria's Masque of 1631', *Ben Jonson Journal*, 9 (2000), 1–22.
7. James, Duke of York, later James II, was born on 14 October 1633. Legal sources suggest the birth and lack of a previous masque after the King's coronation spurred the offer elicited a spontaneous expression from the lawyers, although Thomas Coke claims that the King had invited the masque using Lord Coventry as messenger, see *JCS*, 5.1154–5. Whitelocke, *Memorials*, sig. D2r dates the onset of preparations to 'about *allholantide*' [Hallowtide].
8. Whitelocke's *Diary* attributes the impetus for *The Triumph of Peace* to the lawyers, describing the masque as 'seasonable' due to Prynne's antitheatricalism and the need to differentiate the lawyers from Prynne's views (Whitelocke, *Diary*, p. 73; the same phrase is used in *Memorials*, sig. D1v).
9. Sir John Finch and the Earl of Dorset highlighted the attacks on the Queen but Lord Cottington saw the book as having this more general target: see *Documents Relating to the Proceedings Against William Prynne in 1634 and 1637*, ed. S. R. Gardiner (London: Royal Historical Society, 1877), pp. 10–11, 25, and 16. Cottington's views were echoed by Lincoln's Inn when they expelled Prynne and by the Venetian ambassador (cited in Kim Walker, 'New Prison: Representing the Female Actor in Shirley's *The Bird in a Cage* (1633)', *English Literary Renaissance*, 21 (1991), 385–400, p. 388).
10. Pleasing the Queen after *Histriomastix* may well have figured: Whitelocke claims to have used musicians from the Queen's Chapel, 'the more to please her' (Whitelocke, *Diary*, p. 74). It has also been argued that the choice of Shirley was an attempt to assuage the Queen: see *Three Seventeenth-Century Plays on Women and Performance*, ed. Hero Chalmers, Julie Sanders, and Sophie Tomlinson (Manchester: Manchester University Press, 2006), p. 25.
11. Many aspects of the occasion were the result of collaboration, including musical and theatrical resources, and Whitelocke's *Memorials* stress how the principal members of the Inn and others 'amongst whom some were servants to the King' decided a masque would demonstrate the legal Inns' loyalty (sig. D1v).
12. These are: (1) the shorter manuscript 'diary', published as *The Diary of Bulstrode Whitelocke* (covering 1605–75); (2) the longest manuscript, a

monumental set of 'Annales' (covering 1605–60); and (3) the printed text, sponsored and edited by the Earl of Anglesey in *Memorials of the English Affairs* (1682). The 'Annales' and the *Diary* run in parallel up to 1660, the former supplemented by newspaper material, the latter relying on direct observation. See Whitelocke, *Diary,* pp. 31 and 35–6.

13. Whitelocke, *Diary,* p. 74.
14. Vane, feeling himself 'undervalued in a young lawyer's difference of opinion from his wisdom', tried to block 'such conveniences and accommodation as were requisite and the place did afford', something that Whitelocke in a 'befittingly humble' manner rejected as his 'business' was 'acceptable to both their Majesties' and that the inns, whose servant he accounted himself, were being obstructed: see BL MS Add 53,726, fols. 90v–91.
15. Whitelocke, *Memorials,* sig. D1v. Whiteway shows (see n. 31 below) that others made the same linkage to the sports.
16. Whitelocke, *Memorials,* sig. D2v. Stephen Orgel and Roy Strong, *Inigo Jones: The Theatre of the Stuart Court,* 2 vols. (Berkeley: University of California Press, 1973), 1.64–6, illustrate the confusions about this narrative, noting the rather obvious nature of the 'covert' message and the involvement of the monopoly-defending lawyer, Noy. They also describe the organising committee in terms of left/right politics while admitting that the implications of Charles' policies were not clear in 1633; see Martin Butler, 'Politics and the Masque: *The Triumph of Peace*', *The Seventeenth Century,* 2 (1987), 117–41, pp. 118–19 and 122.
17. Recent studies of *The Triumph of Peace* have stressed its negotiation with critical voices either as a 'tactful but firm caution about the necessity of the constraints of legality' restrained by genre and occasion (Butler, 'Politics and the Masque: *The Triumph of Peace*', p. 122), or as more formally transgressive but despite 'criticism of particular royal policies' broadly aligned with loyalty to the Crown (see Kevin Sharpe, *Criticism and Compliment: The Politics of Literature in the England of Charles I* (Cambridge: Cambridge University Press, 1987), 212–23, esp. p. 222). For Sharpe, the involvement of numerous critics of the Crown, without damage to their later careers, justifies his defence of Caroline court culture as open, various, flexible, and responsive.
18. *Memorials* connects the masque to *The Book of Sports* (*Memorials,* sig. D1v). See Whitelocke, *Diary,* pp. 35–6 on the role of the Earl of Anglesey in the production of *The Memorials* which reshaped events for the Restoration audience.
19. John Peacock, 'The Image of Charles I as a Roman Emperor', in *The 1630s: Interdisciplinary Perspectives,* ed. Atherton and Sanders, pp. 50–73, p. 65.
20. Butler, 'Politics and the Masque: *The Triumph of Peace*', p. 136, notes the tougher implications of the procession.
21. Compare L. Bryant, 'From Communal Ritual to Royal Spectacle', in *French Ceremonial Entries in the Sixteenth Century: Event, Image, Text,* ed. N. Russell and H. Vissentin (Toronto: University of Toronto Press, 2007), pp. 207–45, p. 208, on how entry rituals dramatise and spatialise competing civic and court spheres.
22. W. W. Greg, '*The Triumph of Peace.* A Bibliographer's Nightmare', *The Library,* 5th ser., 1 (1946), 113–26, and 'The Text', in *A Book of Masques,* pp. 306–7.
23. Murray Lefkowitz, 'The Longleat Papers of Bulstrode Whitelocke: New Light on Shirley's *Triumph of Peace*', *Journal of the American Musicological Society,* 18 (1965), 42–60.

24. The masque was also reported in the Venetian ambassador's dispatches, and received a special entry in the *Gazette de France*, 9 March 1634, including a long description of the procession. It was also the only masque text that has been traced to the Bibliothèque du Roi: see Mare-Claude Canova-Green, *La Politique-spectacle au grand siècle: les rapports franco-anglais* (Tübingen: Gunter Narr Verlag, 1993), p. 176.
25. All quotations are taken from *The Triumph of Peace* (1634), ed. Clifford Leech, in *A Book of Masques*, ed. S. Wells (Cambridge: Cambridge University Press, 1967). Confidence here means 'impudence' or 'presumption'.
26. The descriptions suggest the influence of the pseudo-Rabelaisian text *Les Songes Drolatiques* (1565): see Canova-Green, *La Politique-spectacle au grand siècle*, pp. 246–7, and Anne Lake Prescott, 'The Stuart Masque and Pantagruel's Dreams', *English Literary History*, 51 (1984), 407–30.
27. Leech lists these as 'Anti-masque xiii' (*A Book of Masques*, pp. 281, 301), but this misses the point: they are not the antimasque but essential to the masque. See below, pp. 193–4.
28. See George Garrard's and William Drake's letters cited below, pp. 204–5.
29. BL Harleian MS 1026, fol. 50–50v, commonplace book of Justinian Pagitt. This letter is usually cited from John Payne Collier's *The history of English dramatic poetry to the time of Shakespeare, and Annals of the stage to the restoration*, 2 vols. (London: John Murray, 1831), 2.60–1 (as in M. Lefkowitz, *Trois Masques à la Cour de Charles Ier d'Angleterre* (Paris: CNRS, 1970), p. 39), where a partial transcription is offered. Pagitt (1612–68) was a lawyer based in the Middle Temple with musical interests (see *ODNB*, http://www.oxforddnb.com/view/article/66665?docPos=3); his commonplace book mixes letter drafts, sermon notes and instructions on deportment while dancing. See also Wilfrid Prest, *The Inns of Court, 1590–1640* (London: Longman,1972), pp. 162–4.
30. See pp. 194–5 below.
31. William Whiteway, 'Diary', 3 Feb 1634 in BL MS Egerton 784, cited in McGee, '"Strangest Consequence from Remotest Cause": The Second Performance of *The Triumph of Peace*', *Medieval and Renaissance Drama in England*, 5 (1991), 309–42, pp. 320–1. Whiteway's dating is confirmed by Sir Humphrey Mildmay's diary, by Justinian Pagitt's letter, by *The Diary of Sir Richard Hutton 1614–1639*, ed. W. R. Prest (London: Selden Society, 1991), p. 96, and by Herbert's documents that change the date from 2 to 3 February: *JCS*, 5.1156–7. Bentley notes Herbert's altered dating as 'an error', although there may have been earlier negotiations about the masque: Garrard reported to Wentworth (6 December 1633) that it was planned for Twelfth Night (see *The Earl of Strafford's letters and despatches, with an essay towards his life by Sir G. Radcliffe*, ed. W. Knowler, 2 vols. (1740), 1.167).
32. The *Memorials* simply states it 'was agreed to be on Candlemas Night to end Christmas' (sig. D1v) and claims the masquers left Ely House on 'Candlemasday in the afternoon' (sig. D2). Dayrell's tomb (see n. 130 below) places the performance on Candlemas night.
33. Ronald Hutton, *The Rise and Fall of Merry England: The Ritual Year 1400–1700* (Oxford: Oxford University Press, 1994), p. 197; and *The Elizabethan Prayerbook*, cited in C. Hassel, *Renaissance Drama and the English Church Year* (Lincoln, NE: University of Nebraska Press, 1979), p. 95. The feast also

marked the presentation of Christ at the Temple (and was associated with the story of Simeon and with the 'Nunc dimittis').
34. The Queen's Capuchin chapel at St James, devoted to the Virgin Mary, had been opened in 1632: see Erica Veevers, *Images of Love and Religion: Queen Henrietta Maria and Court Entertainments* (Cambridge: Cambridge University Press, 1989), pp. 92–109, esp. pp. 95 and 106.
35. Veevers, *Images of Love and Religion*, pp. 142–3.
36. Hamon L'Estrange, *The Life and Reign of King Charles* (1655), sig. S1r; and compare W. Sanderson, *A Compleat History of the life and raigne of King Charles from his cradle to his grave* (1658), sig. 2C2v.
37. William Prynne, *Histrio-mastix. The Players Scourge or Actors Tragedie* (1633), sig. 5D4v.
38. Whitelocke, *Memorials*, sig. D1v, notes the association of the masque to *The Book of Sports*, describing how 'The King revived his Father's declaration for tolerating lawfull sports . . . on the Lord's day, which gave great distaste to many, both others, as well as those who were usually termed Puritans.' This passage occurs immediately before the discussion of Shirley's masque
39. Whitelocke, *Memorials*, sig. D2r.
40. William Prynne, *A Brief Survey and Censure of Mr Cosins Concerning his Cozening Devotions* (1628), cited in Veevers, *Images of Love and Religion*, pp. 143–4.
41. *The Sermons of John Donne*, ed. E. Simpson and G. R. Potter, 10 vols. (Berkeley: University of California Press, 1953–62), 10.90. Donne also argues that the problem is not the 'use of Candles by day' but that Protestants should avoid 'superstitious Invocations, with magical Incantations'.
42. It is perhaps no accident that Robert Herrick marks the day more indirectly, celebrating the folk customs associated with the feast, such as the removal of the Christmas 'rosemary and bays' and their replacement with 'the greener box', rather than either the feast or its prescribed scriptural texts: see 'Ceremonies for Candlemas Eve', in *Hesperides*: see *Poetical Works of Robert Herrick*, ed. L. C. Martin (Oxford: Oxford University Press, 1956), p. 285.
43. The Wisdom of Solomon, 9:3. The gospel for Candlemas describes the presentation of the young Christ at the Temple in accordance with 'the custom of the law' (Luke 2:27), while the epistle stresses 'charity' (Colossians 2:14) and the communal body. All references are to *The Bible: Authorized King James Version*, ed. R. Carroll and S. Prickett (Oxford: Oxford University Press, 1997).
44. Wisdom, 9:6–7.
45. Wisdom, 9:14 and 18. The other prescribed text, Colossians 3:12, meshes less well with Caroline theology. Colossians may have promoted obedience and hierarchy (notably 2:18–23), but clearly within the context of a righteous and religious regime, and in a language that was open to a much more radical and Protestant interpretation.
46. On Candlemas Day Charles offered seven nobles instead of the usual one: see K. Sharpe, *The Personal Rule of Charles I* (New Haven and London: Yale University Press, 1992), p. 219.
47. Johan P. Sommerville, *Politics and Ideology in England, 1603–40* (Harlow: Longman, 1986), pp. 64–6, and Roy Strong, *Coronation: A History of Kingship and the British Monarchy* (London: HarperCollins, 2005), 238–40. At the

time the Venetian ambassador reported, 'people talk of the possibility of his Majesty not being crowned, so as to remain more absolute, avoiding the obligation to swear to the laws' (*CSPV, 1625–1626*, p. 51).
48. The matter was resolved by 24 January as the Stationers' Register entry refers to the masque as 'to be presented to his majesty at Whitehall the third of February next': see *JCS*, 5.1156.
49. Henry Burton, *For God, and the King* (1636), cited in Veevers, *Images of Love and Religion*, p. 144; John Donne, *Sermons*, 10.85 ('Preached Upon Candlemas Day').
50. Donne, *Sermons*, 10.102.
51. Leech in *A Book of Masques*, pp. 312–13, glosses these lines as 'when seen properly, it will be evident that they are of full age, although factious spirits, light-blinded, cannot see them as such'. 'Foreign persons' are strangers, perhaps glancing at the use of mercenary troops, contrasting with the fully prepared British youth.
52. 'Faction' (634) seems to reverse a term commonly deployed against the religious opponents of the Caroline regime.
53. *Oberon*, 96–7, *Mercury Vindicated*, 146, and *Golden Age Restored*, 126.
54. Shirley's description of 'wings of several-coloured feathers' and a carnation robe, yellow hair, sliver coronet and a white staff and buskins (626–8) differs from the more classical figures of Jonson's masques where Genius is often a old man, and is less clearly the 'Genius of these kingdoms' seen in Carew's *Coelum Britannicum*, who sports 'wings at his shoulder' and carries a cornucopia, see *The Poems of Thomas Carew*, ed. R. Dunlap (Oxford: Oxford University Press, 1948), lines 892–6.
55. *OED*, 'white staff', n., notices the specific association with either the staff of office, or sometimes used as a synonym for the office-holder.
56. The King's arrival at Welbeck (1633) had been compared to a 'fount of light' as if it enacted a moment of masque-like revelation and transformation (*The King and Queen's Entertainment at Welbeck*, 28).
57. Amphiluche appears in *Iliad*, VII, 433 (see *A Book of Masques*, p. 311, note 92).
58. Revelations 12:1–6.
59. *The Purple Island*, canto 6, cited in David Norbook, *Poetry and Politics in the English Renaissance* (Oxford: Oxford University Press, 2002), p. 269. The allusion may be conscious as Fletcher's text had been published in 1633.
60. There may be a further differentiation from the Marian imagery associated with Henrietta Maria as the Morning Star was a common symbol for Mary and was used in several texts for the Queen, for instance *Luminalia* (1637): see Veevers, *Images of Love and Religion*, p. 144.
61. Donne, *Sermons*, 10.84.
62. Donne, *Sermons*, 10.102.
63. Regeneration is, here, a response to Protestant notions of reformation which were applied to the masque in the 1630s, see Norbrook, 'The Reformation of the Masque', in Lindley (ed.), *The Court Masque*, pp. 96, 99–100, and note 7 (p. 107).
64. *Albion's Triumph* (1632) in *The Poems and Masques of Aurelian Townshend*, ed. C. Brown (Reading: Whiteknights Press, 1983), p. 87.
65. *The Poems and Masques of Aurelian Townshend*, pp. 86–7.
66. *The Poems and Masques of Aurelian Townshend*, p. 89.

67. 'In answer of an Elegiacall Letter upon the death of the King of Sweden', in *The Poems of Thomas Carew*, lines 6, 95–8.
68. C. Leech in *A Book of Masques*, p. 311 (note 155) sees the eye and yoke as symbols of vigilance and control. As Leech points out, however, the Hours according to Hesiod were 'tutelary goddesses of agriculture' (*Book of Masques*, p. 279), so the yoke is also an agricultural tool as much as a symbol.
69. Plutarch, 'The Fortunes of Rome', in *Selected Essays and Dialogues*, ed. D. Russell (Oxford: Oxford University Press, 1993), p. 133. Numa's reign was supposed to have lasted forty-three years.
70. T. Godwin, *Romanae historiae anthologia recognita et aucta. An English exposition of the Roman antiquities . . . for the vse of Abingdon Schoole* (1631), sig. A4v.
71. John Peacock, *The Stage Designs of Inigo Jones: The European Context* (Cambridge: Cambridge University Press: 1995), pp. 92–3.
72. Peacock, *The Stage Designs of Inigo Jones*, p. 92 and plates 3 and 4.
73. Peacock, 'The Image of Charles I as a Roman Emperor', p. 62, notes the connection between the grove and the temple. It is possible that Irene's ability to 'make a temple of a forest' echoes this connection.
74. 'Primum / Hunc Arethusa mihi' alludes to Virgil, *Eclogues*, 10.1, where Arethusa is the river associated with pastoral.
75. Edmund Spenser, *The Faerie Queene*, ed. A. C. Hamilton (Harlow: Longman, 2001), 7.7.43 (5–8).
76. 'Assoil' carries suggestions of intellectual labour and effort: see *OED*, 2.6 (to solve a problem, resolve a doubt or difficulty).
77. *The Book of Revelation*, 14:19–20.
78. B. Ravelhofer, '"Virgin Wax" and "Hairy Men-Monsters": Unstable Movement Codes in the Stuart Masque', in *The Politics of the Stuart Court Masque*, ed. David Bevington and Peter Holbrook (Cambridge: Cambridge University Press, 1998), pp. 244–72 (pp. 261–4).
79. H. Langelüddecke, '"The chiefest strength and glory of this kingdom": Arming and Training the "Perfect Militia" in the 1630s', *English Historical Review*, 118 (2003), 1264–1303.
80. Roy Strong, *Van Dyck: Charles I on Horseback* (London: Viking, 1972), pp. 59–63.
81. Sharpe, *The Personal Rule of Charles I*, p. 220.
82. Elias Ashmole, *The Institutions, Laws and Ceremonies of the most noble order of the Garter* (1672), cited in Strong, *Van Dyck: Charles I on Horseback*, pp. 62–3.
83. *The King's Majesty's Declaration to His Subjects Concerning the Lawful Sports to be Used* (1633), sig. C2v. The original *The Book of Sports* (1617, 1618) included in the list- of licit recreations not only 'May-Games, Whitson Ales, and Morris-dances', but also 'Archerie for men, leaping, vaulting': see *The Minor Prose Works of King James VI and I*, ed. J. Craigie and A. Law (Edinburgh: Scottish Text Society, 1982), pp. 107, 239.
84. John Stow, *Annals of London*, cited in William Hunt, 'Civic Chivalry and the English Civil War', in *The Transmission of Culture in Early Modern Europe*, ed. Anthony Grafton and Ann Blair (Philadelphia: University of Pennsylvania Press, 1998), pp. 204–37, p. 219.
85. Hunt, 'Civic Chivalry', pp. 223–5.
86. J. S. A. Adamson, 'Chivalry and Political Culture in Caroline England', in *Culture and Politics in Early Stuart England*, ed. Kevin Sharpe and Peter Lake (Basingstoke: Macmillan, 1994), pp. 161–97, p. 169.

258 Notes

87. Strong, *Van Dyck: Charles I on Horseback*, pp. 61–2.
88. William Barriffe, *Mars, his Triumph. Or, Description of an Exercise performed at the 18 October 1638 in Merchant-Taylors' Hall* (1639). William Barriffe was a military author and later parliamentarian officer: see B. Donagan, 'Barriffe, William (1599/1600–1643)', *ODNB* (Oxford, 2004), http://www.oxforddnb.com/view/article/40628, accessed 27 February 2007.
89. Barriffe, *Mars, his Triumph*, π3.
90. T. Dekker, *Wars, wars, wars* (1628), sig. A2.
91. Dekker, *Wars, wars, wars*, sigs. C2–C2v.
92. Hunt, 'Civic Chivalry', p. 230; *CSPD 1633–34*, p. 443 (nomination of Walter Neale as Captain of the Artillery Garden).
93. *The Letters and Papers of the Earl of Strafford*, ed. Knowler, 1.167.
94. Sharpe, *Personal Rule of Charles I*, p. 233, note 106.
95. Anon, 'Now did heaven's charioteer', cited in M. B. Pickel, *Charles I as Patron of Poetry and Drama* (London: F. Muller, 1936). The poem also appears in a copy in the state papers (NA, SP16/260/14) and in three other poetic miscellanies (BL MS Add 33998, fols. 64v–65r; Rosenbach Library, Philadelphia, MS 232/14, pp. 46–7; Yale, Osborn Collection, MS b 200, pp. 119–20).
96. Interestingly, one copy ascribes this poem to Alexander Gil (the Younger). Gil, a major Latin poet, had toasted the assassin John Felton and circulated verses against the Duke of Buckingham. He had a reputation for political commentary and has been suggested as the author of the 'The Blessing of the Five Senses', the answer to *The Gypsies Metamorphosed*. See Gordon Campbell, 'Gil, Alexander, the younger (1596/7–1642?)', *ODNB* (Oxford: Oxford University Press); online edn., Jan. 2008 (http://www.oxforddnb.com/view/article/10730, accessed 26 February 2014).
97. From a Latin adage, but compare 'In time of peace prepare for war' (Tilley, T300).
98. William Crofts to William Cavendish, Earl of Newcastle, 1 February 1634, BL MS Add 70499, fols. 174–174r; cited from *HMC Portland*, 2.125 in T. Orbison (ed.), *Middle Temple Documents Relating to George Chapman's 'The Memorable Masque' and James Shirley's 'The Triumph of Peace'*, Malone Society Collections, 12 (Oxford, 1983), p. 33.
99. BL Add MS 64907, Thomas Coke to Sir John Coke, 17 October 1633, fol. 44, cited in *JCS*, 5.1155–6 from *HMC Report 12, Cowper MSS*, 2.34. The first part of this passage is cited in Butler, 'Politics and the Masque: *The Triumph of Peace*', p. 137, also from *HMC Cowper*.
100. Prest, *The Inns of Court, 1590–1640*, pp. 113 and 154.
101. *Pleasure Reconciled to Virtue* (1618) illustrates how individual performance and competition could alter the masque, in a text that was designed to moderate the financial demands of courtiers, yet depended – in the end – on a display from precisely the kind of reward–hungry courtiers it sought to police. See Butler, 'Ben Jonson and the Limits of Courtly Panegyric', p. 112.
102. The 'figary', a variant of 'vagary', but perhaps the Tailor's mistake for 'figure', is a kind of 'diversion' from the main route of the masque (*OED*, 'vagary', 1, 3), and also a kind of wandering journey rather than a disciplined dance. The point, though, appears to be that the craftsmen don't know how to dance, but the lawyers, on balance, still do.
103. *The Masque at Coleorton*, line 75.

104. The offstage noise is, in fact, created by both parties, including those who attempt to keep them out (670–1). Shirley here uses *Love Restored* (1611) as a model and he seems to have recognised the issues about speech and slavery voiced in that masque. Many of the same ideas were echoed in the 1628 parliamentary debates: see Chapter 2, pp. 46–7 and p. 225 (note 116).
105. Indeed, their one concern is to 'go off cleanly' (714), so that even their language is sanitised as in the Tailor's warning that they 'may else kiss the porter's lodge' (708) for their interruption. 'Kiss the porter's lodge' may suggest making reverence to the place of punishment, but it also sidesteps the more obvious bawdry, 'kiss the porter's arse'.
106. John Finet, *The Ceremonies of Charles I: The Notebooks of John Finet 1628–1641*, ed. A. J. Loomie (New York: Fordham University Press), p. 41, although Whitelocke's manuscript diary attributed the repeat only to the Queen's enjoyment (Whitelocke, *Diary*, p. 76). Whitelocke, *Memorials*, sig. D3r.
107. Whitelocke, *Diary*, p. 76; Repertory Book, Court of Aldermen, minutes of meeting of 14 February 1634, as transcribed in McGee, '"Strangest Consequence from Remotest Cause"', p. 325.
108. McGee, '"Strangest Consequence from Remotest Cause"', p. 310.
109. William Whiteway, diary entry, 3 February 1634, from *William Whiteway of Dorchester: His Diary 1618 to 1634*, ed. David Underdown, Dorset Record Society Publications, 12 (1991), pp. 138–9. The passage is also cited, transcribed from BL MS Egerton 784, in McGee, '"Strangest Consequence from Remotest Cause"', pp. 320–1.
110. Details taken from Edward Rossingham's letters in *Court and Times of Charles I*, ed. Thomas Birch (1849), pp. 229–30, and the *CSPD, 1633–34*, p. 443 (petition of William Elworthy imprisoned over his opposition to the new soap). See also *Stuart Royal Proclamations, Volume 2: Royal Proclamations of King Charles I, 1625–1646*, ed. J. F. Larkin and P. L. Hughes (Oxford: Clarendon Press, 1983), p. 407.
111. Finet reports that he greeted the King 'on his knee' at his first arrival, and that despite his ill-health he also returned during the banquet to welcome the royal party (*The Ceremonies of Charles I*, p. 43).
112. McGee, '"Strangest Consequence from Remotest Cause"', pp. 311–12.
113. Finet, *The Ceremonies of Charles I*, p. 42.
114. McGee, '"Strangest Consequence from Remotest Cause"', p 313.
115. Finet, *The Ceremonies of Charles I*, p. 41. McGee, '"Strangest Consequence from Remotest Cause"', p. 312, suggests that the walkway constructed between the mayor's house and the Merchant Taylors' Hall was elaborately decorated with the royal coat of arms to draw attention to city loyalty.
116. Peter Heylyn, *Observations on the history of the reign of King Charles* (1656), sig. H6.
117. J. Knowles, '"In the purest times of peerless Queen Elizabeth": Nostalgia, Politics, and Jonson's Use of the 1575 Kenilworth Entertainments', in *The Progresses, Pageants, and Entertainments of Queen Elizabeth I*, ed. Jayne Archer, Elizabeth Goldring, and Sarah Knight (Oxford: Oxford University Press, 2007), pp. 247–67, pp. 265–6
118. William Cavendish to Prince Charles, in Margaret Cavendish, *Life of William Cavendish*, ed. C. H. Firth (London: Routledge, 1907), Appendix II,

p. 186. Later he advised the Prince 'to shew your Selfe Gloryously, to your People; like a God': see Thomas P. Slaughter (ed.), *Ideology and Politics on the Eve of the Restoration: Newcastle's Advice to Charles II* (Philadelphia: American Philosophical Society, 1984), p. 45.

119. Indeed, in 1633 Charles travelled by carriage rather than on horseback, and his 'privatised' mode of transport seemed to some to defeat the purpose of royal ceremony: see Mark Brayshay, 'Long-Distance Royal Journeys: Anne of Denmark's Journey from Stirling to Windsor in 1603', *Journal of Transport History*, 25 (2004), 1–21, p. 17, and my essay cited below.
120. They were also described by Vasari and Serlio: see Andrew Martindale, *The Triumphs of Caesar by Andrea Mantegna in the Collection of Her Majesty the Queen at Hampton Court* (London: Harvey Miller, 1979), p. 97. Martindale notes that a small copy by Rubens, 'Scenes from a Roman Triumph', c.1630, also survives in the National Gallery (p. 107).
121. Peacock, 'The Image of Charles I as Roman Emperor', p. 55.
122. Butler, 'Reform or Reverence: the Politics of the Caroline Masque', in *Theatre and Government under the Early Stuarts*, ed. J. R. Mulryne and Margaret Shewring (Cambridge: Cambridge University Press, 1991), pp. 118–56, p. 134. My reading of *Albion's Triumph* is much influenced by Professor Butler's reading and by John Peacock's 'The Image of Charles I as a Roman Emperor' (see note 19 above).
123. *The Poems and Masques of Aurelian Townshend*, p. 80.
124. Butler, 'Reform or Reverence: The Politics of the Caroline Masque', p. 135.
125. *CSPV, 1632–36*, p. 195, cited in *JCS*, 5.1157. Garrard reported to Strafford that the 'riding show' was the reason for the repetition: *Strafford Letters*, 1.207.
126. *CSPV, 1632–36*, p. 195, cited in *JCS*, 5.1157.
127. John R. Elliott Jr., 'The Folger Manuscript of *The Triumph of Peace* Procession', *English Manuscript Studies*, 3 (1992), 193–215, p. 198.
128. *The Memorable Masque* in *Court Masques*, lines 27–114
129. *The Memorable Masque*, line 34; Whitelocke, *Memorials*, sigs. D2r, D2v.
130. Dayrell, sometimes spelt Darrell or Dorell (of Lillingstone Dayrell, Buckinghamshire), later served as a royalist officer and was knighted in 1634 (see W. A. Shaw, *The Knights of England*, 2 vols. (London: Sherratt and Hughes, 1906), 2.202; E. Dayrell, *The History of the Dayrells of Lillingstone Dayrell* (Jersey: Le Lievre Bros, 1885), p. 31). His appearance in the masque features on his tombstone in the parish church: he was chosen for his 'comeliness of person'.
131. Francis Lenton, *The Inns of Court Annagramatist* (1634), sigs. B1r–B1v.
132. Lenton, *The Inns of Court Annagramatist* (1634), sigs. B1r–B1v.
133. McGee, '"Strangest Consequence from Remotest Cause"', p. 312. The Aldermen were also to ensure that householders prevented their servants or children from throwing squibs or crackers (p. 335).
134. Finet, *The Ceremonies of Charles I*, p. 41, and McGee, '"Strangest Consequence from Remotest Cause"', pp. 312, 335.
135. Jonson, *Royall and Magnificent Entertainment*, 314–457, 548–77.
136. John Harris and Gordon Higgott, *Inigo Jones: Complete Architectural Drawings* (London: Royal Academy of Arts, 1989).

137. M.P., *The Honour of the Inns of Court Gentleman, The second part* (1634), mentions how the chariots, 'a fashion / For mighty Princes and conquerors most fit', attracted 'admiration' from the crowd.
138. On the copy that survives in a volume of plays, collected by an unknown tourist, c.1634, see Chapter 4 (pp. 124 and 243 note 114).
139. M.P., *The second part*, stanza 5.
140. This woodcut might derive from a ballad about the 1617 or 1633 royal progresses to Scotland.
141. Joad Raymond notes a 'sentimental pro-royalist' stance in Parker's post-1640 writings: see Joad Raymond, 'Parker, Martin (*fl.* 1624–1647)', *ODNB* (Oxford: Oxford University Press) (http://www.oxforddnb.com/view/article/21326, accessed 26 February 2014).
142. It is possible that the lines preceded the masque (and they appear there in some copies of Q3), but there are some parallels between the two speeches, notably in 'wish no blessedness but you' (643), which is replaced by 'Acknowledge no triumph but in you' (801), and the lines on the soul (644–5) are matched in 802–4.
143. Parker claimed to have 'ten thousand twopenny customers': see *Harry White his Humour* (1637), sig. A4, cited in Raymond, 'Parker, Martin (*fl.* 1624–1647)' (note 141 above).
144. For the lost publications, see D. S. Collins, *A Handlist of News Pamphlets, 1590–1610* (London: South-West Essex Technical College, 1943), pp. 114–15.
145. *An excellent new ballad, shewing the petigree if our royall King Iames, the first of that name in England* (London: Edward White, 1603) [STC 14423]: see Collins, *Handlist*, p. 65.
146. George Garrard to Wentworth in *Earl of Strafford's Letters and Disptaches*, ed. W. Knowler, cited by Butler, 'Politics and the Masque: *The Triumph of Peace*', p. 137.
147. Kevin Sharpe, *Reading Revolutions: The Politics of Reading in Early Modern England* (London and New Haven: Yale University Press, 2000), p. 144.
148. See Jean Fuzier, 'English Political Dialogues 1641–1651: A Suggestion for Research with a Critical Edition of *The Tragedy of the Cruell Warre* (1643)', *Cahiers Elisabéthains*, 14 (1977), 49–68. Quotations are taken from this edition.
149. It assigns its production as 'Printed in the year of the Cavaliers' cruelty'. Lois Potter, '*The Triumph of Peace* and *The Cruel War*: Masque and Parody', *Notes and Queries*, 27 (1980), 345–8, argues that this blurring shows how the masque is misunderstood, but for all its crudeness, *The Cruel War* echoes a common trope in civil war journalism that comedy has become tragedy and masques have now ushered in antimasques.
150. Susan Wiseman, *Drama and Politics in the English Civil War* (Cambridge: Cambridge University Press, 1998), p. 119.
151. L'Estrange, *The Life and Reign of King Charles* (1655), sig. S1.
152. Whitelocke, *Memorials*, sig. πB, 'The Publisher to the Reader', probably by Arthur Annesley, notes how he 'sometimes writes up to the dignity of an Historian' but 'elsewhere is content barely to set down Occurences Diarywise, without melting down or refining the Ore'. See Whitelocke, *Diary*, pp. 28–9 (dates of copying) and pp. 35–6 (the objections of the Duke of Ormonde to passages about his role in the civil wars).

153. Whitelocke, *Diary*, pp. 73–6.
154. In Whitelocke, *Memorials* Whitelocke says of the masque, 'It would manifest the difference of their opinion from Mr Prynne's new learning' (sig. D1v).
155. Whitelocke, *Memorials*, sig. D1v, notes that *Histriomastix* predated the royal pastoral.
156. Whitelocke, *Memorials*, sig. D1v, says Heylyn 'bare great malice to Prynne for confuting some of his doctrines'.
157. Francis Beaumont and John Fletcher, *The Maid's Tragedy*, 1.1.41–2 in *The Dramatic Works of the Beaumont and Fletcher Canon*, ed. F. Bowers, 10 vols. (Cambridge: Cambridge University Press, 1970), 2.30.

Select Bibliography

Primary sources

Manuscripts

British Library

    MS Add 12,528 (accounts of Sir Sackville Crowe for George Villers)
    MS Add 53,726, MS Add 37,343 (Annales of Bulstrode Whitelocke)
    MS Egerton 784 (diary of William Whiteway)
    MS Harleian 481 (diary of Sir Simonds D'Ewes)
    MS Harleian 1026 (commonplace book of Justinian Pagitt)

Hatfield House, Hertfordshire

    Cecil MSS, 140/125 (verse libel on Buckingham)

National Archives, London

    SC6 (Special Collections: Ministers' and Receivers' Accounts)
    SP14 (State Papers, Domestic, James I)
    SP16 (State Papers, Domestic, Charles I)

National Library of Wales

    MS 5298 E (Herbert of Cherbury booklist)

Printed books

Anon. (1949) *Three Parnassus Plays (1598–1601)*, ed. J. B. Leishman (London: Nicholson and Watson).

―― (1967) *The Masque of Flowers*, ed. E. A. J. Honigmann, in *A Book of Masques*, ed. S. Wells (Cambridge: Cambridge University Press).

Akrigg, G. P. V. (ed.) (1984) *Letters of King James VI & I* (Berkeley: University of California Press).

Anderton, B. (ed.) (1930) 'Selections from the Delaval Papers in the Public Library, Newcastle-upon-Tyne', in *A Volume of Miscellanea, Publications of the Newcastle-upon-Tyne Records Committee* (Newcastle-upon-Tyne: Newcastle-upon-Tyne Records Committee).

Bacon, Francis (1874) *Letters and Life of Francis Bacon*, ed. James Spedding, 7 vols. (London: Longman and Green).

―― (1996) *Francis Bacon*, ed. B. Vickers (Oxford: Oxford University Press).

Barriffe, William (1639) *Mars, his Triumph. Or, Description of an Exercise performed at the 18 October 1638 in Merchant-Taylors' Hall* (London: Ralph Mab).

The Bible: Authorized King James Version, ed. R. Carroll and S. Prickett (Oxford: Oxford University Press, 1997).

Bibliotheca Norfolciana (1681) *Bibliotheca Norfolciana: sive Catalogus libb. manuscriptorum & impressorum in omni arte & lingua, quos ... Henricus Dux Norfolciæ, &c. Regiæ Societati Londinensi pro scientia naturali promovenda donavit*, ed. William Perry (London: Richard Chiswel).

Bingham, John (1616) *The tactiks of Aelian or art of embattailing an army after ye Grecian manner Englished and illustrated with figures throughout* (London: Laurence Lisle).

Birch, Thomas (ed.) (1848) *The Court and Times of Charles the First*, 2 vols. (London: H. Colburn).

—— (1849) *The Court and Times of James the First*, 2 vols. (London: H. Colburn).

Burton, Henry (1636) *For God, and the King* (London: Felix Kingston).

Burton, Robert (1989–2000) *The Anatomy of Melancholy*, ed. Thomas C. Faulkner, Nicolas K. Kiessling, Rhonda L. Blair, with an introduction by J. B. Bamborough, 6 vols. (Oxford: Clarendon Press).

Calendar of State Papers, Domestic, James I (1856–72) *Calendar of State Papers, Domestic series, of the reigns of Edward VI, Mary, Elizabeth, (James I)*, ed. R. Lemon with addenda ed. M. A. E. Green, 7 vols. (London: Longman and Co).

Calendar of State Papers, Domestic, Charles I (1858–97) *Calendar of State Papers, Domestic series, of the reign of Charles I, 1625–[1649]*, ed. J. Bruce and others, 23 vols. (London: Longman and Co).

Calendar of State Papers, Venetian (1864–1947) *Calendar of state papers and manuscripts, relating to English affairs, existing in the archives and collections of Venice, and in other libraries of northern Italy*, ed. Rawdon Brown and others, 38 vols. (London: Longman and Co).

Campion, Thomas (1614) *The Description of a Masque ... and choice airs* (London).

—— (1969) *The Works of Thomas Campion*, ed. W. R. Davis (London: Faber).

Carew, Thomas (1948) *The Poems of Thomas Carew*, ed. R. Dunlap (Oxford: Clarendon Press).

Cavendish, Margaret (1907) *Life of William Cavendish*, ed. C. H. Firth (London: Routledge).

Cecil, Robert (1606) *An Answere to certaine scandalous papers. Scattered abroad under colour of a Catholicke admonition* (London: Robert Barker).

Chalmers, Hero, Julie Sanders, and Sophie Tomlinson (eds.) (2006) *Three Seventeenth-Century Plays on Women and Performance* (Manchester: Manchester University Press).

Chamberlain, John (1939) *The Letters of John Chamberlain*, ed. N. E. McClure, 2 vols. (Philadelphia: American Philosophical Society).

Chapman, George (1614) *Andromeda Liberata* (London: Laurence Lisle).

—— (1614) *A Free and Offenceless Justification of a lately Published and most maliciously misinterpreted poeme entitled Andromeda Liberata* (London: Laurence Lisle).

Charles I (1633) *The King's Majesty's Declaration to His Subjects Concerning the Lawful Sports to be Used* (London: John Bill).

Chaucer, Geoffrey (1988) *The Riverside Chaucer*, ed. Larry D. Benson (Oxford: Oxford University Press).

Croft, Pauline (ed.) (1987) *A collection of several speeches and treatises of the late Lord Treasurer Cecil, and of several observations of the Lords of the Council given to King James concerning his estate and revenue in the years 1608, 1609 and 1610* (London: Royal Historical Society, 1987) [Camden Miscellany, 29].

Daniel, Samuel (1885) *Hymen's Triumph* in *The Complete Works in Verse and Prose of Samuel Daniel*, ed. A. Grosart (London: Hazell, Watson and Viney).
────── (1967) *The vision of the 12. goddesses presented in a maske the 8. of Ianuary, at Hampton Court*, ed. Joan Rees, in *A Book of Masques*, ed. Stanley Wells (Cambridge: Cambridge University Press).
────── (1994) *Hymen's Triumph*, ed. J. Pitcher (Oxford: Oxford University Press).
Dekker, Thomas (1628) *Wars, wars, wars* (London: I. Grismand).
────── (1953-61) *The Dramatic Works of Thomas Dekker*, ed. Fredson Bowers, 4 vols. (Cambridge: Cambridge University Press).
D'Ewes, Simonds (1682) *Journals of All the Parliaments during the reign of Queen Elizabeth* (London: Paul Bowes).
Dio Cassius (1914-27) *The Roman History*, ed. Ernest Cary and Herbert Foster, 9 vols. (Cambridge, MA: Harvard University Press).
Donne, John (1912) *The Poems of John Donne*, ed. H. C. Grierson, 2 vols. (Oxford: Oxford University Press).
────── (1953-62) *The Sermons of John Donne*, ed. E. M. Simpson and G. R. Potter, 10 vols. (Berkeley: University of California Press).
────── (1971) *The Complete English Poems of John Donne*, ed. A. J. Smith (Harmondsworth: Penguin Books).
Donne, John, Jr. (1651) *Letters to Several Persons of Honour* (London: Richard Marriot).
Drummond, William (1711) *The Works of William Drummond* (Edinburgh: James Watson).
Dudley Edwards, Ruth (ed.) (1938) 'The Letter-Book of Sir Arthur Chichester, 1612-1614', *Analecta Hibernia*, 8, 3-178.
Evans, H. A. (ed.) (1897) *English Masques: With an Introduction* (London and Glasgow: Blackie & Son).
Fairholt, F. W. (ed.) (1850) *Poems and Songs Relating to George Villiers, Duke of Buckingham* (London: Percy Society Publications).
Finet, John (1656) *Finetti Philoxenis: som choice observations of Sr. John Finett knight* (London: H. Twyford and G. Bedell).
────── (1987) *The Ceremonies of Charles I: The Notebooks of John Finet 1628-1641*, ed. A. J. Loomie (New York: Fordham University Press).
Fletcher, John (1966-96) *The Dramatic Works of the Beaumont and Fletcher Canon*, ed. F. Bowers, 10 vols. (Cambridge: Cambridge University Press).
Florio, John (1611) *Queen Annas New World of Words* (London: Edw. Blount and William Barret).
Foster, Elizabeth Read (ed.) (1966) *Proceedings in Parliament*, 2 vols. (New Haven: Yale University Press).
Fuzier, Jean (1997) 'English Political Dialogues 1641-1651: A Suggestion for Research with a Critical Edition of *The Tragedy of the Cruell Warre* (1643)', *Cahiers Elisabéthains*, 14, 49-68.
Gardiner, S. R. (ed.) (1862) *Parliamentary debates in 1610* (London: Camden Society).
────── (ed.) (1865) *Letters Illustrating Relations between England and Germany, 1618-19* (London: Royal Historical Society).
────── (ed.) (1868) *Illustrating the Relations between England and Germany at the Commencement of the Thirty Years' War* (London: Camden Society).
────── (ed.) (1877) *Documents Relating to the Proceedings Against William Prynne in 1634 and 1637* (London: Royal Historical Society).
Gawdy, P. (1906) *Letters of Philip Gawdy*, ed. I. H. Jeayes (London: J. B. Nichols).

Gerbier, Balthasar (1662) *A Brief Discourse Concerning the Three Chief Principles of Magnificent Building* (London: Thomas Heath).
Godwin, T. (1631) *Romanae historiae anthologia recognita et aucta. An English exposition of the Roman antiquities. . . . for the vse of Abingdon Schoole* (Oxford: J. Lichfield).
Gordon, Robert (1816) *Catalogue of the Singuler and Curious Library Originally Formed Between 1610 and 1650 by Sir Robert Gordon* (Edinburgh).
Harris, John and Gordon Higgott (1989) *Inigo Jones: Complete Architectural Drawings* (London: Royal Academy of Arts).
Herrick, Robert (1956) *Poetical Works of Robert Herrick*, ed. L. C. Martin (Oxford: Oxford University Press).
Heylyn, Peter (1656) *Observations on the historie of the reign of King Charles: published by H. L. Esq* (London: John Clarke).
Historical Manuscripts Commission (1883–1976) *Report on the Papers of the Marquess of Salisbury*, 24 vols. (London: HMSO).
―――― (1887) *The manuscripts of Henry Duncan Skrine, Esq: Salvetti correspondence*, ed. H. B. Tomkins (London: HMSO).
―――― (1891–1931) *The manuscripts of His Grace the Duke of Portland preserved at Welbeck Abbey*, 10 vols. (London: HMSO).
―――― (1925–95) *Report on the Manuscripts of the Marquess of Downshire, preserved at Easthampstead Park, Berkshire*, 6 vols. (London: HMSO).
Hutton, Richard (1991) *The Diary of Sir Richard Hutton 1614–1639*, ed. W. R. Prest (London: Selden Society).
Hyde, Edward (1978) *Selections from the History of the Rebellion and the Life of Himself*, ed. G. Huehns and Hugh Trevor-Roper (Oxford: Oxford University Press).
James VI and I (1616) *The Workes of the Most High and Mighty Prince James* (London: John Bill).
―――― (1620) *A Meditation Upon the 27, 28, 29 Verses of the XXVII Chapter of St Matthew or a pattern for a King's inauguration* (London: John Bill).
―――― (1621) *His Majesties Declaration Touching his proceedings in the late Assemblie and Convention of Parliament* (London: B. Norton for John Bill).
―――― (1944–50) *The Basilicon Doron of King James VI*, ed. James Craigie, 2 vols. (Edinburgh: William Blackwood & Sons Ltd).
―――― (1955–8) *The Poems of James VI of Scotland*, ed. James Craigie, 2 vols. (Edinburgh: Scottish Text Society).
―――― (1982) *The Minor Prose Works of King James VI and I*, ed. James Craigie and A. Law (Edinburgh: Scottish Text Society).
―――― (1994) *King James VI and I: Political Writings*, ed. Johann P. Sommerville (Cambridge: Cambridge University Press).
Jansson, M. (ed.) (1988) *Proceedings in Parliament 1614 (House of Commons)* (Philadelphia: American Philosophical Society).
Jonson, Ben (1604) *Ben Jon: His Part of King James his Royall and Magnificent Entertainment through his Honorable Cittie of London* (London: Edward Blount).
―――― (1616) *The workes of Benjamin Jonson* (London: William Stansby).
―――― (1816) *The Works of Ben Jonson*, ed. W. Gifford, 9 vols. (London: G. and W. Nicol).
―――― (1925–52) *Ben Jonson*, ed. C. H. Herford, P. Simpson, and E. Simpson, 11 vols. (Oxford: Clarendon Press).

—— (1952) *Jonson's Masque of Gipsies*, ed. W. W. Greg (London: The British Academy).
—— (1969) *The Complete Masques*, ed. S. Orgel (New Haven: Yale University Press).
—— (1971) *Every Man In His Humour: A Parallel Text edition of the 1601 Quarto and the 1616 Folio*, ed. J. W. Lever (London: Arnold).
—— (1985) *Ben Jonson*, ed. I. Donaldson (Oxford: Oxford University Press).
—— (1996) *Poetaster*, ed. Tom Cain (Manchester: Manchester University Press).
—— (2012) *The Cambridge Edition of the Works of Ben Jonson*, ed. David Bevington, Martin Butler, and Ian Donaldson, 7 vols. (Cambridge: Cambridge University Press).
Larkin, J. F. and P. L. Hughes (eds.) (1973) *Stuart Royal Proclamations, Volume 1: Royal Proclamations of King James I, 1603–1625* (Oxford: Clarendon Press).
—— (eds.) (1983) *Stuart Royal Proclamations, Volume 2: Royal Proclamations of King Charles I, 1625–1646* (Oxford: Clarendon Press).
Laud, William (1847–60) *Works*, ed. Philip Bliss, 7 vols. (Oxford: Oxford University Press).
Lauze, François de (1623) *Apologie de la Danse* (Paris: n.p.).
Le Fèvre de la Boderie, Antoine (1750) *Ambassade de Monsieur de la Boderie en Angleterre sous le regne d'Henri IV. et la minorité de Louis XIII. depuis les années 1606 jusqu'en 1611*, 5 vols. (Paris).
Lee, Maurice (ed.) (1972) *Dudley Carleton to John Chamberlain, 1603–1624: Jacobean Letters* (New Brunswick, NJ: Rutgers University Press).
Lefkowitz, Murray (ed.) (1970) *Trois Masques à la Cour de Charles Ier d'Angleterre* (Paris: CNRS).
Lenton, Francis (1634) *The Inns of Court Annagramatist* (London: William Lash).
L'Estrange, Hamon (1655) *The Life and Reign of King Charles* (London: W. Reybold).
Lindley, D. (ed.) (1995) *Court Masques: Jacobean and Caroline Entertainments, 1605–1640* (Oxford: Oxford University Press).
Lucian of Samosata (1915–67) *Lucian*, ed. and trans. A. M. Harmon, 8 vols. (Cambridge, MA: Harvard University Press).
Markham, Francis (1622) *Five decades or epistles of warre* (London: Augstine Matthews).
Middleton, Thomas (2007) *Thomas Middleton: The Collected Works*, ed. Gary Taylor and John Lavignino (Oxford: Clarendon Press).
Mihm, M. T. (ed.) (1984) *The Songe d'Enfer of Raoul de Houdenc* (Tübingen: Niemeyer).
Milton, John (1971) *The Complete Shorter Poems of John Milton*, ed. J. Carey (London: Longman).
Montagut, Barthélemy de (2000) *Louange de la Danse*, ed. B. Ravelhofer (Cambridge: RTM Publications).
Morfill, W. R. (ed.) (1873) *Ballads From Manuscripts*, 2 vols. (London: Ballad Society).
Niccols, R. (1616) *Sir Thomas Overbury's Vision* (London: R. Meighen and T. Jones).
Nichols, John (1828) *The Progesses of James I*, 4 vols. (London: John Nichols).
Orbison, T. (ed.) (1983) *Middle Temple Documents Relating to George Chapman's 'The Memorable Masque' and James Shirley's 'The Triumph of Peace'*, Malone Society Collections, 12 (Oxford: Oxford University Press).
Orgel, Stephen and Roy Strong (1973) *Inigo Jones: The Theatre of the Stuart Court*, 2 vols. (Berkeley: University of California Press).
P[arker], M[atthew] (1634) *The Honour of the Inns of Court Gentleman, The second part* (London).

Plutarch, Lucius Mestrius (1993) *Selected Essays and Dialogues*, ed. D. Russell (Oxford: Oxford University Press).
Prynne, William (1628) *A Brief Survey and Censure of Mr Cosins Concerning his Cozening Devotions* (London: Thomas Cotes).
—— (1633) *Histrio-mastix. The players scourge, or, actors tragaedie* (London: Michael Sparke).
Questier, M. C. (ed.) (1998) *Newsletters From The Archpresbyterate of George Birkhead* (London: Camden Society Publications), 5th Ser., 12.
Rabelais, François (1994) *Gargantua and Pantagruel*, trans. Thomas Urquhart and P. Le Motteux with an introduction by Terence Cave (London and New York: Everyman's Library).
Ralegh, Walter (1999) *The Poems of Sir Walter Ralegh: A Historical Edition*, ed. M. Rudick (Tempe: Arizona Center for Medieval and Renaissance Studies, 1999).
Raymond, Thomas (1917) *Autobiography of Thomas Raymond and Memoirs of the Family of Guise of Elmore*, ed. G. Davies (London: Royal Historical Society).
Ridpath, George (1698) *The Stage Condemn'd* (London: John Salusbury).
Rous, John (1856) *The Diary of John Rous*, ed. M. A. E. Green (London: Camden Society).
Sanderson, W. (1658) *A Compleat History of the life and raigne of King Charles from his cradle to his grave* (London).
Scott, Thomas (1624) *Vox Regis* (Utrecht: A. van Herwicjk).
Seddon, P. R. (ed.) (1975–87) *Letters of John Holles, 1587–1637*, 3 vols. (Nottingham: Thoroton Society).
Shirley, James (1634) *The triumph of peace. A masque* (London: William Cooke).
—— (1967) *The Triumph of Peace*, ed. C. Leech, in *A Book of Masques*, ed. S. Wells (Cambridge: Cambridge University Press).
Slaughter, Thomas P. (ed.) (1984) *Ideology and Politics on the Eve of the Restoration: Newcastle's Advice to Charles II* (Philadelphia: American Philosophical Society).
Spenser, Edmund (2001) *The Faerie Queene*, ed. A. C. Hamilton, text ed. Hiroshi Yamashita and Toshiyuki Suzuki (Harlow: Longman).
Stow, John (1618) *A Survey of London*, ed. A. Munday (London: G. Purslowe).
Suckling, John (1971) *The Works of Sir John Suckling: The Non-Dramatic Works*, ed. T. Clayton (Oxford: Oxford University Press).
Townshend, Aurelian (1983) *The Poems and Masques of Aurelian Townshend*, ed. C. Brown (Reading: Whiteknights Press).
W. T. (1595) *A Pleasant Satire or Poesie: wherein is discovered the Catholicon of Spayne, and the chiefe leaders of the League* (London: Thomas Man).
Wells, Stanley (ed.) (1967) *A Book of Masques; in honour of Allardyce Nicoll* (Cambridge: Cambridge University Press).
Wentworth, Thomas (1740) *The Letters and Papers of the Earl of Strafford*, ed. W. Knowler, 2 vols. (London).
Whitelocke, Bulstrode (1682) *Memorials of the English Affairs* (London: Nathaniel Ponder).
—— (1990) *The Diary of Bulstrode Whitelocke, 1605–1675*, ed. R. Spalding (Oxford: Oxford University Press).
Whiteway, William (1991) *William Whiteway of Dorchester: His Diary 1618 to 1634*, ed. David Underdown, Dorset Record Society Publications, 12 (Dorset: Dorset Record Society).
Wilbraham, Roger (1902) *The journal of Sir Roger Wilbraham, 1593–1616*, ed. H. S. Scott (London: Royal Historical Society) (Camden Society, 3rd ser., 4).

Secondary sources

Adamson, J. S. A. (1994) 'Chivalry and Political Culture in Caroline England', in *Culture and Politics in Early Stuart England*, ed. Kevin Sharpe and Peter Lake (Basingstoke: Macmillan), pp. 161–98.

Akrigg, G. P. V. (1948) 'The Curious Marginalia of Charles, Second Earl Stanhope', in *John Quincy Adams Memorial Studies*, ed. J. G. MacManaway, G. E. Dawson, and E. E. Willoughby (Washington: Folger Shakespeare Library), pp. 785–801.

Anderson, J. and E. Sauer (eds.) (2002) *Books and Readers in Early Modern England: Material Studies* (Philadelphia: University of Pennsylvania Press).

Archer, Jayne, Elizabeth Goldring, and Sarah Knight (eds.) (2007) *The Progresses, Pageants, and Entertainments of Queen Elizabeth I* (Oxford: Oxford University Press).

Astington, John H. (1999) *English Court Theatre, 1558–1642* (Cambridge: Cambridge University Press).

Atherton, Ian and Julie Sanders (eds.) (2006) *The 1630s: Interdisciplinary Essays on Culture and Politics in the Caroline Era* (Manchester: Manchester University Press).

Barker, Nicholas (ed.) (2003) *The Devonshire Inheritance: Five Centuries of Collecting at Chatsworth* (Alexandria, VA: Art Services International).

Barnard, John and Maureen Bell (1994) 'The Early Seventeenth-Century York Book Trade and John Foster's Inventory of 1616', *Proceedings of the Leeds Philosophical and Literary Society*, 24, 17–132.

Bellany, Alastair (2002) *The Politics of Court Scandal in Early Modern England: News Culture and the Overbury Affair, 1603–1660* (Cambridge: Cambridge University Press).

—— (2004) 'Monson, Sir Thomas, First Baronet (1563/4–1641)', *ODNB*, http://www.oxforddnb.com/view/article/18990, accessed 7 January 2007.

—— (2006) 'Singing Libel in Early Stuart England: The Case of the Staines Fiddlers, 1627', *Huntington Library Quarterly*, 69, 177–93.

Bentley, G. E. (1941–68) *The Jacobean and Caroline Stage*, 7 vols. (Oxford: Clarendon Press).

Braunmuller, A. R. (1991) 'Robert Carr, Earl of Somerset, as Collector and Patron', in *The Mental World of the Jacobean Court*, ed. Linda Levy Peck (Cambridge: Cambridge University Press), pp. 230–50.

Bray, A. (1990) 'Male Homosexuality and the Signs of Male Friendship', *History Workshop Journal*, 29, 1–19.

Brayshay, Mark (2004) 'Long-Distance Royal Journeys: Anne of Denmark's Journey from Stirling to Windsor in 1603', *Journal of Transport History*, 25, 1–21.

Britland, Karen (2000) '"All emulation cease, and jars": Political Possibilities in *Chloridia*, Queen Henrietta Maria's Masque of 1631', *Ben Jonson Journal*, 9, 1–22.

Brown, Cedric C. (1994) 'Courtesies of Place and Arts of Diplomacy in Ben Jonson's Last Two Entertainments for Royalty', *The Seventeenth Century*, 9, 147–71.

Bryant, L. (2007) 'From Communal Ritual to Royal Spectacle', in *French Ceremonial Entries in the Sixteenth Century: Event, Image, Text*, ed. N. Russell and H. Vissentin (Toronto: University of Toronto Press), pp. 207–45.

Burgess, Glenn (1996) *Absolute Monarchy and the Stuart Constitution* (New Haven: Yale University Press).

Butler, Martin (1987) 'Entertaining the Palatine Prince: Plays on Foreign Affairs, 1635–7', in *Renaissance Historicism*, ed. A. Kinney (Amherst: University of Massachusetts Press), pp. 265–92.

——— (1987) 'Politics and the Masque: *The Triumph of Peace*', *The Seventeenth Century*, 2, 117–41.
——— (1991) 'Private and Occasional Drama', in *The Cambridge Companion to Renaissance Drama*, ed. A. R. Braunmuller and Michael Hattaway (Cambridge: Cambridge University Press), pp. 131–63.
——— (1991) '"We are one man's all": Jonson's *The Gipsies Metamorphosed*', *Yearbook of English Studies*, 21, 253–73.
——— (1992) 'Ben Jonson's *Pan's Anniversary* and the Politics of Early Stuart Pastoral', *English Literary Renaissance*, 22, 369–404.
——— (1993) 'Jonson's Folio and the Politics of Patronage', *Criticism*, 35, 377–90.
——— (1993) 'Jonson's *News From the New World*, the "Running Masque" and the Season of 1619–20', *Medieval and Renaissance Drama in England*, 6, 153–79.
——— (1993) 'Reform or Reverence? The Politics of the Caroline Masque', in *Theatre and Government under the Early Stuarts*, ed. J. R. Mulryne and Margaret Shewring (Cambridge: Cambridge University Press), pp. 118–56.
——— (1994) 'Ben Jonson and the Limits of Courtly Panegyric', in *Culture and Politics in Early Stuart England*, ed. Kevin Sharpe and Peter Lake (Basingstoke: Macmillan), pp. 91–115.
——— (1995) 'Sir Francis Stewart: Jonson's Overlooked Patron', *Ben Jonson Journal*, 3, 101–27.
——— (1998) 'Courtly Negotiations', in *The Politics of the Stuart Court Masque*, ed. David Bevington and Peter Holbrook (Cambridge: Cambridge University Press), pp. 20–40.
Butler, Martin and David Lindley (1994) 'Restoring Astraea: Jonson's Masque for the Fall of Somerset', *English Literary History*, 61, 807–82.
Campbell, Gordon (2004) 'Gil, Alexander, the younger (1596/7–1642?)', *ODNB* (Oxford: Oxford University Press), online edn, January 2008 (http://www.oxforddnb.com/view/article/10730, accessed 26 February 2014).
Canova-Green, Marie-Claude (1993) *La Politique-spectacle au grand siècle: les rapports franco-anglais* (Tübingen: Gunter Narr Verlag).
Chambers, E. K. (1923) *The Elizabethan Stage*, 4 vols. (Oxford: Clarendon Press).
Chetwood, W. R. (1756) *Memoirs of the Life and Writings of Ben Jonson* (Dublin: W. R. Chetwood).
Clucas, S. and R. Davies (eds.) (2003) *The Crisis of 1614 and the Addled Parliament: Literary and Historical Perspectives* (Aldershot: Ashgate).
Cogswell, Thomas (1989) *The Blessed Revolution: English Politics and the Coming of War, 1621–1624* (Cambridge: Cambridge University Press).
——— (1995) 'Underground Verse and the Transformation of Early Stuart Political Culture', in *Political Culture and Cultural Politics in Early Modern England*, ed. Susan D. Amussen and Mark A. Kishlansky (Manchester: Manchester University Press), pp. 277–300.
——— (1998) *Home Divisions: Aristocracy, the State and Provincial Conflict* (Manchester: Manchester University Press).
——— (2002) 'The People's Love: The Duke of Buckingham and Popularity', in *Politics, Religion and Popularity in Early Stuart Britain Popularity: Early Stuart Essays in Honour of Conrad Russell*, ed. Thomas Cogswell, Richard Cust, and Peter Lake (Cambridge: Cambridge University Press, 2002), pp. 211–34.

—— (2004) '"Published by Authoritie": Newsletters and the Duke of Buckingham's Expedition to the Ile de Ré', *Huntington Library Quarterly*, 67, 1–25.
Cogswell, Thomas, Richard Cust, and Peter Lake (2002), 'Revisionism and its Legacies: The Work of Conrad Russell', in *Politics, Religion and Popularity: Early Stuart Essays in Honour of Conrad Russell*, ed. Thomas Cogswell, Richard Cust, and Peter Lake (Cambridge: Cambridge University Press), pp. 1–18.
Cokayne, G. E (1910–59) *The Complete Peerage of England, Scotland, Ireland, Great Britain and the United Kingdom, Extant, Extinct or Dormant*, ed. V. Gibbs (London: St Catherine's Press).
Colclough, David (1999) '*Parrhesia*: The Rhetoric of Free Speech in Early Modern England', *Rhetorica*, 17, 177–212.
—— (2003) '"Better Becoming a Senate of Venice"? The "Addled Parliament" and Jacobean Debates on Freedom of Speech', in *The Crisis of 1614 and the Addled Parliament*, ed. Stephen Clucas and Rosalind Davies (Aldershot: Ashgate), pp. 51–62.
—— (2005) *Freedom of Speech in Early Stuart England* (Cambridge: Cambridge University Press).
Collier, John Payne (1831) *The History of English Dramatic Poetry to the Time of Shakespeare, and Annals of the Stage to the Restoration*, 2 vols. (London: John Murray).
Collins, D. S. (1943) *A Handlist of News Pamphlets, 1590–1610* (London: South-West Essex Technical College).
Corbett, Margery and Ronald Lightbown (1979) *The Comely Frontispiece: The Emblematic Title-Page in England, 1550–1660* (London: Routledge & Kegan Paul).
Coughlan, Patricia (1989) '"Some Secret Scourge shall by her come unto England": Ireland and Incivility in Spenser', in *Spenser in Ireland: An Interdisciplinary Perspective*, ed. Patricia Coughlan (Cork: Cork University Press), pp. 46–74.
Craik, Katharine A. (2004) 'Reading *Coryats Crudities* (1611)', *Studies in English Literature, 1500–1900*, 44, 79–96.
Croft, Pauline (1991) 'The Reputation of Robert Cecil: Libels, Political Opinion and Popular Awareness in the Early Seventeenth Century', *Transactions of the Royal Historical Society*, 6th ser., 1, 43–69.
—— (1991) 'Robert Cecil and the Early Jacobean Court', in *The Mental World of the Jacobean Court*, ed. Linda Levy Peck (Cambridge: Cambridge University Press), pp. 134–47.
—— (1995) 'Libels, Popular Literacy and Public Opinion in Early Modern London', *Historical Research*, 68, 266–85.
—— (2008) 'Robert Cecil, first earl of Salisbury (1563–1612)', *ODNB*, http://www.oxforddnb.com/?/4890, accessed 5 December 2010.
Crum, Margaret (ed.) (1969) *First-Line Index of English Poetry, 1500–1800*, in *Manuscripts of the Bodleian Library* (Oxford: Clarendon Press).
Cuddy, Neil (1987) 'The Revival of the Entourage: The Bedchamber of James I, 1603–1625', in *The English Court: From the Wars of the Roses to the Civil Wars*, ed. David Starkey (London: Longman), pp. 173–225.
—— (1989) 'Anglo-Scottish Union and the Court of James I, 1603–1625', *Transactions of the Royal Historical Society*, 39, 107–24.
—— (1993) 'The Conflicting Loyalties of a "Vulger Counselor": The Third Earl of Southampton, 1597–1624', in *Public Duty and Private Conscience in*

Seventeenth Century England, ed. J. Morrill, P. Slack, and D. Woolf (Oxford: Oxford University Press), pp. 121–50.

——— (2002) 'The Real Attempted "Tudor Revolution in Government": Salisbury's 1610 Great Contract', in *Authority and Consent in Tudor England: Essays Presented to C. S. L. Davies*, ed. G. W Bernard and S. J. Gunn (Aldershot: Ashgate), pp. 249–70.

Cust, Richard (1986) 'News and Politics in Early Seventeenth-Century England', *Past and Present*, 112, 60–90.

——— (1989) 'Politics and the Electorate in the 1620s', in *Conflict in Early Stuart England: Studies in Religion and Politics, 1603–1642*, ed. Richard Cust and Ann Hughes (Harlow: Longman), pp. 134–67.

——— (1995) 'Honour and Politics in Early Stuart England: The Case of Beaumont v. Hastings', *Past and Present*, 149, 57–94.

——— (2002) 'Charles I and Popularity', in *Politics, Religion and Popularity in Early Stuart Britain*, ed. Richard Cust, Thomas Cogswell, and Peter Lake (Cambridge: Cambridge University Press), pp. 235–58.

——— (2007) 'Prince Charles and the Second Session of the 1621 Parliament', *English Historical Review*, 122, 432–7.

——— (2007) 'The "Public Man" in Late Tudor and Early Stuart England', in *The Politics of the Public Sphere in Early Modern England*, ed. Peter Lake and Steven Pincus (Manchester: Manchester University Press), pp. 116–43.

Cust, Richard and Ann Hughes (1989) 'Introduction: After Revisionism', in *Conflict in Early Stuart England: Studies in Religion and Politics 1603–1642*, ed. Richard Cust and Ann Hughes (Harlow: Longman).

Dahl, Folke (1952) *A Bibliography of English Corantos and Periodical Newsbooks 1620–1642* (London: Bibliographical Society).

Darnton, Roger (2007) '"What is the History of Books?" Revisited', *Modern Intellectual History*, 4, 495–508.

Dayrell, Eleanora (1885) *The History of the Dayrells of Lillingstone Dayrell* (Jersey: Le Lievre Bros).

DeMolen, Richard (1984) 'The Library of William Camden', *Proceedings of the American Philosophical Society*, 128, 327–409.

Donagan, Barbara (1995) 'Halcyon Days and the Literature of War: England Military Education Before 1642', *Past and Present*, 147, 65–100.

Duncan, Douglas (1979) *Ben Jonson and the Lucianic Tradition* (Cambridge: Cambridge University Press).

Dutton, Richard (1983) *Ben Jonson: To the First Folio* (Cambridge: Cambridge University Press).

——— (2000) *Licensing, Censorship and Authorship in Early Modern England* (New York: Palgrave Macmillan).

——— (2008) *Ben Jonson, 'Volpone' and the Gunpowder Plot* (Cambridge: Cambridge University Press).

Elliott, John R., Jr. (1992) 'The Folger Manuscript of *The Triumph of Peace* Procession', *English Manuscript Studies*, 3, 193–215.

Elton, G. R. (1976) 'Tudor Government: The Points of Contact. Part 3: The Court', *Transactions of the Royal Historical Society*, 5th ser., 26, 211–28.

Finkelpearl, Philip (1969) *John Marston of the Middle Temple: An Elizabethan Dramatist in his Social Setting* (Cambridge, MA: Harvard University Press).

Fischer, Jeffrey (1977) '*Love Restored*: A Defense of Masquing', *Renaissance Drama*, 8, 231–44.
Fox, Adam (1994) 'Ballads, Libels and Popular Ridicule in Jacobean England', *Past and Present*, 155, 47–83.
Gilbert, Allan H. (1948) *The Symbolic Persons in the Masques of Ben Jonson* (Durham, NC: Duke University Press).
Goldberg, Jonathan (1983) *James I and the Politics of Literature* (Baltimore: Johns Hopkins University Press).
—— (ed.) (1994) *Queering the Renaissance* (Durham, NC: Duke University Press).
Goldie, Mark (2001) 'The Unacknowledged Republic: Officeholding in Early Modern England', in *The Politics of the Excluded, c.1500–1880*, ed. T. Harris (Basingstoke: Palgrave Macmillan), pp. 153–94.
Gombrich, Ernst (1948) 'Icones Symbolicae: The Visual Image in Neo-Platonic Thought', *Journal of the Warburg and Courtauld Institutes*, 11, 163–92.
Gordon, Donald J. (1975) *The Renaissance Imagination: Essays and Lectures by D. J. Gordon*, ed. Stephen Orgel (Berkeley: University of California Press).
Greenblatt, Stephen (1985) 'Invisible Bullets: Renaissance Authority and its Subversion, *Henry IV and Henry V*', in *Political Shakespeare: New Essays in Cultural Materialism*, ed. J. Dollimore and A. Sinfield (Manchester: Manchester University Press), pp. 18–47.
Greg, W. W. (1939–59) *A Bibliography of the English Printed Drama to the Restoration*, 4 vols. (London: Bibliographical Society).
—— (1946) '*The Triumph of Peace*: A Bibliographer's Nightmare', *The Library*, 5th ser., 1, 113–26.
Griffiths, Antony (1998) *The Print in Stuart Britain, 1603–1689* (London: British Museum).
Gurr, Andrew (1987) *Playgoing in Shakespeare's London* (Cambridge: Cambridge University Press).
Guy, John (1995) 'The Rhetoric of Counsel in Early Modern England', in *Tudor Political Culture*, ed. Dale Hoak (Cambridge: Cambridge University Press), pp. 292–310.
—— (1996) *The Shakespearean Playing Companies* (Oxford: Clarendon Press).
Hadfield, Andrew (2003) 'Tacitus and the Reform of Ireland in the 1590s', in *Early Modern Civil Discourses*, ed. Jennifer Richards (Basingstoke: Palgrave Macmillan), pp. 115–30.
Hanson, Laurence (1938) 'English Newsbooks, 1620–41', *The Library*, 4th ser., 18, 355–84.
Hasler, P. W. (ed.) (1981) *The House of Commons, 1558–1603*, 2 vols. (London: HMSO).
Hassel, Chris (1979) *Renaissance Drama and the English Church Year* (Lincoln, NE: University of Nebraska Press).
Healy, Thomas (2003) 'Drama, Ireland and the Question of Civility', in *Early Modern Civil Discourses*, ed. Jennifer Richards (Basingstoke: Palgrave Macmillan), pp. 131–45.
Heaton, Gabriel (2010) *Writing and Reading Royal Entertainments: From George Gascoigne to Ben Jonson* (Oxford: Oxford University Press).
Held, Julius (1980) *The Oil Sketches of Peter Paul Rubens: A Critical Catalogue*, 2 vols. (Princeton: Princeton University Press).

Henshall, Nicholas (1992) *The Myth of Absolutism: Change and Continuity in Early Modern European Monarchy* (London: Longman).

Hill, Tracey (2010) *Pageantry and Power: A Cultural History of the Early Modern Lord Mayor's Show, 1585–1639* (Manchester: Manchester University Press).

Hirst, Derek (1978) 'Court, Country, and Politics before 1629', in *Faction and Parliament: Essays on Early Stuart History*, ed. Kevin Sharpe (Oxford: Clarendon Press), pp. 105–37.

—— (1981) 'Revisionism Revised: The Place of Principle', *Past and Present*, 92, 79–99.

Holman, Peter (1987) 'The Harp in Stuart England: New Light on William Lawes's Harp Consorts', *Early Music*, 15, 188–204.

Hotson, Leslie (1928) *The Commonwealth and Restoration Stage* (Cambridge, MA: Harvard University Press).

Howarth, David (1997) *Images of Rule: Art and Politics in the English Renaissance, 1485–1649* (Basingstoke: Macmillan).

Hulse, L. (2002) '"Musique which pleaseth myne rare": Robert Cecil's Musical Patronage', in *Patronage, Culture and Power: The Early Cecils*, ed. Pauline Croft (New Haven and London: Yale University Press/Paul Mellon Studies in British Art), pp. 139–58.

Hunt, William (1998) 'Civic Chivalry and the English Civil War', in *The Transmission of Culture in Early Modern Europe*, ed. Anthony Grafton and Ann Blair (Philadelphia: University of Pennsylvania Press), pp. 204–37.

Hutton, Ronald (1994) *The Rise and Fall of Merry England: The Ritual Year, 1400–1700* (Oxford: Oxford University Press).

—— (2004) *Debates in Stuart History* (Basingstoke: Palgrave Macmillan).

Ingram, Martin (1985) 'Riding, Rough Music and Mocking Rhymes in Early Modern England', in *Popular Culture in Seventeenth-Century England*, ed. Barry Reay (Beckenham: Croom Helm), pp. 166–97.

Jardine, Lisa and Alan Stewart (1998) *Hostage to Fortune: The Troubled Life of Francis Bacon, 1561–1626* (London: Gollancz).

Jeanneret, Michel (1991) *A Feast of Words: Banquets and Table Talk in the Renaissance* (Cambridge: Polity Press).

Jones-Davies, M. T and A. J. Hoenselaars (2007) 'The Masque of Cupids', in *Thomas Middleton: The Collected Works*, ed. Gary Taylor and John Lavignino (Oxford: Clarendon Press), pp. 1027–33.

Jowett, John (1991) 'Jonson's Authorization of Type in *Sejanus* and Other Early Quartos', *Studies in Bibliography*, 44, 254–65.

Judson, J. R. and R. O. Eckhart (1999) *Gerrit van Honthorst, 1592–1656* (Doornspijk: Davaco).

Kermode, Frank (1971) 'The Banquet of Sense', in *Shakespeare, Spenser, Donne: Renaissance Essays* (London: Routledge & Kegan Paul, 1971), pp. 84–115.

Kiessling, Nicholas (1988) *The Library of Robert Burton* (Oxford: Oxford Bibliographical Society).

Knowles, James (1999) 'A 1621 Tilt and Its Imprese: Huntington MS. EL 7972', *Huntington Library Quarterly*, 62, 391–400.

—— (2000) 'The "Running Masque" Recovered? A Masque for the Marquess of Buckingham (c.1619–20)', *English Manuscript Studies*, 8, 79–135.

—— (2001) 'Unprofitable Lovers: Cecil, Jonson and the Negotiation of Patronage', in *The Early Cecils: Patronage, Politics and Culture*, ed. Pauline Croft (New Haven and London: Yale University Press/Paul Mellon Studies in British Art), pp. 181–95.

―――― (2003) 'To enlight the darksome night, pale Cinthia doth arise: Anna of Denmark, Elizabeth I and the Images of Royalty', in *Women and Culture at the Courts of the Stuart Queens*, ed. Clare McManus (Basingstoke: Palgrave Macmillan), pp. 21–48.

―――― (2006) 'Jonson in Scotland: Jonson's Mid-Jacobean Crisis', in *Shakespeare, Marlowe, Jonson: New Directions in Biography*, ed. T. Kozuka and J. R. Mulryne (Aldershot: Ashgate), pp. 259–77.

―――― (2006) 'Songs of Baser Alloy: Jonson's *Gypsies Metamorphosed* and the Circulation of Manuscript Libels', *Huntington Library Quarterly*, 69, 53–176.

―――― (2007) 'Introduction: *The Masque of Heroes*', in *The Complete Works of Thomas Middleton*, ed. G. Taylor and J. Lavignino (Oxford: Clarendon Press), pp. 1320–24.

―――― (2007) '"In the Purest Times of Peerless Queen Elizabeth": Nostalgia, Politics, and Jonson's Use of the 1575 Kenilworth Entertainments', in *The Progesses, Pageants, & Entertainments of Queen Elizabeth I*, ed. Jayne Elisabeth Archer, Elizabeth Goldring, and Sarah Knight (Oxford: Oxford University Press), pp. 247–67.

Kyle, Chris (2002) 'Parliament and the Palace of Westminster: An Exploration of Public Space in the Early Seventeenth Century', *Parliamentary History*, 21, 85–98.

Lake, Peter (1996) 'Retrospective: Wentworth's Political World in Revisionist and Post-Revisionist Perspective', in *The Political World of Thomas Wentworth, Earl of Strafford, 1621–1641*, ed. J. F. Merritt (Cambridge: Cambridge University Press), pp. 252–83.

Lake, Peter and Steven Pincus (eds.) (2007) *The Politics of the Public Sphere in Early Modern England* (Manchester: Manchester University Press).

Lake, Peter and M. C. Questier (2000) 'Puritans, Papists and the "Public Sphere" in Early Modern England: The Edmund Campion Affair in Context', *Journal of Modern History*, 72, 587–627.

Langelüddecke, H. (2003) '"The chiefest strength and glory of this kingdom": Arming and Training the "Perfect Militia" in the 1630s', *English Historical Review*, 118, 1264–1303.

Larminie, Vivienne (1995) *Wealth, Kinship, and Culture: The Seventeenth-Century Newdigates of Arbury and Their World* (Woodbridge: Boydell and Brewer).

Lefkowitz, Murray (1965) 'The Longleat Papers of Bulstrode Whitelocke: New Light on Shirley's *Triumph of Peace*', *Journal of the American Musicological Society*, 18, 42–60.

Levy, Fritz (1989) 'The Decorum of News', in *News, Newspapers and Society in Early Modern Britain*, ed. Joad Raymond (London: Frank Cass), pp. 12–38.

Limon, Jerzy (1990) *The Masque of Stuart Culture* (Newark, NJ: University of Delaware Press).

―――― (1994) '"A Silenc'st Bricke-layer": An Allusion to Ben Jonson in Thomas Middleton's Masque', *Notes and Queries*, 41, 512–13.

Lindley, David (1979) 'Who Paid for Campion's *Lord Hay's Masque*?', *Notes and Queries*, 224, 144–5.

―――― (ed.) (1984) *The Court Masque* (Manchester: Manchester University Press).

―――― (1986) *Thomas Campion* (Leiden: E. J. Brill).

―――― (1987) 'Embarrassing Ben: The Masques for Frances Howard', in *Renaissance Historicism: Selections from ELR*, ed. Arthur F. Kinney and Dan S. Collins (Amherst: University of Massachusetts Press), pp. 248–64.

────── (1993) *The Trials of Frances Howard: Fact and Fiction at the Court of King James* (London: Routledge).

────── (2004) 'Campion, Thomas (1567–1620)', *ODNB*, http://www.oxforddnb.com/view/article/4541, accessed 7 January 2007.

Lindquist, Eric (1985) 'The Failure of the Great Contract', *Journal of Modern History*, 57, 617–51.

Lockyer, Roger (1981) *Buckingham: The Life and Political Career of George Villiers, First Duke of Buckingham, 1592–1628* (London: Longman).

Loewenstein, J. (1991) 'Printing and the "Multitudinous Presse": The Contentious Texts of Jonson's Masques', in *Ben Jonson's 1616 Folio*, ed. J. Brady and W. H. Herendeen (Newark, NJ: University of Delaware Press), pp. 168–91.

────── (2002) *Ben Jonson and Possessive Authorship* (Cambridge: Cambridge University Press).

Love, Harold (1998) *The Culture and Commerce of Texts: Scribal Publication in Seventeenth-Century England* (Amherst: University of Massachusetts Press).

Marcus, Leah S. (1986) *The Politics of Mirth* (Chicago: University of Chicago Press).

────── (1998) 'Valediction', in *The Politics of the Stuart Court Masque*, ed. David Bevington and Peter Holbrook (Cambridge: Cambridge University Press), pp. 321–6.

McCavitt, John (1996) 'An Unspeakable Parliamentary Fracas: The Irish House of Commons, 1613', *Analecta Hibernia*, 37, 223–35.

────── (1998) *Sir Arthur Chichester, Lord Deputy of Ireland, 1605–16* (Belfast: Institute of Irish Studies).

McClung, William A. and Rodney Simard (1987) 'Donne's Somerset Epithalmion and the Erotics of Criticism', *Huntington Library Quarterly*, 50, 95–106.

McGee, C. E. (1991) '"Strangest Consequence from Remotest Cause": The Second Performance of *The Triumph of Peace*', *Medieval and Renaissance Drama in England*, 5, 309–42.

McKenzie, D. F. (1975) '*The Staple of News* and the Late Plays', in *A Celebration of Ben Jonson*, ed. W. Blissett, Julian Patrick, and R. W. Van Fossen (Toronto: University of Toronto Press), pp. 83–128.

McManus, Clare (2002) *Women on the Renaissance Stage: Anna of Denmark and Female Masquing in the Stuart Court, 1590–1619* (Manchester: Manchester University Press).

McRae, Andrew (2004) *Literature, Satire and the Early Stuart State* (Cambridge: Cambridge University Press).

Marsh, Christopher (2004) 'The Sound of Print in Early Modern England: The Broadside Ballad as Song', in *The Uses of Script and Print, 1300–1700*, ed. A. Walsham and J. Crick (Cambridge: Cambridge University Press), pp. 171–90.

Martindale, Andrew (1979) *The Triumphs of Caesar by Andrea Mantegna in the Collection of Her Majesty the Queen at Hampton Court* (London: Harvey Miller).

Merritt, J. F. (ed.) (1996) *The Political World of Thomas Wentworth, Earl of Strafford, 1621–1641* (Cambridge: Cambridge University Press).

Milton, Anthony (2007) *Laudian and Royalist Polemic in Seventeenth-Century England: The Career and Writings of Peter Heylyn* (Manchester: Manchester University Press).

Morison, S. (1980) 'The Origins of the Newspaper', in *Selected Essays on the History of Letter-Forms in Manuscript and Print*, ed. David McKitterick (Cambridge: Cambridge University Press), pp. 325–57.

Mulryne, J. R. and Margaret Shewring (eds.) (1993) *Theatre and Government under the Early Stuarts* (Cambridge: Cambridge University Press).

Murphy, Andrew (1999) *But the Irish Sea Betwixt Us: Ireland, Colonialism, and Renaissance Literature* (Lexington: University Press of Kentucky).

Murray, Timothy (1983) 'From Foul Sheets to Legitimate Model: Antitheater, Text, Ben Jonson', *New Literary History*, 14, 641–64.

—— (1987) *Theatrical Legitimation: Allegories of Genius in Seventeenth-Century England and France* (New York and Oxford: Oxford University Press).

Netzloff, Mark (2001) '"Counterfeit Egyptians" and Imagined Borders: Jonson's *The Gypsies Metamorphosed*', *English Literary History*, 68, 763–93.

Nevitt, Marcus (2005) 'Ben Jonson and the Serial Publication of News', in *News Networks in Seventeenth-Century Britain and Europe*, ed. Joad Raymond (London and New York: Routledge), pp. 53–68.

Newton, Richard C. (1982) 'Jonson and the (Re-)Invention of the Book', in *Classic and Cavalier: Essays on Jonson and the Sons of Ben*, ed. C. Summers and Ted-Larry Pebworth (Pittsburgh: University of Pittsburgh Press), pp. 31–55.

Nicol, David (2006) 'The Repertory of Prince Charles's (I) Company, 1608–1625', *Early Theatre*, 9, 57–72.

—— (2012) *Middleton and Rowley: Forms of Collaboration in the Jacobean Playhouse* (Toronto: University of Toronto Press).

Norbrook, David (1984) 'The Reformation of the Masque', in *The Court Masque*, ed. David Lindley (Manchester: Manchester University Press), pp. 94–110.

—— (1986) 'The Masque of Truth: Court Entertainments and International Protestant Politics in the Early Stuart Period', *The Seventeenth Century*, 1, 81–110.

—— (1999) '*Areopagitica*, Censorship, and the Early Modern Political Sphere', in *British Literature, 1640–1789: A Critical Reader*, ed. Robert DeMaria (Oxford: Blackwell), pp. 13–39.

—— (2002) *Poetry and Politics in the English Renaissance*, revised edition (Oxford: Oxford University Press).

O'Callaghan, Michelle (2003) '"Now Thou May'st Speak Freely": Entering the Public Sphere in 1614', in *The Crisis of 1614 and the Addled Parliament: Literary and Historical Perspectives*, ed. Stephen Clucas and Rosalind Davies (Aldershot: Ashgate), pp. 63–80.

—— (2006) 'Performing Politics: The Circulation of the Parliament Fart', *Huntingdon Library Quarterly*, 69, 121–38.

—— (2007) *The English Wits: Literature and Sociability in Early Modern England* (Cambridge: Cambridge University Press).

O'Connell, Sheila (1999) *The Popular Print in England* (London: British Museum).

Oman, C. C. (1957) *English Church Plate* (Oxford: Oxford University Press).

Orgel, Stephen (1968) 'To Make the Boards Speak: Inigo Jones and the Jonsonian Masque', *Renaissance Drama*, NS 1, 121–52.

—— (1975) *The Illusion of Power: Political Theater in the English Renaissance* (Berkeley: University of California Press).

—— (1981) 'The Royal Theatre and the Role of the King', in *Patronage in the Renaissance*, ed. S. Orgel and G. F. Lytle (Princeton: Princeton University Press), pp. 261–73.

—— (2002) 'Afterword: Records of Culture', in *Books and Readers in Early Modern England: Material Studies*, ed. J. Anderson and E. Sauer (Philadelphia: University of Pennsylvania Press), pp. 282–90.

Orrell, John (1977) 'The Agent of Savoy at *The Somerset Masque*', *Review of English Studies*, 28, 302–4.

——— (1978) 'The London Stage in the Florentine Correspondence, 1604–1618', *Theatre Research International*, 3, 157–76.

——— (1979) 'The London Court Stage in the Savoy Correspondence, 1613–75', *Theatre Research International*, 4, 79–94.

Palmer, Barbara D. (1995) 'Court and Country: The Masque as Sociopolitical Subtext', *Medieval and Renaissance Drama in England*, 7, 338–54.

Palmer, Daryl W. (2004) *Writing Russia in the Age of Shakespeare* (Aldershot: Ashgate).

Parks, Stephen and Alan Bell (1986) *The Elizabethan Club of Yale and Its Library* (New Haven: Yale University Press).

Parry, Ross (1999) 'The Careful Watchman: James I, Didacticism and the Perspectival Organisation of Space', in *Disziplinierung im Alltag des Mittelalters und der frühen Neuzeit*, ed. Gerhard Jaritz (Vienna: Der Österreichischen Akademie der Wissenschaften), pp. 275–97.

Paul, James Balfour (ed.) (1904–14) *The Scots Peerage Containing an Historical and Genealogical Account of the Nobility of that Kingdom*, 9 vols. (Edinburgh: David Douglas).

Peacock, John (1991) 'Ben Jonson's Masques and Italian Culture', in *Theatre of the Italian Renaissance*, ed. J. R Mulryne and Margaret Shewring (Basingstoke: Macmillan), pp. 73–94.

——— (1993) 'The Stuart Court Masque and the Theatre of the Greeks', *Journal of the Warburg and Courtauld Institutes*, 56, 183–208.

——— (1995) *The Stage Designs of Inigo Jones: The European Context* (Cambridge: Cambridge University Press).

——— (2006) 'The Image of Charles I as a Roman Emperor', in *The 1630s: Interdisciplinary Perspectives*, ed Ian Atherton and Julie Sanders (Manchester: Manchester University Press), pp. 50–73.

Pearl, S. (1984) 'Sounding to Present Occasions: Jonson's Masques of 1620–5', in *The Court Masque*, ed. David Lindley (Manchester: Manchester University Press), pp. 60–77.

Peck, Linda Levy (1982) *Northampton: Patronage and Policy at the Court of James I* (London: Allen & Unwin).

——— (ed.) (1991) *The Mental World of the Jacobean Court* (Cambridge: Cambridge University Press).

——— (1998) 'Uncovering the Arundel Library at the Royal Society: Changing Meanings of Science and the Fate of the Norfolk Donation', *Notes and Records of the Royal Society*, 52, 3–24.

——— (1999) 'Monopolizing Favour: Structures of Power in the Early Seventeenth-Century English Court', in *The World of the Favourite*, ed. J. H. Elliot and L. W. B Brockliss (New Haven: Yale University Press), pp. 54–70.

Peltonen, Markku (2013) *Rhetoric, Politics and Popularity in Pre-Revolutionary England* (Cambridge: Cambridge University Press).

Perry, Curtis (2002) '"If Proclamations Will Not Serve": The Late Manuscript Poetry of James I and the Culture of Libel', in *Royal Subjects: Essays on the Writings of James VI and I*, ed. M. Fortier and D. Fischlin (Detroit: Wayne State University Press), pp. 205–32.

Pickel, M. B. (1936) *Charles I as Patron of Poetry and Drama* (London: F. Muller).

Portal, E. M. (1915–16) 'The Academ Roial of King James I', *Proceedings of the British Academy*, 7, 189–208.
Potter, Lois (1980) '*The Triumph of Peace* and *The Cruel War*: Masque and Parody', *Notes and Queries*, 27, 345–8.
Prescott, Anne Lake (1984) 'The Stuart Masque and Pantagruel's Dreams', *English Literary History*, 51, 407–30.
Prest, Wilfred (1972) *The Inns of Court, 1590–1640* (London: Longman).
Randall, Dale (1975) *Jonson's Gypsies Unmasked: Background and Theme of 'The Gypsies Metamorphos'd'* (Durham, NC: Duke University Press).
Ravelhofer, Barbara (1998) '"Virgin Wax" and "Hairy Men-Monsters": Unstable Movement Codes in the Stuart Masque', in *The Politics of the Stuart Court Masque*, ed. David Bevington and Peter Holbrook (Cambridge: Cambridge University Press), pp. 244–72.
Raylor, Timothy (2000) *The Essex House Masque of 1621* (Pittsburgh: Dusquesne University Press).
—— (2001) 'The Essex House Masque of 1621: Viscount Doncaster and the Jacobean Masque', *Renaissance Quarterly*, 54, 988–9.
Raymond, Joad (1998) 'The Newspaper, Public Opinion and the Public Sphere in the Seventeenth Century', *Prose Studies*, 21, 109–40.
—— (ed.) (1999) *News, Newspapers and Society in Early Modern Britain* (London: Frank Cass).
—— (2003) '"The Language of the Public": Print, Politics, and the Book Trade in 1614', in *The Crisis of 1614 and the Addled Parliament: Literary and Historical Perspectives*, ed. Steven Clucas and Rosalind Davies (Aldershot: Ashgate, 2003), pp. 98–117.
—— (2003) *Pamphlets and Pamphleteering in Early Modern Britain* (Cambridge: Cambridge University Press).
—— (2004) 'Describing Popularity in Early Modern England', *Huntington Library Quarterly*, 67, 101–30.
—— (2004) 'Parker, Martin (*fl.* 1624–1647)', *ODNB* (Oxford: Oxford University Press), http://www.oxforddnb.com/view/article/21326, accessed 26 February 2014.
—— (ed.) (2005) *News Networks in Seventeenth Century Britain and Europe* (London and New York: Routledge).
—— (2006) 'Perfect Speech: The Public Sphere and Communication in Seventeenth-Century England', in *Spheres of Influence: Intellectual and Cultural Publics from Shakespeare to Habermas*, ed. Willy Maley and Alex Benchimol (Frankfurt: Peter Lang), pp. 43–69.
Ribeiro, Alvaro (1973) 'Sir John Roe: Ben Jonson's Friend', *Review of English Studies*, 24, 153–64.
Richards, Jennifer (ed.) (2003) *Early Modern Civil Discourses* (Basingstoke: Palgrave Macmillan).
Riggs, David (1989) *Ben Jonson: A Life* (Cambridge, MA: Harvard University Press).
Rosser, G. (1991) 'A Netherlandic Triumphal Arch for James I', in *Across the Narrow Seas: Studies in the History and Bibliography of Britain and the Low Countries*, ed. S. Roach (London: British Library), pp. 67–82.
Rowland, Robert (1990) '"Fantasticall and Devilishe Persons": European Witch-Beliefs in Comparative Perspective', in *Early Modern European Witchcraft: Centres and Peripheries*, ed. Bengt Ankarloo and Gustav Heningsen (Oxford: Oxford University Press), pp. 161–90.

Sanders, Julie (1998) 'Print, Popular Culture, Consumption and Commodification in *The Staple of News*', in *Refashioning Ben Jonson: Gender, Politics, and the Jonsonian Canon*, ed. Julie Sanders, Kate Chedgzoy, and Sue Wiseman (Basingstoke: Macmillan), pp. 183–207.

——— (2000) 'Caroline Salon Culture and Female Agency: The Countess of Carlisle, Henrietta Maria, and Public Theatre', *Theatre Journal*, 52, 449–64.

——— (ed.) (2010) *Ben Jonson in Context* (Cambridge: Cambridge University Press).

Sanders, Julie and Ian Atherton (2006) 'Introducing the 1630s: Questions of Parliament, Peace and Pressure Points', in *The 1630s: Interdisciplinary Perspectives*, ed. Ian Atherton and Julie Sanders (Manchester: Manchester University Press), pp. 1–27.

Sanderson, James L. (1966) 'Poems on an Affair of State: The Marriage of Somerset and Lady Essex', *Review of English Studies*, 17, 57–61.

Schrickx, Willem (1986) *Foreign Envoys and Travelling Players in the Age of Shakespeare* (Ghent: Rijksuniversiteit te Gent).

Schuckman, C. and D. De Hoop Scheffer (eds.) (1991) *Hollstein's Dutch and Flemish Etchings, Engravings, and Woodcuts, ca. 1450–1700* (Roosendaal: Koninklijke Van Poll).

Seddon, P. R. (1970) 'Robert Carr, Earl of Somerset', *Medieval and Renaissance Studies*, 14, 48–68.

Sedgwick, Eve (1985) *Between Men: English Literature and Male Homosocial Desire* (New York: Columbia University Press).

Sellin, Paul R. (1980) 'The Performances of Ben Jonson's *Newes from the New World Discover'd in the Moone*', *English Studies*, 61, 491–7.

——— (1986) 'The Politics of Ben Jonson's *Newes from the New World Discover'd in the Moone*', *Viator*, 17, 321–37.

Sharpe, Kevin (1978) 'Parliamentary History 1603–1629: In or Out of Perspective', in *Faction and Parliament: Essays on Early Stuart History*, ed. Kevin Sharpe (Oxford: Clarendon Press), pp. 1–42.

——— (1987) *Criticism and Compliment: The Politics of Literature in the England of Charles I* (Cambridge: Cambridge University Press).

——— (1992) *The Personal Rule of Charles I* (New Haven and London: Yale University Press).

——— (1994) 'The King's Writ: Royal Authors and Royal Authority in Early Modern England', in *Culture and Politics in Early Stuart England*, ed. Kevin Sharpe and Peter Lake (Basingstoke: Macmillan, 1994), pp. 117–38.

Sharpe, Kevin and Peter Lake (eds.) (1994) *Culture and Politics in Early Stuart England* (Basingstoke: Macmillan).

Sharpe, Kevin and Steven Zwicker (eds.) (1987) *The Politics of Discourse: The Literature and History of Seventeenth-Century England* (Berkeley: University of California Press).

Shaw, William A. (1906) *The Knights of England*, 2 vols. (London: Sherratt and Hughes).

Shuger, Debora (1997) 'Irishmen, Aristocrats, and Other White Barbarians', *Renaissance Quarterly*, 50, 494–525.

——— (1998) 'Civility and Censorship in Early Modern England', in *Censorship and Silencing: Practices of Cultural Regulation*, ed. Robert C. Post (Los Angeles: Getty Research Institute for the Arts and Humanities), pp. 89–110.

Simpson, Claude M. (1966) *The British Broadside Ballad and its Music* (Brunswick, NJ: Rutgers University Press).
Sinfield, Alan (1994) *Cultural Politics — Queer Reading* (London: Routledge).
Smith, Bruce R. (1998) *Ancient Scripts and Modern Stage Experience* (Princeton: Princeton University Press).
Smith, James M. (1998) 'Effaced History: Facing the Colonial Contexts of Ben Jonson's *Irish Masque at Court*', *English Literary History*, 65, 297–321.
Smith, Peter J. (1996) 'Ajax by Any Other Name Would Smell as Sweet: Shakespeare, Harington and Onomastic Scatology', in *Tudor Theatre: Emotion in the Theatre*, ed. André Lascombes (Bern: Peter Lang), pp. 125–58.
Smuts, R. Malcolm (1996) 'Art and the Material Culture of Majesty in Early Stuart England', in *The Stuart Court and Europe: Essays in Politics and Political Culture*, ed. R. Malcolm Smuts (Cambridge: Cambridge University Press), pp. 86–112.
────── (1991) 'Cultural Diversity and Cultural Change at the Court of James I', in *The Mental World of the Jacobean Court*, ed. Linda Levy Peck (Cambridge: Cambridge University Press), pp. 99–112.
────── (2006) 'Force, Love and Authority in Caroline Political Culture', in *The 1630s: Interdisciplinary Perspectives*, ed. Ian Atherton and Julie Sanders (Manchester: Manchester University Press), pp. 28–49.
────── (2010) 'The Court', in *Ben Jonson in Context*, ed. Julie Sanders (Cambridge: Cambridge University Press), pp. 144–52.
Somerset, Anne (1997) *Unnatural Murder: Poison at the Court of James I* (London: Weidenfeld & Nicolson).
Sommerville, Johan P. (1986) *Politics and Ideology in England, 1603–40* (Harlow: Longman).
Sotheby and Co (2008) *The Library of the Earl of Macclesfield Removed from Shirburn Castle, Part Eleven: English Books and Manuscripts* (London: Sotheby).
South, Raymond (1981) *Royal Castle, Rebel Town: Puritan Windsor in Civil War and Commonwealth* (Buckingham: Barracuda Books).
Stephens, F. G. (ed.) (1870) *Catalogue of Prints and Drawings in the British Museum: Satirical and Personal Subjects, Volume I, 1320–1689* (London: British Museum).
Stevenson, David (1997) *Scotland's Last Royal Wedding: The Marriage of James VI and Anne of Denmark* (Edinburgh: John Donald).
Stewart, A. (1997) *Close Readers: Humanism and Sodomy in Early Modern England* (Princeton: Princeton University Press).
Strong, Roy (1972) *Van Dyck: Charles I on Horseback* (London: Viking).
────── (2005) *Coronation: A History of Kingship and the British Monarchy* (London: HarperCollins).
Taylor, F. (1941) 'The Books and Manuscripts of Scipio Le Squyer, Deputy Chamberlain of the Exchequer (1620–59)', *Bulletin of the John Rylands Library*, 25, 137–64.
Thurley, Simon (1999) *Whitehall Palace: An Architectural History of the Royal Apartments 1240–1698* (New Haven: Yale University Press).
Tighe, Robert Richard and James Edward Davis (1858) *Annals of Windsor: being a history of the castle and town, with some account of Eton and places adjacent* (London: Longman, Brown, Green, Longman and Roberts).
Tilley, Morris P. (1950) *A Dictionary of The Proverbs in England in the Sixteenth and Seventeenth Centuries* (Ann Arbor: University of Michigan Press).

Travis, Peter W. (2004) 'Thirteen Ways of Listening to a Fart: Noise in Chaucer's *Summoner's Tale'*, *Exemplaria*, 16, 1–19.
Underdown, David (1996) *A Freeborn People: Politics and the Nation in Seventeenth-Century England* (Oxford: Clarendon Press).
Veevers, Erica (1989) *Images of Love and Religion: Queen Henrietta Maria and Court Entertainments* (Cambridge: Cambridge University Press).
Walker, Kim (1991) 'New Prison: Representing the Female Actor in Shirley's *The Bird in a Cage* (1633)', *English Literary Renaissance*, 21, 385–400.
Walsham, A. (1996) 'Impolitic Pictures: Providence, History, and the Iconography of Protestant Nationhood in Early Stuart England', *Studies in Church History*, 33, 307–28.
Warburg, Aby (1999) 'The Theatrical Costumes for the Intermedi of 1589', in *The Renewal of Pagan Antiquity: Contributions to the Cultural History of the European Renaissance*, ed. and trans. David Britt and Kurt W. Foster (Los Angeles: Getty Research Institute), pp. 349–401.
Wilks, Timothy (1989) 'The Picture Collection of Robert Carr, Earl of Somerset (*c.*1587–1645), Reconsidered', *Journal of the History of Collections*, 1, 167–77.
―――― (2001) '"Forbear the Heat and Haste of Building": Rivalries among the Designers at Prince Henry's Court, 1610–12', *Court Historian*, 6, 49–65.
Williamson, Arthur H. (1996) 'Scots, Indians and Empire: The Scottish Politics of Civilisation', *Past and Present*, 150, 57–62.
Wiltenberg, R. (1988) '"What need hast thou of me? or my Muse?": Jonson and Cecil, Politician and Poet', in *The Muses Common-Weale*, ed. C. J. Summers and T. L. Pebworth (Columbia: University of Missouri Press), pp. 34–47.
Wiseman, Susan (1991) '"Adam, the Father of all Flesh", Porno-Political Rhetoric and Political Theory in and after the English Civil War', *Prose Studies*, 14, 134–57.
―――― (1998), *Drama and Politics in the English Civil War* (Cambridge: Cambridge University Press).
Wood, Andy (1999) *The Politics of Social Conflict: The Peak Country, 1520–1770* (Cambridge: Cambridge University Press).
―――― (2001) '"Poore men woll speke one daye": Plebeian Languages of Deference and Defiance in England, *c.*1520–1640', in *The Politics of the Excluded in England, c.1500–1850*, ed. Tim Harris (Basingstoke: Palgrave Macmillan), pp. 67–98.
Wormald, Jenny (1983) 'James VI and I: Two Kings or One?', *History*, 68, 187–209.
Young, Alan (1987) *Tudor and Jacobean Tournaments* (London: George Philip & Son).
Young, Michael B. (1997) *Charles I* (Basingstoke: Macmillan).

Online resources

'Early Stuart Libels: An Edition of Poetry from Manuscript Sources', ed. Alastair Bellany and Andrew McRae. Early Modern Literary Studies Text Series I (2005), http://purl.oclc.org/emls/texts/libels/
OED Online. March 2013. Oxford University Press.
Oxford Dictionary of National Biography (*ODNB*), Oxford University Press, 2004, online edn.

Index

Numbers in **bold** refer to illustrations in the text.

Abercromby, Abraham, 31, 87, 88, 220n51
Achmouty, John, 87, 88
Addled Parliament, 84, 92
Anna of Denmark, Queen, 51, 55, 65–74, 82, 109, 229n62
anti-Scots sentiment, 26–31
Ashmole, Elias, 188
audience, 2, 14–18, 21, 39, 41, 49–51, 78, 87, 95, 97–9, 101, 106, 110–11, 115, 118–19, 121, 124–6, 129–30, 163, 171, 203–4, 207, 216n92
'community of meaning', 17, 121

Bacon, Francis, 4, 58, 59, 79, 82, 97
Bacon, Nathaniel, 122
Barriffe, William, *Mars, his Triumph*, 189–90
Bayly, Lewis, *The Practice of Piety*, 145, 146, 148
Bellany, Alastair, 54, 56, 169
Bolton, Edmund, 96, 157–8
Bowyer, Henry, 31
Bowyer, William, 31
Burkhardt, Jacob, 2, 17
Burton, Henry, 180
Burton, Robert, 97, 127, **128**
Butler, Martin, 2, 136, 139, 140, 143, 156, 197

Cahill, Daniel, 82
Callot, Jacques, 185
Calvert, Samuel, 55, 56, 61
Camden, William, *Britannia*, 87
Campion, Thomas, 113
  The Entertainment at Caversham, 74, 127
  The Somerset Masque, 53, 55, 67–74, 78, 83, 86, 229n64
Carew, Thomas, 184
  Coelum Britannicum, 122, 191, 242n106, 243n112, 256n54

Carleton, Dudley, 10, 122, 131
Carr, Robert, Earl of Somerset, 55–78, 88, 91, 221n54, 226n8, 227n23, 227–8n29
  see also Overbury affair
Carr–Howard marriage, 12, 18, 55–78, 91, 226n8
Catullus, 229n64
Cecil, Robert, 1st Earl of Salisbury, 10–11, 12, 18, 21–2, 43, 47, 58, 221n67, 224n108
  'Great Contract' (1610), 10–11, 18, 21–2, 24–36, 36–7, 40
  unpopularity of, 34–41
censorship, 12, 87, 212n27, 222n85
  see also libel and slander; political communication
Chamberlain, John, 10, 18, 29, 30, 36, 47, 65, 66, 77, 78, 87, 103, 131–2, 149, 152, 153
Chapman, George, 7, 26, 84–5
  A Free and Offenceless Justification, 84
  Andromeda Liberata, 84
  The Memorable Masque, 91, 198
Charles I, Prince of Wales and King of England, 101–3, 173, 180
Chaucer, Geoffrey
  The House of Fame, 167
  The Miller's Tale, 165
  The Summoner's Tale, 166–7
Cicero, 98
civic culture, 173–209
  processions, 20, 56, 77, 91, 103, 118, 175, 176, 191, 194, 196–9, 202–3
  see also civic ritual; political culture; public sphere
civic ritual, 15–16, 118, 175, 196

283

civility, 9, 12, 18, 20, 33–4, 50–1, 53–5, 78–81, 84, 87–8, 110, 132, 152, 160, 164–5, 211–12n27, 222–3n85, 234n142
see also libel and slander; political communication
Clifton, Gervase, 20
Cogswell, Tom, 160
Coke, Thomas, 192
Colclough, David, 4, 14
Cope, Walter, 40
Corbett, Richard, 158–9, 170
Coryat, Thomas, 166
  Crudities, 164
Cosin, John, *Private Devotions*, 179
counsel, 1, 4–7, 11, 22, 24, 33, 39, 45–53, 102, 207–8
  see also political communication
court culture, 1–4, 7–20
  expenditure, 31–2, 53
  factions, 7, 56, 58, 65, 67, 71, 74, 171–2
  patronage, 7, 58–60
  political communication, 33–45
  'polycentric', 7
  sexual politics, 53–92
  tilting, 75, 103
  see also civility; counsel; masque; monarchy
Crane, Ralph, 122
Crichton, Robert, 28
Croft, Pauline, 36, 40
Crofts, William, 192
cultural tourism, 122, 124
Cust, Richard, 6, 214n60

dance, 14, 50, 71, 74, 81, 100, 132, 160, 176–7, 192–3, 259n102
  ballet de cour, 73–4
  see also music
Daniel, Samuel
  Hymen's Triumph, 55, 86–7, 229n60
  Tethys' Festival, 127
  The vision of the 12. goddesses presented in a maske the 8. of Ianuary, at Hampton Court, 121, 127
Davenant, William, *Luminalia*, 179
Davies, John, 81
Day, John, *Isle of Gulls*, 26

Dayrell, Thomas, 198
de Boisschot, Ferdinand, 73
de Lauze, François, *Apologie de la Danse*, 14
Dekker, Thomas, 15–16
  Britannia's Honour, 127
  Lantern and Candlelight, 156
  Wars, wars, wars, 190
Delaval, Francis, 91–2
Devereux, Robert, Earl of Essex, 55, 62–3, 67, 74
d'Ewes, Simonds, 138, 151, 154, 246n23
Donne, John, 37–40, 49, 179, 180–1, 183, 255n41
Drake, William, 205–6
Drayton, Michael, 171
Drummond, Jean, 55, 66
Drummond, William, 43
  Informations, 116
Dutton, Richard, 12
Dyson, Humphrey, 127

Edwards, Philip, 82
Eglisham, George, 249n68
  The Forerunner of Revenge, 158
Elizabeth I, Queen, 23, 32, 104
Elizabeth of Bohemia, 189
Erasmus, Desiderius, *The Praise of Folly*, 5
Erskine, Thomas, 31
Essex Rebellion, 40

farts/farting, 139, 144, 161–71, 250n81, 250n84
  see also scatology
Finet, John, 73, 137, 138, 194, 195
flattery, 1, 3, 208
Fletcher, John, 208
Fletcher, Phineas, 182
Florio, John, 164
Foucault, Michel, 2
Fox, Adam, 168
Foxe, John, *Book of Martyrs*, 147
Fraunce, Abraham, 70
Frederick, Duke of Bohemia, 96
friendship, 42, 51, 52, 59–60, 64, 72–3

Garrard, George, 190, 195, 204
Gerbier, Balthasar, 133

Index 285

Gibson, Abraham, *A Preparative to War*, 95
Goldberg, Jonathan, 13
Goodman, Godfrey, 147
Goodyer, Henry, 37
gossip, 55, 61, 62, 68–9, 78, 97–8, 131
  see also libel and slander
Great Comet (1618), 94, 105
'Great Contract', *see* Cecil, Robert
Greg, W. W., 119
Gunpowder Plot, 36

Hammersley, Hugh, 190
Hawley, James, 28
Hedley, Thomas, 47
Henrietta Maria, Queen, 174, 179
Henry Frederick, Prince of Wales, 23, 25, 26, 31, 51, 58, 102–4, 218n14
Herbert, Edward, 1st Baron Herbert of Cherbury, 122, 242n104
Herbert, Henry, Master of the Revels, 125, 126
Herbert, Philip, Earl of Montgomery, 28, 137
Herbert, William, Earl of Pembroke, 71, 75, 142, 230n71
Heylyn, Peter, 195–6, 208
Hill, Christopher, 54
Hill, Tracey, 15
Holles, John, 28, 66
Hoskyns, John, 29, 39
Howard, Charles, Lord Effingham, 110
Howard, Frances, Countess of Essex, 55, 56, 60, 62–3, 76, 226n14, 230n69
  see also Carr–Howard marriage
Howard, Henry, Earl of Northampton, 56, 59, 62, 65, 67
Howard, Thomas, Earl of Arundel, 122, 143, 185
Howard, Thomas, Earl of Suffolk, 56, 71, 86
Howarth, David, 19
humanism
  feasts, 164, 166
  vir civilis, 4

James VI and I, King, 24–33, 58–9, 80, 95–6, 159, 219n24
  A Meditation Upon the 27, 28, 29 Verses of the XXVII Chapter of St Matthew, 102, 104–5
  Basilicon Doron, 18, 88, 102, 105, 234n142
  Meditation on 1 Chronicles, 100
  The Book of Sports, 164, 174, 178, 179, 189, 207, 208, 255n38
Jones, Inigo, 7, 49, 122, 185
Jonson, Ben
  awareness of audience, 14–18, 21
  creation of the literary masque, 121
  creation of a print identity, 120
  printed texts, 119–30
  self-reflexive writing, 7, 115
  view of masque as educative, 102, 114–15
  view of masque as poetry, 5, 14, 101, 111, 114
  view of monarch and poet as equivalent, 6
  works:
  A Challenge at Tilt, 55, 74–7
  Barriers at a Marriage, 74, 121
  Ben Jon: His Part of King James his Royall and Magnificent Entertainment through his Honorable Cittie of London, 14–15, 16, 121, 124
  Chloridia, 122, 124, 173
  Discoveries, 6
  Eastward Ho, 26
  Every Man In His Humour, 167
  Hymenaei, 16, 121
  Love Restored, In a Masque at Court, 2, 5, 18, 21–52, 88, 111–12
  Love's Triumph Through Callipolis, 17, 122, 173, 196
  Lovers Made Men, 113, 124
  Neptune's Triumph, 5, 124–5
  News from the New World in the Moon, 5, 19, 93–130
  Oberon, 23, 103, 104, 113
  Pan's Anniversary, 18, 119, 148–50
  Pleasure Reconciled to Virtue, 6, 42, 102, 113, 116, 119, 122
  Poetaster, 116, 165, 167

Jonson, Ben – *continued*
  Sejanus His Fall, 121
  The Alchemist, 166
  The Character of Two Noble Masques (see also *The Masque of Beauty* and *The Masque of Blackness*), 121
  The Entertainment at Britain's Burse, 41–2
  The Fortunate Isles, 124–5, 126–7
  The Gypsies Metamorphosed, 19, 113, 114, 122, 131–72
  The Haddington Masque, 5–6, 121
  The Irish Masque at Court, 18, 31, 54, 55, 64–5, 78–92, 135
  The Masque of Augurs, 112–13, 124–5, 126
  The Masque of Beauty, 122, 239n72
  The Masque of Blackness, 15, 122
  The Masque of Queens, 6, 17, 23, 69, 112, 113, 121, 122, **123**,
  The New Inn, 126
  The Staple of News, 93, 126
  The Underwood, 171
  The Vision of Delight, 99, 101, 113, 119
  The workes, 6, 17, 95, 120, 127
  Time Vindicated, 124–5
  Volpone, 134

Knollys, William, 92
Kyle, Chris, 19

Lake, Peter, 10, 11
Laud, William, 9, 179, 180, 182, 208
Lenton, Francis, *Inns of Court Annagramatist*, 198
L'Estrange, Hammon, 207
libel and slander, 9, 10–11, 18–19, 21–2, 34–41, 47, 54, 56–78, 84–5, 131–72, 225n3
  see also news culture; political communication; political culture
Limon, Jerzy, 125
Lindley, David, 14, 46, 57, 72, 73, 87, 226n14
Livingston, John, 30
Loewenstein, Joe, 126
Lotti, Ottaviano, 27
Love, Harold, 10
Lucian of Samosata, 42, 45, 223n98

Lucianic tradition, 5, 212n30, 212n31
Ludlow, Henry, 165

manuscript circulation, 9–10, 40, 54, 105, 122, 126, 129, 131–2, 151, 171
Marcus, Leah, 23, 49, 164
Marsh, Christopher, 168
Marston, John, 26
  The Entertainment at Ashby, 154
Martin, John, 147
masque
  antimasque, 5, 6, 22, 49, 68–9, 80, 85–6, 112–14, 176–7, 240n75
  ethics of, 2, 24, 44
  factional context, 3, 7, 18, 21–2, 56, 58, 65, 67, 71, 74, 171–2
  poetry of opposition, 33–45
  printed texts, 119–30
  running masque, 19, 95, 103, 106, 113, 116, 118, 133, 139, 159–60
  sexual politics, 53–92
  spatial politics, 19, 117–19, 133
  textual culture, 93–130, 150
  theatrics of power, 2
  use of tact, 20, 208
  see also political communication; political culture
Masque of Flowers, The (Anon.), 55, 79, 122, 243n113
Maxwell, James, 28
McClung, William A., 61
McManus, Clare, 70, 74
Middleton, Thomas, 7, 101
  A Game at Chess, 122
  Inner Temple Masque, or Masque of Heroes, 95, 116–17, 127, 185
  Masque of Cupids, 55, 56, 77, 231n94
  The World Tossed at Tennis, 19, 95, 106–11, **107**, 117
mimetic magic, 2, 50
monarchy
  arcana imperii, 22, 159
  Divine Right theory, 2, 19
  limits of royal power, 21–2
  models of kingship, 20, 46
  prerogative power, 8, 10–11, 18, 25, 46–7, 50, 53, 92, 105, 159
  royal finances, 24–33

Monson, Thomas, 73
More, John, 29
Mostyn, Thomas, 122
music, 27, 44, 50, 73–4, 81–2, 85, 148–9, 162, 168–70, 177, 193, 232n114

New Historicism, 3, 215n69
Newdigate III, John, 124
news culture, 9, 19, 93–130, 132, 214n60
  corantos, 93, 98
  Mercurius Britannicus, 157
  newsbooks, 3, 151, 157, 236n20, 236n21
  newsletters, 10, 13, 18, 62, 98, 176, 192, 214n54, 236n21
  see also gossip; libel and slander; political communication
Niccols, Robert, 57, 226n16
Norris, Edward, 31
Norton, Benjamin, 40

O'Callaghan, Michelle, 84, 166, 168, 233n131
Order of the Garter, 188–9
Orgel, Stephen, 2
Overbury, Thomas, 55, 59, 65
Overbury affair, 53–4, 55–78, 226n8
Ovid, 186

Pagitt, Justinian, 178
Palmer, Daryl, 47
panegyric, 3–4, 14
Parker, Martin, *The Honor of the Inns of Court Gentlemen*, 199–203, **200**, **201**
Peacham, Henry, *Minerva Britanna*, 70
Peacock, John, 112, 175
Peasants' Revolt, 167
Peck, Linda, 58
Peltonen, Markku, 4–5
Piggott, Christopher, 26
Pincus, Steven, 10, 11
Platonism, 2
Pliny, 3
Plutarch, *Moralia*, 184
political communication, 1–2, 11–12, 14
  free speech, 4, 39, 46–8, 53
  poetry of opposition, 33–45
  propaganda, 3, 36–7, 85, 106, 130, 132, 151, 156–61

political culture, 7–20, 34, 40, 93–130, 131–72
  tavern societies, 39, 166
  theatrics of power, 2
  see also public sphere
political prints, 97–8
Pory, John, 10, 96, 214n54
Prynne, William, 9
  Histriomastix, 174, 179, 208
public sphere, 10–14, 20, 21–2, 53, 105, 129, 215n81
puns, 36, 44–5, 63–4, 155, 228n47, 235n4, 250n87
Puritanism, 32, 168, 206, 208

Rabelais, François, *Pantagruel*, 163
Ralegh, Walter, 35
  History of the World, 115
Ramsay, William, 28
Ravelhofer, Barbara, 188
rhetoric, 3–5, 8, 14, 15, 53, 79, 143, 188, 195
  'conspiratorial paranoia', 9
  parrhesia, 4
Rich, Barnaby, 81
Roe, John, 51
royal palaces
  Denmark House, 67, 96, 109, 216 n95
  Greenwich, 65
  Richmond, 109
  St James, 109
  Whitehall (Banqueting House), 19, 120

Salvetti, Amerigo, 159
Sanders, Julie, 6, 16, 94
scatology, 56, 80, 81, 83, 98, 134, 135, 139, 144–6, 149, 164, 171
Scott, Thomas, 4
  Vox Populi, 95
Scott, Walter, 3
Sedgwick, Eve, 60
Sharpe, Kevin, 4
Sherburn, Edward, 122
Shirley, James, *The Triumph of Peace*, 13, 20, 173–209
Simard, Rodney, 61
Smuts, Malcolm, 7
Spanish Armada, 9

Spenser, Edmund
  The Faerie Queene, 42, 50, 68, 186–7, 237n36
  View of the Present State of Ireland, 81
Stansby, William, 126
Stone, Lawrence, 54
Stow, John, *Survey of London*, 127
Stuart, Arabella, 31

Tacitus, 83
Testwood, Robert, 147
Throckmorton, John, 55
Townshend, Aurelian, *Albion's Triumph*, 175, 183, 185, 189, 191, 196–7
Treaty of London (1604), 25
Trumbull, William, 27, 55–6
Turner, John, 28

Underdown, David, 54

Vane, Henry, 174, 178
Veevers, Erica, 179

Villiers, George, Duke of Buckingham, 12, 19, 96, 97, 104, 132–4, 136–43, 150–61, 169
Virgil, *Eclogues*, 186

Walkley, Thomas, 157
Warburg, Aby, 17
Wentworth, Thomas, 46, 204
Whitelocke, Bulstrode
  'Annales', 174–5
  Diary, 174–5, 178, 194
  Memorials of the English Affairs, 174–5, 179, 198, 207–8
Whiteway, William, 178, 179, 194
Whitney, Geoffrey, *Choice of Emblems*, 115
Wilbraham, Roger, 59, 226n10
Wilson, Thomas, 96
Winwood, Ralph, 79, 85
Wiseman, Susan, 206
Wither, George, 84, 85